Gadamer and the Limits of the
Modern Techno-Scientific Civilization

Berner Reihe philosophischer Studien

Herausgegeben von
Prof. em. Dr. Andreas Graeser u.a., Universität Bern

Band 43

Diese Reihe versammelt Arbeiten, die im Umfeld des Instituts für Philosophie der Universität Bern entstanden und sich entsprechend der hier weiten Ausrichtung mit sehr unterschiedlichen Thematiken und Denkern verschiedener Observanz auseinandersetzen. Dabei orientieren sich die Autorinnen und Autoren an den Standards von Klarheit und Kohärenz und stellen ihre Beiträge in den Dienst der Sache.

PETER LANG
Bern · Berlin · Bruxelles · Frankfurt am Main · New York · Oxford · Wien

Stefano Marino

Gadamer and the Limits of the Modern Techno-Scientific Civilization

PETER LANG

Bern · Berlin · Bruxelles · Frankfurt am Main · New York · Oxford · Wien

Bibliographic information published by Die Deutsche Nationalbibliothek
Bibliographic information published by die Deutsche Nationalbibliothek
Die Deutsche Nationalbibliothek lists this publication in the Deutsche
Nationalbibliografie; detailed bibliographic data is available on the Internet
at ‹http://dnb.d-nb.de›.

British Library Cataloguing-in-Publication Data: A catalogue record for this
book is available from The British Library, Great Britain

Library of Congress Cataloging-in-Publication Data

Marino, Stefano, 1976-
Gadamer and the limits of the modern techno-scientific civilization / Stefano Marino.
 p. cm. -- (Berner Reihe philosophischer Studien, ISSN 1421-4903 ; Bd. 43)
 Includes bibliographical references (p.   ) and index.
 ISBN 978-3-03-430663-8
 1. Gadamer, Hans-Georg, 1900-2002. 2. Civilization, Modern--Philosophy.
3. Technology and civilization. 4. Technology--Philosophy. 5. Science and
civilization. 6. Science--Philosophy. I. Title.
 B3248.G34M363 2011
 193--dc23
                          2011029209

ISSN 1421-4903
ISBN 978-3-0343-0663-8

© Peter Lang AG, International Academic Publishers, Bern 2011
Hochfeldstrasse 32, CH-3012 Bern, Switzerland
info@peterlang.com, www.peterlang.com

All rights reserved.
All parts of this publication are protected by copyright.
Any utilisation outside the strict limits of the copyright law, without the
permission of the publisher, is forbidden and liable to prosecution.
This applies in particular to reproductions, translations, microfilming,
and storage and processing in electronic retrieval systems.

Printed in Switzerland

This book is dedicated to my newborn son Marco,
with the hope he will live in a less *frenetic*
and a more *phronetic* world

Table of Contents

Acknowledgements 9

1. Gadamer's Long Twentieth Century 11

2. Science and Technology: The Real Roots of Modernity 23

3. The Basic Features of Our Societies: Conformism,
   Bureaucracy and Self-Alienation 51

4. Cosmopolitan Hermeneutics in the Age of the
   "Clash of Civilizations" 65

5. The Possibility of Global Disasters and the Fear
   for the Self-destruction of Mankind 75

6. On the Problematic Character of Ethic and Aesthetic
   Experiences in the Age of Science 91

7. Religious Experience in a Nihilistic Epoch 113

8. Hermeneutics, Techno-Science, Enlightenment:
   A Complex "Constellation" 139

9. The Rehabilitation and Universalization of
   Practical Knowledge and Experience 177

10. Reasonableness, Dialogue and Freedom:
    Ethical-Political Consequences of Hermeneutics 217

Bibliography 255

Index 289

Acknowledgements

I would firstly like to thank my teacher, Professor Carlo Gentili, for having carefully followed my work during the last years, ever since the beginning of my doctoral studies at the University of Bologna in the academic year 2004-2005.
Then, I would like to thank Professor Günter Figal: during the draft of the book I have greatly benefitted from conversations with him on philosophical hermeneutics. I am also indebted to Professor Figal for having invited me to the *Philosophisches Seminar* of the University of Freiburg, where I spent fruitful periods of study with the support of a postdoctoral fellowship provided by the Fritz Thyssen Stiftung.
I thank Professors Beatrice Centi, Mariannina Failla, Gianluca Garelli and Giovanni Matteucci for their ongoing encouragement and valuable suggestions. The countless discussions on philosophical issues and the cooperation in research activities with my colleagues Dr. Francesco Cattaneo and Dr. Rosa Maria Marafioti, as well as the "everyday life philosophizing" with my friends of the SSIS (Institute of Teacher Training at the University of Bologna), have been an important source of inspiration.
I would also like to thank everyone at EnglishEdited.com and Leila Jennings for their precious help in the revision and correction of the whole manuscript.
Most of all, however, my gratitude goes to my family (my parents Giuseppe and Karin, my brother Giulio), for their constant love and support, and to my beloved wife Valeria: like Joseph Arthur sings, "you teach me how most things have *no measure*".

I am particularly grateful to the Fritz Thyssen Stiftung for its support during a one-year postdoctoral fellowship, which gave me the opportunity to fully concentrate on this research project, and devote all my time and energies to its realization.

The Department of Philosophy of the University of Bologna has generously offered financial support for covering the print costs (PRIN 2007 Research Funds). In this regard, a special thanks goes to Silvia Rodolosi for her precious help in dealing with bureaucratic cases.

Finally, I would like to thank the Italian publishing house Mimesis for permission to use and re-elaborate material from my previous book *Ermeneutica filosofica e crisi della modernità. Un itinerario nel pensiero di Hans-Georg Gadamer* (Milano 2009).

***

All the works I have referred to in this book have always been quoted both from the original version (German, French, Italian) and with the English translation, when the latter was available. In the footnotes, I have first reported information about the original version of the text, followed, in square brackets, by information concerning the English translation I have used. When no English translation was available, I have quoted directly from the original version. However, in a few cases (for example, Gadamer's interviews that have only appeared in Italian journals or books) I have translated the quotations into English myself. Full details about Gadamer's works and other sources I have used are reported in the Bibliography.

1. Gadamer's Long Twentieth Century

It is a well known fact that great part of contemporary culture has been characterized by strong feelings of uneasiness, uncertainty and lack of orientation. Apropos of this situation, some thinkers have spoken of a sort of malaise of modernity, i.e. of "features of our contemporary culture and society that people experience as a loss or a decline, even as our civilization 'develops'"[1]. A loss or decline that "people feel [...] has occurred during the last years or decades", or – according to others – "over a much longer historical period": for example, "the whole modern era from the seventeenth century is frequently seen as the time frame of the decline"[2]. Hence, it has been noticed that "in the twentieth century", while on the one hand "the process of modernization expand[ed] to take in virtually the whole world", on the other, it shattered into "a multitude of fragments"[3]. As a result, "the idea of modernity [lost] much of its vividness, resonance and depth", as well as "its capacity to organize and give meaning to people's lives", so that "we find ourselves today in the midst of a modern age that has lost touch with the roots of its own modernity"[4].

On this basis, I think we could say that the whole twentieth century, as well as the first decades of the twenty-first, has been characterized to a wide extent by the general idea or feeling that we are witnessing a particularly critical phase in the history of our civilization. A phase that seems to be characterized, above all, by the preponderance and diffusion of the techno-scientific culture. So, it is not by accident that pessimistic and sometimes even "apocalyptic" expressions like *decline of the West* (Spengler) and *shadow of*

---

1 Taylor 1992, p. 1.
2 Taylor 1992, p. 1.
3 Berman 1983, p. 17.
4 Berman 1983, p. 17.

tomorrow (Huizinga), *crisis of European sciences* (Husserl) and growth of *European nihilism* (Nietzsche, Heidegger, Löwith), *uneasiness in culture* (Freud) and *crisis of the spirit* (Valèry), *eclipse of reason* (Horkheimer) and *crisis in culture* (Arendt), *waning of humaneness* (Lorenz) and *antiquity* or *death of man* (Anders, Foucault), *end of modernity* (Lyotard, Vattimo) and *end of history* (Kojève, Gehlen, Fukuyama), *failure of the modern Enlightenment project* (MacIntyre) and *paradigm lost* (Luhmann), have become veritable keywords of the present age.

It is also a well known fact that the current discussion on these topics is not a prerogative of the philosophical community alone, but rather seems to interest our entire culture and society. Accordingly, not only philosophers, but also journalists, writers, intellectuals, political and religious leaders, opinion-makers, and common people, are used to dealing with these problems and with analogous ones. As has been noted, modernity today is indeed mostly seen as

> enigmatic at its core [...]. We are left with questions where once there appeared to be answers, and [...] it is not only philosophers who realize this. A general awareness of the phenomenon filters into anxieties which press in on everyone[5].

Now, my aim here is *neither* to detail the global historical and cultural background underlying this critical view of the modern age, *nor* to linger on the conceptions of all those authors who, despite their divergences on many other issues, were and are united by the circumstance of having taken part in such a wide and comprehensive critical discourse[6]. Actually what I intend to do, in this book, is to

---

5   Giddens 1991, p. 49.
6   Such a critical discourse seems to range, indeed, from the post-Nietzschean crisis of the early twentieth century to that thing "called 'postmodernism' emerged from [the] chrysalis of the anti-modern" and definable, at least to some extent, as "some kind of reaction to, or departure from, 'modernism'" (Harvey 1990, pp. 3 and 7). With regard to this point, I think it is also important to underline that "many theorists of post-modernity are not celebrators of the condition they diagnose. Their attitude is more generally one of resignation, often tinged with ironic regret at the passing of the more confident modern era.

focus my attention on one single protagonist of the twentieth century intellectual life, the German philosopher Hans-Georg Gadamer, whose 1960 groundbreaking work, *Wahrheit und Methode*, has established once and for all philosophical hermeneutics as one of the leading traditions of contemporary philosophy.

It has been noticed that "Gadamer clarifies our historical situation – clarifies, one might say, our modernity"[7]. As a matter of fact, I think that his philosophy – despite the fact that it cannot be described either as simply "anti-modern", or as "post-modern" – could be included in the abovementioned discourse concerning the crisis of modernity and the limits of its techno-scientifically oriented worldview. From this point of view, I agree with Richard E. Palmer when he says that "Gadamer's philosophical hermeneutics contributes importantly to the effort to think beyond the basic assumptions and thought forms of modernity", that is, he offers "what amounts to a systematic critique of modernity", basically focused on the "critique of scientific objectivity" and the "critique of the lack of dialogical openness to the other in modernity"[8]. More precisely, I will try to show in the course of this book that Gadamer's philosophy entails both a *pars destruens* and a *pars construens*, i.e. it "offers both a critique of modernity and ways of moving beyond it"[9].

[...] The announcement of the end of this or that project or period – 'modernity', 'history' – brings with it little excitement or hope, little sense of a new beginning or something to look forward to in the future. Many commentators seem sunk rather in a mood of resignation or melancholy" (Kumar 1995, pp. 127 and 151).

7 Bruns 1992, p. 10.
8 Palmer 2003, p. 160.
9 Palmer 2003, p. 174. I don't agree with Palmer, however, when he claims that Gadamer "is postmodern, post-subjectivist, post-humanist" (Palmer 2010, p. 129). Rather, I believe that, although "it would be tempting to turn Gadamer into a 'postmodern' thinker, because he throws into question the whole of the evidence of 'modernity'", to speak of postmodernism would probably represent a misunderstanding, since "even the term 'postmodern' in fact suggests the idea of a new departure, of a *tabula rasa*, which is never the case for Gadamer's thought" (Grondin 2003, p. 3). Indeed, while Gadamer surely rejects "the subject-centered philosophy of modernity", he nevertheless does not lose sight

Actually, Gadamer probably represents one of the contemporary thinkers who paid the most attention to these topical problems, and answered them in a very challenging and convincing (though not always clear and unproblematic) way. His fundamental philosophical task being indeed that "to seek the experience of truth that transcends the domain of scientific method wherever that experience is to be found, and to inquire into its legitimacy"[10]. "It would be an error to assert that we no longer need [...] in the age of scientism" the lesson of the great philosophers and writers, i.e. of the "humanists", Gadamer explains in his important essay *Die philosophischen Grundlagen des zwanzigsten Jahrhunderts*:

> The limit they designate over against the total scientific reduction of our world is nothing we must first devise. It is there as something that has always preceded science. What seems to me to be the most hidden and yet the most powerful foundation of our century is its skepticism over against all dogmatism, including the dogmatism of science[11].

In addition to this, I argue that interpreting Gadamer's hermeneutics in this way might prove useful in order to highlight the fundamental "unity" of his philosophy: a "unity" which is obviously not synonymous with "systematicity", at least in the traditional sense[12]. In other

---

of "the pervading humanistic trend of Western civilization. [...] Gadamer unearths in the forgotten tradition of humanism an instance that can fuel a resistance against the illegitimate claims of modern science to encompass all there is to know" (Grondin 1997, pp. 167 and 164).

10 GS 1, p. 1 [TM, p. XXI].
11 GW 4, pp. 21-22 [PH, pp. 128-129].
12 As a matter of fact, Gadamer was always quite mistrustful towards the philosophers' traditional demand for a systematic, i.e. totalizing and all-encompassing comprehension of the real. Not by chance, he clearly stated that today nobody could or should aim at renewing the nineteenth century "systematic projects [...] concerning the unity of all our knowing" (VZW, p. 14 [RAS, p. 7]), and that "die Systembauten [...] sind natürlich grobe Fälschungen" (Gadamer 1994c, p. 6). So, he always understood his own hermeneutic philosophy not "as an 'absolute' position but as a path of experiencing. Its modesty consists in the fact that for it there is no higher principle than this: holding oneself open to the conversation" (GW 2, p. 505 [Gadamer 1997b, p. 36]).

words, my idea is that the many dimensions of Gadamer's thought – aesthetics and human sciences, philosophy of language and moral philosophy, dialogue with the Greeks and interpretation of modern thought, observations on anthropological problems and remarks about socio-political issues – actually represent the different faces of a unitary philosophy.

One way to make this explicit, in my opinion, is to read his hermeneutic philosophy[13] in the light of those questions concerning the crisis of modernity and the limits of the techno-scientific civilization. Finally, it is my strong belief that such an interpretation of Gadamer's hermeneutics might help to throw light on some aspects of his philosophy – most of which were presented in the works he wrote before and after his *magnum opus*, and which were later collected in the ten volumes of his *Gesammelte Werke* – that have received little attention compared to the doctrines on art, history and

---

Apropos of this, it has also been observed that one of Gadamer's first writings, the essay *Zur Systemidee in der Philosophie* (Gadamer 1924), was strongly criticical of the philosophical systematic underlying the so-called "history of problems", i.e. of the Neo-Kantian concepts of history and system (Lembeck 2008, p. 36. See also Grondin 1999, pp. 76-78 [2003, pp. 66-68]). Moreover, it must be said that, in the case of thinkers like Gadamer, "man sollte systematische Ansprüche im traditionellen Sinn nicht mit einer systematischen Orientierung von Philosophie überhaupt verwechseln. Philosophie kann auch ohne enzyklopädische Absichten, ohne deduktive Verfahren und ohne Letztbegründung systematisch sein" (Figal 2007c, p. 95).

13 To be precise, most of the time Gadamer uses the expression "*philosophische Hermeneutik*", and only rarely "*hermeneutische Philosophie*" (see, for instance, GW 10, pp. 199 and 205). In recent times, a powerful and convincing attempt to distinguish philosophical hermeneutics from hermeneutic philosophy has been made by Günter Figal, who interprets the two expressions as embodying two different stages in the development of a full understanding of "the hermeneutical (*das Hermeneutische*)". On this topic, see Figal 1996 (especially pp. 11-31), 2000, 2003 and 2006 (especially pp. 5-58 [2010, pp. 5-47]). Also according to Reiner Wiehl, Gadamer has always been fundamentally uncertain about the relation of philosophical hermeneutics and hermeneutic philosophy (Wiehl 2009, p. 12).

language he presented in the three parts of *Wahrheit und Methode*. As a matter of fact, on the one side it is obviously true that,

> daß Gadamer heute als einer der wichtigsten Philosophen des zwanzigsten Jahrhunderts gilt [...], geht allein auf *Wahrheit und Methode* zurück. Dem Buch folgt kein weiteres nach. Was Gadamer später als systematischen Arbeiten verfasst hat, ist Ergänzung, Modifikation, in mancher Hinsicht auch Selbstkritik seiner – wie der Untertitel des Buches lautet – *Grundzüge einer philosophischen Hermeneutik*[14].

On the other side, however, it is also true that

> Im Lauf seines langen Lebens hat Gadamer sehr viel geschrieben [...]. Selbst *Wahrheit und Methode*, das mühevoll erreichte Ziel, stellt nur eine, wenn auch wichtige Etappe auf seinem Weg von der Phänomenologie zur Dialektik dar. Die Fülle dessen, was er später in mehr als vierzig Jahren hervorgebracht hat, sollte darüber keineswegs vernachlässigt oder gar ignoriert werden, will man die reiche Entfaltung und Differenzierung seiner philosophischen Besinnung nicht allzu sehr verengen. Die Relevanz, die man gewöhnlich *Wahrheit und Methode* zuerkennt, hat nicht nur die nachfolgenden, sondern auch die vorangehenden Schriften in den Schatten gestellt[15].

This is the case, in particular, with the ethical-political dimension of his philosophy, which in my opinion actually represents an aspect of decisive importance[16]. It is a well known fact that "the young

---

14 Figal 2007a, p. 1.
15 Di Cesare 2007, pp. 9-10 [2009, pp. 1-2]. Analogous remarks in Di Cesare 2008 (p. 22) and 2009 (pp. 56-57).
16 By the way, Gadamer's collected papers actually gather only a part of, but not all, his philosophical production. With regard to this question, he declared in an interview: "my very first thought was that I really do not want people to make a classic figure out of me, a person of whom everything I ever wrote is gathered up. So the edition of my writings does not offer my complete works [...] but rather my 'collected' works. I collected some for the edition and left others out" (GLB, p. 294 [GR, p. 426]). As we read in another interview: "I didn't aim at publishing everything [...]. When I am dead, I don't want people to publish everything I wrote, including some platitudes. The experience of Heidegger's complete works has been highly instructive, since it gave me the idea of how much an author can be penalized when everything he wrote appears in print. It is

Gadamer" was in a certain sense a "budding political theorist"[17], as his first works were fully devoted to the interpretation of Plato's and Aristotle's moral and political philosophies (set against the backdrop of the great crisis that affected Germany after the end of the First World War). The attention for the ethical-political dimension in Gadamer's hermeneutics, although "eclipsed" in *Wahrheit und Methode* by the greater attention paid to other questions concerning philosophy and the humanities, later returned to the core of his thought, especially in the 1970s, with the idea of hermeneutics *as* practical philosophy, and in the 1980s-1990s, with what has been called the "almost 'political' or cosmopolitan broadening of his hermeneutics"[18].

I also argue that the present account of Gadamer's philosophy, specifically focused on his concept of techno-science, the instrumental rationality it endorses and the fundamental role played by it in shaping the present human condition, could prove useful to amend some inveterate interpretations of his thought which, in my opinion, are actual misunderstandings. I refer, in particular, to the idea of Gadamer's philosophy – that has become almost commonplace after the famous controversy on hermeneutics and ideology critique of the late 1960s/early 1970s – as *traditionalist, conservative*, and prejudicially contrary to the values of modern Enlightenment. Whereas a close look at the ethical-political dimension of his philosophy shows that it is "*liberal*, liberating, and relevant to the *crisis of modernity* in

---

out of doubt, indeed, that the strength of Heidegger's thought is decreasing because of this complete edition" (Gadamer 2002, p. 224). Analogous considerations can be found in the essay *Das Drama Zarathustras*, where Gadamer obviously expresses appreciation for the scientific value of Giorgio Colli's and Mazzino Montinari's enterprise – due to which "we now have access for the first time to Nietzsche's notebooks in a reliable and sequential form, and therefore do not have to depend on the edition and selection of Nietzsche's notes, arranged by his sister and later editors" – but then adds: "such a complete edition also provides an excellent mode to conceal essential matters among inessential ones" (GW 4, p. 451 [Gadamer 1998b, p. 127]).

17 Sullivan 1989, p. 7.
18 Grondin 1999, p. 370 [2003, p. 329].

which we find ourselves today"[19], i.e. that it actually "leads in a more democratic and less authoritarian direction and that the form of *criticism* it allows is an interpretive form of *democratic* deliberation"[20]. But I also refer to the common vision of Gadamer's hermeneutics as an *anti-scientific* philosophy grounded on an idea of truth that is in principle opposed to the methods of science. In my opinion, it would be more precise to speak of an *anti-scientistic* philosophy, for reasons I will explain in the following chapters.

Now, it is without doubt that Gadamer, due to his extraordinary long life, was a "privileged" observer and a preeminent witness of the events of the twentieth century. As he himself declared at the beginning of the 1985 essay *Die Vielfalt Europas*: "I have lived through this stormy epoch from my childhood until today and may therefore qualify as a witness"[21]. However, since "it was without doubt the most murderous century of which we have record, both by the scale, frequency and length of the warfare which filled it", and also by "the unparalleled scale of the human catastrophes it produced, from the greatest famines in history to systematic genocide"[22], then it might be said that Gadamer had not only the honour, but also the burden[23], to have an overview of the twentieth century, so to speak, from its beginning to its end.

This point clearly emerges from Gadamer's philosophical writings and his autobiographical reflections. As a matter of fact, it was a century that, with regard to "the basic emotional, mental and religious circumstances of [the] time", could be described as suspended in "the uncertain position between belief and disbelief, between hope and despair"[24]. A century that, in a certain sense, began

---

19 Palmer 2003, p. 159 (my italics).
20 Warnke 2002, p. 79 (my italics).
21 EE, p. 7 [EPH, p. 221].
22 Hobsbawm 1996, p. 13.
23 See Gadamer 1999: "Zeuge des Jahrhunderts zu sein ist eine große Last".
24 GW 9, pp. 367-368 [EPH, pp. 111-112].

with the first shipwreck experienced in live broadcast by telegraph[25], and ended with the terrorist attack in New York on the 11th September, 2001, and the fall of the Twin Towers experienced in live broadcast by television and internet: an event upon which the centenarian Gadamer commented: "The world has become quite strange to me (*Es ist mir recht unheimlich geworden*)"[26].

Now, among the historical events which gave the twentieth century its murderous and tragic physiognomy, the First World War is surely the one upon which Gadamer has called the most attention. As Karl Löwith noticed, indeed, "the European war from 1914 to 1918 [...] was the end not simply of a century but rather of an entire epoch"[27], and Gadamer obviously perceived the epoch-making character of this event. In particular, Gadamer often emphasizes that while the nineteenth century had been an epoch of unlimited faith in science and progress, now it was precisely "the proud cultural consciousness of [the] liberal age, with its faith in scientifically based progress", that was "thoroughly defeated"[28]. In such a disoriented world, young people were searching for "a new orientation", while "a mood of catastrophe was spreading more and more, and was bringing about a break with the old traditions"[29]. From this point of view, Jean Grondin is surely right in claiming that

---

25 Quite significantly, Gadamer mentions the sinking of the Titanic on the 15th March, 1912 among his most vivid childhood memories (see PL, p. 7 [PA, p. 1]). According to his biographer Jean Grondin, it is extremely interesting that "Gadamer's memories of childhood were in general inflected by the 'progress of technological civilization', to which he developed an ambiguous relation [...]. This catastrophe fascinated him more completely [...] than the powder keg of the Balkan war – not least because the sinking of the Titanic had something to do with the demise of science, progress, and grandeur in general, just as it also evoked the downfall of the Titans. [...] Even today the world-famous picture of the sinking ship has lost nothing of its poignancy" (Grondin 1999, pp. 38-39 [2003, pp. 36-37]).
26 See Gadamer 2001d.
27 Löwith 1983, p. 477 [1995, p. 175].
28 GW 2, p. 480 [Gadamer 1997b, p. 4].
29 GW 2, p. 480 [Gadamer 1997b, p. 4]. The attention paid to the epoch-making and tragic significance of the First World War obviously does not imply that

Today it is a matter of discourse to discern of "crises" in the most various and vague coincidences. But there was a time so prone to profound crisis as that to which Gadamer belonged in 1918. [...] Modernity – that is, unbridled science as pure technology – apparently led directly to the trench warfare of the First World War [...]. It was not just the obvious inanity of internal politicians; it was not too little Enlightenment, actually, but too much science that had apparently led to catastrophe. [...] This sense of crisis was probably the initial appearance, profoundly troubling at the time, of what is today a widespread and relatively familiar skepticism about science. [...] The decline of science-based culture – that is, the decline of the West – was considered to be the direct consequence of the First World War battles, the *Materialschlachten* (battles of materials) often mentioned by Gadamer, where technology was decisive. [...] It is perhaps not too much to suggest that in his experience of the First World War declining toward its tragic conclusion we can glimpse one of the subterranean roots of Gadamer's thought[30].

Anyway, apropos of the philosophical, artistic, spiritual and cultural mood of those decades, I think that it is also important to differentiate

---

Gadamer was unaware, so to speak, of the enormous dimensions of the Second World War and the events that preceded and followed it, like "the terrible consequences of Hitler's accession to power – the new barbarism, the Nuremberg laws, the terror, [...] and, finally, the inextinguishable shame of the extermination camps" (Gadamer 1988c, p. 178 [1989a, p. 429]). With regard to this, in his autobiography Gadamer speaks of "a terrible awakening [when] the year 1933 broke in. [...] We had underrated Hitler and his kind, and admittedly we made the same mistake as the liberal press in doing this. Not one of us had read *Mein Kampf* [...]. It was a widespread conviction in intellectual circles that Hitler in coming to power would deconstruct the nonsense he had used to drum up the movement, and we counted the anti-Semitism as part of this nonsense. We were to learn differently. [...] Soon enough the fronts became clearer. The Nuremberg Laws put to an end any illusions one had with regard to the demise of anti-Semitism. Our Jewish friends had to leave us or to live quietly [...]. Parting was bitter [and] one felt ashamed to remain" (PL, pp. 51 and 53-54 [PA, pp. 75 and 77]). Finally, Gadamer recalls the moment when the Second World War broke out: "the news was announced over the loudspeaker. An unforgettable moment, especially for someone who had experienced the outbreak of war in 1914 [...]. The war news was received in Leipzig like a report of death. [...] I myself was shattered. I still held to the illusion that such an insane thing simply could not happen" (PL, p. 113 [PA, pp. 94-95]).

30 Grondin 1999, pp. 63-65 [2003, pp. 56-57].

Gadamer's position from those of other intellectuals. In fact, although Gadamer often recalled the particular fascination conveyed by books like Paul Ernst's *Zusammenbruch des deutschen Idealismus*, Oswald Spengler's *Untergang des Abendlandes*, Theodor Lessing's *Europa und Asien*, and Thomas Mann's *Betrachtungen eines Unpolitischen*[31], and although he recognized the basic root of the present problems in "the unquestioned belief in science so characteristic of our age", nonetheless he never identified himself with the "warning voices that have made themselves heard during the past century in the form of a pessimistic cultural critique, predicting the West's impending collapse"[32]. According to him, these warning voices are indeed the expression of "social strata threatened with extinction – [...] the nobility, the *haute bourgeoisie*, and the cultured middle class", and above all "they carry little conviction, if only because they are themselves immersed in the civilization produced by modern science"[33].

More generally, it is surely relevant to notice that Gadamer was always "very skeptical of every kind of pessimism", finding "in all pessimism a certain lack of sincerity"[34]. Gadamer, indeed, always insisted on the inner insincerity of every kind of pessimism, simply "because no one can live without hope"[35]. Even "after the terrible disappointments on the way to democracy in the world" that the twentieth century has caused us, although we must admit that "we cannot be too optimistic", nonetheless we must agree that "hope and forgetting characterize the human feeling of life"[36]. As we will see in the course of the book, this led him to develop a view of the present age that is surely critical, but less desperate than those developed by other leading thinkers of our time.

---

31 See GW 2, p. 480 [Gadamer 1997b, p. 4].
32 GW 2, p. 159 [EPH, pp. 168-169].
33 GW 2, p. 159 [EPH, p. 169].
34 HÄP, p. 71 [GC, p. 83].
35 HÄP, p. 71 [GC, p. 83].
36 Gadamer 1997a, p. 347.

2. Science and Technology: The Real Roots of Modernity

Gadamer always paid a great attention to the important role played by science and technology in our world. More precisely, according to him they actually represent the real roots of modernity. As a matter of fact, it is clear from many of Gadamer's writings that he even identifies the epochal transition to the modern age with the birth and growth of science and technology. That is, he somehow sees what we might define "techno-science" as the fundamental feature of the Western civilization from the seventeenth century on. So, in the essay *Wissenschaft als Instrument der Aufklärung* he poses the questions: "When and how did modernity begin? With the Renaissance? [...] With the discovery of the individual [...], with the discovery of America?" – and then he answers: "Whenever it started, it was certainly the new science that [...] became something quite new and ushered in the new epoch"[1].

According to Gadamer, the great fact of "the mathematical foundation of all empirical sciences" represented indeed "the actual beginning of modernity", which "did not begin on a certain date – this game of the historian has been played enough – but with the methodological ideal of modern science"[2]. To be sure, Gadamer never denies the existence of some historical and philosophical presuppositions in the ancient and medieval culture which set the basis, so to speak, for the development of the modern techno-scientific *forma mentis*. I think it is important to underline this point, because otherwise Gadamer's strong belief in the revolutionary significance of the advent of modern science could be interpreted as contradicting his well-known emphasis

---

1 LT, p. 93 [PT, pp. 75-76].
2 EE, p. 44 [EPH, p. 198].

on tradition, that is, on the basic continuity of history[3]. With specific regard to the question of science, it has thus been noticed that in a "Gadamerian approach", based on

> the ideas of an "effective history of scientific traditions" and an "effective-historical consciousness of scientific communities" [...] incommensurability becomes impossible. [...] In each scientific revolution, no matter how global it is, a class of prejudices remains unchanged. Conceptual change, therefore, is always a change within the realm of an already understood tradition[4].

Nonetheless, Gadamer argues that it was "at the start of modernity" that a revolutionary, completely new worldview took place: namely, a worldview which finally set free – although "not without losses" – "the thinking of Western humanity" from "a conception of nature [...] established [by] Plato and Aristotle"[5]. From that moment on, "the prevalence of science" has veritably become "the determinative mark of the age"[6], and such a "decisive change", Gadamer claims, "cannot [be] overemphasize[d]"[7]. Hence, in the the essay *Geschichte des Universums und Geschichtlichkeit des Menschen* we read:

---

3   So, for example, in his review of Hans Blumenberg's seminal work *Die Legitimität der Neuzeit* Gadamer writes that, for Blumenberg, "den Schein eines absoluten Neuanfangs [ist] sachlich zu berichtigen. [...] Descartes hat also tatsächlich das Gepräge und den Anspruch des neuzeitlichen Denkens grundelegend bestimmt, aber nicht dadurch, daß er der Tradition mit der Gewaltsamkeit eines radikalen Einbruchs und neuen Entwurfs entgegentrat, sondern dadurch, daß er die Implikationen des theologischen Absolutismus einen entscheidenden Schritt weiter explizierte [...]. Daß der Mensch unter den Bedingungen des theologischen Absolutismus mit weniger Wahrheit leben mußte, als es Antike und Hochscholastik ihm zugedacht und zugemutet hatte, erweist sich als Voraussetzung für eine neue Definition von Wissenschaftlichkeit. *Das scheint mir überzeugend*" (GW 4, pp. 54-56 [my italics]). Gadamer specifically refers here to the second part of Blumenberg's long and complex book, concerning the relationship of theological absolutism and human self-assertion (Blumenberg 1966, pp. 75-200 [1985, pp. 123-226]).
4   Ginev 1997, pp. 23 and 63.
5   GW 7, p. 426 [Gadamer 1986e, p. 49].
6   VZW, p. 118 [RAS, p. 145].
7   EE, p. 15 [EPH, p. 225].

wir [leben] in einer Kultur [...], in der sich die Wissenschaft seit Jahrhunderten zu einem bestimmenden Faktor nicht nur in Europa, sondern in der ganzen Welt entwickelt hat. [...] [Die] neue Wissenschaft der Neuzeit [...] war eine wahrhafte Revolution, [...] die sich im 17. Jahrhundert voll durchsetzte. Damals zersprang die homogene Einheit des antiken Weltdenkens [...]. Ein eigentümlicher Riß war damit eingetreten – und ein neues Rechtfertigungsbedürfnis. Es war ein neuer Wissenschaftsbegriff, der sich im 17. Jahrhundert durchsetzte. Gegründet auf das Experiment und auf die Mathematik, war es eine neue Maßgesinnung, die in beständigem Fortschritt und dauernder Selbstüberholung Wissenschaft schließlich zur Forschung umbildete[8].

And still in the important essay *Bürger zweier Welten* he writes:

it is undeniable that the science which developed in Greece represents the differentiating characteristic of the world culture emanating from Europe. Certainly [...] the form of science – in the widest possible sense of the word – received its actual character in Greece and this in a sense which *does not yet incorporate* the specific meaning of the modern empirical sciences, by means of which Europe is changing the world today. [...] In a very broad sense, we can call what happened there and what structured the history of the West "enlightenment", enlightenment through science. What does science mean here? Perhaps it will prove to be true that the awakening of science in Greece, on the one hand, and the development of the scientific culture of modernity, on the other hand, *despite all the continuity* in Western history, will exhibit *so great a difference* that the unity of meaning in the concept of enlightenment will also be affected[9].

---

8 GW 10, pp. 209 and 216.
9 GW 10, pp. 225-226 [EPH, pp. 209-210 (my italics)]. Analogous considerations can be found, among other places, in the essay *Natur und Welt. Die hermeneutische Dimension in Naturerkenntnis und Naturwissenschaft*, where Gadamer asks: "Ist damals, im 17. Jahrhundert, nicht erstmals Wissenschaft im Sinne der mathematischen Naturwissenschaft, die sich auf Messung und Experimente gründete, in Erscheinung getreten, und zwar als etwas Neues, nicht nur gegenüber dem zeitgenössischen Aristotelismus, sondern auch und gerade gegenüber dem gesamten Erbe der durch Aristoteles und Plato begründeten Tradition?" – and then concludes: "Mir scheint das nicht einfach ein anderes Paradigma, das mit Galileis Begründung der Mechanik in der modernen Naturwissenschaft zur Geltung gekommen ist. Es war nicht lediglich ein

As is well known, philosophers and historians of science have been extensively and persistently debating over such questions for decades. Some of them, for example, "such as Butterfield, Kuhn and many others, have seen the science of the seventeenth century as marking a radical departure from the science of all previous periods", whereas others, "such as Duhem and Crombie, [...] have been inclined to trace science back from the seventeenth century into the Renaissance and the Middle Ages"[10]. So, while the former scholars "speak confidently of 'The Scientific Revolution'", the latter play down – at least to some degree – "the novelty of the seventeenth-century scientific movement, emphasising rather the continuities with earlier theories and practices"[11]. Within such an intellectual "diatribe", it would probably be more likely to ascribe Gadamer's ideas on the relation between ancient and modern science to the first line of thought than to the second.

However, apart from these questions that mainly pertain to the history and philosophy of science, what matters in our specific discourse is that the whole modern age, according to Gadamer, "is defined – notwithstanding all disputed datings and derivations – quite univocally by the emergence of a new notion of science"[12]. And if we now ask ourselves what constitutes the very essence of such a scientifically determined civilization, then we will find that Gadamer's answer lies in a simple word that is already present in the title of his *magnum opus*. That is, in the simple word "method". So, for example, in the 1947 lecture *Das Verhältnis der Philosophie zu Kunst und Wissenschaft* Gadamer claims:

> Man wird wohl, wenn man *die Eigenart der abendländischen Kultur* beschreiben will, Übereinstimmung in der Behauptung finden, daß sie von der Wissenschaft entscheidend bestimmt und beherrscht ist. Und fragen wir uns, was *das Wesen dieser durch die Wissenschaft beherrschten Kultur* ist, so liegt die

---

 Paradigmenwechsel – es war eine Umgestaltung dessen, was Wissenschaft überhaupt sein kann" (GW 7, pp. 436 and 439).
10 Oldroyd 1986, p. 48.
11 Oldroyd 1986, p. 48.
12 VZW, p. 13 [RAS, p. 6].

Antwort ebenfalls auf der Hand: Es ist *das Methodische* im Verhalten des Abendländers, das wir damit meinen, das Methodische in der Wissenschaft und ihrem Betrieb, das Methodische der Anwendung der Wissenschaft in der Technik und der Industrie, das Methodische in der Ordnung unseres sozialen Lebens, das Methodische in der Zerstörung. *Planen, Machen, Beherrschen*, das scheint die eigentliche Grundhaltung des durch die Wissenschaft des Abendlandes geprägten Menschentums zu sein[13].

What emerges from these and other analogous passages taken from Gadamer's writings is the planning-controlling-dominating attitude he ascribes on the whole to the methodical, i.e. scientific *forma mentis*. In addition to this, Gadamer actually envisions the tight relations subsisting between modern science, its technological applications and the economic-industrial progress in our societies. As a matter of fact, "the tremendous development of the sciences" in the last centuries has led to "the encompassing technical applications of our new knowledge and abilities, so that one began to call it the 'industrial revolution', which since then has rolled over us in ever new waves"[14]. Hence, he notices that science "has become today the primary productive factor of the human economy"[15].

Now, although the questions regarding science and technology play a central role in his whole thought, one must admit that it is quite hard to find a precise theory of science in Gadamer's works. In the same way, even in *Wahrheit und Methode* there is no specific chapter or section dedicated to this latter concept (method), which is however of decisive importance to understand his own philosophical position. Nevertheless, given the countless hints and indications on this subject that Gadamer included in all of his writings, it is quite easy to derive at least the basic features of his overall concept of science.

The starting point for such an analysis is precisely represented by the concept of method, i.e. by what Gadamer calls "the methodical thinking of modern science"[16]. As is well known, his inquiry in

---

13 KS 1, pp. 22-23 (my italics).
14 EE, p. 20 [EPH, p. 228].
15 GW 4, p. 247 [EH, p. 6].
16 GW 1, p. 29 [TM, p. 21].

Wahrheit und Methode has its origin from a profound "dissatisfaction with the modern concept of methodology"[17]. More precisely, in the very first section of the book Gadamer begins by questioning the supposed universal pertinence of "the inductive method, basic to all experimental science", and concerned with "establishing similarities, regularities, and conformities to law which would make it possible to predict individual phenomena and processes"[18]. Here he refers particularly to John Stuart Mill's ideas on the applicability of inductive logic also to human sciences, and he stresses the fact that Mill belongs to "an English tradition of which Hume has given the most effective formulation in the introduction to his *Treatise*"[19]. Anyway, behind the question concerning "the method of the social sciences, [...] the methodological ideas of the eighteenth century and their programmatic formulation by Hume, ideas that are a clichéd version of scientific method"[20], Gadamer catches the glimpse of another leading figure of modern philosophy, or better the founder of modern philosophical tradition itself: René Descartes.

According to Gadamer, "scientific certainty always has something Cartesian about it", and "Cartesian echoes cannot be missed"[21] in each and every epistemological conception proposed after the seventeenth century. It was Descartes, indeed, who "philosophically grounded for the first time [the] new notion of science and method", that had been "worked out initially in a partial field of study

---

17 GW 1, p. 467 [TM, p. 459].
18 GW 1, p. 9 [TM, p. 3].
19 GW 1, p. 9 [TM, p. 3].
20 GW 1, pp. 364-365 [TM, p. 353].
21 GW 1, pp. 242-243 [TM, pp. 231-232]. As a matter of fact, this last sentence is taken from the section of *Wahrheit und Methode* regarding the conflict between science and life-philosophy within Dilthey's analysis of historical consciousness, and it is specifically directed against "the unresolved Cartesianism" of Dilthey's "epistemological reflections on the basis of the human science" (GW 1, p. 241 [TM, p. 231]) that Gadamer strongly criticizes. In a latter essay Gadamer goes so far as to even speak of a positivistic spirit which would characterize Dilthey's philosophy (see GW 4, pp. 406-424).

by Galileo"[22]. It was Descartes who actually conceived "the idea of the unitary method of knowledge (*Einheitsmethode der Erkenntnis*)"[23], "the idea of a universal method of verification"[24]: namely, the idea that "what is called 'method' in modern sciences remains the same everywhere"[25]. So, it was actually Descartes' mature works, like the *Discours de la méthode*, the *Meditationes de prima philosophia* and the *Principia philosophiae*, as well as his early writing *Regulae ad directionem ingenii* – emphatically defined by Gadamer as his "real treatise on method, [...] the veritable manifesto of modern science" –, that "set a task for an entire age"[26]. From that moment on, things would never be the same in philosophy, science and, more in general, in the whole of Western culture. As Jean Grondin expresses it:

---

22 VZW, p. 13 [RAS, p. 6].
23 GW 4, p. 246 [EH, p. 5].
24 Cfr. LT, p. 95 [PT, p. 77]. As we read in the essay *Wissenschaft als Instrument der Aufklärung*, "Descartes [...] gave the concept of method a new, dominant position. Method is, to be sure, an ancient Greek concept, and the Greek concept of method also meant approaching the thing to be known in a way appropriate to it. But the Greek concept of method took the criterion of its appropriateness from the individual character of the subject under consideration in each case. It was in opposition to this that Descartes developed the idea of a standard method" (LT, p. 95 [PT, p. 77]).
25 GW 1, p. 13 [TM, p. 7].
26 GW 1, p. 464 [TM, p. 456]. In the essay *Philosophie oder Wissenschaftstheorie?* Gadamer even assigns a sort of "primacy" to the *Regulae* over other works of Descartes. In fact, he writes: "His *Discourse on Method*, and still more the elaboration of his ideal of method in the so-called *Regulae*, [...] was meant to develop a novel ideal of knowledge" (VZW, p. 132 [RAS, p. 156]). As John Cottingham has noticed, indeed, "towards the end of the 1620s Descartes produced his first major work, the *Regulae ad Directionem Ingenii*", a book which "was never completed and was not published in Descartes' lifetime", and which testified for the very first time "his lifelong project of establishing a universal method for arriving at the truth. [...] The main inspiration for Descartes' model of knowledge in the *Regulae* is mathematics", and its aim is to "enable the precise nature and structure of each problem", in order to make it "transparently clear" (Cottingham 1986, p. 10).

Descartes is the originator of the idea of method that forms the basis of the scientific project of modern times, or quite simply the modern method. For Descartes, the whole edifice of certain and *indubitable knowledge*, that of science, must be *methodologically* reviewed and made secure [...]. Descartes finds the foundation and model of this certainty in the evidence of the *cogito*, of the "I think" which is true each time I am aware of thinking, even when I take the trouble to doubt it [...]. All other knowledge, following the example of geometry, can be deduced by the same method of *certainty*, and by virtue of the same *clarity*. Based on the *evidence* of the "I think", [...] methodological knowledge is that in which all stages are made secure and which can be verified by others, provided that they follow the rational order [...]. From now on, only evidence and the clarity of rightly ordered thought count. [...] The evidence is found first of all in the *consciousness of the subject*, but it extends to the whole universe of *mathematical* and geometrical truths which share in the same certainty and find their true basis in the certainty of the "I think". It only remains to *extend* this type of methodological certainty to the other sciences[27].

I think this long quotation contains most of the terms which actually form Gadamer's concept of modern science. And these are precisely the terms that I chose to italicize in the passage taken from Grondin's introduction to the philosophy of Gadamer.

In many of his writings Gadamer stresses indeed the relevance of the Cartesian doubt[28] and, most of all, of the "reduction of truth to

---

27 Grondin 2003, pp. 1-2 (my italics).
28 So, in *Wahrheit und Methode* we read: "modern science [follows] the rule of Cartesian doubt, accepting nothing as certain that can in any way be doubted, and adopting the idea of method that follows from this rule. [...] Just as when in his famous meditation on doubt Descartes set up an artificial and hyperbolical doubt like an experiment, which led to the *fundamentum inconcussum* of self-consciousness, so methodical science fundamentally doubts everything that can be doubted in order to guarantee the certainty of its results" (GW 1, pp. 275 and 243 [TM, pp. 273 and 232]). Gadamer obviously here is referring to the Cartesian method of hyperbolic doubt that is meant to finally lead to the absolute and indubitable certainty of the "I think, therefore I am": *"je pense, donc je suis"* (Descartes 1973a, p. 32 [1979, p. 101]); *"ego cogito ergo sum"* (Descartes 1973c, p. 7 [1979, p. 221]). As he explains in his second *Meditation*, "this proposition: I am, I exist, is necessarily true each time that I pronounce it, or that I mentally conceive it. [...] But what am I [...]? [...] I find here that thought is an attribute that belongs to me; it alone cannot be separated from me. I am, I

certainty" that gave birth to "a new, narrower sense of knowledge which first became valid in the modern period"[29]. As a matter of fact, the fundamental aim of modern science consists for Gadamer in deliberately restraining our world-experience's wideness and vagueness. And this finds a clear expression precisely in the concepts of method and scientific objectivity, in the sense that "only what is approached by methodological means, namely 'what is objectified' (*das "Objizierte"*), can become the object (*Gegenstand*) of scientific knowledge"[30]. In other words, in the "new epoch of knowledge of the world" inaugurated by Descartes (but not only by him, as we will see) "the objects of science are defined by the conditions of methodical knowability"[31] – something that Gadamer also expresses with the idea of the primacy of method over the subject matter itself[32]. This, in turn, perfectly fits with the modern claim for a universal way of knowledge, independently from the diversity of its objects.

---

    exist, that is certain (*Ego sum, ego existo, certum est*). [...] I do not now admit anything which is not necessarily true: to speak accurately I am not more than a thing which thinks (*res cogitans*), that is to say a mind (*mens*) or a soul (*animus*), or an understanding (*intellectus*), or a reason (*ratio*)" (Descartes 1973b, pp. 25-27 [1979, pp. 150-152]).

29   ÜVG, p. 184 [EH, p. 148].
30   GW 7, p. 433.
31   GW 2, p. 320 [PT, p. 51].
32   Not by chance, apropos of the differences between natural and human sciences Gadamer says: "The humanities and social sciences [...] may be distinguished from the natural sciences not only through their ways of proceeding but also through the preliminary relationship they have to their subject matter [...]. This is the reason I have suggested that the ideal of objective knowledge which dominates our concepts of knowledge, science, and truth, needs to be supplemented by the ideal of sharing in something, of participation. [...] In other words, knowledge in the humanities and social sciences always has something of self-knowledge in it. This kind of application can never be taken away. [...] In all understanding an application occurs, such that the person who is understanding is himself or herself *right there* in the understood meaning. He or she *belongs to* the subject-matter that he or she is understanding" (HÄP, pp. 14-15 and 23-24 [GC, pp. 40 and 47]). The same observations can also be found, among other places, in GW 2, p. 323.

What emerges from these last quotations is also the close connection between the two new concepts of method and object, or better the centrality of the objectifying attitude for the entire scientific enterprise. As a matter of fact, Gadamer repeatedly underlines how the growing development of the very notion of *Objekt* or *Gegenstand* – "meaning 'object', literally, 'that which stands over against us' [or] 'that which offers resistance' (*Widerstand*)" – has been "wholly in accord with that sense of radical new departure which has dominated modern science since the beginnings of modernity"[33]. More precisely, as he explains in the essay *Die Ausdruckskraft der Sprache*, it was thanks to the new scientific model that this concept was defined, "whereas before there was no such word or thing":

> "*Objekt*" or "*Gegenstand*" is defined through a "method" that prescribes how reality gets made into an object. The aim of methodically researching the object in this way is then essentially to break down the resistance of "objects" and to dominate the processes of it; the basic intentions of technology [...] are an immanent consequence of it, and their reality surrounds us on all sides in the shape of our technological civilization[34].

But the very notion of *object* would not be understandable without its correlative concept, namely the *subject*, which, as we have seen, was assumed as *fundamentum inconcussum* in the philosophy of the modern age[35]. And, in turn, the subject/object dichotomy (according to Gadamer, one of the fundamental elements of the scientific attitude) implicates the basic Cartesian "distinction between the *res extensa* and *res cogitans*", which "signified the dawning of a new epoch" and

---

33 ÜVG, p. 135 [EH, p. 105].
34 LT, p. 154 [PT, p. 127].
35 From this point of view, it has been noticed that, "for Gadamer, subjectivism [is] the other side of objectivism" (Cambiano 1988, p. 43). And this also explains why philosophical hermeneutics precisely aims to establish an alternative point of view "beyond objectivism and relativism" (see Bernstein 1983, pp. 1-49 and 109-169), although it must be said that the notions of subjectivism and relativism, notwithstanding their close relation, are not exactly synonymic.

constitutes "the basis [on which] the whole of modern science rests"[36]. Hence, the capacity of objectification emerges as something indispensable for the acquisition of knowledge in the modern scientific orientation[37].

But "first and foremost here is the ability to weigh and measure"[38], and this leads to still another aspect of modern science: its mathematical component. As a matter of fact, measurement involves quantification, i.e. the idea of progressively reducing the whole of the real to mere quantitative, mathematical relations. In many of his writings Gadamer insists on this particular point: the need for mathematical abstraction from the concrete, effective conditions of our world-experience. As Gadamer expresses it in the very last section of *Wahrheit und Methode*, dedicated to language and universal hermeneutics:

> The objectifying procedures of natural sciences [...] proved to be an abstraction when viewed from the medium that language is. Abstracted from the fundamental relation to the world that is given in the linguistic nature of our experience of it, science attempts to become certain about entities by methodically organizing its knowledge of the world. Consequently it condemns

---

36 ÜVG, p. 184 [EH, p. 148]. On the close relation between the subject/object opposition and the *res cogitans/res extensa* dualism, see, for instance, GW 2, p. 410; GW 7, p. 440

37 This point is expressed in a particularly clear way in the essay *The Relevance of Greek Philosophy for Modern Thought*, where we read that the "fundamental thesis" of modern science "is that nothing can be known, nothing can be scientifically investigated or truly understood, unless it conforms to procedure of method. Henceforth, objectivity was to be the new epistemological watchword [...]. Objectivity in this sense specifies the very limits of our knowledge – what we cannot objectify we also cannot know. Indeed, this expresses the basic principle of modern science", which "bases itself on the ideal of objectivity" (Gadamer 1987, p. 41). As we will see, Gadamer's hermeneutics precisely represents a theory of the limits of *objectifying science*, that is, a philosophy according to which "it is [...] clear that not everything can be achieved by such means" (ÜVG, pp. 127-128 [EH, p. 97]).

38 ÜVG, p. 135 [EH, p. 105].

as heresy all knowledge that does not allow of this kind of certainty and that therefore cannot serve the growing domination of being[39].

Taking into consideration this distinctive feature of the scientific enterprise, he pays specific attention to the role played by another great protagonist of the so-called scientific revolution: Galileo Galilei. Notwithstanding that the importance of the idea of a "universal mathematics (*mathesis universalis*)" was strongly felt by Descartes as well[40], it was mostly due to Galilei indeed if "the mathematical construction of idealized relationships of motion was elevated into the method of knowing reality"[41]. That is, it was mostly due to Galilei – whose ideal of science, formulated in the letter to the grand duchess Cristina, called for both "sense experiences and necessary demonstrations"[42] – if nature, from the seventeenth century onwards, was "subjected [...] to mathematical construction", so as to achieve "a new notion of natural law":

> With Galileian mechanics and the spread of its procedures into the entire field of experience a new idea of science emerged. [...] Inquiry into the laws of nature on the basis of the mathematical abstraction and its verification by means of measuring, counting, and weighing were present at the birth of the modern sciences of nature. They made possible for the first time the complete

---

39   GW 1, pp. 479-480 [TM, p. 471].
40   See Descartes 1974, pp. 378-379 [1979, pp. 13-14].
41   GW 4, pp. 41-42 [PT, p. 23]. As is well known, in the book *Il Saggiatore* we read: "Philosophy is written in [an] all-encompassing book that is constantly open before our eyes, that is the universe; but it cannot be understood unless one first learns to understand the language and knows the characters in which it is written. It is written in mathematical language" (Galilei 2005b, p. 631 [2008, p. 183]). On this topic, let us be reminded of a famous passage of the *Dialogo sopra i due massimi sistemi del mondo* as well, where Galilei distinguishes intensive and extensive knowledge, and then claims: "the human intellect does understand some [propositions] perfectly, and thus in these it has as much absolute certainty as Nature itself has. Of such are the mathematical sciences", with regard to which the human intellect's knowledge "equals the Divine in objective certainty" (Galilei 2005c, p. 135 [1967, p. 103]).
42   Galilei 2005a, pp. 559 and 587 [2008, pp. 116 and 139].

application of science to the technical transformation of nature for humanly conceived purposes. And this has marked our civilization on a planetary scale[43].

In other words, in modern science – and consequently in the modern scientific civilization, i.e. in what Gadamer calls on the whole "the age of science" – "*everything is measured*"[44]. From this point of view, thanks to the development of the new mathematical model the "concrete information concerning observed phenomena" is progressively organized "under general laws": something which undoubtedly constitutes "one of the decisive achievements of modern science"[45].

While considering the central role played by mathematics in modern science, Gadamer also points out the decisive shift that occurred in the meaning of the concept of mathematics itself. In fact, on various occasions he recalls how mathematics "was the uncontested science of antiquity"[46], that is, how it represented already for the Greeks "the obvious model and the quintessence of all science (*das selbstverständliche Vorbild und der Inbegriff aller Wissenschaft*)"[47]. Such a primacy, however, was conceived in a very different way from the way it was in the modern age, characterized by its "empirical science grounded on mathematics"[48]. In ancient Greece (and, more generally, in pre-modern culture) science was indeed "essentially represented by mathematics", because it dealt "with what

43 VZW, p. 131 [RAS, pp. 155-156].
44 ÜVG, p. 128 [EH, p. 98 (my italics)].
45 ÜVG, p. 127 [EH, p. 97]. Even in the essay *Die Gegenwartsbedeutung der griechischen Philosophie* Gadamer explains that "das, was ist, dem berechenden Entwurf – im Sinne der mathematischen Naturwissenschaft – zugeordnet ist: *Berechnung* durch Isolation und Messung der das Naturgeschehen bestimmenden Faktoren war der Weg, auf dem Galilei die klassische Mechanik entwickelte. [...] Der Stolz dieses wissenschaftlichen Weltzugangs ist seine Objektivität: [...] so wird die *Objektivität* der Wissenschaft, wird die *Wißbarkeit* zum Inbegriff des leitenden Seinsverständnisses – und die aus den wißbaren Bedingungen folgende *Machbarkeit*. Das, was wahrhaft ist, ist der berechnete *Gegenstand*" (HE, p. 105 [my italics]).
46 LT, p. 153 [PT, p. 126].
47 GW 7, p. 294.
48 GW 7, p. 438.

is unchangeable", and it was consequently understood as a "genuine [...] science of reason"[49]. Hence, while Gadamer observes – for example, with reference to Plato's *Meno* – that mathematics stood for everything that the Greeks "would call real knowledge or insight"[50], he also underlines that

> if in the end even nature came to be thought of as approximating these [...] pure mathematical and numerical relationships [...], it was still always compulsory assumptions and their consequences, the logic of proof, *apodeixis* (which is most purely embodied in mathematics), that constituted science. On the other hand, though modern science is certainly also familiar with the dominance of the *instrumentarium* of mathematics, what distinguishes it from the sciences of pure reason [...] is that modern sciences understand themselves as sciences of experience. A concept like "science of experience" would have sounded like "wooden iron" to Greek ears. [...] It cannot be denied that the new empirical science with its new ideal of method, applying mathematical projections to nature and natural processes, [...] has paradoxical connotations for the tradition from which our civilization developed. Science that needs only experience in order to be true! What kind of "science" is that? [...] In mathematics, truth is established from concepts through thought's own self-development. As soon as experience comes into it, science can be effective only in a supporting role. And now modernity turns everything upside down[51].

---

49 GW 2, p. 319 [PT, p. 50].
50 GW 7, p. 159 [IGPAP, p. 56]. Gadamer refers here to the famous episode of Socrates' maieutic experiment with the slave boy who, "after he has put the false solutions behind him, [...] recognizes that a square constructed on the diagonal has the double area he seeks" (GW 7, p. 158 [IGPAP, p. 55]). See Plato, *Meno*, 82a-86c [1997, pp. 881-886].
51 LT, pp. 89-90 and 152-153 [PT, pp. 72 and 126]. Analogous considerations on the somehow paradoxical meaning of the very expression "*Erfahrungswissenschaft*" (empirical science, science of experience) can also be found, for instance, in EE, p. 15 [EPH, p. 225] and VZW, p. 12 [RAS, p. 5]. Even in the 1998 essay *Die Philosophie und ihre Geschichte* Gadamer observes: "Der Begriff von Wissenschaft, der in Griechenland entstanden ist, *episteme* (*scientia, science*), war [...] an der Mathematik orientiert. Sie war die einzige reine Vernunftswissenschaft und stand im ausschließenden Gegensatz zur Erfahrung. Der für die neuzeitliche Wissenschaft angemessene Ausdruck 'Erfahrungs-

Among other things, what emerges from this overview is the shift occurred during the modern epoch also in the concept of experience: the progressive reduction of the concept of *experience*, with all its broadness and richness, to that of *experiment*[52]. And this means that the mathematical, methodological, experimental and "artificial" approach of modern science also entails a decisive and indeed unavoidable break with the "natural", i.e. naïve, unsophisticated knowledge provided by our everyday experience. As a matter of fact, according to Gadamer, modern science actually represents "a certain form of access to our world", namely one "that is neither the only nor the most encompassing access that we possess", and that is grounded on abstraction, "methodical isolation and conscious interrogation – in the experiment"[53].

Apropos of this, Gadamer often mentions the example of Galilei's decisive discovery of the law of free fall of heavy bodies. A discovery that actually "was to become the cornerstone of a new physics"[54], and that Gadamer interprets as a "decisive breakthrough", for here was a man, Galilei,

> who explicitly stated on himself and his new science of mechanics, *mente concipio*, I conceive in mind, and meant with this the pure conditions for the appearances of motion in nature. He discovered, for example, the laws for free fall in this manner, since he began from something which he, in fact, could only conceive in his mind: falling in a vacuum. At that time it was not possible to

---

wissenschaft' wäre für den Platoniker so etwas wie ein hölzernes Eisen" (HE, p. 70).

52 This particular topic is at the core of the section of *Wahrheit und Methode* on the concept of experience and the essence of hermeneutic experience (GW 1, pp. 352-368 [TM, pp. 341-355]). Here Gadamer carefully distinguishes his notion of *Erfahrung* both from the concept of *Erlebnis* – which he previously analyzed in the first, aesthetical part of *Wahrheit und Methode* (see GW 1, pp. 66-87 [TM, pp. 53-70]), and which has been predominant in the human sciences since the nineteenth century – and from the concept of *Experiment* – which, in turn, has been predominant in the theory of the natural sciences since Bacon's *Novum Organum* and Galilei's *Dialogo sopra i due massimi sistemi del mondo*.
53 GW 2, p. 186 [GR, p. 94].
54 Drake 2001, p. 5.

construct an experiment where one could observe a body falling without resistance. [...] The power of abstraction, which was necessary to have this thought, and the power of imaginative construction, which was required to isolate the conditioning factors, to measure them quantitatively, to symbolize and relate them to one another – these were in fact new things, which would cause the fateful change in the relationship of humans to the world[55].

A new approach of humans to the world, breaking once and for all with the traditional world-image of a "large homogeneous structure of determined order and goals" that characterized the "humanistic physics of Aristotle"[56]. In which physics was based on reasoning such as: "a stone falls because it wants to be in its very own place together with other stones", and "fire ascends because it wants to unite itself so to speak with the great fiery space in the sphere of the stars"[57]. Now, Gadamer surely concedes that such a world-explanation may appear "comical to us"[58], "more amusing than serious"[59]. And he also admits that the abandonment of the ancient teleological approach was highly important for the "great victory march" of science "through the whole of modernity up to our age"[60]. Nonetheless, he adds that a world-image like the ancient one represented "an *understandable* whole which *appeared to the senses* as the order of events in nature", and which "completely corresponded to the way humans *acted*", i.e. to

---

55   EE, p. 16 [EPH, p. 226]. Galilei's discovery of the law of free fall and his famous formula *"mente concipio"* are also mentioned, for instance, in GW 2, p. 186 [GR, p. 94]; GW 2, p. 496 [Gadamer 1997b, p. 28]; GW 4, pp. 216-217 [RAS, p. 70]. About the expression *"mente concipio* (imagine, conceive)", see Galilei 2005d, p. 770 [2010, p. 244]. In a famous passage of the *Dialogo sopra i due massimi sistemi del mondo*, Filippo Salviati – the character who defends the Copernican theory and actually presents the ideas of Galilei himself – recommends Simplicio, his Aristotelian counterpart in the conversation, to observe things "if not with one's actual eyes, at least with those of the mind", in order to present "a more suitable experiment" (Galilei 2005c, p. 184 [1967, p. 143]).

56   EE, pp. 17-18 [EPH, pp. 226-227].
57   GW 7, p. 428 [Gadamer 1986e, p. 51].
58   EE, p. 17 [EPH, p. 226].
59   GW 7, p. 428 [Gadamer 1986e, p. 51].
60   GW 7, p. 428 [Gadamer 1986e, p. 51].

their *"purposeful* work"[61]. In other words, the old Aristotelian conception allowed

> a uniform understanding of the whole of the world surrounding us, in the same way as we understand (*verstehen*) ourselves in our actions. [...] Ever since the start of modern experimental sciences we are exposed to [a] tension which permeates our entire culture and which has made the talk of two worlds possible. The one [world] is the research of nature represented by modern science. [...] The other [world] is the teleological ordering of the world which holds self-evidently in the linguistic picture of the world which we all share. It permits us even after the Copernican turn to speak of sunrise and sunset – and not of the earth's rotation[62].

Finally, beside objectivity, methodology, experimentalism, mathematical constructivism, and the reduction of the idea of truth to that of certainty and exactness, there is at least another point that Gadamer emphasizes. It is the aspect of the basic theoretical framework of modern science that concerns technology, or better the inseparability of science and technology. In fact, he claims that "technology is not a mere secondary consequence of the new knowledge of nature, or only of its technical presuppositions"[63]. Rather, technology "lies in the very essence of science", since the latter "understands itself precisely as a kind of knowledge that is guided by the idea of transforming nature [...] by means of rationally controlled projective 'construction'"[64].

---

61 EE, p. 17 [EPH, pp. 226-227 (my italics)]. An interesting contribution on these particular issues is that of Griffero 2004, who – notwithstanding some criticism towards the Gadamerian approach – highlights various relevant points common to both the philosophy of hermeneutic experience and the so-called naïve physics or the theory of the structures of the common-sense world.
62 GW 7, p. 428 [Gadamer 1986e, p. 51]. The example of the persistent attitude which makes us talk about sunrise and sunset, even in a post-Copernican world, is also mentioned by Gadamer on other occasions. See, for instance, GW 1, pp. 452-453 [TM, pp. 445-446]; LT, pp. 153-154 [PT, pp. 126-127].
63 LT, pp. 94-95 [PT, pp. 76-77].
64 GW 4, p. 272 [EH, p. 39]. With regard to this last point, the founding father of modern science that Gadamer has in mind is probably Bacon (even more than Descartes or Galilei), whose basic understanding of the scientific enterprise is notoriously contained in the idea of a *scientia activa*, that is, a science in which

According to Gadamer, indeed, the modern mathematical-experimental model of science "corresponds less to the Greek concept of science, *episteme*, than to the Greek concept of *techne*"[65]. So, in the essay precisely entitled *Theorie, Technik, Praxis*, he writes:

> One must make clear the full significance of the innovation which came into the world with the experimental sciences and the underlying idea of method. If one contrasts "science" with the whole of that knowledge of former times derived from the heritage of antiquity and which was still dominant throughout the high Middle Ages, it is apparent that the conceptions both of theory and practice have fundamentally changed. Naturally there was always application of knowledge to practice, as indicated by the very terms "science" and "arts" (*epistemai* and *technai*). "Science" [...] understood itself, however, as pure *theoria* [...]. It is thus not altogether wrong to say that modern natural science – without detracting from the purely theoretical interest that animates it – means not so much knowledge as know-how. This means [...] that science makes possible knowledge directed to the power of making, a knowing mastery of nature. This is technology[66].

Now, I think it is clear from this overall presentation that such a conception of science and technology has been strongly influenced, at least in certain aspects, by the work and ideas of other philosophers and theorists. In other words, Gadamer's basic understanding of modern science reveals the traces of some profound theoretical debts.

The most evident influence on Gadamer's thought is probably that of his teacher, Martin Heidegger, who explicitly includes science

---

"those twin objectives, human *Knowledge* and *Power*, do in fact come together", and which "is no mere matter of contemplative success but of human welfare and fortune, and of all power to carry out works" (Bacon 2004, p. 44 [2004, p. 45]). Gadamer emphasizes the role of Bacon as a foreshadower of the new age of techno-science in GW 1, pp. 13, 354-355 and 457 [TM, pp. 7, 343-344 and 450].

65 GW 2, pp. 22-23 [Gadamer 1997b, p. 56].
66 GW 4, pp. 245 and 247 [EH, pp. 4-6]. On the lost significance of the original Greek concept of *theoria* as pure contemplation, as "being purely present to what is truly real", see also GW 1, pp. 129-130 and 458-460 [TM, pp. 122 and 450-452]; GW 4, p. 216 [RAS, p. 69].

and technology among the "essential phenomena of modernity"[67] in his seminal 1938 essay *Die Zeit des Weltbildes*. An essay apropos of which Gadamer, in a late interview, emphatically asks: "Is this essay something from yesterday or is it not rather from tomorrow? Or even the day after tomorrow?"[68]. In *Die Zeit des Weltbildes* Heidegger takes indeed the essence of modern techno-science into consideration, and proposes an interpretation that has a great deal in common with Gadamer's one. In this way, he referers to the almost incommensurable difference between the ancient *episteme*, the medieval *doctrina*, and the modern concept of science as research[69]. Heidegger then underlines the importance of "method (*Verfahren*)" – clearly indicated as an "essential characteristic of research" – and the role played by mathematics, or better by "a quite specific kind of [it]"[70], if compared to the Greek concept of mathematics. In fact, "it is only because contemporary physics is a physics that is essentially mathematical that it is capable of being [also] experimental"[71]. Finally, Heidegger mentions "calculation" and "the objectification of beings (*Vergegenständlichung des Seienden*)" among the basic features of the modern scientific enterprise, tracing the latter back to Descartes' original reduction of truth to "the certainty of representation" and reduction of being to "the objectness of representation": "only what becomes, in this way, an object *is* – counts as in being"[72]. More

---

67 Heidegger 1977b, p. 75 [2002, p. 57].
68 GLB, p. 295 [GR, p. 427].
69 Heidegger 1977b, p. 77 [2002, p. 59].
70 Heidegger 1977b, pp. 78-80 [2002, pp. 59-60].
71 Heidegger 1977b, p. 80 [2002, p. 61].
72 Heidegger 1977b, pp. 86-87 [2002, pp. 65-66]. On the modern reduction of the whole of being to a mere realm of objects that is at the subject's disposal, see, for instance, the observations contained in the sixth section of Heidegger's 1944-45 lecture course *Einleitung in die Philosophie. Denken und Dichten*: "durch [die] neuzeitliche Wesensbestimmung des Menschen als des sich-auf-sichselbststellenden Subjektes [...] alle 'Objekte' als solche in ihrer Objektivität bestimmt sind", "alle Dinge zugleich und erst zum Gegenstand [...] werden. [...] Der Mensch im Aufstand und die Welt als Gegenstand gehören zusammen. In der Welt als Gegenstand steht der Mensch im Aufstand. Der aufständische Mensch

precisely, Heidegger points out how the Cartesian grounding of all knowledge in the subject's self-assurance and self-certainty has led to "the necessary interplay between subjectivism and objectivism", which is so characteristic of the modern age, and thus to the transformation of

> the essence of humanity [...] in that man becomes the subject. To be sure, this word "subject" must be understood as the translation of the Greek *hypokeimenon*. The word names that-which-lies-before, that which, as ground, gathers everything onto itself. [In the modern age] man becomes the primary and genuine *subiectum*[73].

Beside this obvious Heideggerian heritage, it is perhaps possible to identify even a Husserlian heritage in Gadamer's conception of modern techno-science. As a matter of fact, *Die Krisis der europäischen Wissenschaften und die transzendentale Phänomenologie* is probably the work of Husserl that Gadamer quotes the most in his own writings[74]. And a central role in Husserl's last masterpiece is

---

läßt nur die Welt als Gegenstand zu. Die Vergegenständlichung ist jetzt das Grundverhalten zur Welt. Das heute noch verborgene innerste Wesen der Vergegenständlichung [...] ist die Technik" (Heidegger 1990, p. 111).

73 Heidegger 1977b, p. 88 [2002, p. 66]. On this last issue, i.e. on the modern translation/reinterpretation of *hypokeimenon* as *subiectum*, and the dominance of subjectivism in our epoch, see also Heidegger 1997a, pp. 124-130 [1982, pp. 96-101]. Gadamer refers frequently to this last Heideggerian insight, for example in the essay *Die deutsche Philosophie zwischen den beiden Weltkriegen*, where we read: "Heidegger zeigte [den] unerkannte[n] Hintergrund unserer ganzen modernen Probleme mit der Subjektivität [...]. Das Wort *subiectum* zeigt es uns an. Es hat nämlich sprachlich und begriffsgeschichtlich nichts mit Bewußtsein zu tun. *Subiectum* ist das, was darunter liegt (was in der griechischen Sprache *Hypokeimenon* heißt) und das Substrat aller Veränderungen ist. Was wir 'Subjekt' nennen, ist nur der ausgezeichnete Fall eines solchen Zugrundeliegenden, nämlich, daß jemandes Vorstellungen alle die seinen sind, seinem Selbstbewußtsein angehören" (GW 10, p. 723).

74 Specifically dedicated to a close examination of the basic themes of this book are Gadamer's essays *Die Wissenschaft von der Lebenswelt* (GW 3, pp. 147-159 [PH, pp. 182-197]), and *Zur Aktualität der Husserlschen Phänomenologie* (GW 3, pp. 160-171). Furthermore, Gadamer deals with Husserl's *Krisis* in the long

precisely played by a critical analysis of Galilei's "geometrical and natural-scientific mathematization"[75] of the real, to which he devotes the whole § 9 (the longest section of the book, which is in turn divided into eleven subsections).

Here, he claims that Galilei represents "the discoverer [...] of physics", the one who discovered "mathematical nature, the methodical idea", and blazed "the trail for the infinite number of physical discoveries and discoverers"[76]. In other words, it is with Galilei that the ideas, which would form the theoretical framework of modern science, appeared "for the first time, so to speak, as full-blown"[77]. Accordingly, Husserl places Galilei "at the top of the list of the greatest discoverers of modern times"[78], and even goes so far as to assign him a sort of historical and theoretical "primacy" over other fundamental thinkers of the seventeenth century. In Husserl's eye, indeed, Hobbes' idea of the merely subjective character of all qualitative phenomena[79], Leibniz's concept of algebraic thinking[80], Spinoza's demand for a whole new metaphysics created *more geometrico*[81], and even Descartes' notion of universal mathematics[82] somehow imply the effects of "the weight of the theoretical and practical successes [of science]" which began "immediately with Galileo"[83]. Anyway, for the specific purposes of this work, it is not necessary to take thoroughly into consideration Husserl's long and

---

essay *Die Phänomenologische Bewegung* (GW 3, pp. 105-146 [PH, pp. 130-181]), and in *Wahrheit und Methode* as well (GW 1, pp. 251-254 [TM, pp. 238-241]). On Gadamer's critical confrontation with Husserl (in general) and the *Krisis der europäischen Wissenschaften* (in particular), see the accurate reconstruction provided by Gregorio 2008, pp. 15-86.

75 Husserl 1976, p. 51 [1970, p. 51].
76 Husserl 1976, p. 53 [1970, p. 52].
77 Husserl 1976, p. 58 [1970, p. 57].
78 Husserl 1976, p. 53 [1970, p. 53].
79 Husserl 1976, p. 54 [1970, p. 54].
80 Husserl 1976, p. 44 [1970, p. 45].
81 Husserl 1976, p. 65 [1970, p. 64].
82 Husserl 1976, p. 62 [1970, p. 61].
83 Husserl 1976, p. 62 [1970, p. 61].

rich considerations about "the *origin of the modern spirit* [in] mathematics and mathematical natural science"[84]. Rather, for Husserl's own account of the scientific enterprise, it is enough to underline the centrality of the Galileian mathematization of nature, which we have just pointed out as one of the basic elements of Gadamer's understanding of modern science.

Finally, given the increasing interest that has been expressed in recent times by some scholars of philosophical hermeneutics in Gadamer's early Neo-Kantian "roots"[85], it might be interesting to inquire into the possibility of Neo-Kantianism influencing his own view of science. For example, one might argue whether the thoughts of Paul Natorp, Gadamer's very first teacher in Marburg, about objectivity, lawfulness and method as the essential characteristics of science, somehow influenced the conception he presented in his mature works, from *Wahrheit und Methode* on. On the one side, it is indeed true that Gadamer explicitly defines Natorp as "the strictest method fanatic and logician of the Marburg School"[86], going so far as to describe the latter's interpretation of Platonic ideas "from the point of view of natural law, in the sense in which it is fundamental to Galilean and Newtonian science", as "one of the most paradoxical theses ever presented in historical research"[87]. On the other side,

---

84 Husserl 1976, p. 58 [1970, p. 57]. With regard to the this topic, it has been noticed that, in general, Husserl argues that "the Galileian and Cartesian picture of a material world *an sich*, which is in some sense 'mathematical', is the product of a [...] hypostatization of the mathematical method". In particular, "in order to apply mathematical physics to [...] the sensuous contents of life-world objects [...], Galileo had to assume that variations in sensuous qualities are causally related to variations in shape, so that they might be measured indirectly by directly measuring these shapes. To the extent that this hypothesis was corroborated by the discovery of specific causal relations and by the invention of measuring instruments, physics could be mathematized. But this is a method only, and it does not mean that the world itself is mathematical, as Galileo and Descartes thought" (Philipse 1995, pp. 302-303).
85 See, for example, Lembeck 2008 and Grondin 2010a.
86 PL, p. 62 [PA, p. 23]. See also GW 10, p. 376.
87 PL, p. 66 [PA, p. 25]. See also GW 10, pp. 378-379.

however, it is also true that Gadamer strongly emphasizes the shift occurred in Natorp's late philosophizing, when the idea of "the transcending of method (*Überschreitung der Methode*)" became his key concept, and he did not restrict his thinking anymore "to the fact of the sciences and its a priori foundations", but rather opened up to other aspects of life, such as "moral action and artistic activity, [...] *praxis* and *poiesis*"[88]. Anyway, inquiring into the influence of Neo-Kantianism on Gadamer would necessarily require a long and complex analysis, which goes far beyond the scopes of this research.

Apart from these historical-philosophical remarks, however, it might be asked whether Gadamer's understanding of modern science is really adequate and appropriate to capture its very essence, especially with regard to its twentieth-century revolutionary developments[89]. In this connection, for example, it has been observed that although Gadamer's masterpiece is entitled *Wahrheit und Methode*, the latter concept "does not play a major role in the book's discussions", that is, "method is not the main focus of the book"[90]. I think that this observation might perhaps be reformulated this way: on the one hand, it is clear that Gadamer's whole philosophical project deals with the "disciplinary *hubris*" or "disciplinary imperialism [...] of the

---

88 PL, p. 63 [PA, p. 23]. See also GW 10, p. 376.
89 It is worth noticing that Gadamer somehow denies the revolutionary dimensions of the scientific changes occurred at the beginning of the last century (relativity theory, quantum physics), or at least considers them not so revolutionary as those occurred in the seventeenth century (see, for instance, GW 7, pp. 435-436). So, he observes that "the nuclear physics of our century [*scil.* the twentieth] has reached limitations since it became apparent that the idea of an 'absolute observer' is untenable, because the act of measurement in the atomic realm always implies a disturbing influence in the system", and he concedes that this "certainly modified the fundamental concepts of classical physics. However, this does not at all touch the sense of objective cognition and science. Science knows how to state *this* belongingness of the observer to the observed in the mathematical exactness of equations". Considering this, twentieth-century physics appears to Gadamer "the consistent continuation of Galileo's physics" (GW 10, p. 232 [EPH, p. 215]).
90 Palmer 2010, p. 125.

natural sciences"[91]; on the other hand, however, it offers no systematic and satisfactory interpretation of what we might define the logic of scientific discovery[92]. In addition to this, it has been noticed that his concept of modern science could be a little "outdated", that is, perhaps it does not fit with the current state of the discussion on scientific methodology[93]. Finally, some interpreters have pointed out that Gadamer's statements on modern science "remain ambivalent", in the sense that

> in reference to the natural sciences, Gadamer determines that they have been "abstracted out of the fundamental relation to the world". Their ideal of objectivity betrays, according to Gadamer, an "ontological prejudice", i.e. the picture of the world as a "being-in-itself" that is the object of scientific investigation. The result, he says, is a "false methodologism". On the other hand, Gadamer allows that the natural sciences are "able to serve the growing domination of being". But, one asks, is this compatible with his criticism? If the natural sciences rest on a false ontological estimation, how can their control of nature be explained?[94].

To be true, it is not my intention here to take such criticism specifically into consideration and try to determine whether or not Gadamer's view of science is fully appropriate. After all, Gadamer is not a philosopher of science *stricto sensu*, and so it is also understandable if his account of science and technology is not as complete and consistent as that of other contemporary thinkers who are veritable "experts" of these topics. Furthermore, I must add that this is

---

91 Madison 1997, p. 357.
92 I obviously borrow this last expression from the title of Karl Popper's 1935 epistemological treatise *Logik der Forschung*.
93 So, for example, Neuser 2004 (p. 33) observes that "Gadamer in sehr hohem Maße an dem Induktionskonzept von John Stuart Mill anknüpft. […] Am Konzept der Induktion, das Mill stark macht, macht Gadamer fest, was Naturwissenschaften tun und wie Naturwissenschaften mit Erfahrung umgehen. Damit knüpft Gadamer an ein Konzept von Naturwissenschaften an, das mit der klassischen Physik verknüpft ist, das aber sicherlich nicht mehr das Verständnis ist, das wir heute wissenschaftstheoretisch von den Naturwissenschaften haben".
94 Nagl-Docekal 1997, pp. 194-195.

not the ideal place to undertake such discussions, since for the specific purposes of the present inquiry it is enough to understand the decisive role that Gadamer assigns to techno-science in shaping the culture of the present age, i.e. its radical and all-influencing impact on our civilization.

Anyway, in concluding this chapter I would like to point out that Gadamer has sometimes suggested the existence of relevant affinities between his own understanding of science and that of some leading epistemologists of the twentieth century[95]. So, for example, in his 1985 *Versuch einer Selbstkritik* he claims that after the publication of *Wahrheit und Methode* he realized that "Karl Popper's critique of positivism also contained motifs similar to those in [his] own orientation"[96]. A claim that, by the way, has somehow been confirmed by Popper himself, who in a letter to Claus Grossner affirmed:

> 1934 veröffentlichte ich mein Buch *Logik der Forschung*. Das war eine Kritik des Positivismus. [...] *In Wahrheit bin ich ebensoweit vom Positivismus entfernt wie (zum Beispiel) Gadamer*. Ich habe nämlich entdeckt – und darauf begründet sich *meine* Kritik des Positivismus –, daß die Naturwissenschaft *nicht* positivistisch vorgeht, sondern im wesentlichen eine Methode verwendet, die mit "*Vorurteilen*" arbeitet; nur verwendet sie womöglich neue Vorurteile und *Vorurteile, die kritisierbar sind*, und unterwirft sie einer strengen Kritik. [...]

---

95 It is highly interesting that in a collection of essays in honour of the philosopher of science Patrick Heelan, the latter has been explicitly indicated as the one who somehow "succeeded in showing Gadamer, against the widespread academic opinion, that the intellectual operations of the natural sciences embody indispensable elements of interpretation that make them effectively 'hermeneutic'" (Toulmin 2002, p. 25). On the same topic, see also Janik 2002 (p. 95 note), and Heelan's own statement: "In this volume Stephen Toulmin and Allan Janik have represented me as the person who converted Hans-Georg Gadamer to the recognition that the natural sciences and technology are hermeneutical, like history, art, the humanities, and the social sciences. That is, they are constituted by human meanings embodied in language, symbols, and cultural practices. [...] I still recall with excitement my encounter with Gadamer at Boston College in April 1974 when I spoke up to challenge him about his exclusion of the natural sciences and technology from the umbrella of human hermeneutic constitution" (Heelan 2002, p. 445).

96 GW 2, p. 4 [Gadamer 1997b, p. 40].

> Daher: Was mich von Gadamer trennt, ist ein besseres Verständnis der naturwissenschaftlichen "Methode", eine logische Theorie der Wahrheit, und die *kritische* Einstellung. Aber meine Theorie ist genauso anti-positivistisch wie seine[97].

Then, in the essay *Natur und Welt* he expresses an explicit appreciation for "the hermeneutical aspect" which is present in Michael Polanyi's theory of the tacit dimension of science, in Stephen Toulmin's analysis of the concept of phenomenon, and in Thomas Kuhn's notion of paradigms[98]. Thanks to Kuhn's groundbreaking work *The Structure of Scientific Revolutions*, indeed, we now know that "the hermeneutical dimension plays a basic role in all experience of the world and therefore also plays a role even in the work of the natural sciences"[99]. In still another essay, *Philosophie oder Wissenschaftstheorie?*, Gadamer affirms:

---

97 Popper 1971, pp. 284-285. On the affinities between Popperian philosophy of science and philosophical hermeneutics, see, for instance, Antiseri 1997. However, it must be said that while Popper sees the point of convergence in the fact that "Textinterpretation (Hermeneutik) mit echt naturwissenschaftlichen Methoden arbeitet" (Popper 1971, p. 285), Gadamer vice versa sees it in the fact that also natural sciences actually rely on the background of a practical and interpretive fore-understanding! Accordingly, he criticizes all those philosophies of science that dismiss "any inquiry that cannot be meaningfully characterized as a process of trial and error", or do not recognize "the fact that [the] 'logic of scientific investigation' [alone] is not sufficient, since at any given time the viewpoints that select the relevant topics of inquiry and foreground them as subjects of research cannot themselves be derived from the logic of investigation" (GW 2, pp. 452-453 [TM, p. 558]).

98 GW 7, p. 434. Gadamer's references to the books of Kuhn (*The Structure of Scientific Revolutions* [1962]) and Polanyi (*Personal Knowledge: Towards a Post-critical Philosophy* [1958] and *The Tacit Dimension* [1966]) are explicit, while he does not explain to which work of Toulmin he actually refers to. Hints to Polanyi's works can also be found in GW 2, pp. 257, 431 and 505.

99 GW 2, p. 114 [GR, p. 67]. In his reflections on his own philosophical journey Gadamer even draws Kuhn's *Structure of Scientific Revolutions* close to Heidegger's abovementioned *Zeit des Weltbildes*, insofar as "both make clear that the reigning 'paradigm' is decisive both for the questions research raises and for the data it examines, and these are apparently not just the result of methodical research" (GW 2, p. 496 [Gadamer 1997b, p. 28]).

it does not seem to me at all contradictory to the logic of inquiry when Thomas Kuhn elaborated the significance of the paradigm for the progress of research. His theory of revolution in science rightly criticizes the false linear stylization supposedly connected with the progress of science. It shows the discontinuity effected by the dominance of any given time of basic paradigmatic frameworks. The whole problem area of the relevance of questions depends on this, and that constitutes a hermeneutic dimension[100].

---

100 VZW, p. 142 [RAS, p. 164].

3. The Basic Features of Our Societies: Conformism, Bureaucracy and Self-Alienation

After having shown how, according to Gadamer, science and technology actually represent the roots of modernity (from the seventeenth century up to nowadays), let us now take into consideration what we might define as Gadamer's "phenomenology" of the modern techno-scientific world and its "pathologies". I will begin my examination by taking into account some socio-economic issues that are scarcely present in *Wahrheit und Methode* – in which the critical attitude towards "the naive self-esteem of the present moment"[1] is directed at issues regarding art, history and language – but that are widely and extensively discussed in many of the essays published in the collections *Vernunft im Zeitalter der Wissenschaft*, *Lob der Theorie* and *Das Erbe Europas*.

First of all, Gadamer notices that "the economic and technical processes are the real dominant figures of our day", and that "the immanent lawfulness" of such processes "is largely independent of the various democratic and totalitarian political systems on which our states are organized"[2]. According to him, indeed, what is typical of the present age is people's tendency to rely on the "illusion to think that only a rational system of utilities, so to say, a religion of world economy, could regulate human coexistence on this constantly smaller planet"[3]. This illusion, however, has been repeatedly confuted in the last centuries, i.e. "in the time of multinationals, in the age of world economy"[4], when the overwhelming logic of the *homo oeconomicus* has brought an increase of social and economic inequalities, rather

1   GS 1, p. 2 [TM, p. XXI].
2   LT, pp. 112-113 [PT, p. 92].
3   GW 10, p. 237 [EPH, p. 219].
4   EE, p. 10 [EPH, p. 222].

than a reduction of the disparities. Gadamer, then, proves to be fully aware that we live in an age in which "economic, social, and political power-interests [...] prevail against all constitutional, democratic, or socialist principles"[5]. Furthermore, with regard to the predominant role played by economic factors in structuring people's lives, Gadamer proves to be particularly worried by the fact that "the system of needs", instead of being "subordinated [...] to the spiritual forms of ethical life",

> in our day [is] bound up with the vicious circle of production and consumption, which drives humanity ever more deeply into alienation from itself because natural needs are no longer "taken care of" themselves; that is, they may be shown to be more the product of some alien interest than of the direct interest in the satisfaction of a need[6].

Gadamer pays attention to both parts of this process, that is, to the *production* of goods, a seemingly unstoppable tendency of mankind, and to its irrepressible urge for *consumption* and waste. In the 1969 essay, *Vereinsamung als Symptom von Selbstentfremdung*, he piercingly points out human work as "the only new god of our age", "the last worldly god of the polytheistic tradition still to be honored among us", and he stresses the fact that, in modern times, work "becomes alien to man"[7]. As a consequence, man becomes "a stranger in the world and in the human world as a whole", i.e. he becomes self-alienated, the concept of self-alienation being "an expression of a social sickness – perhaps also of suffering in the society"[8]. Quite significantly, in this essay Gadamer explicitly refers to Friedrich Schiller's letters *Über die ästhetische Erziehung des Menschen*[9]: more

---

5 LT, p. 51 [PT, p. 37].
6 VZW, p. 22 [RAS, pp. 12-13].
7 LT, p. 128 [PT, p. 105].
8 LT, pp. 127-128 [PT, pp. 104-105].
9 In fact, Schiller can be considered, at least to some extent, as the forerunner of a critical discourse on modernity that has been carried out during the nineteenth and twentieth centuries. As we read indeed in one of the most famous and beautiful of his letters upon the aesthetic education of man (the sixth): "How different with us Moderns [*scil.* the Greeks]! With us too the image of the

precisely, to the latter's idea of the free activity of man and of a state of freedom set up against "the dead, soulless machine-state in which each individual works only as a cog or a link without [...] his individual consciousness being connected with the activity of the whole"[10]. And in that same essay Gadamer also refers to Karl Marx, "who put the self-alienation of man down to the artificial relations of production, the fetishization of money, and the commodification of human labor"[11]. According to Gadamer, however,

> The self-alienation of man then [*scil.* in the nineteenth century] applied to a particular class situation, and designated the employers' exploitation of the proletariat. When we reconsider the phenomenon of self-alienation, the problem arises under greatly altered circumstances. Today the self-alienation of man in society can no longer be spoken of as the domination of one class by another class that alone enjoys freedom [...]. We live in a modern social welfare state. What we experience there is that we all lack freedom, and that seems to me to be the self-alienation that concerns us today[12].

Significant and serious "pathological" aspects, however, are also noticeable in the modern tendency to the consumption and waste of

---

human species is projected in magnified form into separate individuals – but as fragments [...]. With us, one might almost be tempted to assert, the various faculties appear as separate in practice as they are distinguished by the psychologist in theory, and we see not merely individuals, but whole classes of men, developing but one part of their potentialities [...]. It was civilization itself", Schiller continues, "which inflicted this wound upon modern man. Once the increase of empirical knowledge, and more exact modes of thought, made sharper divisions between the sciences inevitable, and once the increasingly complex machinery of State necessitated a more rigorous separation of ranks and occupations, then the inner unity of human nature was severed too, and a disastrous conflict set its harmonious powers at variance. [...] I do not underrate the advantages which the human race today, considered as a whole and weighed in the balance of intellect, can boast in the face of what is best in the ancient world. But it has to take up the challenge in serried ranks, and let whole measure itself against whole" (Schiller 1962, pp. 322-323 [1983, p. 33]).

10   LT, p. 129 [PT, p. 106].
11   LT, p. 129 [PT, p. 106].
12   LT, pp. 129-130 [PT, pp. 106-107].

things. According to Gadamer, it is indeed alarming that people today are more inclined than ever to "glorify" consumption such as it is, and that this tendency is a sort of logical counterpart of the "idolatry" of work and production such as they are. In addition to this, Gadamer appears to be worried about the fact that today even the more basic human needs, far from being spontaneous or "natural" anymore, are influenced by specific socio-economic interests. With regard to this question, Gadamer explicitly speaks of "artificial creation of needs" in our world, "above all by means of modern advertising"[13]. And he warns us that

> the compulsion to consume [is] something that hardly anybody can avoid who does not possess a great measure of inner freedom. For the organization of consumption and selling is virtually compelled by our whole economic system. It is not really possible to escape, in any kind of free determination of needs, from the consumer goods provided by industry and the economy, when the flood of uniformly generated consumer desires sweeps us, so to speak, in through the doors of the department stores. [...] Every area of our lives has been integrated into this system and is now administered by it alongside everything else. Its influence extends from so-called family life to the so-called culture industry. It seems inevitable: economics is our fate[14].

Now, it is a well known fact that analogous theses were presented and discussed during the twentieth century by other relevant thinkers, many of whom were philosophically and politically sometimes quite distant from each other. For example, Henri Bergson, in his late masterpiece *Le deux sources de la morale et de la religion*, had already observed that "the concern for comfort and luxury [...] has apparently become the main preoccupation of humanity", so that "new needs arise, just as imperious and increasingly numerous"[15]. "Without disputing the services" that science and mechanization have "rendered to man by greatly developing the means of satisfying *real needs*", Bergson thus argued they had to be reproached for "having too strong-

---

13 GW 4, p. 256 [EH, p. 18].
14 LT, pp. 131 and 117 [PT, pp. 108 and 95-96].
15 Bergson 1962, pp. 317-318 [2002, p. 332].

ly encouraged *artificial ones*", and concluded saying that humanity had to "set about simplifying its existence with as much frenzy as it devoted to complicating it"[16]. Similar considerations can also be found in Hannah Arendt, as well as in other works of relevant philosophers and sociologists of our time. So, for example, in her masterpiece *The Human Condition* we read:

> In our need for more and more rapid replacement of the wordly things around us, we can no longer afford to use them, to respect and preserve their inherent durability; we must consume, devour, as it were, [them]. The ideals of the *homo faber*, the fabricator of the world, which are permanence, stability, and durability, have been sacrificed to abundance, the ideal of the *animal laborans*. [...] In this as in other respects, the specter of a true consumers' society is more alarming as an ideal of present-day society than as an already existing reality. [...] A hundred years after Marx we know [that] the spare time of the *animal laborans* is never spent in anything but consumption, and the more time left to him, the greedier and more craving his appetites. [...] One of the obvious danger signs [...] is the extent to which our whole economy has become a waste economy, in which things must be almost as quickly devoured and discarded as they have appeared in the world, if the process itself is not to come to a sudden catastrophic end. [...] The danger is that such a society, dazzled by the abundance of its growing fertility and caught in the smooth functioning of a never-ending process, would no longer be able to recognize its own futility[17].

As Axel Honneth has recently noticed, "in the German-speaking world of the 1920s and 1930s", the concept of reification (*Verdinglichung*) – tightly linked, as we know, to the concept of alienation or estrangement (*Entfremdung*) adopted even by Gadamer – "constituted a leitmotiv of social and cultural critique", that is, an expression of "the historical experiences [...] that gave the Weimar Republic its distinctive character"[18]. In particular, it was Georg Lukács' groundbreaking 1923 collection of essays *Geschichte und Klassenbewußtsein* which succeeded in moving "an entire generation of philosophers and sociologists to analyze the forms of life under the then-

---

16   Bergson 1962, pp. 327-328 [2002, p. 338].
17   Arendt 1959, pp. 109-110 and 114-117.
18   Honneth 2005, p. 11 [2008, p. 17].

prevailing circumstances as being the result of social reification"[19]. Honneth carefully observes, however, that after the Second World War "these notions lived on in the writings of the Frankfurt School"[20]. Let's think of, for example, the famous chapter of Horkheimer's and Adorno's *Dialektik der Aufklärung* on cultural industry[21], or Herbert Marcuse's analysis of the one-dimensional society: an analysis that precisely begins with the distinction between "true and false needs"[22].

With regard to these questions, it is surely worthy of notice that Gadamer admitted to have always seen himself "in agreement with [...] the Frankfurt School [...] on a whole series of points"[23]. As is well known, when Gadamer accepted the professorship in Heidelberg, after having taught philosophy in Frankfurt in 1948-1949, he "suggested that Adorno might succeed him in the only chair of philosophy in Frankfurt"[24], and in 1950 he participated together with Horkheimer and Adorno to a famous radio broadcast entitled *Über Nietzsche und uns. Zum 50. Todestag des Philosophen*[25]. As we also read in Gadamer's autobiographical reflections:

19 Honneth 2005, pp. 11-12 [2008, p. 17].
20 Honneth 2005, p. 12 [2008, pp. 17-18].
21 See Horkheimer and Adorno 2003, pp. 141-191 [2002, pp. 94-136].
22 Marcuse 1991, p. 4. "Most of the prevailing needs", Marcuse explains indeed, "belong to this category of false needs. Such needs have a societal content and function which are determined by external powers over which the individual has no control; the development and satisfaction of these needs is heteronomous" (Marcuse 1991, pp. 4-5).
23 HÄP, p. 71 [GC, p. 83].
24 Wiggershaus 1986, p. 449 [1995, p. 404].
25 See Horkheimer, Adorno and Gadamer 1950. As has been noted, the fiftieth anniversary of Nietzsche's death was celebrated in Germany "with several more public occurrences, including [some] major radio shows", among which the aforementioned radio broadcast *Über Nietzsche und uns*: "The participants in the Frankfurt studio represented supposedly rival wings of German philosophy: Adorno and moderator Horkheimer for Marxian critical theory; and Gadamer for Heideggerian fundamental ontology translated into philosophical hermeneutics and the philosophy of 'dialogue'. [...] Thus, this intended 'dialogue' was bipartite, incorporating 1) all three philosophers in dialogue with Nietzsche, and 2) dialogue between Gadamer on the 'right' and his two interlocutors on the

He [*scil.* Adorno] and I presented extreme contrasts in style, appearance, and behavior. Nonetheless, [...] when his *Negative Dialectics* was published [*scil.* in 1966], at the urging of my students I resolved to take a detailed position on it. Occasionally during my reading of the book, I had noted to my students how curiously the attempted construction and critique of Hegel converged with the line of thought of Heidegger – except that the adherents of the Frankfurt School fall victim to a curious blindness whenever they hear the magic word "ontological". Then they fail to see where they really are. I wanted to put this idea forth in hopes of producing a fruitful discussion. And so I stood in the railroad station at the beginning of a vacation trip, the book in my luggage, when my student Reiner Wiehl happened by and told me that the radio had just announced Adorno's death [*scil.* in 1969]. I was a little too late[26].

After this short parenthesis on the affinities between Gadamer and the Frankfurt School on the question of modern alienation and reification, let us now return to the problems we were previously discussing. Within the context of Gadamer's problematization of the life conditions of our industrial, de-individualized societies, another element that is surely of great importance is the role played by the *réclame*, i.e. the mass media persuasion towards consumption and its "ostentation". Anyway, however dangerous the mass media might be

---

'left'. [...] In the 1950 Frankfurt 'conversation', despite minor differences of opinion about Nietzsche [...], there turned out to be remarkably few real bones of contention" (Waite 2004, pp. 191-192). According to Gadamer's biographer, "this turned out to be the single philosophical exchange between Gadamer and his Frankfurt colleagues" (Grondin 1999, p. 295 [2003, p. 263]). Gadamer also recalls the 1950 radio broadcast in his 1999 essay *Nietzsche und die Metaphysik* (HE, pp. 136-137), while in the 1986 interview *The 1920s, the 1930s, and the Present* he says: "These people, Horkheimer, Adorno, appeared to us as amazingly sophisticated intellectuals, and yet we must say not very substantial. And we were used to a much higher degree of competence, not to put too fine a point on it, through the teaching of Heidegger. We did not think that the Frankfurt school were so terribly competent. [...] To hear us talk, you would think we had a superiority complex, and of course hidden behind that, there was an inferiority complex" (Gadamer 1992e, p. 141).

26 PL, pp. 175-176 [PA, p. 142]. In a late interview, however, Gadamer recalls to have met Herbert Marcuse too, "the most flexible, broadminded and sympathetic" among "the Frankfurter thinkers of the old generation", while Adorno was typically "factious and intransigent" (Gadamer 2006, p. 90).

in urging people to consume more and more, according to Gadamer they are even more dangerous in moulding and manipulating public opinion, because in doing so their activity remains almost imperceptible. Apropos of this, in the essay *Über die Macht der Vernunft* he warns us against "the power of convincing speech" and "the new rhetoric of the modern mass media", which "forestalls all critical consideration and summons the power of the self-evident"[27]. And in the interview *An der Sklavenkette*[28] he points out the dangers of the contemporary television-society (*Fernsehgesellschaft*), with its eminently political function of "domesticating" the masses and "putting to sleep" people's capacities of critical thinking and judgement[29].

According to Gadamer, these and other "experiences of compulsion" – such as, for example, the compulsion to consume (*Konsumzwang*) or the belief-compulsion (*Meinungszwang*), i.e. the compulsion "to believe certain things [...] just because they come sugared with the sweet poison of information politics" – must be set and understood within the broader context of a more general "rational obligation (*rationaler Sachzwang*) that dominates us all", and that "we experience [...] again and again in all sorts of ways"[30]. "Our thoroughly rationalized society", Gadamer says with a sort of Frankfurter-style critical accent, "suffers from something similar to what psychiatrists call the repetition compulsion", which "seems a good simile for the essence of 'administration' (*Verwaltung*)"[31]. In order to clarify these processes, Gadamer sometimes uses even more dramatic and harsh expressions, like for example "domination of the technical-industrial Jacobinism (*Herrschaft des technisch-industriellen Jakobi-*

---

27 LT, p. 60 [PT, pp. 44-45].
28 See Gadamer 1995b.
29 On this topic, see also Gadamer's remarks in his conference from the 19th May, 1999 *Erziehung ist sich erziehen*: "Die Gefahr, die [...] Massenmedien für das eigentliche Menschsein sind, kann man gar nicht hoch genug einschätzen. Es geht doch vor allem darum zu lernen, eigene Urteilsbildung zu wagen und auszuführen. Das ist gar nicht ganz leicht" (ESE, p. 20).
30 LT, pp. 131-132 [PT, pp. 107-108].
31 LT, p. 131 [PT, p. 107].

nertums)"[32]. And in the essay *Über die Planung der Zukunft* he goes so far as to describe "the ideal to which the outlook and the political convictions of the most advanced nations are committed" as

> the idea of a perfectly administered world (*Idee einer perfekt verwalteten Welt*) [...]. Moreover, it seems significant to me that this ideal is presented as one of perfect administration (*Ideal der perfekten Verwaltung*) and not as a vision of the future with a predetermined content. [...] Contained in the ideal of administration is a conception of order which does not specify its content. The issue is not which order should rule, but that everything should have its order; this is the express end of all administration[33].

Among the basic features of our industrialized, alienated, bureaucratized and administrated societies, Gadamer also mentions the tendency to instil in people's mind an hedonistic-consumerist mentality and promote a trivial attitude of mass conformity. Such mass conformity, moreover, paradoxically seems to go hand in hand with its own opposite, i.e. with the widespread diffusion of strong individualistic and unconventional manners[34]. According to Gadamer,

---

32 GW 2, p. 432.
33 GW 2, p. 160 [EPH, p. 169]. It is not hard, I think, to see some affinities between Gadamer's critical ideas on the "Zeitalter der industriellen Revolution, [...] Zeitalter der steigenden Bürokratisierung aller Lebensverhältnisse", in which "fehlen uns in dem Geregelten die Freiräume" (Gadamer 1997d, p. 189), and the famous Weberian conception of modernity, according to which the unstoppable impact of rationalization, instrumentalization, and disenchantment, has progressively led to the transformation of society into "*ein stahlhartes Gehäuse*", that is, an "iron cage" or a "shell as hard as steel" (Weber 1978, p. 203 [2002, p. 121]). As a matter of fact, Gadamer clearly acknowledges that Weber had already predicted, at the beginning of the twentieth century, some social processes that we are experiencing today, and he agrees with Weber's idea, "daß die industrielle Gesellschaft von der Bürokratisierung bedroht sei" (Gadamer 1992a, p. 61). Still in his last interviews with Silvio Vietta, Gadamer recalls that "wir haben uns als junge Philosophiestudenten für Max Weber sehr interessiert", and he even agrees with his interviewer that "Die ganze Vernunft- und Rationalitätskritik des 20ten Jahrhunderts ist ja an [dem] Max-Weberschen-Begriff der Rationalität orientiert letztendlich" (IG, pp. 49-50).
34 With regard to this question, in her interpretation of the modern age through the filter of one of its most flashy phenomena, i.e. fashion, Elizabeth Wilson

however, these manners are just the expression of fictitious non-conformity, that is, they are actually functional to the de-individualizing rules of mass society. Hence, in the essay *Die Idee der Toleranz 1782-1982* he writes:

> The wave of industrialization and bureaucratization sweeping over us has dissolved once self-evidently binding traditions into untested arbitrariness. This happens in the name of the "freedom that I love". But what does this freedom look like? Let's take an example: the feeling of freedom that, especially for young people, comes from having their own car is coupled with an enormous dependency, and leads to both a levelling and an isolation unknown to travellers of earlier times. People do certainly gather together in front of the television screen [...]. But in fact it signifies the end of conversation, the extreme isolation of each individual [...]. In the same way, the freedom of the new unconventionality that pervades our whole social life – especially of the young – is coupled in a peculiar way with a feeling of helplessness and impotence[35].

All this finally leads to a strong tendency, so characteristic of the present age, towards depriving people of responsibility. This is a very important problem to Gadamer, who connects it to "the major role now taken on by the scientific expert in our social and political life"[36].

This issue is at the core of Gadamer's important essay *Die Grenzen des Experten*, in which he first clarifies the particular position assumed today by the experts, i.e. those specialists who have to mediate "between the scientific culture of modernity and its social manifestations in practical life", "between science and research on the one hand and decision making in law and social policy, on the other hand"[37]. Accordingly, Gadamer then says that the expert "is not the

---

> poignantly observes: "Identity becomes a special kind of problem in 'modernity'. [...] The industrial period is often, inaccurately, called the age of 'mass man'. Modernity creates fragmentation, dislocation. It creates the vision of 'totalitarian' societies peopled by identical zombies in uniform. The fear of depersonalization haunts our culture. [...] Yet modernity has also created the individual in a new way [...]. Modern individualism is an exaggerated yet fragile sense of self – a raw, painful condition" (Wilson 2003, pp. 11-12).

35 LT, p. 112 [PT, pp. 91-92].
36 EE, p. 137 [EPH, p. 182].
37 EE, pp. 136-138 [EPH, pp. 181-182].

authority for final decisions", as "he does not – or [...] should not – take the place of the actual decision maker"[38]. The problem, however, is that in his opinion "today the expert has become, in many cases, the most sought-after person and is often [...] the decisive one", and the "increasing importance of the role which the expert plays in our society is rather a serious symptom for the increasing ignorance of the decision makers"[39].

For Gadamer, while there is obviously nothing wrong with having "recourse to the knowledge and ability of others" – since "our nature as social beings is such that we never are in the position to provide for ourselves in all life situations merely by using our own knowledge and ability": "an aspect of human reality and not just one of a bureaucratized society" –, on the other side it is a veritable deformation of our rationalistically, or should we better say techno-scientifically oriented society to think that "all decisions must depend on those who know as the final authority"[40]. In fact, there are decisions in the social and political *praxis* "which I can never discharge to the knowledge of another", and this is exactly what defines "the concept of responsibility (*Verantwortlichkeit*) and, in a certain sense, also the concept of conscience (*Gewissen*)", that is, the idea that everyone has to be "responsible for the results of his decisions"[41]. But this is also exactly where the problem with the new role assumed by the experts in our societies occurs. As has been noted, indeed,

> On Gadamer's view, modernity is characterized by a faith in science which assumes that all problems are technical problems amenable to technical solutions and dependent upon advances in science. Indeed Gadamer argues that the "expert" has replaced the "man of practical wisdom". Social decisions are not the result of a reasoned discussion in an informed public sphere but instead the decisions of small groups of experts [...]. Gadamer argues that such a society of experts is also a "society of functionaries". What becomes important is not the capacity to make responsible decisions on one's own but rather the willingness

---

38 EE, p. 137 [EPH, p. 181].
39 EE, pp. 137-138 [EPH, pp. 181-182].
40 EE, pp. 149-150 [EPH, pp. 188-189].
41 EE, p. 151 [EPH, p. 189].

to adapt to decisions others have made for one, decisions that, in addition, largely follow the logic of technological imperatives. [...] The effect of this reversal of the roles of practical-moral deliberation and scientific-technical reason [...] is an increase in "social irrationality"[42].

On this basis, some interpreters[43] have suggested to closen Gadamer's hermeneutical view on techno-science to the theses of the counter-Enlightenment theorists of the so-called "technocratic conservatism": Arnold Gehlen, Hans Freyer and Helmut Schelsky. Anyway, although such comparisons are surely conceivable and perhaps even plausible (at least to some extent), I argue that they should not be overestimated.

First of all, Gadamer never actually arrives to the technocratic conservatives' extreme theses according to which there is no alternative today "to a modern, differentiated and complex society. [...] Human beings are determined and created according to their functions and relations within the system. Of course, this means alienation", but these thinkers see "no problem with the system, the problem is if people do not adapt to the system"[44]. Secondly, I think that it is highly relevant to notice how Gadamer, on a few but nonetheless important occasions, explicitly distanced himself from Gehlen's theories: for example, from the latter's conception of modernity and art[45], and above all from his strongly conservative conception of social and cultural institutions. In fact, in his 1993 interview with Carsten Dutt on practical philosophy Gadamer admits that "Arnold Gehlen with his neoconservativism was right in asserting that institutions actually take a load off of us and our society", but when his interviewer adds that "Gehlen was nostalgic about institutions" and "wanted to regress, to go back. Away with discussion and back to obedience", Gadamer says:

> But that is absolutely impossible! And this is the reason I have directed my thinking toward formulating a philosophy of rational self-responsibility and

---

42 Warnke 1987, p. 163.
43 See, for instance, Grossner 1971, p. 63 n.
44 Dahl 1999, pp. 71-72.
45 See GW 8, pp. 305-314.

toward showing the communicative character of our *praxis*. We must find the paths ourselves: the paths of solidarity and of reaching understandings. [...] We have largely shaken [...] self-evident customs [...] off today, and I find this very pleasing in many ways. One is not bossed around as much[46].

---

46 HÄP, p. 67 [GC, p. 80].

4. Cosmopolitan Hermeneutics in the Age of the "Clash of Civilizations"

In the *Introduction* I have already mentioned Jean Grondin's significant observation that Gadamer's recognition of the "dimension of world-historical importance" of the "hermeneutic openness to the other" brought him, especially in the 1980s and 1990s, "to an almost 'political' or cosmopolitan broadening of his hermeneutics", which he developed "mostly in lectures, [...] as well as in the numerous interviews on questions of the moment", where "he appears alarmed by the consequences of the Industrial Revolution"[1]. Now, it is surely interesting to notice that Gadamer's attention to what I have previously defined the pathologies of the industrial world also led him to point out how the Western bureaucratic and "levelling" socio-political model, during the last centuries, somehow expanded to the whole world. With regard to this phenomenon, Gadamer explicitly speaks of an "epoch of the new *Oikoumene*"[2], or even of a new and more sophisticated kind of "intellectual colonialism (*geistiger Kolonialismus*)"[3] that could eventually lead to the establishment of a standardized global civilization. So, in the 1989 essay *Heidegger und das Ende der Philosophie* we read:

> Brought into being by the West, [...] our civilization [...] has nevertheless spread its net over the greater part of the world. It concerns the world view which lies at the root of science and scientific theorizing, a world view which is characteristic of our epoch [...] Contemporary civilization strives this destiny, or so it seems, a destiny which will bring the whole of humanity under the sway of the industrial revolution. [...] It is well known how the West managed to "demystify the world" as a result of [the] breakthrough in modern science. The

---

1   Grondin 1999, p. 370 [2003, pp. 328-329].
2   GW 10, p. 269.
3   HE, p. 75.

industrial exploitation of scientific research eventually made it possible for the West to emerge as the dominant planetary power by installing an all-powerful economic and communications system[4].

However, such an indiscriminate "exportation" in the rest of the world of our ideas of cultural, industrial and technological development is not easy nor harmless nor painless, so to speak. Rather, it is likely to produce devastating consequences on a political and "civilizational" level. "We do have to face the problem of the gap between the developed and the underdeveloped countries", Gadamer explains in an interview, "but I do not believe that the answer is to export the West"[5]. And in still another interview he declares: "die westliche Zivilisation heute den ganzen Erdball überzieht und zugleich auf Widerstände stößt"[6].

The process of homologation and bureaucratization dictated by the inevitability of "progress" indeed puts a great strain on the countries in which this process is "exported", and this situation can generate, as a reaction, a renewed devotion to ancient, local traditions. Consequently, according to Gadamer,

> The tendency toward the unification of our world-picture and our relation to the world, which corresponds to the leveling tendency and the growing mobility of today's human society, is countered by a tendency toward differentiation and toward a new articulation of previously hidden distinctions. [...] Many countries

---

4   HE, pp. 197-199 [Gadamer 1992b, pp. 17-19]. An early awareness of these tendencies that strongly characterize our "globalized" age already emerges from the 1967 essay *Herder und die geschichtliche Welt* (which, in turn, is the revision of the text of a 1941 lecture), where Gadamer writes: "Wir leben in einer Epoche, in der neue rationale Ordnungsformen der industriell-technisch entwickelten Welt das alte, von Tradition und geschichtlichem Bewußtsein gesättigte Europa in einer Ausgleichskultur aufgehen lassen. [...] Im Blick auf diese sich ausbreitende Weltkultur reden wir wohl vom Ende des Kolonialismus, aber es gehört zur Dialektik der Geschichte, daß es just die vom Kolonialismus entwickelte Zivilisationsform ist, die sich heute wie ein Überzug technisch-wirtschaftlich-administrativer Apparatur über die diversesten bodenständigen Lebensformen breitet" (GW 4, p. 318).
5   Gadamer 1988a, p. 32.
6   Gadamer 1986c, p. 98.

in this world are in search of a form of civilization which would accomplish the trick of uniting their own traditions and the deeply rooted values of their forms of life with ideas of economic progress derived from Europe. The greater part of humanity is facing this question. It addresses us as well. Are our schools and educational programs actually employed in the right way, when we export them to the Third World? Or are they in the end only grafted, causing more alienation of the elite from their ancestral traditions, rather than contributing to the future of these countries? [...] [Is] what we have to offer, what we control, scientific-technological perfection, really always a gift? One can doubt this even if we enhance our economic aid with the export of know-how. Sooner or later the disparity between their own being and that of the Europeans will arise in the consciousness of the people of the Third World; and then, all new efforts which we are presently pursuing could prove to be just subtle forms of colonization and likewise fail. Signs for this are present today[7].

It is clear that all these problems brought to our attention by Gadamer have in someway related to the delicate question of the relationship between different civilizations, which has become particularly relevant in recent years. As is well known, with regard to this last issue one of the keywords of our age has surely become that of the "clash of civilizations", introduced by Samuel P. Huntington and extensively used since then by political theorists and politicians. I obviously refer here to Huntington's influential book *The Clash of Civilizations and the Remaking of World Order*, whose central theme is that "culture and cultural identities, which at the broadest level are civilization identities, are shaping the patterns of cohesion, disintegration, and conflict in the post-Cold War world"[8]. Namely, in a world in which, for the first time in history,

> global politics has become multipolar *and* multicivilizational. [...] Nation states remain the principal actors in world affairs. [...] The most important groupings of states [however] are no longer the three blocs of the Cold War but rather the world's seven or eight major civilizations. [...] The rivalry of the superpowers is replaced by the clash of civilizations. In this new world the most pervasive, important, and dangerous conflicts [are] between peoples belonging to different

---

7   EE, pp. 57 and 48-49 [EPH, pp. 205 and 200-201].
8   Huntington 1998, p. 20.

cultural identities. [...] The key issues on the international agenda involve differences among civilizations[9].

Gadamer deals with analogous topics in some of his later works: for example, in his 1999-2000 interviews with Riccardo Dottori, in which he says that "an understanding with Islam, [...] at the moment, is the most difficult thing of all but also, in a certain sense, the most essential"[10]. Now, Gadamer surely belongs to those thinkers who have always been strongly critical towards the "expansionistic" attitude of the Western civilization. So, for example, in the 1993 essay *Europa und die Oikoumene* we read:

> Es ist wohl kein Zufall, daß sich die Dinge zwischen den Völkern vielfach sogar noch zuspitzen. Zwar liegen die Religionskriege weit hinter uns, soweit sie im christlichen Europa ausgetragen wurden; und wenn wir nach dem Ende der Türkenkriege heute wieder innerhalb der islamischen Völkerwelt religiöse Energien erwachen sahen, so war das eine Überraschung. Wenn vor fünfzig oder vierzig Jahren vom Islam die Rede war, haben die besten Kenner des Islam immer gesagt, das werde nie ein wirkliches politisches Problem werden, da sie

---

9   Huntington 1998, pp. 21 and 28-29. Strong criticism towards this approach has been expressed, among others, by Amartya Sen, who has noticed that "the 'clash of civilizations' was already a popular topic well before the horrifying events of September 11 sharply added to the conflicts and distrust in the world. But these terrible happenings have had the effect" of increasing the "interest in the theory of civilizational clash forcefully presented in Samuel Huntington's famous book" (Sen 2006, p. 40). According to Sen, however, "the difficulty with this approach begins with unique categorization, well before the issue of a clash – or not – is even raised. Indeed, the thesis of a civilizational *clash* is conceptually parasitic on the commanding power of a unique *categorization* along so-called civilizational lines [...]. The alleged confrontations of religious differences are incorporated into a sharply carpentered vision of one dominant and hardened divisiveness. [...] Thus, the deficiency of the clash thesis begins well before we get to the point of asking whether the disparate civilizations [...] must necessarily – or even typically – clash" (Sen 2006, pp. 10 and 41). It is also remarkable that Fred R. Dallmayr, moving from Gadamerian premises and presuppositions, has developed a sort of hermeneutic "counterbalance" to the civilizational clash theory, explicitly speaking of "dialogue among civilizations" (see Dallmayr 2002, pp. 17-30).

10 UD, p. 143 [CP, p. 140].

sich nie untereinander einigen werden. Nun hat sich die Lage in der Zwischenzeit verändert, wir sehen die Folgen. Da war und ist die Gründung des durch und durch europäischen Staates Israel mitten im Lebensbereich des Islam. Da ist der neue wirtschaftliche Schwerpunkt, durch das in diesen Ländern geförderte Erdöl, und damit die Bildung einer europäisch geschulten intellektuellen Oberschicht und ihre Wirkungen. Das sind Veränderungen, die am Ende überall bevorstehen. Überall ist es so, daß die industrielle Revolution in andere Kulturwelten eindringt und unvorhergesehene Folgen zeitigt. Der Ausbreitung der europäischen Rationalität zum Trotz – und gerade in ihrer Folge – entsteht überall neuer Nationalismus und Regionalismus, und es häuft sich neuer Konfliktstoff an[11].

At the same time, however, although Gadamer certainly does not belong to the uncritical "apologists" of our own civilization and its worldview, but rather to its critics, I think it is important to underline that he never makes the opposite error, so to speak, of developing an "Occidentalist" perspective. By "Occidentalism", some political scientists and journalists intend actually a sort of counterpart of the so-called "Orientalism"[12], i.e. a constellation of subtle, persistent and false assumptions underlying the attitudes towards certain cultures: the culture of the Middle East as observed by Western intellectuals and peoples, in the latter case, the Western culture as observed by Eastern peoples and some Western intellectuals as well, in the former. The authors of a book entitled *Occidentalism* write:

> The dehumanizing picture of the West painted by its enemies is what we have called Occidentalism. [...] Occidentalism, like capitalism, Marxism, and many other modern isms, was born in Europe, before it was transferred to other parts of the world. The West was the source of the Enlightenment and its secular, liberal offshoots, but also of its frequently poisonous antidotes. [...]

---

11 GW 10, p. 271.
12 I obviously refer here to Edward W. Said's famous book *Orientalism*, according to which, "so far as the West was concerned during the nineteenth and twentieth centuries, an assumption had been made that the Orient and everything in it was, if not patently inferior to, then in need of corrective study by the West. [...] Orientalism, then, is knowledge of the Orient that places things Oriental in class, court, prison, or manual for scrutiny, study, judgment, discipline, or governing" (Said 1994, pp. 40-41).

> Occidentalism is [the] hateful caricature [...] of Western modernity [...]. There are, of course, perfectly valid reasons to be critical of many elements that go into the venomous brew we call Occidentalism. Not all the critiques of the Enlightenment lead to intolerance or dangerous irrationalism. [...] But criticism of the West, harsh as it might be, is not the issue here. The view of the West in Occidentalism is like the worst aspects of its counterpart, Orientalism, which strips its human targets of their humanity. [...] Occidentalism is at least as reductive; its bigotry simply turns the Orientalist view upside down. To diminish an entire society or civilization to a mass of soulless, decadent, money-grubbing, rootless, faithless, unfeeling parasites is a form of intellectual destruction[13].

Now, I think that Gadamer could have subscribed to such an anti-reductive view about our own civilization and its relationship with other cultures. A view that, in my opinion, is particularly appropriate in the case of such relevant and living matters like the relation between the Western culture and those (e.g. the so-called Muslim fundamentalists) who reject *a priori* and *en bloc*, so to speak, most of its basic features[14]. According to Gadamer, it is absolutely urgent and necessary indeed "to bring ourselves to an understanding with Islam",

---

13   Buruma and Margalit 2004, pp. 5-6 and 10. To be honest, at the end of *Orientalism* Said himself explicitly declared: "If this book has any future use, it will be [...] as a warning: that systems of thought like Orientalism, discourses of power, ideological fictions – mind-forg'd manacles – are all too easily made, applied, and guarded. Above all, I hope to have shown my reader that the answer to Orientalism is not Occidentalism" (Said 1994, p. 328).

14   I think that it is important to notice that although Gadamer's dialogical perspective surely relies on the recognition of the value and dignity of "the other", nevertheless it never leads to a denial of one's own identity or a complete subjection to that of "the other". According to him, indeed, "with such ideas of the coexistence of differences, one must take care not to introduce a false claim for tolerance or better a false concept of tolerance. It is a widespread mistake to take tolerance to be a virtue which abandons insisting on one's own position and represents the other one as equally valid. [...] However, one may still say this: Only where strength is, is there tolerance. The acceptance of the other certainly does not mean that one would not be completely conscious of one's own inalienable Being. It is rather one's own strength, especially the strength of one's own existential certainty, which permits one to be tolerant. Practice in such tolerance [is] a good preparation for the greater tasks which await the world" (EE, p. 59 [EPH, pp. 206-207]).

and to this end the existence of "a right and a left in the Islamic world, too" might prove to be useful, in the sense that there is "even a movement there that doesn't just stick strictly to what it had previously learned – it says, 'We need to adapt ourselves to the modern world – we could risk it'"[15].

Moreover, for the last few decades these socio-political and cultural trends closely affect not only the international relations between different states, but also the intra-national processes that occur within our society. We have "a variety of minorities who presumably want to integrate themselves into the society and yet have a very strong sense of their own community", so that "we are faced with the problem of their coexistence within the society"[16]. Gadamer then notices that on the one hand "this sense of community inhibits clashes between a minority and its adopted society", while on the other hand "the problem is exacerbated because some conflicts do arise": as a consequence, the adopted society may feel threatened, and closes "itself off from minorities", rejecting "every immigrating minority and, ultimately, [...] immigration as such"[17]. According to Gadamer, however, it is "no longer possible in Europe, and especially in the developed societies, to close oneself off from immigration": hence, "the problem of resolving the conflict between minorities and their adopted society as well as the conflicts among the minorities themselves" appears today as "an unavoidable one"[18].

---

15 UD, p. 143 [CP, p. 140]. I think it is interesting to notice how, according to Richard Rorty, i.e. a philosopher who always claimed to endorse himself a "hermeneutical or Gadamerian attitude", the idea of a dialogue with Islam is actually meaningless or at least useless, since there was "no dialogue between the *philosophes* and the Vatican in the eighteenth century, and there is not going to be one between the mullahs of the Islamic world and the democratic West. The Vatican in the eighteenth century had its own best interests in mind, and the mullahs have theirs. [...] With luck, the educated middle class of the Islamic countries will bring about an Islamic Enlightenment, but this Enlightenment will not have anything much to do with a 'dialogue with Islam'" (Rorty 2005, p. 73).
16 UD, p. 118 [CP, p. 115].
17 UD, p. 118 [CP, p. 115].
18 UD, p. 118 [CP, pp. 115-116].

Gadamer's interest in such phenomena should hardly appear as surprising. Indeed, if there is a strand in contemporary thought whose affinity with the idea and practice of dialogue and fusion of cultural horizons appears undisputable in principle, this is philosophical hermeneutics[19]. In fact, the very notion of *Horizontverschmelzung* "means that we can open ourselves dialogically to rival horizons: the boundaries are expandable, and we can in principle – through inter-civilizational dialogue [...] – liberate ourselves from the opinions of our own cave"[20]. From this point of view, I think it is highly significant that a thinker like Charles Taylor, in discussing the question concerning the relations between different cultures, and searching for "something midway between the inauthentic and homogenizing demand for recognition of equal worth, on the one hand, and the self-immurement within ethnocentric standards, on the other", finally claims: "What has to happen is what Gadamer has called a 'fusion of horizons'"[21]. According to Taylor, indeed,

> We learn to move in a broader horizon, within which what we have formerly taken for granted as the background to valuation can be situated as one possibility alongside the different background of the formerly unfamiliar culture. The "fusion of horizons" operates through our developing new vocabularies of comparison, by means of which we can articulate these contrasts[22].

In some of his last interviews, Gadamer stresses especially the role that the dialogue between different religions could have in paving the way for the establishing of a sort of world *ethos* and international

---

19 I borrow this observation from Garelli 2005, p. 153.
20 Beiner 2004, p. 148.
21 Taylor 1994, pp. 72 and 67.
22 Taylor 1994, p. 67. On Gadamer's hermeneutics and the problems of our multicultural age, see also the interesting contributions of Vasilache 2003 (based on a comparison between the philosophical approaches of Gadamer and Foucault), Rodi 2004 (who offers a sort of introduction to the relation between hermeneutics and intercultural understanding), Schönherr-Mann 2004 (who places the questions of inter- and multi-culturalism within the broader context of hermeneutics *as* ethics), Ataman 2008, pp. 31-52 (who focuses on the question of understanding other religions, and especially Islam), and Zaccaria 2008.

justice. For example, in the interview *Weltethos und internationale Gerechtigkeit* Gadamer says:

> Mich beschäftigt diese Frage seit langem im Bezug auf die Weltreligion. Ich bin der Meinung, wenn es uns nicht gelingt, so etwas wie ein Weltethos zu schaffen, dann werden wir selbst das 3. Jahrhundert nicht erleben. [...] Die Weltreligion, die dem Weltethos zugrunde liegt, muß nicht mit einer Gesamtheit von Dogmen und von universell anerkannten Wahrheiten identifiziert worden. Sie nimmt eher immer noch die Bedeutung des Gesprächs ein und ist dadurch mit Gerechtigkeit verbunden. [...] Die Weltreligion ist daher [eine] antidogmatische Haltung [...]. Jedenfalls sind Menschenrechte von wesentlicher Bedeutung. Wenn wir jedoch auf internationale Gerechtigkeit zielen, sollten wir uns nicht bloß an ihnen festhalten und sie mit absoluten Werten verwechseln: wir sollten eher versuchen, ein Weltethos zu verwirklichen, indem wir auf die Quelle der Menschenrechte zurückgreifen [...]. Ich würde also glauben, daß die Weltreligion dabei helfen könnte, die gegenwärtigen Konflikte zu lösen [...]. Eine gemeinsame Religion würde dabei eine wichtige Rolle spielen[23].

In the abovementioned dialogue with Riccardo Dottori he hints at the possibility of a "dialogue between the various world religions, which philosophy should prepare because it discovers within everyone an instance of the great chain that we call transcendence"[24]. And then he states:

> I am also of the opinion that philosophy is preparing the ground for a global conversation, and we must take advantage of this opportunity to develop a dialogue, or we will be lost. [...] *A conversation among the religions*. Certainly, because the great world religions do exist. But, then...not really "among" the religions. [...] Let's ask, rather, *"How is the Enlightenment comprehended among these religions?"* [...] I want to say again that, on the whole, one must frame the question from the very beginning by pointing out that we should not understand this conversation as a conversation between the representatives of religions or between philosophers [...]. These accomplish nothing; they are infinitesimally small accommodations. [...] The problem is whether this dialogue of the religions themselves is possible and whether one can actually

---

23 Gadamer 2001a, pp. 12-14 and 17.
24 UD, p. 74 [CP, p. 73].

arrive at it by going beyond the philosophical discussion. I say this because I am convinced that we are in *a hopeless situation*, and that it is, in fact, the necessary *consequence of the one-sidedness of a purely scientific knowing*[25].

---

25 UD, pp. 74-75 [CP, pp. 73-74 (my italics)].

5. The Possibility of Global Disasters and the Fear for the Self-destruction of Mankind

It is a well known fact that the twentieth century has been, among other things, a century anguished and "obsessed" by the terrible shock of the atomic bombing of Hiroshima and Nagasaki. Indeed, these events pushed the "planetary iron age" into the phase of the "Damoclean threat"[1]. From then on, we are all drawn into the common adventure of a planetary era, all threatened by nuclear death.

> En 1945, la bombe d'Hiroshima a fait entrer l'âge de fer planétaire dans une phase damocléenne. [...] La potentialité d'auto-anéantissement accompagne désormais la marche de l'humanité. [...] La bombe d'Hiroshima a ouvert en 1945 une phase nouvelle, où l'arme nucléaire est suspedue en permanence audessus de l'humanité entière. Cette situation damocléenne s'est installée avec les énormes arsenaux capables de détruire plusieurs fois le genre humain, les missiles porteurs de mégamorts tapis par milliers dans les silos, sillonnant les océans dans les sous-marins nucléaires, volant sans discontinuer dans les superbombardiers. L'arme se répand, se miniaturise et sera bientôt à la disposition de potentats et/ou de terroristes déments[2].

An outstanding sociologist of our time, Ulrich Beck, has recently contextualized the Hiroshima and Nagasaki trauma within a specific type of "dialectics of modernization", namely the so-called "dialectics of anti-modernity"[3]. As he expresses it:

> Hiroshima: [...] Dieses Ereignis, *hervorgegangen aus den Erfolgen der Naturwissenschaften*, in diesem Fall der Kernphysik, hat die radikalen Ambivalenzen des "Fortschritts" sichtbar gemacht und menschheitsweites Erschreken erzeugt. [...] Erst das alle Begriffe sprengende, alle Vorstellungen überholende Ausmaß der Zerstörung machte offenbar, *was in der alltäglichen Normalität von Wissen-*

---

1 I borrow these expressions from Morin and Kern 1993.
2 Morin and Kern 1993, pp. 31 and 111-112.
3 See Beck 2007, pp. 394-407.

schaft, Forschung und Theorie verdeckt geblieben war: Aus dem Sieg der Moderne war eine Höllenwaffe hervorgegangen, die das Schicksal der Menschheit in die Hände derer legte, die die politischen Machthebel hatten – oder sich Zugang dazu verschafften. Der Untergang der Menschheit [...] wurde *mit dem Fortschreiten des Fortschritts* [...] zur realen Möglichkeit, zu einem Weltrisiko eben, das – weil es nicht mehr aus der Welt zu schaffen ist – eine neue Situation schafft und die Grundlagen aller Zukünfte für immer verändert. [...] Es sind die enormen Erfolge der Moderne, ihre Leistungen, ihre Durchsetzungskraft, die die Möglichkeit der Selbstvernichtung der Menschheit eröffnet haben. [...] Die Atombombe zerstört nicht nur potentiell die Moderne, die Antizipation der Selbstvernichtung zerstört zunächst auch die Selbstgewißheit, die Grundbegriffe und Theorien der Moderne[4].

As the examples of Karl Jaspers (*Die Atombombe und die Zukunft des Menschen*) and Günther Anders (*Die Antiquiertheit des Menschen*) clearly show, even philosophers have deeply meditated on the *potestas annihilationis* (a sort of opposite of the *creatio ex nihilo*) that the atomic bomb has given to man. I think it is interesting to notice that even Gadamer belongs to that group of thinkers who have constantly reflected upon the atomic bomb and its effects on the human condition.

In some of his writings, indeed, he makes insistently reference to "the breathtaking specter of all mankind's self-destruction through misuse of atomic energy"[5]. "For the first time", he says, "an arsenal of weapons has been created, whose use does not guarantee victory, but would rather result only in the collective suicide of human civilization"[6]. Meditating on the dramatic context and situation in which we find ourselves, Gadamer then asks: "how will it be possible to save mankind from itself (*die Menschheit vor sich selbst zu retten*)?"[7]. It is clear that neither Gadamer nor anyone else possesses a clear and unambiguous answer to such urging questions, so all he can suggest is to never lose sight of the important role played by emotions like fear in influencing our decisions even in the sphere of interna-

4   Beck 2007, pp. 395-397.
5   LT, p. 52 [PT, p. 38].
6   EE, p. 11 [EPH, p. 223].
7   GW 8, p. 339.

tional relations between different nations. Hence, in a 1991 interview he explains:

> Wenn wir uns fragen, was kann unsere Welt wieder in Ordnung bringen, so gibt es doch Kräfte, sehr starke emotionale Kräfte. Ich nenne zum Beispiel die Angst, ich rede hier gar nicht von Nächstenliebe oder Menschheitsrechten. Im Augenblick stehen wir vor dem möglichen neuen großen Tod. [...] Einen dritten Weltkrieg dürfte die Menschheit wohl kaum überleben. [...] Ja, deshalb antworte ich mit der Angst. Bisher haben wir aus keinem anderen Grund Frieden gehabt. Die beiden Mächten [*scil.* U.S.A. and U.S.S.R.] hatten voreinander Angst. Das nennt man Freiheit. [...] Wenn es nicht die Angst gäbe, könnte man verzweifeln. Angst ist nicht nur etwas, was einfach in uns ist, aus gutem Grunde, Angst schärft auch unser Bewußtsein. Wir wollen den kollektiven Selbstmord der Menschheit vermeiden[8].

As is well known, however, after the fall of the communist regimes in Soviet Union and Eastern Europe, beside an obvious, great relief due to the end of the Cold War, an unceasing and even dangerous change in the geopolitical balance has been also observed. So, the end of the sharp contrast between the two big ideological "blocs" (each equipped with enormous, terrifying military powers) has paradoxically produced "an enormous zone of political uncertainty, instability, chaos and civil war", destroying "the international system that had stabilized international relations for some forty years"[9]. This has generated a situation even more dangerous than the preceding one, because of the lack of whatever form of geopolitical "order" or stability.

As Clifford Geertz has noticed, "after the fall of the Berlin Wall, it is clear that we are once more in [a] disrupted place, at [a] disjointed time": in fact, the world of "compact powers and contending blocs" in which "we have been living in [...] since Sedan and Port Arthur", the world of "arrangements and rearrangements of macro-alliances – is no more"[10]. What there is instead is a "much more pluralistic pattern of relationships among the world's peoples", whose form however "re-

---

8 Gadamer 1991a, pp. 491-492.
9 Hobsbawm 1996, p. 10.
10 Geertz 2000, p. 219.

77

mains vague and irregular, scrappy, ominously indeterminate"[11]. This means, among other things, that today it is perhaps possible to count *only* on the mutual fear of the political enemies as a warranty for a condition of peace (or, at least, as a guarantee for the absence of global, all-annihilating conflicts). For these reasons, in still another interview from the last years of his life Gadamer fearfully asks:

> How could we ever foresee that there will not be another madman [*scil.* like Hitler]? [...] In the case of a nuclear war, nobody will be safe, because there is no atomic power station that cannot be easily destroyed by an aeroplane crash. It is almost desirable that someday a madman succeeds in that, without setting the whole world on fire however [...]. At that point, those who have atomic energy at their disposal will probably try to reach an understanding. The agreement will be achieved through intimidation and threat. The highly industrialized nations have an arsenal of atomic bombs at their disposal, and probably even nations like Iran [will]. [...] What could lead to worldwide solidarity? Only the fear of a catastrophe, which has an enormous power. [...] If some madman dropped a bomb in some part of the world – and I expect it to happen already in the next century – the fear of such an event would produce solidarity. [...] As I said, mutual fear is needed in such a compromised world situation[12].

Beside all this, another relevant aspect of Gadamer's cosmopolitan broadening of hermeneutics is surely represented by his attention to the possibility of global calamity by still other means than nuclear wars, such as for example ecological catastrophes and analogous phenomena. As Jean Grondin noticed, indeed, "for Gadamer, the sheer survival of our species is in question", and in the last decades of his life he "appeared especially concerned with the ecological crisis, remarking pessimistically that probably no one knows how to solve it", but also glimpsing "some possibilities in the quasi-political broad-

---

11   Geertz 2000, p. 219. According to Geertz, indeed, the developments that have followed the collapse of Soviet Union, "and others induced by them [...], have not produced a sense of a new world order. They have produced a sense of dispersion, of particularity, of complexity, and of uncenteredness. The fearful symmetries of the postwar era have come unstuck, and we, it seems, are left with the pieces" (Geertz 2000, p. 220).
12   Gadamer 2002, pp. 218-219 and 221.

ening of his hermeneutics"[13]. Even in this case, however, one of the reasons of the gravity and seeming "insolubility" of the problem is represented by its global significance and consequences: in particular, by the extraordinary difficulty of "developing institutions or principles of international law that limit national sovereignty", in order to oblige "all the major industrial nations" to commit themselves "to doing something about this"[14].

Now, the question concerning the worldwide diffusion of mass-destruction weapons and technology has already shown us the darkest and most "apocalyptic" side of Gadamer's thought. This dark or apocalyptic side, however, probably becomes even more visible and conspicuous if one takes into consideration his reflections on the ecological question. As a matter of fact, he pessimistically observes that "our world is at an end if it keeps going on this way, as if it were always about to 'move forward'"[15]. And in the essay *Wieweit schreibt Sprâche das Denken vor?*, he sarcastically adds that "this is no mere

---

13 Grondin 1999, p. 371 [2003, p. 329]. On this basis, Vittorio Hösle has developed a veritable *philosophy of the ecological crisis*, claiming that "die Anthropologie und die Metaphysik können nicht unberührt bleiben von der *Möglichkeit* der Apokalypse. [...] Ökologische Katastrophen sind das Verhängnis, das in einer gar nicht mehr weit entfernten Zukunft auf uns lauert – trotz aller kollektiven Anstrengungen, dies zu verdrängen, trotz aller Beschwichtigungs- und Abwiegelungsstrategien hat sich diese Überzeugung inzwischen im Bewußtsein der meisten Menschen festgesetzt [...]. Einerseits hat die Kultivierung dieses Gefühls etwas Widerliches an sich – denn nur zu leicht kann sie zur Resignation und zur Apathie [...] führen [...]. Andererseits darf diese Gefahr aber nicht herhalten zu einer Legitimierung der Verdrängung und damit des lemminghaften Weiterrasens auf den Abgrund zu – dies gilt für jedermann, und erst recht für die Philosophie. [...] [Die] demographische Entwicklung, die Erhitzung der Atmosphäre, die Zunahme giftiger Chemikalien im Wasser, die Erosion des Bodens, die Verdünnung der Ozonschicht, die Abnahme der Nahrungsmittel, die Verringerung der Artenvielfalt müssen eine Situation schaffen, in der es zu ökologischen Katastrophen kommen wird. [...] Strittig ist höchstens der Zeitpunkt dieser Katastrophen" (Hösle 1991, pp. 14-15 and 25).
14 Singer 2002, p. 50.
15 LT, p. 99 [PT, p. 80].

gloomy picture painted by a philosopher living in Cloud-cuckoo-land"[16].

Quite interestingly, with regard to these questions, Gadamer sometimes hints at some possible resemblances between his own ideas and those of another German thinker of his generation, another pupil of Heidegger, who has become internationally known for his search of an ethic for the technological age: Hans Jonas. As is well known, in *Das Prinzip Verantwortung* Jonas tries to give an outline of the foundations of a prescriptive ethics appropriate for "the excessive dimensions of the scientific-technological-industrial civilization"[17]. So, what he has in mind is an ethics that is prompted by the assumption "that we live in an apocalyptic situation", that is, by "the threat of a universal catastrophe" that might be caused by "power over nature through scientific technology [...] if we let things take their present course"[18]. Now, in some of his writings Gadamer expresses analogous preoccupations – although it must be said that he never develops a systematic ethical-political perspective comparable to Jonas' one. So, for example, in the essay *Die Vielfalt Europas* he writes that our problems concern "the whole existence of humans in nature, [...] the task of controlling the development of our abilities and our mastery over natural powers in such a manner that nature will not be destroyed

16 GW 2, p. 202 [TM, p. 549]. At the beginning of this essay, Gadamer claims indeed that "in our contemporary situation, faced as we are with an increasingly widespread anxiety about the future of mankind, the issue is the suspicion slowly seeping into the consciousness of all that, if we go on this way, if we pursue industrialization, [...] and turn our earth into one vast factory as we are doing at the moment, then we threaten the conditions of human life" (GW 2, p. 199 [TM, p. 546]). The same idea is also reasserted in the essay *Europa und die Oikoumene*, where he writes: "Die gesamte technische und industrielle Entwicklung hat inzwischen ein solches Ausmaß erreicht, daß nun die ökologische Krisis allgemein bewußt geworden ist, und wir wissen bisher überhaupt noch nicht, ob sie von der Menschheit wird gemeistert werden können. Im Gespräch mit einem bedeutenden Naturforscher habe ich einmal gesagt, es sei doch nun wirklich fünf Minuten vor zwölf. Er sah mich ernst und antwortete: 'Nein, es ist halb eins'" (GW 10, p. 269).
17 Jonas 1984, p. 251 [1984, p. 140].
18 Jonas 1984, p. 251 [1984, p. 140].

and laid waste by us, but preserved together with our existence on this earth"[19]. On this basis, as I said, Gadamer sometimes points out the existence of relevant points of affinity with Jonas, and even gives him credit for having made us aware of the new dimensions of human responsibility in the techno-scientific age[20].

It must be said, however, that beside these affinities Gadamer highlights some divergences with Jonas as well. For example, he calls Jonas' basic presupposition into question: the idea of the altered nature of human action, that is, the "contention that with certain developments of our powers the *nature of human action* has changed, and, since ethics is concerned with action, it should follow that the changed nature of human action calls for a change in ethics as well"[21]. According to Jonas, indeed, "the qualitatively novel nature of certain of our actions" (namely, the "novel powers [...] of modern *technology*") "has opened up a whole new dimension of ethical relevance for which there is no precedent in the standards and canons of traditional ethics"[22]. For this reason, in the first sections of *Das Prinzip Verantwortung* he clearly distinguishes his new ethical imperative, "responding to the new type of human action and addressed to the new type of agency that operates it", from Kant's traditional categorical imperative: while the latter "was addressed to the individual, and its criterion was instantaneous", the former extrapolates indeed "into a predictable real *future* as the open-ended dimension of our responsibility"[23]. According to Gadamer, however, the change in the dimensions and consequences of our moral responsibil-

---

19 EE, p. 28 [EPH, p. 232].
20 See, for instance, the essay-review *Ethos und Ethik*, where Gadamer takes *Das Prinzip Verantwortung* into account and writes: "Ich sehe [das] Verdienst [der] neueren Arebeiten von Jonas [...] darin, die ungeheuere Maßstabveränderung zum Bewußtsein zu bringen, die über die Verantwortlichkeit des Menschen gekommen ist. Sein unermeßlich gesteigertes Handelnkönnen ist ein Handeln und Entscheiden geworden, das weithin für kommende Generationen schicksalhaft ist" (GW 3, p. 369).
21 Jonas 1984, p. 15 [1984, p. 1].
22 Jonas 1984, p. 15 [1984, p. 1].
23 Jonas 1984, pp. 36-37 [1984, pp. 11-12].

ity is not so radical and "revolutionary" as Jonas seems to argue[24], and so in the essay *Hermeneutik – Theorie und Praxis* he writes:

> Zur Verantwortung gehört auch Wissen und Sachkenntnis. [...] Hans Jonas irrt, wenn er seine Darstellung der Ethik der Verantwortung gegen Kant abheben will. Was sich geändert hat, ist lediglich die Rechtweite der Verantwortung, die etwa politische Entscheidungen in unserer heutigen zugespitzten Kultursituation bekommen haben, seit es um das Überleben der Menschheit überhaupt geht. Das gilt etwa angesichts der ökologischen Krisis, daß die Verantwortlichkeit für die kommenden Geschlechter auf unsere Entscheidungen einwirken muß, und nicht nur das, was wir im Augenblick als vorteilhaft empfinden. [...] So ist also nicht etwa die Verantwortungsethik eine neue Erkenntnis, wohl aber ist es verdienstlich, an die Maßstäbe zu erinnern, in denen diese Erkenntnis uns heute bindet. So würde ich Jonas durchaus zustimmen, daß der Gedanke der Verantwortung uns alle binden muß, und doch sollten wir dabei zugleich klug genug sein, die Eingerechte der Kulturkreise und ihrer Wertbegriffe mitzubeachten. Das sind wahrlich spannungsvolle Aufgaben, die eine Politik auf lange Sicht verlangt[25].

I will conclude this overview on Gadamer's reflections on the most troubling and disquieting aspects of the present world, by taking into consideration his ideas on some issues raised by the application of scientific discoveries to the medical field.

Gadamer had a profound and long standing interest in the problems of health care and the art of medicine which arise in our techno-scientific age, as testified by his 1993 collection of papers *Über die Verborgenheit der Gesundheit* that gathers thirteen essays written between 1963 and 1991. However, this is not the appropriate place to undertake an overall and detailed analysis of Gadamer's "philosophy of medicine", so to speak. In general, what worries Gadamer about the art of healing in a scientific age is the growing diffusion of strong tendencies to one-sided rationalization, technol-

---

24 Hence, in the abovementioned essay-review *Ethos und Ethik* we read: "[ich] glaube [...] nicht, daß diese Veränderung des Maßstabes die grundsätzliche Bedeutung hat, die Jonas ihr zuschreibt. Unbedingter als der kategorische Imperativ kann auch im größten Maßstab nichts werden. Die Klugheit der Aufklärung unseres Jahrhunderts findet die gleiche Grenze wie die der Aufklärung des 18. Jahrhunderts. Das kann man von Kant lernen" (GW 3, p. 369).
25 HE, p. 6.

ogization and bureaucratization in matters that concern living human beings. Strong tendencies which, according to him, are progressively leading to the forgetting and denial of the complexity of the healing process, "this inner proportion, this inner correspondence that cannot be measured and yet must always be taken into account"[26]. So, in the essay precisely entitled *Über die Verborgenheit der Gesundheit*, Gadamer reminds us that

> The role of the doctor is to "treat" or "handle" the patient with care in a certain manner. The German word for treating a patient is *behandeln*, equivalent to the Latin *palpare*. It means, with the hand (*palpus*), carefully and responsively feeling the patient's body so as to detect strains and tensions which can perhaps help to confirm or correct the patient's own subjective localization, that is, the patient's experience of pain. [...] Something is never just a "case" of illness. Perhaps it is not so very strange, although it is certainly disturbing, that when someone attends a large hospital today they lose their own name and are allocated a number instead. This has its own logic. It is necessary that [...] it is revealed to the patient that he or she is a "case" of something. [...] What is important [however] is to recognize the other in their otherness, as opposed, for example, to the tendency towards standardization promoted by modern technology [...]. Treatment (*Behandlung*) always also involves a certain granting of freedom. It does not just consist in laying down regulations or writing out prescriptions[27].

Having said this, I would like to now linger on the specific issue of Gadamer's interest for those questions concerning the basic human phenomena of birth, life and death. Questions that, as is well known, deeply trouble the conscience of our age, at least for the last few decades, and that are currently of great concern in almost every sphere of public debate. As has been noted, indeed, "the advances of medical technology have forced us to think about issues that we previously had no need to face": no matter what we think about it and what our perspective is on these questions, it is without doubt that such technological advances have provoked and are still provoking "major shifts deep in the bedrock of Western ethics. We are going through a

---

26 ÜVG, p. 139 [EH, p. 108].
27 ÜVG, pp. 139, 142 and 140 [EH, pp. 108, 110-111 and 109].

period of transition in our attitude to [...] human life. Such transitions cause confusion and division"[28].

With regard to the problem of rethinking death in the age of science and technology, Gadamer firstly draws attention to the problem of "the postponing of death", which undoubtedly "presents an excessive demand upon a doctor of today that, counter to his Hippocratic oath, [...] 'permits' someone to die"[29]. As a matter of fact, "for a seemingly endless length of time he [*scil.* the doctor] can carry on a meaningless, vegetative functioning of the organism with machine support", until he finally summons his courage and takes "upon himself the torturous responsibility of saying, Now, an end to it!"[30]. So, in the essay *Die Erfahrung des Todes*, Gadamer concludes that thanks to "these enormous technological advances, with their goal of the artificial preservation of life", and thanks to the "anaesthetic drugs developed by modern pharmaceutics [that] can completely sedate the suffering person", in the end the whole process "culminates in the gradual disappearance of the experience of death. [...] The prolongation of life finally becomes a prolongation of death", and death itself "becomes like an arbitrary reward dependent on the decision of the doctor treating the case"[31]. These same issues are also at the centre of Gadamer's 1986 intervention at a forum of the CDU-coalition of Baden-Württemberg, in which he says:

> Für mich ist in den letzten 30 Jahren [...] eines der wichtigsten Phänomene dieser Art die Frage gewesen, wie ein moderner Arzt oder Klinikchef mit dem hippokratischen Eid fertig wird, angesichts der Tatsache der künstlichen Lebensverlängerung, die uns durch unsere technischen Möglichkeiten anvertraut ist. Ich sage das jetzt nicht in dem Sinne, daß diese Leute ihren hippokratischen Eid etwa nicht ernst nehmen. Ich sehe es eher umgekehrt: daß sie einen Begriff von hippokratischem Eid auch dort festhalten, wo der Sinn desselben sich in Unsinn verkehrt hat. Es ist oft passiert, daß, wenn ich über solche Dinge sprach, ein Klinikchef zu mir kam und etwas erregt und betroffen sagte: Es ist wirklich

---

28 Singer 1995, pp. 19 and 1.
29 GW 4, p. 226 [RAS, p. 84].
30 GW 4, p. 226 [RAS, p. 84].
31 GW 4, p. 289 [EH, p. 62].

wahr, es hängt von mir ab, als ob ich der liebe Gott wäre, wann etwa die Aufrechterhaltung des künstlichen Vegetationsprozesses eines Organismus abgestellt wird, wann also man den Menschen sterben läßt[32].

Anyway, this evidently does not mean that Gadamer denies the legitimacy and relevance of all the efforts of modern medicine to prolong life or, at least, to reduce the patients' sufferings before their decease. Rather, what worries him is the global tendency – so characteristic of our age, according to him – to a veritable and systematic "denial" of the experience of death and its basic human significance. More precisely, what Gadamer sees in our epoch is a tendency to reduce dying to "one of the innumerable processes of production within the modern economic life, albeit a negative one": that is, a "real depersonalization of death [...] in the modern hospital", and a reduction of the human being to "a link in the chain of causal processes" through the "artificial maintenance of the vegetative functions of the organism"[33].

I think that even Gadamer's late observations on the "denial", in our society, of the basic human significance of the experience of suffering and pain, belong to this constellation of ideas. As he explains in his very last public intervention of the 11th November, 2000, although "die Befreiung von schweren Schmerzen seit jeher zu den Erfahrungen des menschlichen Lebens gehört", and although it is

---

32 Gadamer 1986b, pp. 26-27. I also think that it is important to notice how Gadamer, when dealing with such topical and controversial questions, often expresses very "open" and "liberal/libertarian" opinions, based on the idea of a basic duty consisting of the need to respect every free decision of each and every individual. So, for example, to an interviewer who asks him "if there is a right to death, like there is a right to life", he answers without any hesitation: "Yes! As long as we are free agents, and as long as the goal of medical therapy always presupposes the person, i.e. it presupposes someone whose free will must always be respected and accepted, we have this right to death as well. From this point of view, I think it is not hard to answer your question. In practice, however, everything becomes harder and more difficult, because the process of dying, the agony itself, can cause a slow paralysis of the possibility to freely decide that characterizes self-conscious and healthy people" (Gadamer 1991b).

33 GW 4, p. 288 [EH, p. 62].

clear that "wir ohne die chemische Industrie vielfältige Mittel und Methoden der modernen Medizin gar nicht zur Verfügung hätten", nevertheless

> wir sind im Schmerz und können ihn nicht von uns trennen. Der Schmerz umgreift gleichsam unser Leben und fordert beständig neu heraus. Es ist viel, was der Schmerz verlangt. [...] In diesem Sinne ist der Schmerz eine große Chance, vielleicht die größte Chance, endlich mit dem "fertig zu werden", was uns aufgegeben ist. Die eigentliche Dimension des Lebens wird im Schmerz erahnbar, wenn man sich nicht über*winden* lässt. Hierin sehe ich auch die größte Gefahr des technologisierten Zeitalters, daß diese Kräfte unterschätzt werden[34].

After having briefly sketched Gadamer's ideas on the problem of *death* and the major ethical-political changes due to the advances of medical science and technology, let us now move on to some problems related to the opposite phenomenon, i.e. *birth*. Even in this case, what worries him the most – as he writes already in the 1965 essay *Über die Planung der Zukunft* – are "the technical possibilities of our scientific discoveries": namely, "the possibilities of applying genetics to the breeding of the human species, in regard to which man still entertains unresolved elemental fears"[35].

From this point of view, I think it might be said that Gadamer precociously envisioned what Jürgen Habermas recently defined the risks and perils of the new "liberal" varieties of eugenics[36]. So, for

---

34 SCH, pp. 22, 29 and 27. Perhaps it is possible to see here another affinity with Jonas: more precisely, with his conviction that we should conceive our mortality (with the load of suffering and pain that it inevitably entails) not just as a burden, but also as a blessing. From this point of view, mortality represents "the simple truth of our finiteness", and hence "not even the fountains of youth, which biotechnology may have to offer one day to circumvent the physical penalties of it, can justify the goal of extorting from nature more than its original allowance to our species for the length of our days" (Jonas 1996, p. 98). The relevance of the dimension of human finiteness for hermeneutic philosophy has been correctly pointed out, among others, by Di Cesare 2004, especially pp. 69-83.
35 GW 2, p. 159 [EPH, p. 168].
36 I obviously refer here to Habermas' influential study on the future of human nature, and his ideas on the moral limits of eugenics and the necessary ban on

example, in the 1986 interview *Traditionen sind der Wissenschaft oftmals weit überlegen*, Gadamer clearly expresses a non-alarmed, but nevertheless cautiously fearful attitude towards the "Schöpferspiel des Gen-Technologen", and poses the question: "wie weit der Gefahrenpunkt in der Gen-Technik erreicht oder erreichbar ist"[37]. Then, in the abovementioned intervention at the CDU-forum, apropos of the "Probleme der modernen Gen-Forschung" and the possible "Mißbrauch der Gen-Technik", he observes that "selbstverständlich stehen wir alle unter dem Eindruck, daß wir hier wiederum [...] vor gewaltigen Veränderungen, fast Revolutionen stehen"[38]. And still in his very last interviews from August-December 2001 he agrees with Silvio Vietta in defining astonishing "was auf einmal technisch-biologisch möglich ist": that is, "die möglichen Eingriffe in unsere anthropologische Ausstattung"[39]. So, he concludes: "Noch sind wir der Tatsache nicht gewachsen, welche Zerstörungsmöglichkeiten die Großmächte haben"[40].

Now, it is clear that everyone who deals with these topics today cannot be absolutely sure of being able to distinguish truthful predictions from science fiction scenarios: legitimate and well-founded fears from unmotivated alarmism and catastrophism. Gadamer proves to be fully aware of this, and so in those of his writings which contain observations on these problems he never lapses into apocalyptic descriptions of future "brave new worlds" founded on some sort of eugenic totalitarianism. Rather, he limits himself, so to speak, to hints and allegations which never lead to explicit and definitive thesis on genetics and technology, but somewhat aim at highlighting the still unresolved problems in this field and at encouraging each of us to autonomously reflect on them.

---

the self-instrumentalization of the species (see Habermas 2001b [2003, pp. 16-100]).
37 Gadamer 1986d, p. 83.
38 Gadamer 1986b, pp. 18 and 26.
39 IG, p. 42.
40 IG, p. 42.

In addition to this, it is also clear that when dealing with such complex, delicate and radically new questions, nobody can claim to possess simple answers or comfortable certainties. The awareness of this circumstance probably represents one of the basic reasons why Gadamer, in "the development of his practical philosophy" (and especially in the case of his observations on ecology, eugenics and technological medicine), chooses "a path which stops prematurely" and suddenly "becomes silent about such things"[41]. Obeying to a sort of "instinctive" and distinctive cautiousness about bioethical problems, Gadamer limits himself indeed to suggesting that, "in the question of gen technology and its misuse", there must be the "presupposition by means of which that, which is abhorred and rejected by all, is effectively prevented"[42]. A presupposition which, once again, must be intended only as a precautionary and prudential principle, looking forward to a new appropriate ethics for "our swiftly changing age"[43]. So, for example, in the 1987 essay *Die deutsche Philosophie zwischen den beiden Weltkriegen* we read:

41 Foster 1991, pp. 227 and 225. To be true, Foster does not limit this criticism to Gadamer's occasional and often fragmentary remarks on bioethical problems, but rather extends it to the whole Gadamerian conception of ethics. So, he observes that "the notable points [...] of Gadamer's practical philosophy [...] are encouraging and sometimes intriguing, but too often unsatisfying: they are vague, or over-generalized, or merely hints [...]. We encounter grand visions left unexplored and enigmatic principles unexplained. Conflicting statements are not unknown. [...] He articulates no theory of society or power, no investigation of justice or friendship, no clear concept of moral anthropology, [...] and no political philosophy or program". His "silence on such subjects draws objection as well as attention. Upon overall reflection, it seems as though Gadamer emasculates his practical philosophy at the moment he most elevates it. [...] He simply stops there, seeming to think that enunciation of [...] his hermeneutical ethic [...] is enough to satisfy the core requirements of a practical philosophy". However, "this is [only] half a practical philosophy" (Foster 1991, pp. 222-224). Even according to Derksen 1983 (p. 255), "Gadamer is by no means a superficial thinker", but "in the end, many questions remain unanswered, mainly because Gadamer believes there is no answer possible anymore".
42 EE, p. 153 [EPH, p. 190].
43 GW 1, p. 3 [TM, p. XXII].

Probleme wie der Streit [...] um die Gentechnologie im Bereiche der biologischen Forschung [haben] auch philosophische Aspekte, insbesondere im Sinne eines Rufes nach einer neuen Ethik. Das darf freilich kaum als eine philosophische Ethik angesehen werden, wonach hier das Zeitbewußtsein verlangt[44].

---

44   GW 10, p. 371.

6. On the Problematic Character of Ethic and Aesthetic Experiences in the Age of Science

In the previous chapters we have mostly dealt with moral and political questions, and I think it has been shown how, from a Gadamerian point of view, one might speak of a problematic character of ethic experience in our age. As a matter of fact, since the end of the nineteenth century we have probably been living in an unprecedented epoch of moral crisis. An epoch characterized by a "situation of disorientation arisen when the traditional ideals and values failed": that is, when the "traditional orientation points were eroded by the disenchantment of the world", and the "techno-scientific rationalization produced [...] the polytheism of values and the equipollence of decisions"[1]. In a word, an epoch that has violently thrown us "into the shadow of nihilism (*im Schatten des Nihilismus*)"[2]. According to Gadamer, nihilism, "relativism, historicism [and] fragmentarism" represent indeed "the undeniable principles of our own world-situation (*die unleugbaren Grundzüge unserer eigenen Weltsituation*)"[3].

Given all this, it is not by accident that Gadamer devoted many observations to moral and political questions, including the dismissal of those ethic concepts he felt unsatisfactory, and the consequent revaluation of those he felt were instead satisfactory and successful. Among the first ones, I think one might mention Kant's philosophy of practical reason and the phenomenological value-ethics of Max

1   Volpi 2005, pp. 4 and 175. On this topic, see also Volpi 2000.
2   To be exact, "*Im Schatten des Nihilismus*" is the title of an essay dedicated by Gadamer to the interpretation of modern German poetry (GW 9, pp. 367-382 [EPH, pp. 111-123]). However, I think that this expression has a wider meaning in Gadamer – as testified by the fact that he employed it even in other contexts (see, for instance, GW 3, p. 407) – and consequently might be intended as embodying his thought on a whole variety of problems.
3   GW 10, p. 263.

Scheler and Nicolai Hartmann. In the essays *Das ontologische Problem des Wertes* and *Wertethik und praktische Philosophie*[4], Gadamer criticizes indeed Scheler's and Hartmann's ambition to grasp *a priori* and intuitively an ontological order of absolute values. While his critiques of "Kantian formalism" are mostly based on his reliance on "Hegel's well-known critique of [the] ethics of the pure Ought"[5], and his critical confrontation of Kant's moral philosophy with Aristotle's[6].

In my opinion, Plato, Aristotle and Hegel represent indeed the authors upon whom Gadamer mostly relies in his own efforts in the field of ethics. What he envisions in their ethical views is the claim for the autonomy of the practical, i.e. moral domain, and its irreducibility to the theoretical or technical domains. For example, "the distinction drawn by Aristotle between ethical know-how (*phronesis*) and theo-

---

4 See, respectively, GW 4, pp. 189-202 and 203-215 [HRE, pp. 58-75 and 103-118].
5 GW 4, pp. 180-181 [HRE, pp. 25-26].
6 As a matter of fact, in the 1963 essay *Über die Möglichkeit einer philosophischen Ethik* Gadamer claims that "Aristotle's view" – which is "focused more intensely on the dependence of the individual decision on the practical and social determinants of the time, and less on the unconditionality that pertains to the ethical phenomenon" – succeeds "in rendering the nature of moral knowledge so clear that [...] it covers just as much the subjectivity that judges in the case of conflict as the substance of law and custom which determines its moral knowledge and its particular choices" (GW 4, p. 183 [HRE, pp. 28-29]). Hence, the theorization of what forms "the *ethos* of humankind prior to all appeals to reason", which makes "such appeals possible in the first place, is "the heart of Aristotle's ethics, and Kant does not do it justice" (GW 4, p. 187 [HRE, p. 34]). On other occasions, however, while maintaining his fundamental appreciation of Aristotle, Gadamer has also specified that Kant's position "can be rightly understood only if it is seen in polemical opposition to the Enlightenment thinking of the time" and to the thought "of his followers", who somehow aimed at "making action consistent with scientific knowledge. [...] Despite all criticism of the narrowness of Kant's distinctions", Gadamer concludes, "he is right about the main thing: validating the moral task in the face of the ever growing expansion of scientific and technological power" (GW 7, p. 394 [HRE, pp. 159-160]). For an interesting but quite critical confrontation with Gadamer's interpretations of Aristotle and Kant, see Ernst Tugendhat's essay *Antike und moderne Ethik* (Tugendhat 1984, pp. 33-56).

retical or scientific knowledge (*episteme*)"[7] is particularly relevant for philosophical hermeneutics. By the way, according to Gadamer, this distinction was already present in Plato's philosophy, although not so explicitly as in Aristotle's. As is well known, indeed, Gadamer on the one side obviously indicates Aristotle as the thinker who drew the fundamental distinction between *theoria, praxis* and *poiesis*, and thus recognized for the first time practical knowledge in its full autonomy as "a different kind of knowing (*allo eidos gnoseos*)"[8]. He, however, also tries to point out that "in Plato too, 'knowledge of the good' was a special kind of knowledge 'beyond' the 'sciences'": namely, "a mode of knowing that had a different epistemological structure from *techne*", and that "Socrates' exemplary life displays"[9]. "Considering the evidence of these similarities", Gadamer thus concludes, "the traditional opposition between Plato and Aristotle could be less and less confirmed, for both are ruled by the enduring urgency of the Socratic question of the good"[10].

Now, just like ethical knowledge "hermeneutical knowledge, too, must reject an objectivist style of knowing", and just like "the ethical subject or knower" also the hermeneutical subject or knower is not

7 PCH, p. 53 [PHC, p. 118].
8 GW 7, p. 146 [IGPAP, pp. 33-34].
9 GW 7, pp. 202 and 146 [IGPAP, pp. 131 and 34]. So, also according to Plato there is "an essential difference between technical-theoretical reasonableness and practical reasonableness [...]. Dialectic is not general and teachable knowledge, even if Plato often follows customary language usage and also speaks of it as *techne* or *episteme*. It is not in the least surprising, however, that he can call dialectic *phronesis* too. Dialectic [...] is 'reasonableness'. [...] Dialectic is not so much a *techne* – that is, an ability and knowledge – as a way of being. It is a disposition, or *hexis* in Aristotle's sense of the word" (GW 7, pp. 147-149 [IGPAP, pp. 35 and 37-39]).
10 Gadamer 1991d, p. 19. Even in the interview with Glenn Most *Die Griechen, unsere Lehrer*, he criticizes "the dogmatic rigidness of sharply contrasting Plato and Aristotle", and explains that "Aristotle was not really so different from Plato; his motives and impulses were not far from those found lodged in Platonic and Greek culture in general. Aristotle [...] belonged in the Platonic world", so that the real task is "to think Aristotle *together with Plato*" (Gadamer 1994a, pp. 140 and 143 [GC, pp. 91 and 94-95]).

"found simply confronting an entity it must verify", but rather "finds itself concerned with and invested by its object"[11]. Furthermore, Gadamer emphasizes the attention paid by the abovementioned philosophers to the embeddedness of all individual moral decisions in a social context. Something which, in turn, he thinks has been discredited or profoundly misunderstood by the modern subjectivist and individualistic culture. So, in the essay *Freundschaft und Selbsterkenntnis* Gadamer writes:

> the ontological constitution of society cannot be at all properly understood from the modern nominalist viewpoint that gave birth to modern science. In this regard, modern subjectivist thought must be forced to concede that "mind" (*Geist*) must also, and preeminently, be thought of as objective mind, for as such it forms state and society. Hegel understood this and, by implication, everything else that has since occurred in the sciences of state and society. But what did the Greeks, who had no such concept of science and "mind", think about this? The fact that Plato could think of world, city, and soul all in one, and that Aristotle, despite detaching ethics from the universal teleology of the good, avoided narrowing it to an ethics of disposition, [...] makes Greek practical philosophy in many respects a paradigm for the critique of subjectivity that still occupies our thought today[12].

And even more explicitly in the essay *Bürger zweier Welten* he develops the same theme on an almost cosmopolitan level, and writes that both "the ancient *polis* [and] the modern technocratic metropolis" are actually based on "the same unchanging fundamental presupposition":

> I would like to call it the presupposition of solidarity (*Voraussetzung der Solidarität*). I mean that self-evident communality (*selbstverständliche Gemeinsamkeit*) which alone allows for the common establishment of decisions which each considers to be correct in the areas of moral, social, and political life. For the Greeks this insight was in an undiscussed manner self-evident and even was reflected in their use of language. The Greek concept of the friend articulated the complete life of society. [...] It appears to me that the important presuppositions for solving the modern world's problems are none other than the ones formu-

---

11 PCH, pp. 52-53 [PHC, pp. 117-118].
12 GW 7, pp. 398-399 [HRE, p. 131].

lated in the Greek experience of thought. In any case the progress of science and its rational application to social life will not create so totally different a situation that "friendship" would not be required, that is a sustaining solidarity (*tragende Solidarität*) which alone makes possible the organized structure of human coexistence. It would certainly be a misunderstanding, if one believed that in a changed world a past thinking as such could be renewed. What is important is rather to use it as a corrective and to recognize the bottleneck of modern subjectivism and modern voluntarism[13].

Anyway, beside the problematic character of ethical experience in the age of science, it must be noticed how Gadamer pays no less attention to the problematic character of aesthetic experience – as well as to that of religious experience, as we will see in the next chapter. As a matter of fact, I think it can be said that, in Gadamer's view, we live in an age in which it has become more and more difficult having "authentic" experiences with art.

From a theoretical point of view, this is the result of the gradual tendency in modern thinking to devalue and bring discredit on any type of knowledge that does not satisfy the conditions of scientific methodology. According to Gadamer, the key role in this whole event was played by Kant, whose first *Kritik* definitively "limited [the] concept of knowledge wholly to the possibility of 'pure natural science'"[14]. His third *Kritik* consequently limited the validity of our experience of art and beauty to the extra-cognitive or "irrational" domains of genius and taste.

Now, the first attestation of Gadamer's interest in the *Kritik der Urteilskraft* is probably represented by a short essay entitled *Zu Kants*

---

13   GW 10, pp. 235-236 [EPH, pp. 218-219].
14   GW 1, p. 89 [TM, p. 72]. The fact that Gadamer, in his writings, mostly pays attention to Kant's *Kritik der praktischen Vernunft* and *Kritik der Urteilskraft* – which, in his eye, actually represented "a turning point", "the end of a tradition but also the beginning of a new development" (GW 1, p. 46 [TM, p. 36]) – absolutely does not mean that he underestimates the extraordinary relevance of the *Kritik der reinen Vernunft*, which he emphatically defines in a 1981 essay as "the beginning of a new epoch in the history of the world" (see GW 4, p. 336-348 [Gadamer 1985]).

Begründung der Ästhetik und dem Sinn der Kunst[15], in which he paid special attention to the §§ 16, 17 and 42 of the third *Kritik*, and analysed some important Kantian themes with which he would also confront in his later writings. So, for example, in the 1958 essay *Zur Fragwürdigkeit des ästhetischen Bewußtseins* he explicitly points out the epoch-making meaning of Kant's third *Kritik*[16], and in the 1960 essay *Die Wahrheit des Kunstwerkes* (first published as introduction to the Reclam edition of Heidegger's famous writing *Der Ursprung des Kunstwerkes*) he claims that it is necessary to "gain some insight into the prejudices that are present in the concept of a philosophical aesthetics", or even "to overcome the concept of aesthetics itself"[17]. Accordingly, Gadamer turns to the *Kritik der Urteilskraft*, which "established the problem of aesthetics in its systematic significance", and claims that

> in the subjective universality of the aesthetic judgment of taste, [Kant] discovered the powerful and legitimate claim to independence that the aesthetic judgment (*ästhetische Urteilskraft*) can make over against the claims of the understanding and morality. [...] What sets the beautiful apart [...] manifests itself in a subjective factor: the intensification of the *Lebensgefühl* [life feeling] through the harmonious correspondence of imagination and understanding. What we experience in beauty – in nature as well as in art – is the total animation and free interplay of all spiritual powers. [...] We must acknowledge that this justification of the autonomy of art was a great achievement in the age of the Enlightenment [...]. Basing aesthetics on the subjectivity of the mind's powers was, however, the beginning of a dangerous process of subjectification [and] the grounding of aesthetics led inevitably to a radical subjectification in further development of the doctrine of the freedom of the genius from rules[18].

Finally, in the first two chapters of *Wahrheit und Methode*[19] Gadamer harshly questions the Kantian subjectivization of aesthetics, which, according to him, is the issue on which the whole philosophy of art of

---

15 Gadamer 1939.
16 See GW 8, pp. 9-17 [Gadamer 1982b].
17 GW 3, p. 253 [HW, p. 100].
18 GW 3, pp. 253-254 [HW, pp. 100-101].
19 See GW 1, pp. 9-87 [TM, pp. 3-70].

the last two centuries lay. Here, he mostly focuses his attention on the decline, in the modern age, of the guiding concepts of humanism, namely those of culture (*Bildung*), commonsense (*sensus communis*), judgment (*Urteilskraft*), and taste (*Geschmack*). In short, Gadamer's basic criticism of the Kantian "transcendental justification of aesthetic judgment" concerns the fact that the limitation of "the idea of taste to an area in which, as special principle of judgment, it could claim independent validity", gave birth to an epoch-making and "radical subjectivization"[20] of our experience with art. Consequently, Gadamer also accuses Kant of having deprived the abovementioned humanist concepts of their intrinsic cognitive and ethic-political significance[21].

Now, Gadamer's critical interpretation of Kant's *Kritik der Urteilskraft* and its overall influence on the development of nineteenth and twentieth-century aesthetics is very long, rich and complex, and it is not possible here to dwell over it anymore. By the way, such an interpretation of Kant's aesthetics is not only very original and interesting, but also problematic (at least to some extent). For example, it should be noticed that Gadamer, in stressing only the subjective element of Kant's concepts of commonsense and taste, actually ends up ignoring some subtle distinctions introduced in the §§ 20 and 40 of the third *Kritik*[22], and even seems to forget that Kant speaks of a "sub-

---

20   GW 1, pp. 46-47 [TM, p. 36].
21   It is quite interesting that such an interpretation of Kant stands in almost complete opposition to Hannah Arendt's well-known interpretation of the *Kritik der Urteilskraft* as a work "of eminent political significance" (Arendt 1992, p. 14). I owe this insight into the strong contrast between these two Kant-interpretations to Beiner 1992 (pp. 135-136) and Forti 2006 (pp. 342-343).
22   Here, indeed, Kant explains that common sense "is essentially different from the common understanding (*vom gemeinen Verstande*) that is sometimes also called common sense" (Kant 1913b, p. 238 [2000, p. 122]). Then, he clearly distinguishes "common sense (*Gemeinsinn*; *sensus communis*)", i.e. "the idea of a communal sense", from the "common human understanding (*gemeiner Menschenverstand*)" or "merely healthy understanding (*bloß gesunder Verstand*)", calling the first one *sensus communis aestheticus* and the second one *sensus communis logicus* (Kant 1913b, pp. 293 and 295 note [2000, pp. 173 and 175 note]). I owe this insight to Menegoni 2008, p. 101.

jective universality" of the judgements of taste[23], so that it might be said that Kant's "aesthetic judgment [is] intersubjective as well as subjective"[24]. Anyway, for our specific purposes I think it is enough to underline that, although "Kant made heroic efforts to define [the] non-objective validity" of aesthetic and artistic pleasure, it is without doubt that he saved objective universality, i.e. true knowledge, for science only: hence, "the Kantian foundations for aesthetics has pretentions to scientific objectivity as its backcloth", and in this context "aesthetics must be something else" than knowledge "if it wants to be autonomous"[25].

According to Gadamer, the polarization-opposition between full objectivity (science, technology) and mere subjectivity (art and, in general, the whole of unmethodical experience) has gradually led to a false alternative: the interpretation of the aesthetic-artistic dimension either as a sphere of higher spirituality and truth (Romanticism) or as a sphere of groundlessness, irrelevance and superfluity (Positivism). Neither approach, however, brings full justice to the relevance and significance of art[26]. Gadamer also argues that the incapacity to de-

---

23 More precisely, Kant speaks of a "claim to the consent of everyone", which is based on the "subjective universal communicability of the kind of representation in a judgement of taste" (Kant 1913b, pp. 216-217 [2000, pp. 101 and 103]).
24 Makkreel 1990, p. 157. In this regard, I think it is surely relevant to notice how Gadamer, in the later essay *Anschauung und Anschaulichkeit*, clearly admitted that *Wahrheit und Methode* only gave a partial and one-sided account of the *Kritik der Urteilskraft* (GW 8, p. 201-202).
25 Grondin 2003, p. 32. As Gadamer explains at the end of *Wahrheit und Methode*, a world dominated by a techno-scientific worldview can surely accept "the beauty of nature, the beauty of art, and the disinterested pleasure they give – but only at its own frontiers, the frontiers of the achieved domination of nature" (GW 1, pp. 483-484 [TM, pp. 474-475]).
26 In a certain sense, this is also connected to the question concerning the use of scholarly methodologies in the study of art. Gadamer believes indeed that scientific methods "can deal thematically with much about the work of art, but not with the one and all of its *Aussage*" (GW 8, p. 50 [GR, p. 148]). In other words, as we read in the essay on Paul Celan *Wer bin Ich und wer bist Du?*, "all the methods developed by scholarship can be hermeneutically profitable", but only "if one uses them correctly and does not forget that a poem is not a fact

velop an alternative to this "either/or" has actually influenced in a negative way our ability to make "authentic" aesthetic experiences. From this point of view, it has been correctly noticed that, in Gadamer's eye, "the approach of modern philosophy of consciousness" on the whole

> fails to thematize the broader constitutive conditions of aesthetic experience. [...] Aesthetic theory in general is a relatively modern philosophical endeavour, one made possible by the Cartesian turn to the subject and driven by epistemological (rather than metaphysical or ontological) questions and concerns[27].

However, beside the purely theoretical question concerning the "aesthetic consciousness (*ästhetisches Bewußtsein*)" Gadamer also sees a more "concrete" aspect, which is in turn closely related to the theoretical one. According to him, the primacy of a subjectivistic approach to the aesthetic dimension in the modern age has gradually led to the confinement of art to the realm of the imaginary, the unreal, the mere apparent, i.e. of "fiction"[28].

On the one side, this process of autonomization of the aesthetic dimension has obviously had positive effects, and it has also led to "the creation of specific 'sites' for art" that are often "carefully separated from the rest of civic reality, which is dominated by the hard realities of science and economics"[29]. On the other side, however, this same process has also had negative consequences, in the sense that conceiving art "as appearance *sui generis*", and turning it "into an

---

which can be explained as an instance of something more general, the way that an experimentally valid fact is an instance of the law of nature" (GW 9, p. 447 [GOC, p. 161]).

27 Hance 1997, p. 134. In other words, it might be said that "der wichtigste Aspekt der Kunstdiskussion in *Wahrheit und Methode* [ist] die Überführung der philosophischen Ästhetik in die Hermeneutik. Gadamer hat die methodische Erschließung des Kunstwerks als unwahr gebrandmarkt und *die Ästhetik* abgelehnt, weil sie *sich an dem naturwissenschaftlichen Wahrheits- und Objektsbegriff orientiert*" (Hammermeister 1999, p. 78 [my italics]).

28 GW 1, p. 90 [TM, p. 73].

29 Grondin 2003, pp. 36-37.

autonomous world of production and creation", cuts it off "from the rest of reality"[30]. So, the abovementioned specific sites for art – among which Gadamer mentions "the 'universal library' in the sphere of literature, the museum, the theater, the concert hall", and even such twentieth-century innovations as the "techniques of reproduction, which turn buildings into pictures" – assume the form of areas where "the 'aesthetic differentiation' performed by aesthetic consciousness also creates an external existence for itself"[31]. Namely, the form of institutions where "the work loses its place and the world to which it belongs":

> aesthetic differentiation is an abstraction that selects only on basis of aesthetic quality as such. It is performed in the self-consciousness of "aesthetic experiences". [...] By disregarding everything in which a work is rooted (its original context of life, and the religious or secular function that gave it significance), it becomes visible as the "pure work of art". In performing this abstraction, aesthetic consciousness [...] differentiates what is aesthetically intended from everything that is outside the aesthetic sphere. It abstracts from all the conditions of a work's accessibility. Thus it is a specifically aesthetic kind of differentiation. It distinguishes the aesthetic quality of a work from all the elements of content that induce us to take up a moral or religious stance towards it[32].

30 Grondin 2003, p. 37. Thus, it has been noticed that, in Gadamer's view, "the consequences of 'aesthetic consciousness' are mixed [...]. What is good about it is that it separates the aesthetic from everything nonaesthetic and thus, in principle, allows the work of art to be seen in its true being as autonomous appearance. What is negative, and ultimately outweights the positive contribution, is that the work is abstracted from the world in which it has meaning and now belongs only to the world of aesthetic consciousness: the work is autonomous but meaningless" (Kelly 2004, p. 111).
31 GW 1, pp. 92-93 [TM, pp. 75-76].
32 GW 1, pp. 93 and 91 [TM, pp. 76 and 74]. As Gianni Vattimo has noticed, from a Gadamerian point of view "the museum understood as a social institution is only a correlation of aesthetic consciousness, its most significant incarnation. In the museum, too, objects are presented in the condition of absolute abstraction of the purely aesthetic stage. In other words, they are withdrawn from their concrete historical links (i.e., their religious, social, political, or everyday 'uses') by means of an activity that situates all of them at the same level of the objects

With regard to these topics, it could be perhaps intriguing to draw close the remarks made by Gadamer in the first part of *Wahrheit und Methode* to those made by "pragmatism's most active and influential twentieth-century figure, John Dewey", for whom "aesthetics was a very central concern"[33]. As a matter of fact, the first chapter of Dewey's major aesthetic writing, the 1934 treatise *Art as Experience*, deals precisely with a strong critique of the "museum conception of art" or "compartmental conception of fine art": that is, the predominant conception in the modern age, which sets artwork "apart from human experience", isolating it "from the human conditions under which it was brought into being and from the human consequences it engenders in actual life-experience"[34].

As has been noted, in this way Dewey takes a very critical position against "the presumed gap between life and art", i.e. against the modern "idea of art and the aesthetic as a separate realm": an idea that, according to him, reduces "art and the aesthetic [to] something to be enjoyed when we take a break from reality", and thus produces a "sequestration and fragmentation of our experience of art"[35]. Like Gadamer, Dewey also denounces the tendency to "set Art upon a remote pedestal" and relegate it "to the museum and gallery", explaining that "when artistic objects are separated from both conditions of origin and operation in experience, a wall is built around them that renders almost opaque their general significance"[36]. Once, Dewey notices, "the arts of the drama, music, painting, architecture" were "part of religious rites and celebrations", and thus had "no peculiar connection with theaters, galleries, museums. They were part of the significant life of an organized community", whereas today the "works of art are set in a niche apart instead of being celebrations,

---

of a 'taste', which in turn has become absolute and total" (Vattimo 1967, p. 171 [2010, p. 126]).
33 Shusterman 2000, p. 3.
34 Dewey 1989, pp. 12, 14 and 9.
35 Shusterman 2000, pp. 53, 20 and 13.
36 Dewey 1989, pp. 11-12 and 9.

recognized as such, of the things of ordinary experience"[37]. This, in turn, has wide and profound consequences on the life and the activity of the artist himself, who has gradually been

> pushed to one side from the main streams of active interest. Industry has been mechanized and an artist cannot work mechanically for mass production. He is less integrated than formerly in the normal flow of social services. A peculiar esthetic "individualism" results. Artists find it incumbent upon them to betake themselves to their work as an isolated of "self expression". In order not to cater to the trend of economic forces, they often feel obliged to exaggerate their separateness to the point of eccentricity. Consequently artistic products take on to a still greater degree the air of something independent and esoteric. [...] Finally we have, as the record of this chasm, accepted as if it were normal, the philosophies of art that locate it in a region inhabited by no other creature, and that emphasize beyond all reason the merely contemplative character of the esthetic[38].

Hence, for Dewey, the problem with modern artistic theory – tightly connected, as we have seen, to the problem with modern artistic practice – mostly lies in the fact that "existing theories [...] start from a ready-made compartmentalization, or from a conception of art that 'spiritualizes' it out of connection with the objects of concrete experience"[39]. Something which, in my opinion, presents, at least to a certain extent, some undeniable resemblances with Gadamer's critique of the "aesthetic differentiation (*ästhetische Unterscheidung*)" by means of his original concept of "aesthetic non-differentiation (*ästhetische Nichtunterscheidung*)".

With regard to these topics, some interpreters have spoken indeed of a veritable "destruction of aesthetics (*Destruktion der Ästhetik*)" carried out in the first part of *Wahrheit und Methode*[40], whereas other scholars have preferred to speak of an "overcoming of aesthetics

---

37 Dewey 1989, pp. 13 and 16.
38 Dewey 1989, pp. 15-16.
39 Dewey 1989, p. 17.
40 See, for instance, Grondin 2001, pp. 112-113; Grondin 2003, pp. 22-28; and Liessmann 2003.

(*Überwindung der Ästhetik*)"[41] in Gadamer's case. Now, "destruction" and "overcoming" are concepts that Heidegger coined in different phases of his way of thought, in order to clarify his critical attitude towards the whole history of Western ontology or metaphysics[42]. Hence, it can be said that both expressions recall the Heideggerian legacy present in Gadamer's critical attitude towards modern culture, including modern aesthetics – even though Jean Grondin has noticed that Gadamer already used the term *Destruktion* in his early review of Hartmann's *Grundzüge einer Metaphysik der Erkenntnis*[43], before it became a Heideggerian keyword. Anyway, given the very different philosophical presuppositions that, in my view, underlie Heidegger's and Gadamer's philosophies of art[44], I think that their respective attempts to "destroy" or "overcome" modern aesthetics actually lead in different directions[45].

Now, like every strong and ambitious philosophical stance, even Gadamer's "destruction" or hermeneutic "disenfranchisement"[46] of aesthetics have decidedly raised controversial comments and critiques. So, for example, Oskar Becker objected that the project of transcending aesthetic consciousness somehow takes for granted, and relies on, the belief in the fundamental unity of artistic, religious and

41 Fehér 2003, p. 26.
42 Just to mention two examples, see Heidegger 1977a, pp. 27-36 [2010, pp. 19-26] for the concept of *Destruktion der Geschichte der Ontologie*, and Heidegger 2000a, pp. 67-98 [2003, pp. 84-110]) for that of *Überwindung der Metaphysik*.
43 Gadamer 1923-24. See Grondin 2008, pp. 100-101.
44 On this topic, let me remind the reader of my paper *Gadamer on Heidegger: Is the History of Being "just" Another Philosophy of History?* (Marino 2010a, especially pp. 297-299).
45 For example, it has been noticed that even if both thinkers aim at re-establishing "the connection between art and truth", and analyze "the ontological depth of art" and "the *Ereignis* in which the work itself is", nonetheless "the truth that is taken to be served by art, at least according to certain of Gadamer's analyses, seems to be limited to ontic truth, to the truth of beings; it seems in certain instances not to extend to truth in the originary sense in which Heidegger [...] understands it, namely, as unconcealment" (Sallis 2007, p. 55).
46 This last expression is clearly modelled on the title of A.C. Danto's famous book *The Philosophical Disenfranchisement of Art*.

political-ideological significance. This, however, is only a rare and fortunate case[47]. Still, according to Giovanni Matteucci, Gadamer's critique of aesthetic consciousness would actually result in an absolutization and hypostatization of artistic "play (*Spiel*)", conceived as a sort of "super-subject", as a "mighty *Subjektivität*"[48]. Whereas others have claimed that his "critique of aesthetic consciousness as an alienated abstraction from the experience of truth in art" actually "reinforces rather than overcomes a fissure between consciousness and experience"[49]. Finally, in his recent development of a phenomenological aesthetics entitled *Erscheinungsdinge*, Günter Figal has taken into careful consideration Gadamer's thesis that "das ästhetische Erleben ist [...] durch eine 'Abstraktion' charakterisiert, die er 'ästhetische Unterscheidung' nennt", but then has objected that

---

47 See Becker 1962, pp. 235-236: "[Gadamer] ist in allen seinen Analysen stets darauf aus, den unauflösbaren historisch-hermeneutischen Zusammenhang eines Kunstwerks mit außerästhetischen Phänomenen aufzuzeigen [...]. Kritisch wäre hier doch wohl anzumerken, daß z.B. die religiöse und die künstlerische Bedeutung eines Werkes durchaus auseinanderfallen können. [...] Die Einheit der religiösen oder politisch-ideologischen Bedeutung und der künstlerischen 'Aussage' ist keineswegs selbstverständlich oder a priori notwendig; sie ist vielmehr ein seltener Glücksfall".

48 See Matteucci 2004, especially pp. 149-152. For a strong critique of Gadamer's hermeneutic aesthetics, specifically focused on the latter's conception of the ontological valence of the picture, see Matteucci 2011.

49 Kelly 2004, p. 103. According to Kelly, indeed "the alienation of aesthetic consciousness, as Gadamer describes it, [...] is due to the wrong conception of subjectivity. [...] Gadamer aims to break from the philosophical dichotomy between subject and object which is characteristic of modern philosophy. [...] Gadamer opposes experience to consciousness and sides with the former". But his own aesthetic theory "is more subjective than he would have us believe [...]. Gadamer's underlying concern is rather to balance subjectivity with its other 'dimension' rather than to overcome it. [...] Gadamer is therefore not against subjectivity *tout court*; rather, he is offering an alternative conception of it. What he is interested in is a historically situated subjectivity rather than an abstract, alienated subjectivity in the form of aesthetic consciousness" (Kelly 2004, pp. 111-112 and 115-116).

Gadamers Kritik der "ästhetischen Unterscheidung" ist [...] nicht [...] im Hinblick auf die im emphatischen Sinne verstandene Kunst überzeugend. Die These, nach der sich die ästhetische Unterscheidung einer Abstraktion verdankt, kommt selbst durch Abstraktion zustande; von der Komplexität der Kunsterfahrung sieht sie auf mehrfache Weise ab. [...] Auch Gadamers These, das ästhetische Verständnis der Kunst beruhe auf einer Versammlung des Heterogenen, die von dessen "Weltzugehörigkeit" absehe, ist problematisch. Zwar ist das Bild des imaginären Museums darin zutreffend, daß die ästhetisch erfahrbare Kunst sehr verschiedene Werke umfassen kann; gemessen an der Art und Herkunft der Werke kann deren Zusammenstellung willkürlich erscheinen. Aber diese Willkür ist nur vermeintlich, wenn die versammelten Werke als solche der *schönen* Kunst einleuchtend sind[50].

Anyway, it is not my aim to dwell over such controversies and criticisms. Indeed, what matters for our specific discourse is simply the fact that Gadamer, on the whole, interprets the modern subjectivistic attitude and the tendency to the musealization of art, as symptoms of a growing problematicity in our aesthetic experience, and that he actually envisions that the latter critical symptoms derive (although in a very indirect and mediated way) from "the domination of the scientific model of epistemology"[51].

50 Figal 2010, pp. 39 and 41. The ground of this critique probably lies in the presumed inadequacy of Gadamer's account of artistic beauty. Figal writes that, "wenn das Schöne erfahrbar ist, kann es nicht das Ergebnis einer subjektiven Anmutung sein. Dann ist es auch kein der Lebenswirklichkeit entgegengesetztes 'Ideal', keine 'scheinhafte Maskierung, Verschleierung oder Verklärung', als die es in Gadamers Deutung von Schillers Briefen zur ästhetischen Erziehung erscheint. Gadamer kann sich auf Schillers Briefe zur ästhetischen Erziehung nur berufen, weil er von der Erfahrungsqualität, die das Schöne für Schiller hat, absieht. [...] Bei Heidegger und Gadamer ist im Hinblick auf die Kunst wenig von Schönheit und dafür umso mehr von Wahrheit die Rede. [...] Die Möglichkeit, daß Kunstwerke in ihrer Schönheit eine eigene [...] Evidenz haben könnten, kommt bei Gadamer nicht in Betracht" (Figal 2010, pp. 41 and 44-45).
51 GW 1, p. 89 [TM, p. 73]. To be precise, Gadamer writes these last words with reference to "the shift in the ontological definition of the aesthetic", that is, the modern proliferation of "such ideas as imitation, appearance, irreality, illusion, magic, dream", which assume that "art is related to something different from itself: real being". Such a shift "has its theoretical basis in the fact that the domination of the scientific model of epistemology leads to discrediting all the

In addition to this, in the first part of *Wahrheit und Methode*, as well as in the long essay *Die Aktualität des Schönen*[52], he points out the difficult situation in which artists find themselves in the modern age. Beside the positive aspect of the achievement of an unprecedented creative freedom, Gadamer also recalls the negative aspect of the artists' loss of their place in the world. In fact, "the complete independence of his creativity" has gradually turned the artist into "an outsider" or a "bohemian", making him "an ambiguous figure" whose task is now the ongoing search for "new symbols or a new myth that will [...] create a community"[53]. But since every artist in the present age seems to find "his own community", then "the particularity of such communities", according to Gadamer, "merely testifies to the disintegration that is taking place"[54]. In the end, the modern artist

> does not live within a community, but creates for himself a community as is appropriate to his pluralistic situation. Openly admitted competition combined with the claim that his own particular form of creative expression and his own particular artistic message is the only true one, necessarily gives rise to heightened expectations. This is in fact the messianic consciousness of the nineteenth-century [and twentieth-century] artist, who feels himself to be a "new savior" (Immermann) with a claim on mankind. He proclaims a new message of reconciliation and as a social outsider pays the price for this claim, since with all his artistry he is only an artist for the sake of art[55].

Finally, it is interesting to notice how Gadamer sometimes pays attention to the hold that socioeconomic and political factors have on the art-making process. Indeed, he points out the ever-growing influence of modern world economy on artistic activities[56], and he even

---

possibilities of knowing that lie outside this new methodology" (GW 1, pp. 89-90 [TM, pp. 72-73]).
52 See GW 8, pp. 94-142 [RB, pp. 3-53].
53 GW 1, pp. 93-94 [TM, p. 76].
54 GW 1, p. 94 [TM, p. 76].
55 GW 8, p. 98 [RB, p. 7].
56 So, in the 1989 essay *Kunst und ihre Kreise* we read: "es besteht auf dem Gebiet des kulturellen Schaffens eine weltweite Abhängigkeit von den ökonomischen Umständen der Länder oder ihrer Finanzpläne. Das gilt nicht zuletzt für die

reminds us of the influence of mass media, modern technology and cultural planning upon the artistic revolutions of the last century. Gadamer, for instance, points out "the multiplication of imagery by the mass media" which "has an enormously levelling effect, so that art must make very special efforts to be seen and heard about"[57]. This, by the way, "is the reason why modern art is so hard to make sense of": that is, "we are so flooded by information that only very provocative forms of composition can attract the concentration of an audience"[58].

In this context, it might be intriguing to investigate into the potential similarities and differences between Gadamer's reflections on the fate of art in the modern techno-scientific civilization and, for example, Arnold Gehlen's relevant interpretation of the twentieth-century artistic revolutions in the book *Zeit-Bilder* (1960), Theodor W. Adorno's intense meditation on "the possible death of art" in the present world, i.e. his idea that "art may have entered the age of its demise"[59], or even Walter Benjamin's groundbreaking observations on the artwork in the age of mechanical reproducibility (1936). In a 1988 interview Gadamer hints indeed at the possibility of a comparison with Adorno's modernist aesthetics, and he concedes to "agree with Adorno [...] with regard to the crucial part played by the mass media" in influencing the artistic production: from this point of view,

---

    bildenden Künste [...]. Die Verflechtungen der modernen Weltwirtschaft sind überall spürbar. [...] Wie unser Wirtschafts- und Finanzwesen auf abstrakteste Weisen den Erdball fast zur Gleichzeitigkeit und Allgegenwart umgestaltet hat, so ist auch die wirtschaftliche Macht des Kunsthandels auf das Kunstschaffen, auf das Leben der Künstler und auf die Gefolgschaft der Schaffenden von steigendem und oft lähmendem Einfluß. Das, was früher den Lebenskreis von Schaffenden und an ihnen Teilnehmenden durch alle Bereiche des Gesellschaftslebens hindurch belebte, das ist heute durch abstrakte Verlagerungen, wie etwa die Finanzströme oder die industrielle Expansion beherrscht, die den ganzen Erdball verändern" (HE, pp. 176-177).

57 Gadamer 1988a, p. 32.
58 Gadamer 1988a, p. 32.
59 Adorno 2003, pp. 12-13 [2004, p. 4].

Gadamer explains, "the difficulty of modern art is a necessary difficulty"[60].

On a few but significant occasions he also hints at the interest (although a critical one) raised in him by Gehlen's conception of the *peinture conceptuelle* or by Benjamin's theory of the vanishing *aura*. In the essay *Begriffene Malerei?*, Gadamer praises indeed the detailed historical-sociological explanation of modern artistic revolutions provided by Gehlen[61]. He even endorses the latter's observations about the role of "the experimental (*das Experimentelle*)" in twentieth-century art[62]. Nevertheless, Gadamer proves to be quite mistrustful of Gehlen's key concepts of the "image's rationality (*Bildrationalität*)", "eye's rationality (*Rationalität des Auges*)" and "reflexive art (*Reflexionskunst*)", which he interprets as witnessing Gehlen's intention to somehow reduce modern painting to "scientificity (*Wissenschaftlichkeit*) or affinity with science (*Wissenschaftsähnlichkeit*)"[63].

---

60 Gadamer 1988a, p. 32. On this topic, see Lang 1981 (especially pp. 96-100 and 183-196) and Fornet-Ponse 2000 (especially pp. 9-20 and 117-128), who draw the two thinkers close together on the basis of their common interest in artistic truth. See also Davey 2003 (who proposes an interesting comparison of Gadamer's, Adorno's and Iser's conceptions of the meaning of art), Wiehl 2006, and Figal 2010, pp. 24-28, who somehow opposes Gadamer and Adorno as outstanding representatives of classicism (*Klassizismus*) and avant-gardism (*Avantgardismus*), that is, as advocates of philosophies of art respectively centred on the concepts of the classic (*das Klassische*) and the radical modern (*die radikale Moderne*).

61 See GW 8, p. 305. Still in his 2001 interviews with Silvio Vietta, Gadamer explicitly agrees with his interlocutor that Gehlen's *Zeit-Bilder* is "an extremely interesting book (*ein hochinteressantes Buch*)" (IG, p. 65).

62 See GW 8, p. 313.

63 See GW 8, pp. 306, 310 and 308 note. "Hier liegt aber doch wohl ein Mißverständnis", Gadamer writes indeed. "Daß es möglich ist [...] Zusammenhänge dieser Kunst mit [...] Theorien zu untersuchen, ist gar nicht der strittige Punkt, sondern, ob solche Zusammenhänge in dem behaupten Sinne bestehen, nämlich in dem Sinne, daß die Prinzipien das erste sind und daß in einer Art variierender Anwendung derselben die subjektive Phantasie des Künstlers dieselben nachträglich überflute. [...] Die Leitidee der Bildrationalität wird m.

Finally, for that which regards Walter Benjamin, in a late interview Gadamer defines him as a "rich, explosive, brilliant personality", who had "an unpredictable and extraordinary genius", comparable only to "heavyweights like Carl Schmitt or Martin Heidegger"[64]. This, however, does not prevent him from taking a critical stance to Benjamin's famous theory of the vanishing of the *aura* after the advent of the technological reproducibility of artworks. So, in the essay *Bildende und sprachliche Kunst am Ende des XX. Jahrhunderts* we read:

> Walter Benjamin [...] war der Meinung, die Aura, die die Kunst auszeichnet, sei vorbei, seit durch die Reproduktion aller Werke der Kunst mit Hilfe einer neuen Technik in alle Kammern und in alle Säle der Menschheit eindringen. Es gibt bei genialen jungen Leuten mitunter falsche Prophezeiungen. Und so meine ich, daß es jetzt dank der Zunahme dieser reproduktiven Technik und ihrer zuckenden Leinwände wohl gerade umgekehrt ist. Wir suchen nach der Stille und nach der Ruhe dessen, was ein originales Gebilde eines Künstlers geschaffen hat. Es ist etwas von der Aura des Unberührbaren[65].

Anyway, even without detailing anymore this particular issue, we can surely say that Gadamer has strongly felt and powerfully dealt with the question concerning the problematic character of artistic creativity in the techno-scientific world. As he explains it at the end of the 1985 essay *Ende der Kunst?*:

> In Zeiten, in denen Informationstechnik und Reproduktionstechnik eine beständige Reizflut über die Menschen ausgießen, ist diese Verwirklichung des

---

E. dann entstellt, wenn Rationalität hier konstruktiven Aufbau aus Prinzipien im Sinne von Anwendung einer zuvor aufgestellten Theorie bedeuten soll" (GW 8, pp. 308 and 312). According to Matteucci 2010 (p. 91 note), however, this represents a "radical misunderstanding of *Zeit-Bilder*": Gadamer would have missed the real point of "the plasticity of the Gehlenian notion of 'image's rationality', and thus the anthropological ground of the iconical construct's manifestativity".
64 Gadamer 2006, pp. 88-89.
65 Gadamer 1997c, pp. 58-59. Analogous considerations on Benjamin's *Das Kunstwerk im Zeitalter seiner technischen Reproduzierbarkeit* can be found in the essay *Kunst und ihre Kreise* (HE, pp. 177-178).

> Kunstwerkes freilich eine schwere Aufgabe geworden. Ein heutiger Künstler, welcher Kunst auch immer, hat gegen eine Flut zu kämpfen, die jede Empfänglichkeit abstumpft. Eben deshalb muß jeder heutige Künstler Verfremdungen aufbieten, damit die Überzeugungskraft seiner Gestaltung zur Ausstrahlung kommt und die Verfremdung in eine neue Heimatlichkeit zurückbildet. Der Pluralismus des Experimentierens ist daher in unserer Epoche unvermeidlich geworden. Verfremdung bis an die Grenze der Unverständlichkeit ist das Gesetz, unter dem sich die bildende Kraft der Kunst in einem Zeitalter wie dem unsrigen am ehesten erfüllen kann[66].

For all these reasons, Gadamer seems to believe that a "withering aesthetic culture (*absterbende ästhetische Kultur*)", namely a culture which "has more of the character of a well-cared-for sanctuary than something that belongs in our world and in which we would feel at home", is progressively expanding and is typical of "the industrial age that we live in"[67].

Now, when Gadamer deals with the question of the crisis of aesthetic experience, he is mostly referring to *aesthetic* experience as *artistic* experience. However, in the essay *Der Mensch und seine Hand im heutigen Zivilisationsprozess* he deals with this same subject, namely the crisis of aesthetic experience, but intends the latter as *sensorial, perceptive* experience, in conformity with the original etymological meaning of the Greek term *aisthesis*. So, he explains that the "omnipotent bureaucracy and stagnating progress in technology and civilization" have somehow determined "a loss in cultivated senses", so that today we must reinstate a "genuine equilibrium between our sensuous and moral powers", in order to attempt "to humanize our lives in our state, society, and administration"[68]. And thus he writes:

> calculation, not so much intellect, mind, or understanding, is the *omnipotent* power organizing our lives. It is what is underneath the complete mediation of our life by *industrial civilization*: no one even knows the calculations his own hand-outs depend on, which is what makes life so unsatisfactory and so unintu-

---

66 GW 8, pp. 219-220.
67 GW 3, p. 330 [HW, p. 192].
68 LT, pp. 145 and 147-148 [PT, pp. 119 and 121].

itive. [...] We need to see how the *hand* can coexist with *calculation*. [...] *Both sides* must obviously be cultivated. [...] The *senses* have a certain intelligence [...]. *Cultured senses*: that ultimately means developing the human capacity for choice and judgment. [...] Little has fundamentally changed since Schiller hoped *aesthetic education* would give us a way of progressing toward *freedom from the soulless mechanism* of the state apparatus[69].

In general, Gadamer seems to argue that our world tends to become everyday "more and more alike (*immer ähnlicher*)", due to "a levelling of all forms of life (*Nivellierung aller Lebensformen*)" that is gradually leading to the transformation of aesthetic/artistic experience into nothing more than the "mere filling of spare time (*beliebige Ausfüllung bloßer Freizeiträume*)"[70]. On the whole, in Gadamer's view, this obviously represents another critical symptom of the present condition of our civilization. So, in one of his last essays on art and aesthetics, *Der Kunstbegriff im Wandel* (1995), we read:

> In ruhelosen Versuchen [...] leben Kunst und Künste am Rande der Gesellschaft. Im ausgesparten Freiraum einer durchgeplanten Arbeitswelt ist es überdies mehr der Bildungsgenuß vergangener Kunstschöpfungen, als der künstlerische Beitrag der eigenen Gegenwart, der Resonanz findet. Das war und

69 LT, pp. 144-145 and 148 [PT, pp. 118-119 and 121 (my italics)].
70 GW 4, pp. 158-159. Notwithstanding this critical stance to the current way of enjoying, or better "consuming" art and culture, I think it would be a mistake to ascribe an elitist conception of aesthetic experience to Gadamer, like for example D'Angelo 2003 (pp. 426-427) somehow seems to do. As a matter of fact, if compared to "the most critical and 'militant' of aesthetics, such as that of Adorno, [who] can only oppose kitsch with an avant-gardist affirmation of the purity of art that changes systematically into aphasia", Gadamer's hermeneutic aesthetics "shows itself to be more attentive to the social existence of art, and even to the more problematic aspects of 'mass' art such as rock music" (Vattimo 2002, pp. 89-90 [1997, p. 72]). Vattimo makes reference here to a passage from the essay *Die Aktualität des Schönen*, where Gadamer concedes that rock concerts, big music events and "the records of modern songs so popular with the young people of today, are equally legitimate" as "the great works of Greek tragedy" or even "the Passion music of J. S. Bach", in that "they too have a capacity to establish [...] real communication" and thus create a "genuine experience of community" (GW 8, p. 141 [RB, pp. 50-51]). On the same topic, see also the remarks of Vattimo 2010, pp. 281-282.

ist unleugbar ein Symptom für das Auseinanderfallen der Inhaltsbedeutung des Kunstwerkes und seiner gestalterischen Qualität. Es ist die Verdrängung der Begegnung mit der Kunst durch den Bildungsgenuß[71].

---

71 HE, pp. 152-153.

7. Religious Experience in a Nihilistic Epoch

Closely connected to the preceding discourse about the problematic character of ethic and aesthetic experiences in our time is also Gadamer's discourse about the problematic character of religious experience. The basic presupposition for such a tight connection is obviously the link that Gadamer sees between these different dimensions of human experience. For that which regards the relation of aesthetics and ethics, I have elsewhere argued that in Gadamer's case one might perhaps speak of "the morality of the beautiful"[1] – an expression which was clearly modelled on the title of his essay *The Relevance of the Beautiful*. In short, I think that such a relation is firstly testified by Gadamer's attempt to overcome the typically modern denial of any influence of aesthetics on ethics, as in the case of Kantian criticism[2]. Secondly, it is also testified by his ongoing appeal to the classical Greek doctrine of the *kalonkagathia*, that is, of the unity of the beautiful (*kalon*) and the good (*agathon*)[3].

---

1   See Marino 2009a, especially pp. 13-23.
2   This question emerges in various points of Gadamer's critical examination of Kantian aesthetics in the first part of *Wahrheit und Methode*, where he goes as far as to rehabilitate the idea of "an ethics of good taste", i.e. the idea that, in a sense, "all moral decisions require taste": an idea which, according to him, "admittedly sounds strange to our ears" precisely because we are still deeply influenced by Kant's second and third *Critiques* (GW 1, pp. 45-46 [TM, pp. 35-36]). As a matter of fact, even though Gadamer obviously does not ignore that Kant actually imagined "at least six specific connections between aesthetics and ethics", in the §§ 17, 29, 30, 42, 51, 59 and 60 of the *Kritik der Urteilskraft* (Guyer 2006, p. 324), he always draws attention to the fact that Kant's greatest "achievement in moral philosophy" was to purify "ethics from all aesthetics and feelings" (GW 1, p. 46 [TM, p. 36]).
3   On this topic, see, for instance, GW 1, pp. 481-486 [TM, pp. 472-477]; GW 5, pp. 150-151 [PDE, pp. 208-209]; GW 8, p. 380 [GR, p. 203]; UD, p. 48 [CP, p. 44]. Gadamer openly borrows this theme from Plato's metaphysics – mostly

Regarding the relation of aesthetic and religious experiences, I think it is enough to recall the claim he makes in the essay *Die Aktualität des Schönen* that "the experience of the beautiful, and particularly the beautiful in art, is the invocation of a potentially whole and holy order of things, wherever it may be found"[4]. To be sure, this absolutely does not mean that Gadamer "mixes" or "confuses" aesthetics and religiosity, quite the opposite: he is very careful in underlining both "the affiliation and the discrimination"[5] between these forms of human experience, as we may read in the essay *Religious and Poetical Speaking*[6]. As he explains it in still another essay, *Ästhetische und religiöse Erfahrung*:

> it would be quite meaningless to construct an opposition between art and religion, or even between poetic and religious speech [...]. In every expression of art, something is revealed, is known, is recognized. There is always a disturbing quality to this recognition, an amazement amounting almost to horror,

---

from the *Symposium* (210a-211c [1997, pp. 492-493]), the *Philebus* (64e-65a [1997, p. 454]) and the *Phaedrus* (250 b-e [1997, p. 528]) – and its conception of the "important ontological function [of] beauty", namely, "that of mediating between idea and appearance" (GW 1, p. 485 [TM, p. 476]). According to Gadamer (GW 8, p. 123 [RB, p. 33]; GW 8, p. 211), a trace of this classical theory still survives in Hegel's philosophy of art; more precisely, in the latter's famous definition of art and beauty as "the sensuous presentation of the Absolute itself (*sinnliche Darstellung des Absoluten*)": "the content of art", Hegel explains indeed, "is the Idea, while its form is the configuration (*Gestaltung*) of the sensuous material" (Hegel 1970d, p. 100 [1998, p. 70].

4   GW 8, p. 123 [RB, p. 32].
5   Gadamer 1980a, p. 88.
6   More precisely, Gadamer's aim in this essay is to inquire into the relation of aesthetic and religious experience by paying a special attention to the question of their respective languages. So, he offers "a hermeneutical description of the relationship between poetical and religious texts" – claiming that they are both "autonomous texts", i.e. "texts which interpret themselves insofar as one needs no additional information about the occasion and the historical circumstances of their composition" in order to understand them – and then claims that they "are inseparable", although there is also "a basic difference between religious and poetical texts, between scripture and literature, and that is the difference in their form of anonymous address" (Gadamer 1980a, pp. 86, 88 and 90).

that such things can befall human beings and that human beings can achieve such things. At the same time, the claim of the Christian message transcends this and points in the opposite direction: it shows what we cannot achieve. This is what gives rise to its specific claim and accounts for the radicality of its message[7].

Anyway, what matters for our specific discourse is only the critical situation in which, according to Gadamer, religious experience too finds itself today. This has something to do, among other things, with the aforementioned question concerning the "shadow of nihilism" that "fell upon Europe in our [*scil.* the twentieth] century"[8].

Now, it must be said that Gadamer does not represent a true theorist of *nihilism,* in the sense that the question of nihilism is probably not so central and crucial in his thought as it is for other contemporary thinkers. Such a non-nihilistic or rather anti-nihilistic attitude is perhaps to be connected to Gadamer's peculiar unconcern or even "indifference" to Nietzsche[9], probably the most essential figure

---

[7] GW 8, p. 155 [RB, p. 153]. To be true, in this essay Gadamer does not take into consideration the Christian religion alone (as it might appear from the quotation above), but also "the Greek tradition, in which it is impossible to separate specifically poetic and religious language" (GW 8, p. 145 [RB, p. 143]). Among the so-called revealed religions, however, he only takes into account Christianity, or better "the Judaeo-Christian tradition", and rather ignores "Islam, whose religious proclamation represents a special problem", Gadamer explains, "that I cannot go into now since I have no knowledge of Arabic whatsoever" (GW 8, p. 149 [RB, p. 147]).

[8] GW 3, p. 407.

[9] On Gadamer's "failed" encounter with Nietzsche's philosophy, see, for instance, GW 4, pp. 448-449 [Gadamer 1998b, p. 124]; IG, p. 27; Gadamer 2006, p. 73. Worthy of notice is also the fact that Gadamer sometimes explicitly outdistances himself from Nietzsche's "radical, all too radical" positions. For example, in his letter to Richard J. Bernstein, where we read: "Don't we all then run the risk of a terrible intellectual *hubris* if we equate Nietzsche's anticipations [...] with life as it is actually lived with its own forms of solidarity? Here, in fact, my divergence from Heidegger is fundamental" (Gadamer 1983, p. 264). I have tried to inquire into Gadamer's basic "mistrust" for Nietzsche, specifically focusing my attention on his work *Das Drama Zarathustra* (GW 4, pp. 448-462), in Marino 2009b.

for the theorization of nihilism and its further development throughout the whole twentieth century. Nevertheless, an exhaustive study of his writings reveals that Gadamer also saw nihilism as one of the key problems of our time. It is certainly one of the merits of Donatella Di Cesare's recent portrait of Gadamer to have accurately and strongly stressed this point, explaining that although he obviously used the term "nihilism" (even if not so often as other thinkers), his philosophical hermeneutics is not a nihilistic philosophy and, in particular, is not to be confused with the so-called "weak thought"[10]. As she expresses it:

> Wenn er auch ein origineller Interpret der philosophischen Hermeneutik geworden ist, so hat Vattimo doch seine eigene Philosophie entwickelt, deren Bezugspunkte Nietzsche und Heidegger sind. In dem Maße, in dem sie im Lauf der Zeit immer deutlicher ihren Abstand von Gadamers Hermeneutik betont, erweist sie sich als eigenständiges Projekt. [...] "Nihilismus" wird zu ihrem Schlüsselwort. [...] Das schwache Denken [...] sieht im Nihilismus "den einzig möglichen Weg der Ontologie" [und] dekliniert sich [...] in ein unendliches Spiel von Interpretationen. [...] Damit bewegt sich die schwache Ontologie im Gefolge Nietzsches und erkennt sich in jenem "völligen" Nihilismus wieder, der nach dem Verschwinden aller Werte feststellt, daß er die Wahrheit nicht mehr besitzt, daß die Wahrheit nur in den unendlichen perspektivistischen Wirkungen der Interpretationen gegeben ist. [...] Nietzsches Perspektivismus spielt hier eine entscheidende Rolle und setzt [...] eine Philosophie der Interpretation in Gang. In sie mündet die nihilistische Interpretation der Hermeneutik[11].

---

10 See Di Cesare 2007, pp. 279-283 [2009, pp. 265-271]. "Weak thought (*Il pensiero debole*)" is the title of a collection of essays edited by Gianni Vattimo and Pier Aldo Rovatti in 1983, but it also stands for the whole later development of Vattimo's own nihilistic hermeneutics. I think it is interesting to notice that Richard Rorty – another thinker who has provided important, original, but not at all unproblematic interpretations of Gadamer (see Rorty 2009, pp. 315-393, and Rorty 2004) – has hinted at the resemblances between his own philosophy and Vattimo's weak thought (see Rorty 1991b, p. 6). For a first overview on these topics, see the chapter *Nihilism in Italy* in Franca D'Agostini's recent book *The Last Fumes* (D'Agostini 2009, pp. 187-202).
11 Di Cesare 2007, pp. 279-280 [2009, pp. 267-268]. I think that these clarifications are surely of great relevance, most of all with regard to the reception of Gadamer's thought in Italy that has been strongly conditioned by the "media-

In general, Gadamer seems to connect the so-called "problem of historical consciousness" with concomitant phenomena like the "challenge of historicism (*Herausforderung des Historismus*)", the question of "historical relativism (*historischer Relativismus*)", or still the "threat of scepticism (*Gefahr der Skepsis*)"[12]. All phenomena that, according to him, represent both "a privilege" and "a burden [for] contemporary man", and are at the basis of many "immense spiritual upheavals of our times"[13]. Hence, in his 1957 lectures Gadamers goes so far as to define "the problem of historical consciousness", i.e. "the appearance of historical self-consciousness", as "the most important revolution among those we have undergone since the beginning of the modern epoch": a revolution which has given us "the full awareness of the historicity of everything present and the relativity of all opinions"[14].

In other words, what Gadamer points out is the risk for the present age to swiftly, subtly and almost automatically move from historicism to relativism and then to nihilism, without being fully aware of the radical and pernicious consequences of such a shift. So,

---

tion" of Vattimo, who is the Italian translator of *Wahrheit und Methode* and probably the best-known Italian hermeneutic philosopher. In fact, Di Cesare's clarifications allow us to do justice to the differences between Gadamerian hermeneutics and Vattimo's "weak thought" – namely, a thought based on a veritable apology of nihilism, seen as today's "only possibility of freedom" (Vattimo 1998, p. 38 [1991, p. 29]) – and at the same time to appreciate the autonomy and inner coherence of the philosophy of Vattimo. Apropos of Vattimo's relation to Gadamer, see also his autobiographical reflections (Vattimo 2008, pp. 38-40, 126 and 131-133 [2010, pp. 28-29, 103 and 108-110]), and the following observation in his retirement *lectio magistralis*: "the idea that interpretation can fail [...] has always limited my agreement with Gadamer's theory of the 'fusion of horizons' and, in general, of every kind of hermeneutic dialogue, which I actually find too optimistic and conciliatory" (Vattimo 2009b, p. 11). For an insight into the Italian (but not only) reception of Gadamer's hermeneutics, see also Bianco 2004, pp. 169-195.

12   GW 10, pp. 34, 175 and 181.
13   PCH, p. 7 [PHC, p. 89].
14   PCH, p. 7 [PHC, p. 89].

in the first draft of *Wahrheit und Methode* (written around 1956 but published only thirty-six years later) he warns us that already

> Diltheys friedvoller Verzicht, "mit Bewußtsein ein Bedingtes zu sein", offenbart innere Spannung von dämonischer Gewalt. [...] Der Schatten Nietzsches wird sichtbar. [...] Die wirklichen Lebensverhältnisse der modernen Menschheit sind von diesem Relativismus zutiefst bestimmt. Die Wissenschaften selber und die Philosophie vor allem werden als Mittel, als Instrumentierungen der sich selbst durchsetzenden Macht beansprucht, indem sie die einander widerstreitenden und selber zu Machtmitteln der Herrschaftsausübung ausgebildeten Weltanschauungen begründen[15].

It is not hard to see that we are faced with some of the most controversial and extensively discussed issues in contemporary philosophy. Regarding this, one might perhaps speak of two main "waves" of relativistic and nihilistic thought: a first "wave" emerged from the psychologism, historicism and *Lebensphilosophie* of the late nineteenth century/early twentieth century, and a second "wave" stemmed in the last decades of the past century from the philosophical currents of epistemological anarchism, neopragmatism and "negative hermeneutics" or "hermeneutic nihilism"[16]. From this point of view, I

---

15   Gadamer 1992-93, p. 140. To be more precise, the passage from Dilthey's *Das Wesen der Philosophie* quoted by Gadamer says: "dieses [*scil.* das geschichtliche Bewußtsein] aber lebt in dem Zusammenfassen aller Zeiten, und es gewahrt in allem Schaffen des einzelnen die diesem mitgegebene Relativität und Vergänglichkeit. [...] Denn in dem Philosophen der Gegenwart trifft das eigne Schaffen zusammen mit dem geschichtlichen Bewußtsein [...]. Sein Schaffen muß sich wissen als ein Glied in dem historischen Zusammenhang, in welchem er mit Bewußtsein ein Bedingtes erwirkt" (Dilthey 1924, p. 364). I owe this insight into the partial "inexactness" of Gadamer's quotation of Dilthey to Piccini 2003.

16   I borrow these last concepts from Mura 1997 (pp. 374-401). In this context, it may be noticed how Gadamer, on a few occasions, has used the concept of "hermeneutic nihilism (*hermeneutischer Nihilismus*)" with specific reference to the "untenable" idea that "a work of art is not, in itself, completable", so that "it must be left to the recipient to make something of the work. One way of understanding a work, then, is no less legitimate than another. There is no criterion of appropriate reaction" (GW 1, p. 100 [TM, p. 82]). One must also notice, how-

think it might be said that, since Western philosophy has existed, the twentieth century has actually represented the age mostly characterized by the widespread diffusion of a "sceptical *koinē*"[17] and, in Vattimo's and Rorty's words, by the ambition to say once and for all "farewell to truth" given its pragmatic uselessness[18]. According to the latter, indeed, "the question that matters [is] whether the resolution of [a] debate will have an effect in practice, whether it will be useful", his fundamental conviction being that "if a debate has no *practical* significance, then it has no *philosophical* significance":

> The philosophical distinction between justification and truth seems not to have practical consequences. That is why pragmatists think it is not worth pondering. […] I am perfectly ready to admit that one cannot identify the concept of truth with the concept of justification or with any other. But that is not a sufficient reason to conclude that the nature of truth is an important or interesting question[19].

Gadamer, however, is not to be confused with a deflationist, minimalist or nihilist theorist about truth, since the latter notion still "retains a central role […] in his philosophy" and, like Davidson ("the analytic thinker who is most often seen as standing in some proximity to Gadamer"), he "argues for truth as a central and indispensable concept"[20]. As Jeff Malpas has noticed, indeed, thinkers like Rorty

---

ever, that for Gadamer the process of interpretation is constitutively open and, so to speak, never-ending. So, for instance, in his study on Paul Celan's cycle *Atemwende* he says: "Conclusive interpretation simply does not exist. Every interpretation seeks only to be an approximation", and it "must strive, of course, for its own retraction" (GW 9, p. 443 [GOC, pp. 146-147]).

17 D'Agostini 2002, p. XXXV.
18 See, for instance, *Addio alla verità* (Vattimo 2009a [2011]), and *What's the Use of Truth?* (Rorty 2007).
19 Rorty 2007, pp. 34 and 44-45.
20 Malpas and Zabala 2010, p. XVI. On Gadamer and Davidson, see the interesting contributions of Stueber 1994, Hoy 1997, Weinsheimer 2000, Malpas 2002, McDowell 2002, and Picardi 2004. In general, as Jürgen Habermas has noticed: "Die hermeneutische Unterstellung, […] daß der auszulegende Text nur als Äußerung eines vernünftigen Autors einen klaren Sinn haben kann […], zeigt eine verblüffende Verwandtschaft mit Davidsons Prinzip der Nachsichtigkeit. Die

and Vattimo "view the very concept of truth as problematic and even dangerous, urging its abandonment in favour of a more open concept of conversational engagement", but from a Gadamerian-Davidsonian point of view the idea that "we can indeed say 'farewell' to truth, is deeply problematic, since we can no more farewell truth than we can farewell ethics or politics"[21]. In other words, "in using Gadamer as his witness for declaring the end of the philosophical pursuit of truth, Rorty [...] misinterprets the Gadamerian notion of *Bildung*"[22]; "thinkers like Rorty can only enlist Gadamer in their cause by ignoring or dismissing the fundamental Gadamerian concern with truth"[23].

In addition to this, it is surely worth noticing that Gadamer pays the same high level of attention to the theoretical and practical aspects

---

Verwandtschaft reicht sogar weiter. Wie der radikale Interpreter seinen Blick auf die Umstände lenken muss, unter denen ein fremder Sprecher eine präsumtiv für wahr gehaltene Äußerung macht, so muss auch Gadamers Interpret den Blick gleichzeitig auf den Text *und* auf die darin verhandelte Sache selbst richten. [...] Das ist die hermeneutische Version des Grundsatzes der formalen Semantik, wonach der Sinn eines Satzes durch dessen Wahrheitsbedingungen bestimmt ist" (Habermas 2005, pp. 71-72). In this context, Habermas specifically refers to Gadamer's influential notions of "fore-conception of completeness" and "fusion of horizons" (GW 1, pp. 271-274, 298-301 and 307-312 [TM, pp. 269-272, 293-295 and 301-306]), and to Davidson's seminal concepts of "radical interpretation" and "triangulation" (see, respectively, Davidson 2001a, pp. 125-139; and Davidson 2001b, pp. 86-88, 117-121, 128-129, 202-203 and 212-213).

21 Malpas 2009, pp. 20-21.
22 Stueber 1994, p. 173. On the "uncertain legacy" of *Wahrheit und Methode*, with specific regard to its reception by postmodern thought, see also Grondin 2009 (especially pp. 25-28 and 33-36).
23 Wachterhauser 1999, p. 24. On Gadamer's overall conception of truth, see Grondin 1994 (especially pp. 122-194) and Sonderegger 2003, as well as the essays gathered in Wachterhauser 1994. In his essays *Hermeneutics as Phenomenology* (Figal 2009) and *Hermeneutische Wahrheit* (Figal 2011), Günter Figal has proposed an intriguing interpretation of the hermeneutic concept of truth, together with its correlated concepts of language and understanding, from a phenomenological perspective. See also his pregnant definition of Gadamer's "oft [...] unklar oder rätselhaft empfundenem Begriff der 'Wahrheit' [als] die Manifestation und Erfahrung [des] erfahrbaren Sinns von Welt- und Lebenszusammenhängen" (Figal 2001, p. 104).

of these debates. Rather, I think one could say that the nodal point for Gadamer is not represented by the need of overcoming relativism or nihilism from a theoretical point of view (for example, by means of a renewed form of "philosophy as a rigorous science"[24]), but by the need to properly understand the consequences of relativism and nihilism on a practical and historical level.

For example, looking back at the past century from the beginning to the end – for, as we saw in the *Introduction*, Gadamer had the privilege, but also the burden, of seeing it in its entirety – and reflecting on the dramatic years of the Third Reich, Gadamer observes that "Nietzsche's catchword about the death of god has been confirmed again and again in the twentieth century"[25]. In an analogous way, in his review of Pierre Bourdieu's influential study *Die politische Ontologie Martin Heideggers* he somehow connects "the tragedy of the Weimar Republic", "Hitler's 'legal' *Machtergreifung*", and the intellectual climate of "resolute nihilism (*entschlossener Nihilismus*)" that was so diffused in "the conservative ideology"[26] of the time. A similar point of view can also be found in two important lectures, *Zum 300. Geburtstag von Gottfried Wilhelm Leibniz* and *Die Bedeutung der Philosophie für die neue Erziehung*, given between September 1945 and July 1946, i.e. in the aftermath of the fall of the Nazi regime. Here, indeed, Gadamer tries to discover in the history of modern German philosophy from Leibniz onwards the "Vorformen

---

24 Here I am obviously referring to Husserl's famous essay *Philosophie als strenge Wissenschaft*, in which he affirms in the strongest possible terms that "it is easy to see that historicism, if consistently carried through, carries over into extreme sceptical subjectivism. The ideas of truth, theory, and science would then, like all ideas, lose their absolute validity". So, although he acknowledges "the extraordinary value of history in the broadest sense for the philosopher", Husserl finally looks upon "historicism as an epistemological mistake", whose "conesquences must be just as unceremoniously rejected as was naturalism" (Husserl 1987, pp. 43 and 46-47 [1981, pp. 186 and 188]).

25 Gadamer 1997a, p. 257. In this context, it has been noticed that Gadamer's "precise analysis of our spiritual situation could be summarized in the Nietzschean slogan of the death of God" (Dottori 2004, p. 186).

26 GW 10, p. 50.

und Wegbereiter jener Krise des Nihilismus und jener Verzweiflung an der Vernunft, deren Formen uns schmerzhaft bewußt sind"[27]. Among such pre-forms and forerunners, he mentions "jenen romantischen Irrationalismus [...], dessen Wirkungen bis in die Verhängnisse unserer Tage reichen"; or still "jene[n] historischen Individualismus und Relativismus, der im 19. Jahrhundert das historische Bewußtsein und das historische Denken der deutschen Wissenschaft besonders stark bestimmt hat"; or finally "de[n] methodische[n] Subjektivismus [...] der neuen Zeit"[28]. Then, in the other lecture, he talks about the twentieth century "Zersetzung des bürgerlichen Idealismus und der konkreten Lebensformen bürgerlicher Tradition und Sitte", and about "[die] Schwächung des Wertens [und] Aushölung der Werttafel des bürgerlichen Moralismus", and then concludes:

> Diese Aushölung des Idealismus hat dann ihre extreme Zuspitzung in dem gefunden, was Nietzsche den Nihilismus gennant hat und was wir als Wirklichkeit einer jüngsten Vergangenheit erlebt haben. Diese Aushölung des Idealismus ist der Boden der Verkehrung des Wahren geworden, die wir in der nationalsozialistischen Epoche an uns erfuhren[29].

After this short digression on hermeneutics and nihilism, let us now return to the main theme of this chapter, namely the problematic character of religious experience in our time. It is noticeable indeed that such a critical view of our "nihilistic" age has sometimes been converted by Gadamer into an analysis of the gradual decline of any genuine religious sensibility in the present age. So, on various occasions he speaks of our epoch as of the "age of growing mass atheism"[30], or even as the time of "a new type of atheism which is based on indifference" and which "increasingly seems to characterize the attitude of the younger generation in the industrialized world"[31].

---

27 GW 10, p. 305.
28 GW 10, pp. 304-305.
29 KS 1, pp. 15-16.
30 GW 4, p. 291 [EH, p. 65].
31 Gadamer 1995a, p. 199 [Gadamer 1998c, p. 202].

According to Gadamer, it is precisely the growing diffusion of such an attitude of "atheism of indifference" that represents one of the more salient features of the present age, and that defines "the uniqueness of today's situation"[32]. At the end of the very last paragraph of the essay *Ästhetische und religiöse Erfahrung*, Gadamer explains indeed that "the radicality of [modern] Enlightenment" lies in the fact that "for the first time in the history of mankind, religion itself [was] declared to be redundant and denounced as an act of betrayal or self-betrayal"[33]. But in the opening lines of the essay *Reflexionen über das Verhältnis von Religion und Wissenschaft* he then explains that the situation in which religion finds itself today is probably different, or better it is "a unique situation":

> For the first time the important thing is no longer the pro and contra that have been connected from time immemorial with the claim that religions raise. It is no longer waging war for the true god against the false ones or defending one's own religion against the attacks of the unbelievers, whether those belonging to another faith or that of scientific atheism. Today the issue is much more the question whether humanity needs religion at all. Of course, the critique of religion in the manner of Epicurus, Feuerbach, and Marx, as well as of Freud, long ago posed this question and anticipated the answer. But the uniqueness of today's situation seems to me that even the question about the meaning of religion becomes pointless when more and more people actually live without religion. The atheism of indifference does not even recognize the question anymore[34].

I think it is without doubt that such problems are dear, so to speak, to Gadamer's heart, so that he interprets the fact that "modern science has contributed to the dissolution of the various religions and so created a vacuum"[35] as another pathology of our techno-scientific age. From Gadamer's point of view, indeed, the various religions present "forms of objectification (*Objektivierungen*) that offered protection against the [human] anxiety of existence", and so "over thousands of

32 GW 8, p. 156 [HRE, p. 119].
33 GW 8, p. 155 [RB, p. 153].
34 GW 8, p. 156 [HRE, p. 119].
35 ÜVG, p. 197 [EH, p. 159].

years of human history" they have "successfully provided a framework for the attempt to make ourselves at home [...] in the world"[36]. But in the present "age of anonymous responsibility" (in Karl Jaspers' words, that Gadamer explicitly quotes) this fundamental process of making oneself at home (*Sich-Einhausen*) "presents us with particular difficulties because the future seems so devoid of hope", and we all experience the anxiety "which is clearly inseparable from life itself [...] as something nameless, and thus as something which is increasingly difficult to grasp"[37]. Hence, according to Gadamer, it is not at all mistaken to speak of "an anxiety peculiar to modern civilization", an "anxiety which is part of today's civilization (*Zivilisationsangst von heute*)", and which is "something atmospheric; we say that it is 'in the air'"[38].

Anyway, I think that it would represent a veritable misunderstanding if we were to interpret this whole discourse in a strictly religious or even "denominational" sense. To be precise, Gadamer's warnings seem to concern less the crisis of religious sensibility as such, and more the crumbling away of "the deep solidarities (*tieferliegende Solidaritäten*) underlying all norms of human life": something which, in turn, is connected to "the loss of the unifying power of religion and of the churches [...] in the last centuries"[39]. From this point of view, the real problem for Gadamer seems to consist in the close connection between the decline of religious faith, the loosening of social ties, i.e. of "what we truly have in common and what unites us (*das wahrhaft Gemeinsame und alle Verbindende*)"[40], and the spread of a profound sense of malaise, indifference and nihilistic anxiety. On this basis, I thus argue that Gadamer's concern for the twilight of religion, although strong and relevant in itself, is better understood however if contextualized, that is, if it is situated within a

---

36 ÜVG, p. 196 [EH, p. 159].
37 ÜVG, p. 197 [EH, p. 159].
38 ÜVG, pp. 196-197 [EH, p. 159].
39 EE, p. 157 [EPH, p. 192].
40 EE, p. 157 [EPH, p. 192].

broader context[41]. Namely, the context of his general concern for the current atomization or "liquidification"[42] of our lives, and the dissolution of such fundamental social institutions as culture, education, family and community relationships.

On the basis of all these elements, some interpreters have interestingly pointed out the existence of relevant affinities between philosophical hermeneutics and so-called communitarianism. For example, it has been noticed that a "contemporary writer whose work shows great similarities to that of Gadamer is Alasdair MacIntyre, who criticized the rationalism of some modern moral philosophers as the attempt to stand outside any specific moral tradition and to judge human action purely by formal criteria"[43]. As a matter of fact, I think that some resemblances between the two thinkers actually exist. For example, the idea that "the breakdown" of the modern "project of an independent rational justification of morality" provides "the historical background against which the predicaments of our own culture can

---

41 An interesting observation is that made by Nicholas Davey, according to whom "philosophical hermeneutics contends that some features attributed to religious experience are not specifically religious but are, as the instance of hermeneutic transcendence exemplifies, integral elements within the dynamics of profound experience itself" (Davey 2006, p. 28). I think that this is a perfectly fitting observation, which explains how and why Gadamer often makes use of theological or religious categories to clarify such hermeneutic experiences like those of art and language, at the same time maintaining an absolutely "laical" attitude.

42 With this word I obviously refer to Zygmunt Bauman's influential theory of the "liquidification" of our forms of life in the twentieth century. According to him, it is indeed possible today "to deploy 'fluidity' as the leading metaphor for the present stage of the modern era", and thus "to consider 'fluidity' or 'liquidity' as fitting metaphors when we wish to grasp the nature of the present, in many ways *novel*, phase in the history of modernity" (Bauman 2000, p. 2). Accordingly, he even speaks of a shift "from heavy to light modernity" (Bauman 2000, pp. 113-118), and claims: "The 'melting of solids', the permanent feature of modernity, has therefore acquired a new meaning […]. The solids […] which are in the process of being melted at the present time, the time of fluid modernity, are the bonds which interlock individual choices in collective projects and actions" (Bauman 2000, p. 6).

43 Sokolowski 1997, p. 228.

become intelligible"[44], and that such a breakdown therefore urges a rehabilitation of the tradition of virtue ethics[45] and especially of the virtue of the *phronesis*. Also, the strong anti-Nietzschean and pro-Aristotelian stance that both Gadamer and MacIntyre take, and the project of overcoming the abstract dichotomy existing between reason and tradition/authority[46]. Finally, the idea that in the modern age "the exercise of practical intelligence" has degenerated into or remained "from the outset merely a certain cunning capacity for linking means to any end rather than to those ends which are genuine goods for man"[47].

Furthermore, one might also make possible comparisons between Gadamer's thoughts regarding the influence of prejudices and pre-reflexive or "implicit" understanding on reflexive or "explicit" reasoning, and MacIntyre's ideas on the rationality of traditions, i.e. the embeddedness of every form of reason in a tradition[48]. However, not-

---

44   MacIntyre 1985, p. 39.
45   See MacIntyre 1985, pp. 109-255.
46   As is well known, this project plays a central role in one of the most famous and most discussed sections of *Wahrheit und Methode* (see GW 1, pp. 276-290 [TM, pp. 274-285]). In the fourth chapter of *After Virtue*, for his part, MacIntyre notices that in the present age "the notion of authority and the notion of reason" are usually considered "not [as] intimately connected, but [as] mutually exclusive. Yet this concept of authority as excluding reason is [...] itself a peculiarly, even if not exclusively, modern concept, fashioned in a culture to which the notion of authority is alien and repugnant, so that appeals to authority appear irrational. But the traditional authority of the ethical", for example, "was not of this arbitrary kind" (MacIntyre 1985, p. 42).
47   MacIntyre 1985, p. 154. As we will see, Gadamer deals in many of his essays with the question of the historical transformations of reason, and especially with the strong tendency in the modern age to interpret reason only in terms of "calculating thinking" or "instrumental rationality". On this topic, see above all the essay *Rationalität im Wandel der Zeiten* (GW 4, pp. 23-36 [Gadamer 1979]).
48   See MacIntyre 1988, pp. 349-369. It has been argued that "the question of at least an indirect influence of Gadamer's thought upon MacIntyre is an intriguing one. There is no indication of it in *After Virtue* though that book treats many Gadamerian themes [...]. However in the later *Whose Justice? Which Rationality?* [...] there is frequent reference to 'tradition-constituted and tradition-

withstanding the relevance and appeal of such comparisons, I fear they might also be misleading and, for example, might be seen as supporting the idea of Gadamer's hermeneutics as a conservative or even authoritarian philosophy[49]. This is an idea that became almost commonplace after the latter's famous controversy with Habermas, but I consider this point of view inadequate and inexact.

Anyway, that Gadamer's concern for the loss of a genuine religious experience must be contextualized and thus connected to his wide-ranging ethical and socio-political interests is somehow proven by his development of the complex and fascinating idea of a sort of world religion (*Weltreligion*) or common religion (*gemeinsame Religion*) that would eventually pave the road for the establishment of a veritable world *ethos*[50]. Furthermore, it should be noticed that Gadamer rarely speaks of God, and rather seems to prefer more neutral or impersonal expressions like "transcendence" or "the divine". So, apropos of the concept of *transcendence*, he says that it is "a very good expression to use for saying that we aren't certain what there is in the beyond or what it is like. [...] Transcendence is not simply believing in God", but rather "something incomprehensible": "the *ignoramus*", that is, "the finitude beyond which we are not allowed to go", is "the fundament of transcendence"[51]. In relation to the concept of *the divine*, Gadamer makes reference to the peculiarity of Greek re-

---

constitutive' inquiry [...]. The idea is certainly Gadamerian" (Smith 1991, p. 94 note).

49 It is not by chance that the abovementioned book of Paul Christopher Smith ends with a chapter entitled *Gadamerian Conservatism* (Smith 1991, pp. 267-282). In this context, however, it is surely worth mentioning that on a few occasions Gadamer and MacIntyre have confronted each other on philosophical and ethic-political issues, conceding that some resemblances actually exist, but also stressing their mutual divergences (see MacIntyre 2002 and GW 3, pp. 350-356). On this topic, see also the following observation made by MacIntyre himself: "From Gadamer I have learned a great deal about intellectual and moral tradition. I am very close to all in Gadamer that comes from Aristotle; that which comes from Heidegger I reject" (MacIntyre 1994, p. 151).
50 On this topic, see, above all, Gadamer 2001a.
51 UD, pp. 76 and 80 [CP, pp. 74 and 78-79].

ligious life and explains that "generally the Greeks preferred to use the neuter gender: *to theion*", an expression that "signifies a fundamental human experience connected in an indefinite manner with the presence of something surpassing through its power the expectations of our daily life. [...] In the neuter", he says, "one hears something peculiar, as much mysterious as ungraspable"[52]. Accordingly, the divine is not to be understood as "a definite thing of a certain kind", but rather as "an atmospheric datum", as "something that pervades and determines everything, without being itself determinate", as something that always maintains "its peculiar ungraspable distance"[53].

Finally, regarding the entwinement of religious questions with ethical and political questions, it is surely relevant what Gadamer affirms in the last section of his extended interview with Riccardo Dottori – a section significantly entitled *Verso una nuova religiosità*, that is, *Towards a New Kind of Religiosity*, but translated in the English edition of the book as *The Last God*. Here, indeed, Gadamer claims that humanity is "likely to go down [a] semi-catastrophic road", and asks himself if our angst for possible global calamities could bring "humanity to a halt"[54]. In this way, he says, there might be a hope for people to come to "an understanding of some sensible conception of transcendence", and perhaps begin "asking themselves why

---

52 GW 7, pp. 85 and 87 [Gadamer 1986f, pp. 54-55]).
53 GW 7, p. 87 [Gadamer 1986f, p. 55]. Analogous remarks can be found in the essay *Articulating Transcendence*, where Gadamer claims that "the Greek philosophy is [...] the first opening for the dimension of transcendence", and then points out the specificity of "the neuter: 'the divine'", confirming that "the neuter is one of the most mysterious things in human language wherever it is preserved. German and Greek have the excellence of preserving the neuter. [...] To use the neuter [...] expresses something of ungraspable presence", like "filling in the empty space" or "the plenitude of presence, the omnipresence of something. Hence, the divine is indeed an expression for such an omnipresence" (Gadamer 1984d, pp. 1 and 5). Gadamer also underlines the peculiarity of the use of the neuter in Greek and German language in the first of his lessons on the beginning of Western philosophy, where he explains that "the neuter [...] has to do not with the quality of a being, but the quality of a whole space, 'being', in which all things appear" (IFO, p. 19 [BP, p. 14]).
54 UD, p. 144 [CP, p. 142].

we are born without being asked, why we die without being asked, and so on"⁵⁵. In the final analysis, Gadamer concedes his interlocutor that these are surely religious questions, although not theological ones. They are questions addressing our "religious sentiment" – religious sentiment being definable as "an unavoidable question for us", as "a hope", or even as "a task that unites us all in our mutual understanding": an *"ultimate ethical task* [that] cannot be separated from the one task of questioning and understanding our own existence"⁵⁶.

That a "laical" interpretation of the religious question in Gadamer's thought is possible and indeed correct is also testified, in my opinion, by a simple biographical and intellectual fact, namely his agnosticism. To be true, it must be said that on a few occasions Gadamer has clearly defined himself as "a Protestant"⁵⁷, which obviously contrasts with my preceding observations. However, it has been noticed that Gadamer's "claim to be a Protestant" can be interpreted as "an attempt to distinguish himself from Heidegger's Catholicism", from "his teacher's 'theological' path"⁵⁸. From a biographical point of view, Gadamer's agnosticism could be traced back to the "atmosphere of intellectual atheism determined by his father, a pharmaceutical chemist", while his vaguely religious disposition "following the rules of Protestantism" probably derives from his mother, whose "Pietistic religiosity" represented in the first four years of

---

55 UD, p. 145 [CP, p. 142].
56 UD, p. 145 [CP, pp. 142-143 (my italics)]. On the difference between genuine religious questions and theological questions, Gadamer explains: "this abuse [*scil.* that of wanting to impose its standards on humanity, of wanting to dominate it] occurs again and again throughout the whole of theology. [...] I have nothing against theology, [...] I only want to warn of the misuse that one makes of a theological doctrine when it turns into an instrument of the imperialism of a church within a state. The blame rests not with theology as such, but with the subjection of theology to a doctrine and of the concomitant religious sentiment being subjected to the power of a church" (UD, p. 145 [CP, p. 142]).
57 See, for instance, GW 8, p. 126 [RB, p. 35]; Gadamer 1995a, p. 197 [Gadamer 1998c, p. 200]; Gadamer 2001a, p. 14; Gadamer 2001b, p. 126.
58 Di Cesare 2002, pp. 60-61. The same observation on Heidegger and Gadamer is also made by Grondin 1999, p. 20 [2003, p. 21].

Gadamer's life (she untimely died in 1904) "a counterweight" to his father's "faith in scientific progress"[59]. Anyway, notwithstanding the cultivating of "especially close relations with theology and the church [...] during his whole life" – let's think of his friendship with Rudolf Bultmann, or his collaboration with Christian schools and institutions in the U.S.A., where he repeatedly served as visiting professor after his 1968 retirement from German university – and notwithstanding his appeal in *Wahrheit und Methode* to "church fathers such as Augustine, Thomas Aquinas, and Nicolas of Cusa", Gadamer always maintained "an agnostic, even Socratic distance from the church and even from religious faith"[60]. In other words, although he "always had the highest respect for people who could summon up [...] the 'courage' to believe, [...]" he had to admit with regret that he himself could not do so": that is, it seems he never believed "in a personal God and an otherwordly life"[61].

This point emerges quite clearly in a tape-recorded conversation of the 18th September, 1994, reported in Grondin's biography, as well as in some of his last interviews. Here, in fact, Gadamer explicitly claims to have "no religious faith at all"[62], to be an "unredeemed agnostic"[63], and to believe not in an afterlife, "at least not in the sense the religious do"[64]. So, in accordance to the "laical" or "secular"

---

59 Di Cesare 2002, p. 60. The expression "vaguely 'religious disposition' (*vage 'religiöse Veranlagung'*)" is taken from the biography of Gadamer written by Jean Grondin, who reports that Gadamer himself used those words in a private conversation of July 1989 (see Grondin 1999, p. 19 and note [2003, pp. 21 and 384 note]). On the probable influence of the religious and meditative disposition of Gadamer's mother on her son, see Grondin 1999, pp. 18-24 [2003, pp. 20-26].
60 Grondin 1999, pp. 20-21 [2003, p. 22].
61 Grondin 1999, pp. 23 and 20 [2003, pp. 25 and 22].
62 Grondin 1999, p. 23 [2003, p. 25].
63 Gadamer 1993b (quoted by Grondin 1999, p. 21 and note [2003, pp. 23 and 385 note]).
64 Gadamer 1993a, p. 22 (quoted by Grondin 1999, p. 21 and note [2003, pp. 22 and 385 note]). In the interview with Giovanni Reale *Platone scopritore dell'ermeneutica* Gadamer says: "I believe that the existence of something beyond reason is undeniable. Yet, the claim to be able to say what this beyond actually is, is something different. I don't think that our reason's ongoing re-

interpretation I have tried to give so far, what Grondin defines Gadamer's "vaguely '*religious* disposition'" might also be intended as indicating the latter's "receptiveness to what exceeded the boundaries of reason and science, which he himself would perhaps call the *aesthetic* or *artistic*"[65].

Now, I think that within this discourse a very relevant point is represented by the abovementioned difference between Heidegger's and Gadamer's approaches to philosophy *and* religion. Given the broadness and complexity of this theme, it is obviously not my intention to deal extensively with it here. Rather, what I would like to point out is simply that this theme actually throws light on one of the basic features of Gadamer's whole interpretation of his teacher's philosophy, namely its emphasis on "the inner urgency of the question concerning religion and theology in Heidegger's thought (*die innere Dringlichkeit des Problems der Religion und der Theologie im Denken Heideggers*)"[66]. It is thus not by accident if one of his main contributions on this subject, later collected in the book *Heideggers Wege*, is precisely entitled *Die religiöse Dimension*[67], and if the title chosen by Gadamer for his introduction to the so-called *Natorp-Bericht* – a text written by Heidegger in 1922 that went lost for decades and was finally found and published at the end of the 1980s[68] – sounds: *Heideggers "theologische" Jugendschrift*[69]. As a matter of fact, Gadamer repeatedly stresses the fact that "Heidegger's whole life was the life of a God-seeker"[70], that "at one point in his life he lost

---

    search can reach its final point, i.e. a first principle. Anyway, I believe that the question concerning God and religion remains a mystery; a mystery without which we just cannot live, however" (Gadamer 2001b, pp. 125-126). With regard to this last statement, Mariannina Failla has even spoken of "a sort of 'intellectual' deism (*eine Art 'intellektuellen' Deismus*)" in Gadamer, probably inherited from his father (Failla 2008, p. 31 [2009, pp. 48-49]).

65 Grondin 1999, pp. 19-20 [2003, p. 21 (my italics)].
66 GW 10, p. 7.
67 GW 3, pp. 308-319 [HW, pp. 167-180].
68 See Heidegger 2005, pp. 343-419 [1992].
69 See Gadamer 1989b.
70 Gadamer 1995c, p. 117.

God, and so he spent his entire life searching for Him"[71]. Hence, according to Gadamer, "the question that motivated him [*scil.* Heidegger] and pointed out his way of thinking", "his original and constantly advancing question", was: "How can we speak of God without reducing him to an object of our knowledge?"[72]. As he confirms in the interview *Die Logik des verbum interius*:

> Sie müssen immer bedenken, daß die eigentliche Frage Heideggers [...] war: [...] Wie kann man glauben? Das ist seine Frage. Er ist ein Gottsucher, und sein ganzes Leben ist er ein Gottsuchender geblieben[73].

Now, I argue that these remarks can help us understand the substantial difference between the two thinkers' responses to the questions of nihilism and "the loss of the gods (*Entgötterung*)"[74] in our techno-scientific age. In fact, Gadamer never hesitated when distancing himself from the eschatological *pathos* of his teacher's thought, claiming that Heidegger "was an extremist" and openly pronouncing himself against the latter's "vision of the complete forgetfulness of being, something which parallels the last man of Nietzsche"[75]. "Complete forgetfulness of being cannot be achieved", Gadamer confidently states, thus confirming that he does not follow Heidegger "when he says that only a God can save us"[76] or "when he talks about new gods and similar things"[77].

---

71 UD, pp. 125-126 [CP, p. 122].
72 GW 3, pp. 321 and 331 [HW, pp. 183 and 194-195].
73 Gadamer 1997-98, p. 27.
74 Heidegger 1977b, p. 76 [2002, p. 58].
75 Gadamer 1988a, p. 26.
76 Gadamer 1988a, p. 26.
77 Gadamer 1984c, p. 10. "When he [*scil.* Heidegger] first started coming out with his mysterious allusions to the return of the gods, we were really shocked", Gadamer admits. "I contacted him again and saw that that was not what he had in mind. It was a *façon de parler*. Even his famous statement, *Nur ein Gott kann uns retten*, means only that calculating politics is not what will save us from the impending catastrophe. Nevertheless, I would criticize that too" (Gadamer 1984c, p. 11).

In a few cases, Gadamer makes some remarks on Heidegger that may even sound a little bit sarcastic. For example, in the interview with Giovanni Reale *A scuola da Platone* he declares: "Heidegger spent his whole life in search of God: this is the key to understand his whole thought. [...] He believed that a new 'missionary' of God would come within a hundred years. He never claimed it in public, but that was his conviction"[78]. And still: "Heidegger had a very special talent [...] but I must admit that perhaps he had an exaggerated and unreasonable self-esteem: he thought that in two hundred years he would have been considered as a real saviour"[79]. Finally, in an interview with Riccardo Dottori he says: "Heidegger was a deeply religious man and a frustrated thinker", who surely "had a great deal of imagination": "in the end, [...] we might even take Heidegger for an imaginative madman"[80]. In short, however, in the abovementioned 1994 tape-recorded conversation with Grondin he openly acknowledges that his

> life mission was very different from Heidegger's, [...] who was searching for a more appropriate language than that of Catholicism – that is, he was searching for a religious language. That was something Bultmann could never give him. Finally it was Hölderlin who did so – though to my mind in a very bizarre way. So my religious background – like that of so many Protestants – actually has little to do with the church[81].

In conclusion, the crucial point of Gadamer's argument about religious experience and its problematic character in the age of nihilism lies, in my opinion, in what has been defined his "especially solid

---

78 Gadamer 2001c, pp. 135-136.
79 Gadamer 2002, p. 222. In the 1986 interview *The German University and German Politics: The Case of Heidegger*, Gadamer even adds some "biographical and psychological explanation": "The truth is that as a little boy Heidegger was all too much admired and adored at home. He never learned how to lose. A person who, in the first three years of life as a child, never learns how to lose will never learn that his whole life long. That is my opinion on this point" (Gadamer 1992c, pp. 11-12).
80 UD, pp. 144 and 140 [CP, pp. 141 and 137].
81 Grondin 1999, p. 22 [2003, p. 24].

sense of human limits"[82]. As we have already seen, Gadamer's retrieval of such concepts as "transcendence" or "the divine" is entirely based on his sensibility for the mystery of our finitude, that is, on the fact that "we simply can't say anything about a lot of things – about the mysteries of birth, life, and death"[83].

Not by chance, one of the recurring anthropological questions in his writings precisely concerns "the in-built capacity of man to think beyond his own life in the world, to think about death", and the consequent "fundamental phenomenon of becoming human" represented by "the burial of the dead"[84]. Apropos of this phenomenon, belonging to "the immutable anthropological background for all the human and social changes, past or present"[85], in the essay *Die Erfahrung des Todes* he dares speak of a "unique status of the rite of death":

---

82   Grondin 1999, p. 24 [2003, p. 26].
83   UD, p. 76 [CP, pp. 74-75].
84   GW 4, p. 220 [RAS, pp. 74-75].
85   GW 4, p. 219 [RAS, p. 74]. Unlike Heidegger, whose mistrust of anthropology is well-known and documented both in the first and the second phase of his path of thought (see, for instance, Heidegger 1976, pp. 202 and 237 [1998, pp. 154 and 181]; Heidegger 1977a, pp. 22-23, 60-67, 175, 243 and 265 [2010, pp. 16-17, 44-49, 128, 177 and 192]; Heidegger 1977b, pp. 93, 99, 111-112 and 249 [2002, pp. 70, 75, 84 and 186]; Heidegger 1991, pp. 208-214 [1997, pp. 146-150]), Gadamer has repeatedly shown a certain openness to philosophical and cultural anthropology. This is testified, for instance, by his frequent references to Scheler, Plessner and Gehlen, the founding fathers of twentieth-century philosophical anthropology (see GW 2, pp. 204, 257 and 431-432; GW 4, pp. 250-253 [EH, pp. 9-13]; GW 8, pp. 136 and 355; GW 10, pp. 380-387). Furthermore, it is worthy of mention that between 1972 and 1975 he co-edited the collection of essays in seven volumes *Neue Anthropologie*, for which he also wrote an interesting *Schlußbericht* (Gadamer 1975). With regard to his philosophy of language, Günter Figal has even claimed that in his later works Gadamer, quite in contrast to the ontological conception he had presented in the third part of *Wahrheit und Methode*, rather opted for a quasi-anthropological "description of life-world comportment [and] ritual" as "a complex of behavior patterns to which one must become accustomed to be able […] to say that which has meaning in the context of customary behavior" (Figal 2002a, p. 123).

> the experience of death – Gadamer explains – occupies a central place in the history of humankind. We could perhaps even say that this experience initiated the process of our becoming human. As far as human memory extends we can recognize as an undisputed characteristic of human beings that they perform some kind of funeral rites. [...] In this humankind stands unique among all the other creatures, as unique as in the possession of language. Or perhaps it is something even more original. [...] For every living person there is something incomprehensible in the fact that this human consciousness capable of anticipating the future will one day come to an end. [So] the repression of death (*Verdrängung des Todes*) must be conceived as an elementary human reaction to death and one which each human being takes up with respect to their own lives. [...] By looking at [the] secularized forms of remembrance it is possible to understand [how] here both religious faith and purely secular attitudes concur in honouring the majesty of death[86].

This, in turn, is connected with the basic theme of the present book, i.e. the predominance of techno-scientific approaches in our civilization and the potential problems that such an unopposed primacy can bring. In Gadamer's view, indeed, "the contribution of the scientific Enlightenment reaches an insuperable limit in the mystery of life and of death"[87]. "We can make good use of the natural sciences", he confidently concedes, "but the idea that we can now solve all our problems, like birth and death, history and purpose of life, with this [*scil*. the scientific] conception of truth – that makes no sense"[88].

On the other hand, in the secularized societies of the Western world today Gadamer sees the diffusion of a paralyzing indifference not only to religious faith itself, but more generally to "the really astonishing character of [our] own finite being", of "our finitude"[89]. A paralyzing indifference that goes hand in hand with the tendency in our time to "an almost systematic repression of death"[90] and, above

---

86   GW 4, pp. 289-290 and 292 [EH, pp. 62-64 and 67].
87   GW 4, p. 293 [EH, p. 67].
88   UD, p. 76 [CP, p. 74].
89   GW 3, p. 236 [HW, p. 78].
90   GW 4, p. 290 [EH, p. 63].

all, to its "anonymization", i.e. its transformation into an anonymous event[91].

This finally leads to the loss of the broadly speaking "metaphysical" questions connected to the insurmountable "ungraspability of death (*Unbegreiflichkeit des Todes*)"[92] which greatly contribute to our being and becoming human. On this topic, let me also remind the reader of Gadamer's pregnant observations in the essays *Vergänglichkeit* and *Die Unsterblichkeitsbeweise in Platos "Phaidon"*, in which we read:

> Auch in Zeiten, in denen Wohlstand und Gedeihen so etwas wie ein behagliches Glück versprechen, ist in unserem Daseinsgefühl das Wissen um die eigene Endlichkeit immer rege. Es gehört zur Grunderfahrung des Menschen, daß er um seinen Tod weiß und zugleich nicht weiß, wann oder wie bald er abberufen wird. Wissen um den Tod hat die Menschheit schon Jahrtausendelang vor aller bezeugten Überlieferung begleitet. Dafür gibt es ein unumstößliches Zeugnis. Die Menschen haben ihre Toten bestattet[93].

And still:

> [the] proof of the ontological relationship of idea, life, and soul, as marvelous as it might be, is incapable demonstrating anything more than the character of the universal *eide*, and [...] it most certainly cannot allay the fears which the specific individual soul has of being destroyed, fears which pervade its self-understanding. [...] As convincing as the discussion [*scil.* in the *Phaedo*] might have been, the conclusion is drawn that the proofs are not sufficient and that one must continue to test their premises insofar as is humanly possible. Evidently in questions of this sort one cannot expect greater certainty. [...] This brings us back to the splendid metaphor of the child in us, whose fears of death are never quite to be allayed by rational arguments, however convincing. [...] And how

---

91 In the interview *Was bleibt?* with Günter Figal and Heimo Schwilk, Gadamer says: "Noch nie war der Tod so stark in der Öffentlichkeit gegenwärtig und wurde zugleich so wenig ernst genommen. Heute könnte man den Tod sogar ins Warenhaus verlegen. Wir verkaufen den Tod, machen ein Geschäft daraus. Dennoch müssten wir eigentlich wissen, dass zum Wissen das Wissen von den Grenzen unseres Wissens gehört. Der Tod bleibt ein Geheimnis" (Gadamer 1999).
92 GW 4, p. 161.
93 GW 9, p. 171.

indeed should the phenomenon of death in all its immensity ever become comprehensible for human reason and insight, and yet how much even so does it continue to demand from human beings a response to its imponderability. Evidence of this fact is provided above all by that silent yet eloquent ancestor worship and tomb art which projects human feeling and imagination beyond the inner certainty of one's own being alive to those departed in death[94].

In the end, I think that the basic reasons for Gadamer's concern for the importance of a religious disposition (even a "vague" one, as we have seen), in a techno-scientific and even nihilistic age like ours, are somehow contained in the final lines of his 1977 essay *Herméneutique et théologie*. Here, Gadamer hints at certain affinities between hermeneutic and religious experiences ("cette structure générale que j'appellerais la situation herméneutique est aussi valuable pour la théologie", he says), and then concludes:

> la tâche de l'enseignement religieux, qui consiste à clarifier la conscience du croyant, est extrêmement précaire. Surtout dans le temps modernes, le premier moment de cette tâche *n'est pas de nous introduire dans la grande tradition théologique* vécue dans l'Eglise, mais de *surmonter l'oubli moderne et le*

---

[94] GW 6, pp. 198-200 [DD, pp. 36-37]). An analogous remark can be found in Gadamer's commentary to the *Phaedo* (105c-107b [1997, pp. 90-92]), where we read: "Plato will mit seinem Beweise nicht nur das Wesensverhältnis von Seele und Lebendigkeit geltend machen. Er meint damit auch über die konkrete Einzelseele etwas ausgemacht zu haben. Freilich ist er sich darüber im klaren, daß solche rationale Beweisführung die Angst vor dem Tode nicht wirklich überwinden kann. Er spricht in diesem Zusammenhang von der Schwäche des menschlichen Herzens, für die auch ein gelungener Beweis nie endgültig sein kann. Was die Art von Beweisanspruch betrifft, die Plato mit seiner Beweisführung verbindet, so habe ich glaubhaft zu machen versucht, daß diese Beweisführung nur in dem negativen Sinne Geltung beansprucht, daß sie die Widerlegung der Unsterblichkeit der Seele, d.h. die materialistische Argumentation, mit der das ganze Gespräch anhebt, als unhaltbar erweist. Ein positiver Beweis für die Unsterblichkeit der konkreten Einzelseele, in dem Sinne, in dem der einzelne Befreiung von seiner Angst wünschen mag, kann darin nicht liegen" (PTI, p. 79).

désespoir radical de l'être humain concernant la mort, la souffrance, la *finitude*. [...] Ouvrir les yeux à l'*expérience du divin, en un sens très general,* est la condition préliminaire à l'accueil du message chrétien[95].

---

95 Gadamer 1977, pp. 396-397 (my italics).

8. Hermeneutics, Techno-Science, Enlightenment: A Complex "Constellation"

In the second chapter we have seen how the "splendid development of the natural sciences" from the seventeenth century onwards, together with the "technological and economic development" provided by the rational and consistent exploitation of "the practical possibilities that result from the scientific discoveries"[1], have actually been considered by Gadamer as the real roots of the modern age. On this basis, Gadamer has offered an extensive and profound analysis of the present condition of mankind, which is, according to him, a very critical condition that keeps us in suspense, almost breathless[2].

Following his diagnosis, it might seem that the responsibility for every particular aspect of today's critical situation falls upon the shoulders of science and the technological civilization it has created. As we read, for instance, in the essay *Theorie, Technik, Praxis*:

> the scientific-technical mastery of nature [...], the technical exploitation of natural resources and the artificial transformation of our environment [have] become so carefully planned and extensive that [their] consequences endanger the natural cycle of things and bring about irreversible developments on a large scale. [...] Issues such as the city, the environment, population growth, the world food supply, problems of the aged, etc., thus justly acquire a privileged place among the scientific themes of our knowledge of man. The atom bomb proves itself more and more to be only a special case of the self-endangering of human beings and their life on this planet to which science has led[3].

---

1 GW 4, pp. 3-4 [PH, p. 108].
2 So, in the essay *Humanismus und industrielle Revolution* Gadamer speaks of "[die] spannungsvolle und kritische Weltlage der Menschheit", and still of "die uns bis heute in Atem haltende und sich immer mehr zuspitzende Krise" (HE, pp. 28-29).
3 GW 4, pp. 247-248 [EH, pp. 6-7].

Now, on the one side, Gadamer's words contain an undeniable and self-evident truth. In order to understand this point, all one has to do is think about those extremely problematic phenomena of our time such as ozone depletion, environmental pollution or some of the bioethical issues in medical genetics and human cloning research; or, to recall such dramatic events of our time as Auschwitz and Hiroshima, or, again, more recently, the Chernobyl disaster and even this year's nuclear accident in Fukushima. All phenomena and events which, although in very different ways, somehow seem to be "the visible expression of [the] totalization of technical civilization (*Totalisierung der technischen Zivilisation*)"[4] and the mechanical, bureaucratic rationalization of life that this kind of civilization model endorses[5].

To be precise, for that which regards the abovementioned disasters related to the use of nuclear energy and atomic weapons, I think that the link with techno-scientific development is clear. Not quite as clear, however, would appear to be the connection between technoscience and all that is embodied in the name "Auschwitz", i.e. the apocalyptical reality of concentration camps and genocide.

Now, it is obviously not my intention to put the blame on technoscience for what Adorno defined "Auschwitz [and] the world of torture which has continued to exist after Auschwitz and of which we

---

4   GW 4, p. 248 [EH, p. 7].
5   In this regard, see Gadamer's observations in the essay *Hegel und die Sprache der Metaphysik*: "Wir stehen hier wirklich alle gemeinsam Rede, wenn wir uns über [den] Schicksalsweg des Abendlandes Gedanken machen. Es geht um die Entstehung der Wissenschaft unter den Griechen und die Wiederaufnahme dieses Antriebs unter den veränderten Bedingungen der christlichen Kirche und ihrer Theologie, die dann im 17 Jahrhundert die neuzeitlichen Erfahrungswissenschaften zur Entwicklung gebracht haben. Diese Entwicklung erweist sich heute mehr und mehr als die Umgestaltung unseres Planeten zu einer Fabriklandschaft. […] Wir haben inzwischen eine gewaltige Zahl von Problemen vor uns, die sich daran knüpfen. Man denke an das Geburtenproblem, an das Nuklearproblem, an das ökologische Problem – überall scheint es so, als ob die Wissenschaft gerufen wäre und ihre Experten es sein müßten, die das, was sie durch ihr wissenschaftliches Können erst ermöglicht haben, nun auch für die Menschheit zum Guten zu steuern und zu vollenden hätten" (Gadamer 1991e, pp. 12-13).

[have received] the most horrifying reports from Vietnam"[6] – and since then, one may add, from Cambodia, Bosnia, Ruanda, Darfur...Rather, what I would like to point out is that, although we usually interpret genocides as momentary lapses into barbarousness and obscurantism, a connection between genocidary terror and some instruments, institutions or expressions of modernity probably exists. In other words, as Bernard Bruneteau has argued: "les génocides du XXe siècle concrétisent tous un projet rationnel indissociable de la dimension prométhéenne de l'esprit de modernité"[7]. I think that this somehow holds true even if one agrees with Peter Singer that "the horrific mass killings of the twentieth century were not a new phenomenon, except insofar as *modern technology and communications* enabled the killers to murder far more people in a relatively brief period of time than had ever happened before"[8].

6   Adorno 1998, p. 160 [2001, p. 101].
7   Bruneteau 2004, p. 227.
8   Singer 2002, pp. 108-109 (my italics). To support his thesis that "genocide and crimes against humanity [are] not a new phenomenon", Singer provocatively but convincingly quotes from the Bible. More precisely, from the *Book of Numbers* (31: 1-18), which "tells of a time when Israelite men were succumbing to the charms of the women of a neighboring tribe, the Midianites. Worse still, it seems that these women succeeded in persuading their Israelite lovers to follow the Midianite religion: 'And the LORD spake unto Moses, saying, Avenge the children of Israel of the Midianites. And Moses spake unto the people, saying, Arm some of yourselves unto the war, and let them go against the Midianites, and avenge the LORD of Midian. [...] And they warred against the Midianites, as the LORD commanded Moses; and they slew all the males. [...] And Moses said unto them, [...] Now therefore kill every male among the little ones, and kill every woman that hath known man by lying with him. But all the women children, that have not known a man by lying with him, keep alive for yourselves'. [...] Here we have an example of genocide", Singer comments, "in which the genetic advantage to the perpetrators is as clear as anything can be. [...] Midianite males were potential competitors and of no genetic use to the Israelites. So Moses ruthlessly eliminated them, men and boys alike. Killing all the Midianite women who are not virgins ensured that there were no pregnant women who might carry male Midianite children, and it was an effective way of ensuring that there would be no one of full Midianite descent in the next generation. Allowing the captains to keep the young Midianite females for themselves

Once again, this whole discourse is absolutely not meant to say that the norms and standards of the modern techno-scientific civilization "automatically" lead to mass deportation and extermination, which would be an absurd, untenable and even ignominious thesis. Rather, I think that one could agree with Zygmunt Bauman's proposal to treat the Holocaust "not [as] an antithesis of modern civilization and everything (or so we like to think) it stands for", but rather "*as a rare, yet significant and reliable, test of the hidden possibilities of modern society*"[9]. In fact, without modern civilization, that is, without "its technology, its rational criteria of choice, its tendency to subordinate thought and action to the pragmatics of economy and effectiveness", and without its "*routine bureaucratic procedures*: means-ends calculus, budget balancing, universal rule application" – without all this, "the Holocaust would be unthinkable"[10]. As Bauman puts it:

> Modern civilization was not the Holocaust's *sufficient* condition; it was, however, most certainly its *necessary* condition. [...] It was the *rational world of modern civilization* that made the Holocaust thinkable. [...] We know of many massacres, pogroms, mass murders, indeed instances not far removed from genocide, that have been perpetrated without *modern bureaucracy*, the skills and *technologies* it commands, the *scientific principles* of its internal management. The Holocaust, however, was clearly unthinkable without such bureaucracy. The Holocaust was not an irrational outflow of the not-yet-fully-eradicated residues of pre-modern barbarity. It was a legitimate resident in the house of modernity; indeed, one who would not be at home in any other house[11].

---

      increased the number of their own descendants" (Singer 2002, pp. 106-108 and 110).
9   Bauman 1989, pp. 7 and 12.
10   Bauman 1989, pp. 13 and 17.
11   Bauman 1989, pp. 13 and 17 (my italics). In this context, I would like to quote Gadamer's significant statement in the essay *Die Menschenwürde auf ihrem Weg von der Antike bis heute*, according to which "der Holocaust hat nicht nur das Unheimliche mit sich gebracht, daß eine Staatsführung Mitbürger wegen ihrer Rasse austilgte, sondern auch, daß dies in maschineller Form vor sich ging" (Gadamer 1988b, p. 106).

Anyway, *on the one side*, as I said before, Gadamer's speech about the consequences of techno-science for the self-endangering of human beings and, in general, of life on planet earth, are quite understandable and reasonable. *On the other*, however, that same speech might suggest that he puts the blame on techno-science for all the problems of the present age, which would obviously be an untenable argument. Furthermore, it could seem as if Gadamer, by saying so, adopts a sort of "philosophocentric perspective"[12], namely one which grounds all historical or socio-political transformations on changes in the realm of philosophical (and scientific) concepts. An attitude, the latter, which is indeed characteristic, at least to a certain extent, of many philosophers, such as for example Heidegger – who notoriously considers "the fundamental metaphysical positions [as] the ground and realm of what we know as world history", and nihilism, i.e. the happening of the forgetfulness of being originated by the oblivion of the ontological difference, as "the lawfulness of history", "its *inner logic*", "what determines the historicity of this history"[13] – or perhaps even Husserl,

---

12 Cambiano 1988, p. 63.
13 Heidegger 1997a, p. 79 [1982, p. 53]. In the so-called second phase of Heidegger's way of thought, namely that dominated by his "new *seynsgeschichtlich* approach", i.e. by the idea of being as "the history of unfolding epochs of self-manifestation" (Guignon 1993, p. 15), metaphysics is viewed indeed as virtually coinciding with nihilism. The latter, in turn, is interpreted by Heidegger "not just [as] one historical phenomenon among others", but "on the contrary [as] the fundamental movement of the history of the West", the "scarcely recognized fundamental process in the destiny of Western peoples [that] moves history" (Heidegger 1977b, p. 218 [2002, p. 163]). Metaphysics and nihilism thus represent to him the "concealed ground of our historical *Dasein*", the "happening that grounds history", that "runs through Western history from the inception onward": an happening that "the eyes of all historians will never reach, but which nevertheless happens" (Heidegger 1983, pp. 100, 42 and 40 [2000, 99, 41 and 39]). This obviously confers to history a singular fateful nature, since its essence appears determined by destining (*Geschick*), by "the sending that gathers (*versammelnde Schicken*), that first starts man upon a way of revealing" (Heidegger 2000a, p. 25 [1993, p. 329]). So, the history of metaphysics is compared to "the destiny of being itself", "the unthought – be-

who somehow "reduces" the crisis of the whole Western civilization to that of European philosophy and science alone.

To be true, by reading some of Gadamer's writings one can actually get the impression that the aforementioned "suspects" are being confirmed. For example, he mostly concentrates on cultural and "ideal" aspects, rather than providing specific, appropriate and deep analysis of the economic and socio-political factors which have contributed to the shaping of the present civilization (although the interest in such factors and phenomena is not entirely absent from his works, as we have seen in the previous chapters); also, in most of his writings he takes a strong stand on the dangerous side of technoscience. On this basis, one might even go so far as to consider Gadamer as a mortal enemy of science and technology, or better still, as one of the many twentieth-century "radical critics" who have "exaggerated the real power of technology", and thus "personified it, demonized it" and interpreted it as a sort of "omnipotent demiurge"[14]. In other words, it seems as if "the twentieth-century prevailing attitude towards technology in the field of the humanities has been by far a radically critical one"[15]: something which also finds confirmation in the contemporary intellectuals' overall relationship to modernity. As an important observer like Alain Touraine noticed,

> la modernité [...] est mise en cause, rejetée ou redéfinie aujourd'hui. [...] L'idée de modernité, sous sa forme la plus ambitieuse, fut l'affirmation que l'homme est ce qu'il fait, que doit donc exister une correspondance [...] d'une culture

---

cause withheld – mystery of being itself", which forms "the historical ground of the world history" (Heidegger 1977b, pp. 264-265 [2002, pp. 197-198]).

14 Nacci 2000, pp. 9 and 13.

15 Nacci 2000, p. 11. According to this scholar, indeed, science and technology have been mostly defined in the last century "through the features of precision, mathematization, objectivity, planning, control, exploitation, [...] anthropocentrism and subjectivism. [...] Twentieth-century intellectuals have misunderstood technology, they have created a myth and produced a lot of misunderstandings [...]. With a few exceptions, twentieth-century philosophers have conceived technology in a distorted, deformed way", often putting the blame on it for "totalitarian regimes, oppressive societies, human standardization and even for the end of the Western civilization" (Nacci 2000, pp. 9 and 12-13).

scientifique, d'une société ordonnée et d'individus libres [...]. L'humanité, en agissant selon ses lois, avance à la fois vers l'abondance, la liberté et le bonheur. C'est cette affirmation centrale qui a été contestée our rejetée par les critiques de la modernité. [...] Si notre siècle [*scil.* the twentieth century] apparaît aux technologues et aux économistes comme celui de la modernité triomphante, il a été dominé intellectuellement par le discourse antimoderniste. [...] ce siècle dit de progrès a été pensé, en Europe au moins, comme un siècle de crise et souvent de déclin ou de catastrophe. La grande poussée de l'industrialisation occidentale [a] été accompagnée d'un vaste mouvement intellectuel de critique de la modernité[16].

In my opinion, however, although Gadamer certainly belongs to what we could define as the great chain of the twentieth-century critics of techno-scientific modernity, and although he has sometimes expressed his opinions on this topic in quite a radical or drastic way, he has nevertheless not gone so far as to conceive science and technology as omnipotent and perhaps even monstrous forces. I think indeed that Gadamer has clearly acknowledged that one cannot put the blame on science for all the dangers and risks of the present age[17]. Furthermore, he has repeatedly invited one to consider modern science as "one of the major fruits of the modern Enlightenment" and as "an impressive embodiment of critical freedom that is to be marvelled at"[18]. And he openly acknowledges that "without the continuing productive development of science, without scientific developments and their ingenious technical applications", we could "neither maintain the stand-

---

16 Touraine 1992, pp. 11, 15 and 121.
17 So, for instance, in the essay *Über die Ursprünglichkeit der Wissenschaft* he first states that "die Wissenschaft", together with "die moderne Maschinentechnik und [...] die ganze moderne Industrie", "die wesentliche Grundlage der neuzeitlichen Kultur überhaupt ist". Then, he specifies: "Daß [die] Beherrschung der Natur sich so furchtbar gegen die menschliche Natur überhaupt auswirken konnte, möchte den Wert der Wissenschaft für die Menschheit fragwürdig machen und als eine Schuld der Wissenschaft erscheinen. Niemand kann jedoch zweifeln, daß *die Schuld nicht bei der Wissenschaft und der Technik liegt*, wenn sie der Zerstörung dienen, *sondern bei den Menschen*, die sie dazu benutzen" (GW 10, p. 289 [my italics]).
18 ÜVG, p. 155 [EH, p. 122].

ard of our civilization nor look forward to improved living conditions for mankind as a whole"[19].

It is finally remarkable, I think, that Gadamer never calls the scientific claim for objective knowledge and truth into question. Rather, besides recognizing the full legitimacy of such a claim, he "simply" reminds us of how this particular kind of knowledge does not exhaust the whole question about truth, knowledge and experience. In other words, it is my opinion that Gadamer, though surely sharing with other thinkers some strong criticism towards the idea that *extra scientiam nulla salus*, nonetheless had no intention of abruptly suppressing the separation of science from non-science, thus drawing scientific knowledge close to myth, magic or witchcraft – like, for example, Paul Feyerabend has done. Nor did he dare level the genre distinction between literature, philosophy and science, thus reducing the latter to just another kind of writing – like, for example, Richard Rorty has done[20].

---

19 LT, pp. 143-144 [PT, p. 188].
20 I obviously refer here to Rorty's provocative idea that philosophy "is delimited, as is any literary genre, not by form or matter, but by a tradition – a family romance involving, e.g., Father Parmenides, honest old Uncle Kant, and bad brother Derrida" (Rorty 1982, p. 92). Rorty surely represents the most radical, resolute, and consistent interpreter of the philosophy-as-literature line of thought. In fact, he seems to praise "a general turn against theory and towards narrative" (Rorty 1989, p. XVI), and promote "the idea of a seamless, undifferentiated 'general text'", with the consequent reduction of metaphysics to "that genre of literature which attempted to create unique, total, closed vocabularies" (Rorty 1991b, pp. 87 and 105). Rorty indeed hypothesizes "an intellectual life" which "would not make much of the line between 'philosophy' and something else, nor try to allot distinctive cultural roles to art, religion, science, and philosophy" (Rorty 1991a, p. 76). From this point of view, he also declares he agrees "with the late Heidegger" when he says "that the science/poetry/philosophy distinctions we have lived with are outmoded" (Rorty 2006, p. 21). In my essay *Philosophy and Poetry – Philosophy as a Kind of Writing*, I have tried to explain why, in my view, Rorty's interpretation of Heidegger actually represents a misinterpretation, although surely a relevant and original one (see Marino 2011a).

Notwithstanding all this, I have already said in the *Introduction* that Gadamer's hermeneutics has often been interpreted as an *antiscientific* philosophy. Among the reasons for such an interpretation one can probably mention the title itself of Gadamer's masterwork, *Wahrheit und Methode*, which has often been interpreted as a sharp antithesis: "truth or method", "truth but not method", "truth without method"[21]. Just to mention a few examples, let us recall Jürgen Habermas' idea of "an antiscientific [and] traditionalistic Gadamer", whose philosophy is wholly summarized by "the contrast (*Gegensatz*) between 'truth' and 'method'"[22]. Or let us still recall Paul Ricoeur's opinion that the real question about Gadamer "is to what extent the work deserves to be called *Truth AND Method*, and whether it ought not to be entitled instead *Truth OR Method*"[23].

However, Gadamer's basic conviction seems not to be that genuine truth is in principle opposed to knowledge acquired through scientific methods, but rather that "method should be complemented with truth"[24]. The same thing has been observed, among others, by Lawrence K. Schmidt, Paul Giurlanda and Jean Grondin. According to the first author, Gadamer's "central theme is that the universalistic claim of the scientific method to be the *only* way to justify truth is wrong"[25], while the second argues that "it is hardly method itself which Gadamer opposes, only the attempt to turn method into an infallible tool"[26]. Accordingly, Grondin explains that it would be misleading to read *Wahrheit und Methode* as a plea against method and

---

21 Moda 2000, p. 18.
22 Habermas 1999, pp. 91-92 [2003, pp. 73-74]. To be precise, the English translator of Habermas' book had used here the term "antiscientistic". However, since I am trying to stress the difference between an antiscientistic and an antiscientific attitude, and since the German word used by Habermas is "*antiszientifisch*", I have decided to translate it as "antiscientific".
23 Ricoeur 1986, p. 107 [1991, p. 71].
24 Bianco 1997, p. 12.
25 Schmidt 2010, p. 210.
26 Giurlanda 1987, p. 41.

thus to draw it close to Feyerabend[27], just like it would be misleading to draw Gadamer close to the so-called postmodern thinkers. As Grondin explains it, indeed:

> For postmodernism, criticism of the infatuation with method and with scientific certainty ends in questioning *all truth*, all notion of the adequacy of consciousness and of reality. [...] What Gadamer takes issue with is not the link between truth and method. The *dependence of truth on method* is so obvious that it would be useless to try to repeat it once more. What he criticizes is the *method's attempt to exercise a monopoly on the notion of truth*. [...] A similar mistake is to think again that Gadamer stands *against method* and instrumentalism. But *this is not the case at all*: [...] instead, he has learnt a lot from the methodologies of understanding, for which he has the highest praise. For him, they are evidence and gain. *He never challenges science*, but only the fascination which emanates from it and which threatens to reduce the understanding to an instrumental process[28].

Given all this, it is thus understandable why Gadamer, in the years following the publication of *Wahrheit und Methode*, has often returned to this topic, for example admitting in an interview: "Ma formule est effectivement si ambiguë que le premiers critiques ont cru voir dans le

27 See Grondin 2000a, p. 26. I obviously make reference here to Paul Feyerabend's famous book *Against Method*, whose aim is not only that of dismantling "the idea of a method that contains firm, unchanging, and absolutely binding principles for conducting the business of science", but also that of outlining "an anarchist methodology and a corresponding anarchist science": "the idea of a fixed method, or of a fixed theory of rationality", Feyerabend explains, "rests on too naïve a view of man and his social surroundings. To those who look at the rich material provided by history, and who are not intent on impoverishing it in order to please their lower instincts, their craving for intellectual security in the form of clarity, precision, 'objectivity', 'truth', it will become clear that there is only one principle that can be defended under *all* circumstances and in all stages of human development. It is the principle: *anything goes*" (Feyerabend 1993, pp. 13-14 and 18-19). I think it is worthy of notice that probably the first one who actually emphasized "the parallels between this book [*scil. Wahrheit und Methode*] and Paul Feyerabend's *Against Method*" was precisely Richard Rorty, according to whom "Gadamer's book" could be reasonably be called "a tract against the very idea of method" (Rorty 2009, p. 358 note).
28 Grondin 2003, pp. 3 and 20 (my italics).

livre tantôt la dernière méthode pour atteindre la vérité, tantôt une condamnation radicale de la méthode!"[29]. "I am not at all against method", Gadamer openly admits: "I merely maintain that it is not only method the route of access"[30]. In yet another interview he states that "a title is just a means to draw attention. It is not something unambiguous and it can even be interpreted in different ways": the title-slogan of his 1960 book, however, "is correctly interpreted this way: not all truth is achievable through scientific method"[31]. And in the lectures *Metafisica e filosofia pratica in Aristotele* from 1990 (thirty years after *Wahrheit und Methode*) he still declares that such a title "does not mean at all to be against science, but simply to go against an illegitimate spread of scientific objectivism"[32]. So, I think it is correct to say that to interpret "*Wahrheit und Methode* [...] as *Wahrheit versus Methode*" actually represents "a one-sided polarization" and "an excessive radicalization of Gadamer's theses"[33].

For all these reasons, I thus argue that, in Gadamer's case, it would be more precise to speak of *anti-scientistic* rather than *anti-scientific* philosophy, scientism being describable as "an exaggerated and often distorted conception of what science can be expected to do or explain for us"[34]. In this perspective, I think, what Gadamer writes in the *Nachwort zur 3. Auflage* of his masterpiece is reasonable: na-

---

29 Gadamer 1984b, p. 232.
30 Gadamer 1995c, p. 121. Analogous remarks can be found in HÄP, pp. 14-17 [GC, pp. 40-42].
31 Gadamer 1991c.
32 MET, p. 64.
33 Gentili 1996, p. 33. By the way, Jean Grondin has pointed out that *Wahrheit und Methode* is not even the original title of the book, in the sense that "the book was originally to be called *Fundamentals of a Philosophical Hermeneutics*. Gadamer's publisher found the title somewhat exotic. [...] So Gadamer decided to make the original title the subtitle. [...] At that time Gadamer considered the title *Event and Understanding*, which he perhaps rejected because of its similarity to a title of Bultmann's (*Belief and Understanding*). Only during the printing did the new, Goetheske title, *Truth and Method* occur to him" (Grondin 1992-93, p. 73 [1995, pp. 37-38]).
34 Dupré 2001, p. 1.

mely, that "it was, of course, a flat misunderstanding when people accused the expression 'truth and method' of failing to recognize the methodical rigor of modern science", since nobody "can really doubt that methodical purity is indispensable in science"[35]. "What hermeneutics legitimates", he claims, "is something completely different", which "stands in no tension whatever with the strictest ethos of science": that is, hermeneutics legitimates the simple fact that "what constitutes the essence of research is much less merely applying the usual methods than discovering new ones" by means of "the creative imagination of the scientist"[36]. As Josef Bleicher has noticed, "by referring to the universality of the hermeneutic experience", Gadamer aims at overcoming "scientistic restrictions of knowledge", emphasizing that "the understanding taking place in science represents only one segment of the basic understanding that underlies all our activities and which contains conditions of truth preceding those of the logic of science"[37]. As a matter of fact, from a hermeneutic point of view,

> Methodically derived experiences [...] are abstracted from the totality of human existence and are characterized by their indifference towards capturing the essence of things through qualitative determinations. Such an approach to "things" underlies methodical science, which concerns itself with phenomena that can be objectified and controlled by a, seemingly, autonomous subject. Scientistic conceptions, of course, regard this kind of experience as the only legitimate one [...]. Science follows the laws of its subject-matter and can only be judged in relation to that. When it transgresses its legitimate sphere of activity – that of objectifiable objects – and when it usurps the role of purveyor of all truth, hermeneutic consciousness will assert the legitimacy of a discipline of questioning and inquiry in which the methods of science cannot take hold; and it will re-affirm the fact that method cannot guarantee truth, but only secure degrees of certainty about controllable processes[38].

---

35 GW 2, p. 449 [TM, p. 555].
36 GW 2, p. 449 [TM, p. 555].
37 Bleicher 1980, pp. 118-119.
38 Bleicher 1980, pp. 118 and 120.

This, in turn, seems to confirm my previous suggestion that Gadamer probably represents an *anti-scientistic* thinker, but surely not an *anti-scientific* one.

Now, this last difference might perhaps appear as a subtle and inessential one; however, I think that it is actually of decisive importance, unless one does not want to enlist among the so-called "enemies" of modern science thinkers like, for example, Hilary Putnam or John McDowell. The former claims indeed that at least "part of the problem with present day philosophy is a *scientism* inherited from the nineteenth century – a problem that affects more than one intellectual field" and that prevents giving "a sane and human description of the scope of reason"[39]. While according to the latter "the presumably deep-rooted block that produces [the] uncomfortable situation" of modern thought – which is suspended, in McDowell's view, between the two equally unsatisfactory positions of "rampant Platonism" and "bald naturalism" – lies in a kind of *scientism* that "tends to represent itself as educated common sense, but […] is really only primitive metaphysics"[40].

As the examples of Putnam and McDowell clearly show, it is thus possible to criticize scientism, i.e. the "absolutism" of scientific knowledge, without for this reason aiming to abandon the secure path of method or to return to the "common mediaeval outlook", according to which "what we now see as the subject matter of natural science

---

39 Putnam 1981, p. 126 (my italics). I borrow the idea of such a possible comparison of Gadamer and Putnam from Richard Rorty's interesting essay *Being That Can Be Understood Is Language* (Rorty 2004, pp. 21-22). At the same time, however, it must be noticed that Putnam seems to reject any comparison with Rorty himself, whom he accuses of shifting from a correct critique of scientism to "a relativist" and finally "deconstructionist position" (Putnam 1992, p. 108). "Relativism à la Rorty", Putnam says, "is rhetoric" (Putnam 1992, p. 71). Furthermore, in his book *Pragmatism. An Open Question* Putnam critically hints at Gadamer too, presenting his hermeneutics as nothing more than an "unsuccessful" theory of the "contrast between fact and interpretation" (Putnam 1995, p. 62) – which, in my opinion, is a reductive and largely unsatisfactory account of Gadamer's philosophy.

40 McDowell 1996, pp. 69 and 82.

was conceived as filled with meaning, as if all of nature were a book of lessons for us"[41]. It is indeed "a mark of intellectual progress that educated people cannot now take that idea seriously, except perhaps in some symbolic role"[42]. But this, in my opinion, seems to perfectly match Gadamer's own view of present day philosophical and scientific problems.

As a matter of fact, Gadamer surely thinks that the typically modern "naive faith in scientific method" that "denies the existence of effective history", and so causes "an actual deformation of knowledge"[43], must be contrasted. At the same time, however, he does not even hint at the possibility of weakening the importance and validity of the modern scientific enterprise, leveling the distinctions between scientific and non-scientific knowledge (although he obviously aimed at reassessing the latter's autonomous significance), or perhaps returning to ancient, outdated explanation schemes. For example, explanation schemes according to which "fire moves upwards because it is at home there with the shining stars", or "a stone falls because that

---

41 McDowell 1996, p. 71.
42 McDowell 1996, p. 71. McDowell probably represents one of the most relevant cases of analytic philosophers who are really interested in Gadamer's hermeneutics and even draw inspiration from him. In fact, in the last chapter of his groundbreaking work *Mind and World* McDowell explicitly says he borrows "from Hans-Georg Gadamer a remarkable description of the difference between a merely animal mode of life, in an environment, and a human mode of life, in the world" (McDowell 1996, p. 115). McDowell refers here to, and directly quotes from, the section of *Wahrheit und Methode* on language as experience of the world, where Gadamer distinguishes animal from human forms of life and, accordingly, the concept of *Umwelt* (environment) from that of *Welt* (world) (see GW 1, pp. 446-456 [TM, pp. 440-448]). However, as I have tried to show in a recent essay (Marino 2011b), what McDowell calls "Gadamer's thesis", or "Gadamer's account of how a merely animal life, lived in an environment, differs from a properly human life, lived in the world" (McDowell 1996, pp. 115 and 117), is actually not an original Gadamerian insight, since he, in turn, borrows the distinction between *Umwelt* and *Welt* from German biologists and philosophers like Üxkull, Scheler and Gehlen (see GW 1, pp. 448 note and 455 [TM, pp. 489 note and 448]).
43 GW 1, p. 306 [TM, p. 300].

is where all other stones are and it belongs there"[44] – which is precisely what McDowell calls "Aristotle's innocence" and "mediaeval superstition"[45].

Given all this, I think that the idea of Gadamer as an irreducible enemy of science and technology can be definitively put aside. Rather, what he strongly and consistently criticizes is the fact that, in modernity, techno-science has veritably become the fundamental and undisputed *forma mentis* of our whole civilization, i.e. something that sometimes appears as a sort of new "ideology". As we read at the end of the essay *Bürger zweier Welten*, the errors of our technological civilization are caused "not so much by human beings as such, and not by science, and not through science, but by the superstitious faith in science held in modern society"[46]. In this context, Gadamer unequivocally speaks of "new [scientific] dogma"[47], "technological dreams (*technologische Träume*)" and "intoxications by technocratic frenzy (*Berauschungen des technokratischen Taumels*)"[48] as basic features of our age. An age "credulous about science to the point of superstition"[49]. So I think it is no surprise if Gadamer's hermeneutic effort, "in the context of the philosophy of science and technology", has been interpreted as having "an essentially critical and even demythologizing function"[50].

Another element which is surely of great importance in this context is that of the peculiar form of rationality that the modern techno-scientific civilization endorses. We encounter here a topic which has been highly relevant for the whole twentieth-century philosophy, namely that concerning the so-called "calculative thinking (*rechnendes Denken*)" or "instrumental reason (*instrumentelle Ver-*

---

44   EE, p. 17 [EPH, p. 226].
45   McDowell 1996, p. 109. On this topic, let me remind the reader of my paper on Gadamer and McDowell *Seconda natura, libertà e corporeltà* (Marino 2011c).
46   GW 10, p. 236 [EPH, p. 219].
47   LT, p. 158 [PT, p. 130].
48   GW 10, p. 313.
49   GW 2, p. 450 [TM, p. 556].
50   Fehér 1999, p. 8.

nunft)". As is well known, the first concept is a somehow original coinage of Martin Heidegger, who sees in the modern age the triumph of "*ratio* [as] calculus, reckoning", of "reason [as] an account", and then emphatically invites us not to "give up what is worthy of thought in favor of the recklessness of exclusively calculative thinking and its immense achievements", but rather to "find paths upon which thinking is capable of responding to what is worthy of thought"[51]. The second concept, instead, is mostly ascribable to the philosophical and sociological production of the Frankfurt School, although its origins can probably be found in Max Weber's concept of "purposeful" or "goal-oriented" rational action (*Zweckrationalität*)[52], and György Lukács' theory of the reification of human existence in modern society[53], both of which had a strong influence on Horkheimer, Adorno and many other thinkers.

In what is probably the founding text of the Frankfurt School, *Dialektik der Aufklärung*[54], the question of instrumental reason is presented and delineated as an inquiry into "the tireless self-destruction of enlightenment" and "the destructive side of progress"[55], while in *Eclipse of Reason* Horkheimer directly copes with "the concept of rationality that underlies our contemporary industrial cul-

---

51 Heidegger 1997b, pp. 155, 174 and 189 [1996, pp. 103, 119 and 129].
52 As is well known, in the first chapter of his posthumous treatise *Wirtschaft und Gesellschaft* Weber explains indeed that "social action, like all action, may be oriented in four ways. It may be: 1) *instrumentally rational* (*zweckrational*) [...]; 2) *value-rational* (*wertrational*) [...]; 3) *affectual* (especially emotional) [...]; 4) *traditional*" (Weber 1972, p. 12 [1978, pp. 24-25]).
53 See Lukács 1968, in particular pp. 257-397 [1971, pp. 83-222].
54 For a defence of this thesis, let me remind the reader of the first chapter of my book *Un intreccio dialettico* (Marino 2010b, pp. 17-51). As a support to my opinion on the centrality of *Dialektik der Aufklärung* for the whole development of the Frankfurt School, let me simply mention here Rolf Wiggershaus' influential interpretation of "*Eclipse of Reason* [as] Horkheimer's 'Dialectic of Enlightenment'", "*Eros and Civilization* [as] Marcuse's 'Dialectic of Enlightenment'", and "*Negative Dialectics* [as] Adorno's continuation of *Dialectic of Enlightenment*" (Wiggershaus 1986, pp. 384-390, 553-565 and 663-675 [1995, pp. 344-350, 496-507 and 597-609]).
55 Horkheimer and Adorno 2003, pp. 11 and 13 [2002, pp. XIV and XVI].

ture"[56]. Here he points out the "profound change of outlook that has taken place in Western thinking in the course of the last centuries", and that he interprets as a subjectivization and formalization of reason, that is, as a transformation of reason into the mere "ability to calculate probabilities and thereby to co-ordinate the right means with a given end"[57]. Hence, Horkheimer stigmatizes today's replacement of "truth [with] calculability", the "triumph of the means over the end", and the "reduction of reason to a mere instrument": something that, on the whole, has led to an "abasement of reason" and "a state of irrational rationality"[58].

Now, Gadamer's affinity and perhaps even indebtedness to Heidegger and his concept of calculative thinking is clear and undisputed, although I think that Gadamer, given his fundamental criticism of Heidegger's being-historical perspective, has finally developed this theme in a different direction to that of his teacher[59]. Namely, in the direction of a rehabilitation of practical reason and, in particular, of the Aristotelian virtue of the *phronesis*, which he always

---

56 Horkheimer 2004, p. V.
57 Horkheimer 2004, p. 4.
58 Horkheimer 2004, pp. 30-31, 37 and 61.
59 On the resemblances and differences between Heidegger's and Gadamer's philosophies, and on their different relationship with the whole tradition of Western metaphysics, see, for instance, Donadio 2002 and Gentili 2006. According to Martin Kusch, Gadamer's ideas on language are "freed from Heidegger's *Geschick*", since he "does not make the history of Being part and parcel of his philosophy of language" (Kusch 1989, pp. 242-243), while John D. Caputo writes: "Gadamer's thought is historical, but it is not Being-historical, not thought in the terms of the *Geschick*, of Being's sending-withdrawal. It is historical but not epochal, for it does not see the *epoché* of the *Seinsgeschick* in any given epoch. [...]. His is a kind of Heideggerianism without the scandal of the *Ereignis* and the play of the epochs" (Caputo 1987, pp. 114-115). See also Gadamer's critical stand against Heidegger's concept of *Geschick* in the 1986 interview *Historicism and Romanticism*: "Heidegger in his later years [...] introduced a kind of necessity into his ideas [...]. But the poeticizing mode of speech used by the later Heidegger, when he spoke of *Geschick* and the like – that bothered me. It made it easy to raise the charge of mythological thinking against him" (Gadamer 1992d, pp. 127-128).

interpreted as reasonableness (*Vernünftigkeit*); whereas the later Heidegger rather tends to oppose modern calculative thinking to an original form of contemplation, meditation or detachment (*Gelassenheit*). So, for example, in his writing actually entitled *Gelassenheit* Heidegger explains that there are

> two kinds of thinking [...]: calculative thinking and meditative thinking. [...] Calculative thinking computes. [...] This calculation is the mark of all thinking that plans and investigates. [...] We depend on technical devices [but] suddenly and unaware we find ourselves so firmly shackled to these technical devices that we fall into bondage to them. Still we can act otherwise. [...] Therefore, the issue is the saving of man's essential nature. Therefore, the issue is keeping meditative thinking alive[60].

In addition to this, I also think that some relevant affinities between Gadamer's critique of techno-scientific rationality and the Frankfurt School's critique of instrumental reason actually exist. Not by chance, Gadamer himself has sometimes pointed out the nearness of "the eclipse of reason, the increasing forgetfulness of being (*Seinsvergessenheit*)", and "the tension between truth and method"[61]. For example, in the essay *Mythos und Vernunft* he diagnoses with a perfect Frankfurter-style critical accent the present day "devaluation of the concept of reason (*Abwertung des Begriffs von Vernunft*)", explaining that

> sie [*scil.* die Vernunft] ist nicht mehr das Vermögen der absoluten Einheit, nicht mehr das Vernehmen der letzten unbendigten Zwecke, sondern vernünftig heißt nunmehr die Findung der rechten Mittel zu gegebenem Zwecke, ohne daß die Vernünftigkeit dieser Zwecke selbst ausgewiesen wäre. Die Rationalität des modernen Zivilisationsapparates ist daher in ihrem letzten Kerne eine rationale Unvernunft, eine Art Aufstand der Mittel gegen die beherrschenden Zwecke – kurz, die Freisetzung dessen, was wir auf allen Lebensgebieten Technik nennen[62].

---

60 Heidegger 2000b, pp. 520, 526 and 529 [1966, pp. 46, 53-54 and 56].
61 GW 2, p. 251.
62 GW 8, p. 167.

What Gadamer sees is thus a connection between the "overbearing scientism (*herrschender Szientismus*)" that characterizes our epoch and the "erroneous reduction of reason to technological rationality (*falsche Verkürzung der Vernunft auf technische Rationalität*)"[63]. Specifically dedicated to these questions is the 1979 essay *Rationalität im Wandel der Zeiten*, in which he moves from the Greek concept of *logos* and attempts to clarify "how the idea of rationality was developed in Greek thought and how 'rationality', in alliance with the developing science, [...] has defined its place among all philosophical concepts"[64]. Hence, Gadamer explains that Galilei's original use of "the rational potential of mathematics for the experimental way of research", and his creation of "a new science [...] in the realm of the contingent, observable and quantifiable", actually was "a revolutionary event in the history of human knowledge, and represented a new form of rationality"[65]. From this point of view, Gadamer argues that

> In the age of science which is ours today, it became a prevailing tendency [...] to recognize no other form of rationality than the rationality of critical-scientific method – and at its best the general rationality of solving problems by trial and error [...]: one sees Rationality in the context of science and confined within its limits. But now, it was exactly this form of rationality achieved by the sciences, which was to push the process of the rationalisation of the world of human labor and of social life into that extreme which characterises the industrial and technological age. As a matter of fact rationality is here reduced to the rationality of the means towards the end, which themselves are given as self-evident. That is a gigantic process, Reduction and Expansion in the same moment, and with the consequence, that all that cannot be reached by rationalisation through the sciences remains a pure relict, which must be surrendered to the irrationality of decisions by moral or religious faith, and loses in any case every rational justification[66].

What Gadamer points out, then, is the fact that such a rationalized and techno-scientific worldview seems to lead today to "a rational system

---

63 GW 4, pp. 67 and 61.
64 GW 4, p. 23 [Gadamer 1979, p. 3].
65 GW 4, p. 27 [Gadamer 1979, p. 6].
66 GW 4, pp. 29-30 [Gadamer 1979, pp. 8-9].

of well-balanced world-administration", which "may be able itself to produce the type of man needed, a man completely adapted to the technological ideal of rational administration and regulation"[67].

On this basis I think it becomes more understandable why, in Gadamer's view of "the tragic fate of our modern civilization", the critical condition in which we find ourselves today basically derives from "science and the technical application of scientific knowledge", which have led to "a domination of the natural world to an unparalleled extent"[68]. As a matter of fact, far from being a prerogative of the so-called "enemies" of science, these critical views and opinions have actually been shared by many thinkers who are not "suspect" to hard feelings, so to speak, against science and technology. Just to mention a few examples, let us think of Bertrand Russell's 1924 essay *Icarus, or The Future of Science*, with its distrust of the capacity of human beings to take real advantage of the benefits of science, and its gloomy foreshadowing of big troubles and perhaps even catastrophes as a result of techno-scientific achievements. Or, still, taking a leap forward of about seventy years, let us recall Edgar Morin's influential idea that

> Notre devenir est plus que jamais animé par la double dynamique du développement des sciences et du développement des techniques qui s'entrenourissent l'un l'autre [...]. Ainsi, la techno-science mène le monde depuis un siècle. [...] La foi en la mission providentielle de la techno-science a nourri la certitude du progrès, les grandioses espérances du développement futur. La techno-science n'est pas seulement la locomotive de l'ère planétaire. Elle a envahi tous les tissus des sociétés développées [...]. Elle a opéré ses *crackings* sur la pensée en lui imposant disjonctions et réductions. La techno-science est ainsi noyau et moteur de l'agonie planétaire[69].

According to Gadamer, in view of the modern tendency to reduce all knowledge to scientific knowledge and all reason to technical-instrumental rationality, the right thing to do is not to deny the value and

---

67 GW 4, p. 30 [Gadamer 1979, p. 9].
68 ÜVG, pp. 130-131 [EH, pp. 100-101].
69 Morin and Kern 1993, pp. 101-102.

importance of science and technology, which are fully justified and needed in their own way. Rather, like the Italian philosopher Enrico Berti noticed, what Gadamer aims at is to revaluate the plurality of the "ways of reason", in order to "outline an alternative to scientific rationality", without at the same time falling into the post-Nietzschean "global crisis of reason"[70].

In this connection, it is worthy of notice that Gadamer has often distanced himself from the so-called "hermeneutics of suspicion", which has played an important role in the twentieth-century philosophy. So, in the essay *The Conflict of Interpretations*, he explains that "it was mainly Nietzsche that brought about [a] new style of interpretation", namely one which aims at "unmasking *pretended* meaning and signification. [...] Then of course both the critique of ideology and psychoanalysis call for the same new sense of interpretation"[71]. Given this, however, Gadamer asks: "how can we hope to reconcile this radicalism of interpretation as unmasking with an attitude of participation in a cultural heritage which forms and transforms itself in a process of mediation?"[72], i.e. with the kind of hermeneutics precisely presented in *Wahrheit und Methode*? "In posing this question", Gadamer says, "we are confronted by the two extremes" represented on the one side by "interpretation in the Nietzschean sense that refers to any form of interpretation as was practiced by Marx or by Freud", while on the other side "there is the experience of life in communicative processes, the actual working out of daily life, where communication [...] structures the whole of social reality and encompasses the cultural features of this reality"[73]. Any-

70 Berti 1987, pp. 28-29 and 17.
71 Gadamer 1982a, p. 299.
72 Gadamer 1982a, p. 301.
73 Gadamer 1982a, p. 303. The same idea is confirmed, for instance, in the essay *The Hermeneutics of Suspicion*, where Gadamer moves from Paul Ricoeur's famous opposition of "hermeneutics in the classic sense of interpreting the meaning of texts" and "radical critique of and suspicion against understanding and interpreting. This radical suspicion", he says, "was inaugurated by Nietzsche and had its most striking instances in the critique of ideology on the one hand and of psychoanalysis on the other". According to Gadamer, "the dichotomy of

way, according to Gadamer "going behind, unmasking [...] is something besides communication", and "the preeminent model" always remains that of "the *dialogue*", which we must assume as "the basis of our social life" and intend as "sharing in a social act"[74]. "In this sense", Gadamer concludes, "even the conflict of interpretations could have a resolution. For the critique of ideologies, psychoanalysis, and every radical form of critique should be and needs to be reintegrated into [the] basic process of social life"[75].

Actually, one of the basic reasons for the famous 1981 Parisian controversy between Gadamer and Derrida is probably to be found here. As a matter of fact, the latter challenged Gadamer's "absolute commitment to the desire for consensus in understanding", his "axiomatic precondition of interpretive discourse which [he] calls *Verstehen*" and intends as the basis "for any community of speakers, even regulating the phenomena of disagreement and misunderstanding"[76]. More precisely, what Derrida questioned was Gadamer's "appeal to good will", claiming that even behind the good will to understand the other, there is probably a Nietzschean will to power secretly concealed, and, more in general, that such a "way of speaking, in its very necessity, belong[s] to a particular epoch, namely, that of a metaphysics of the will"[77]. But Gadamer, for his part, simply replied by admitting he found "it difficult to understand [the] questions that ha[d] been addressed to [him]", and ironically adding: "I am hoping he [*scil*. Derrida] will excuse me if I try to understand him"[78]! Then, he said that by good will he only meant an attitude which is "essential [...] for any understanding at all to come about",

---

the belief in the integrity of texts and the intelligibility of their meaning, and the opposed effort to unmask the pretentions hidden behind so-called objectivity [...] is too sharp to allow us to rest content with a mere classification of the two forms of interpretation", and there is "no way of reconciling the two" (Gadamer 1984a, 54 and 58).

74 Gadamer 1982a, pp. 303-304.
75 Gadamer 1982a, p. 304.
76 Derrida 1984, pp. 341 and 343 [1989, pp. 52-53].
77 Derrida 1984, pp. 341-342 [1989, pp. 52-53].
78 Gadamer 1984e, pp. 59 and 61 [DDGD, pp. 55 and 57].

since it is evident that "whoever opens his mouth wants to be understood; otherwise, one would neither speak nor write"[79]. So, according to him, "this is not at all a kind of metaphysics, but the presupposition that any partner in a dialogue must assume, including Derrida", who speaks and writes "in order to be understood"[80]. In other words, for Gadamer

> dialogue is neither a manifestation of subjectivity nor a true philosophical beginning. In conversation the intentions of the interlocutors renounce to their fullness to achieve reciprocal understanding. Furthermore dialogue does not make any philosophical claim; it is not a beginning, but it is the natural premise, the zero degree of any understanding. Any conversation is based on a "good will to understand each other", which is not metaphysically determined as a transcendental of communication[81].

Anyway, with regard to the aforementioned question of the "essence" of rationality and its destiny in the age of techno-science, I think that Gadamer's "modest" proposal, in the end, consists in emphasizing the fact that "human reason occurs in manifold forms", such as "our experience of the world by language, [...] works of art", and in some sense even "the religious tradition"[82]. "All that", he says in the final lines of the essay *Rationalität im Wandel der Zeiten*, "originates from the one

---

79 Gadamer 1984e, p. 59 [DDGD, p. 55].
80 Gadamer 1984e, pp. 60-61[DDGD, pp. 56-57]. On the same topic, see also Gadamer's remarks in HÄP, pp. 43-44 [GC, pp. 61-62], in which we read: "The question is whether Derrida is capable of engaging in a genuine conversation. It could be that the character of his thinking excludes this. Still, he has a speculative mind, and for this reason I have sought to engage him as a real conversation partner [...]. Derrida's incapacity for dialogue [is] manifest. Dialogue is not his strength. His strength is in the artful spinning of a yarn further and further, with unexpected new aspects and surprising reversals".
81 Ferraris 1997, p. 283 [1996, p. 185]. In this context, it is surely worthy of notice that Gadamer, a few years later, has openly paid tribute to "Habermas' vorzügliche Derrida-Kritik in *Der philosophische Diskurs der Moderne*" (GW 2, p. 23 note): more precisely, to Habermas' critique of Derrida's critique of phonocentrism (see Habermas 1985, pp. 191-218 [1987, pp. 161-184]).
82 GW 4, p. 36 [Gadamer 1979, p. 14].

and unique excellence of man, to have reason"[83]. Similar remarks can also be found, for instance, at the end of the essay *Die Vielfalt der Sprachen und das Verstehen der Welt*, in which Gadamer, after having hinted at Max Weber's anticipation of "bureaucratization [as] the actual fate of our civilization (*das eigentliche Schicksal unserer Zivilisation*)", emphasizes the everlasting relevance of "being in conversation (*im Gespräch sein*)" and then claims:

> Ich möchte sagen, wir hätten damit einen besseren Begriff von Vernunft gewonnen. Das ist nicht etwas Irrationales, weil es freilich nicht nur Kalkulieren oder logisch zwingendes Schließen ist. Es ist im Gegenteil ein vielseitiger Anblick von Vernunft[84].

Now, this discourse leads us to one last point, namely that concerning Gadamer's attitude towards modern Enlightenment. As is indeed well known, after the famous debate with Habermas of the late 1960s/early 1970s, *Wahrheit und Methode* has often been read as an example of a radically anti-modern philosophical stance, or even as a mere expression of an anti-illuminist revaluation of prejudices and traditional customs. So, for example, at the time of the controversy on hermeneutics and ideology critique, Gadamer's hermeneutics was presented as a kind of conservatism based on the "hypostatization of the context of tradition (*Hypostasierung des Überlieferungszusammenhangs*)" and limited by the "already accepted and traditionally settled convictions of the socio-cultural life-world (*anerkannten und traditionell eingelebten Überzeugungen der soziokulturellen Lebenswelt*)"[85], or even as a "general devaluation of the Enlightenment (*generelle Abwertung der Aufklärung*)" which is actually "totally rejected (*in toto abgelehnt*)"[86]. Many years later, Terry Eagleton described Gadamer's philosophy as "a grossly complacent theory of history", according to which "tradition holds an authority to

---

83 GW 4, p. 36 [Gadamer 1979, p. 14].
84 GW 8, pp. 348-349.
85 Habermas 1971, pp. 153-154 and 157. For an overall and accurate reconstruction of the Gadamer-Habermas debate, see Nicholson 1991.
86 Bormann 1971, pp. 88 and 115.

which we must submit", and "past and present, subject and object, the *alien* and the *intimate* are [...] secretly coupled together by a Being which encompasses them both"[87]. According to Eagleton, Gadamer postulates indeed "beneath all history, silently spanning past, present and future", the existence of

> a unifying essence known as "tradition". [...] It might be as well to ask Gadamer whose and what "tradition" he actually has in mind. For his theory holds on the enormous assumption that there is indeed a single "mainstream" tradition [...] and that the prejudices which "we" (who?) have inherited from the "tradition" are to be cherished[88].

---

[87] Eagleton 1983, pp. 72-73 (my italics). That Gadamer's hermeneutics fails to do justice to the radical otherness of "the alien (*das Fremde*)" is also Bernard Waldenfels' claim, according to whom "in der Hermeneutik, wie sie bei Hans-Georg Gadamer ihren wirkkräftigsten Ausdruck gefunden hat, gibt der Versuch einer Überwindung des Fremden durch *Verstehen* zu der Gegenfrage Anlaß, ob nicht die radikale Fremdheit eben dadurch bestimmt ist, daß Fremdes *als solches* keinen Sinn hat, keiner Regel unterliegt und eben damit den hermeneutischen Zirkel sprengt. [...] Die entscheidende Frage lautet: Läßt sich das Fremde auf dem Boden der Hermeneutik bewältigen, oder ist dieses dazu angetan, die Hermeneutik selbst noch in Frage zu stellen? [...] Es gehört zu den Grundvoraussetzungen einer hermeneutischen Philosophie, daß Fremdheit nicht unüberwindlich ist. Es handelt sich lediglich um eine *relative Fremdheit für uns*, und nicht um eine *Fremdheit in sich selbst*. [...] So erscheint es nicht verwunderlich, daß Gadamer [...] die Überwindung der Fremdheit zur eigentlichen Aufgabe der Hermeneutik erklärt" (Waldenfels 1999, pp. 15-16, 67 and 71).

[88] Eagleton 1983, p. 72. According to still another scholar, Bernd Auerochs, "Gadamers Traditionsbegriff [ist] in sich widersprüchlich konzeptualisiert", and, above all, "Gadamer [denkt] das Überlieferungsgeschehen (bzw. die Wirkungsgeschichte) als Quasisubjekt": something which presupposes "daß das Überlieferungsgeschehen als Totalität, ja letztlich als Subjekt der Geschichte gedacht wird" (Auerochs 1995, p. 296). On the possible affinity between Gadamer's hermeneutic view of tradition and classical philosophies of history (an affinity which, in my opinion, should not be overestimated), see also Pannenberg 1963 and Schulz 1970. Gadamer, however, has clearly stated that his thesis "that the tradition poses questions and points the way to answers, in no way entails that the tradition is some kind of 'supersubject'" (HÄP, p. 30 [GC, p. 51]).

Thirty years after the publishing of the collection *Hermeneutik und Ideologiekritik*, a distinguished scholar such as Pascal Michon confirmed this line of interpretation, claiming that

> L'œuvre de Gadamer s'inscrit dans le mouvement *anti-Aufklärung* qui traverse la pensée européenne depuis le début du XIXe siècle et qui s'est encore accentué au cours du XXe. Et en cela elle n'est pas très originale. La plupart de ses thèmes ont déjà été développés de nombreuses fois avant elle. Sur le plan de la conaissance, elle reprend les vieilles critiques philosophiques, religieuses et parfois littéraires qui ont toujours contesté la pertinence du savoir des sciences de la nature, puis de sciences humaines. Sur le plan politique et éthique, Gadamer retrouve une position typique des milieux intellectuels conservateurs confrontés aux révolutions industrielles et à la démocratisation des sociétés européennes, positions qui voit dans la science et la technique des machines folles prêtes à tout asservir, qui dénie aux hommes toute capacité à faire leur histoire de manière rationelle, volontaire et donc démocratique, et qui en appelle finalement, contre tout ce qui est moderne, aux exemples grecs et médiévaux[89].

On this basis, I think that it is correct to say that "[depuis] la fin des années 1960 [...] la critique du conservatisme de Gadamer est devenue un lieu commun [...] – quoique Habermas ait plus tard grandement teméré ce jugement"[90]. As Brice Wachterhauser has noticed, indeed, ever since this moment Gadamer has always been "suspected of a reactionary politics", and such criticism has become "something approaching a new orthodoxy in some quarters", although

---

89 Michon 2000, pp. 11-12.
90 Ipperciel 2004, p. 610. As a matter of fact, in two writings appearing thirty years after his "cannonade" of ideology critique, Habermas has openly defined Gadamer as a *"liberalen* Geist", characterized by "eine bewundernswerte Unabhängigkeit des Urteils" (Habermas 2000, p. 53 [my italics]), whose *"liberal-konservative* Antwort [auf] die Frage, ob wir in der reflexiv gebrochenen Einstellung des inzwischen verbreiteten historischen Bewußtseins zu einer Weise der Traditionsaneignung zurückfinden können, die die Verbindlichkeit überzeugungskräftiger Traditionen unbeschädigt läßt", essentially differs from "die *konservativ-revolutionäre* Antwort Heideggers" (Habermas 2001a, p. 91 [my italics]).

"Gadamer's overtly political statements show him to be a strong advocate of parliamentary democracy"[91].

To be sure, the question of prejudices discredited by the Enlightenment, and their consequent rehabilitation as conditions of understanding as such, plays an important role in the second part of *Wahrheit und Methode*[92]. So, even though Gadamer later stated that "what Kant calls enlightenment in truth corresponds to what hermeneutics has in view"[93], it is not my intention to turn him into an Enlightenment thinker, at least not in the traditional sense. Nevertheless, I argue that the common view that Gadamer's "radical contrast to the Enlightenment" and "radical anti-Enlightenment views" are "central to his philosophizing"[94], and that his philosophical hermeneutics represents nothing more than "a late product of the 'romantic reaction to the Enlightenment' (*ein spätes Produkt der 'romantische[n] Reaktion gegen die Aufklärung'*)"[95] – I argue that such a view of Gadamer's philosophy is actually poor and inadequate. In fact, like Richard J. Bernstein points out, all those "critics (and defenders) of Gadamer [who] stress the conservative implications of philosophical hermeneutics" actually neglect "the latent radical strain implicit in Gadamer's understanding of hermeneutics as practical philosophy",

91 Wachterhauser 1999, pp. 45-46.
92 See GW 1, pp. 275-290 [TM, pp. 273-285].
93 Gadamer 1997a, p. 287.
94 Detmer 1997, p. 275.
95 Keuth 1998, p. 82. The last words of Keuth's sentence are taken indeed from the section of *Wahrheit und Methode* on the discrediting of prejudice by the Enlightenment, where Gadamer writes: "the criteria of the modern Enlightenment still determine the self-understanding of historicism. They do so not directly, but through a curious refraction caused by romanticism. This can be seen with a particular clarity in the fundamental schema of the philosophy of history that romanticism shares with the Enlightenment and that precisely through the romantic reaction to the Enlightenment became an unshakable premise: the schema of the conquest of *mythos* by *logos*. [Romanticism] shares the presupposition of the Enlightenment", namely that "of the progressive retreat of magic in the world", and "only reverses its values, seeking to establish the validity of what is old simply on the fact that it is old" (GW 1, pp. 277-278 [TM, p. 275]).

which lies "in his emphasis [...] on freedom and solidarity that embrace all of humanity"[96]. From this point of view, I think it is rather correct to say that "l'opposition de Gadamer à l'*Aufklärung* n'est pas absolue, contrairement à ce que laisse supposer Habermas. [...] Refusant l'objectivisme, elle [*scil.* l'herméneutique] ne s'identifie pas à un retour romantique à la tradition"[97]. Even more clearly, in the essay *Hermeneutics, Critical Theory and Deconstruction* Bernstein has noticed that

> Gadamer does not reject the idea of emancipation. He even agrees that it is implicit in Reason itself [and] intrinsic in hermeneutic understanding. [...] Gadamer has always been critical of what he takes to be the *excesses* of the Enlightenment. [...] In the development of his philosophical hermeneutics, Gadamer emphasizes the role of the tradition in determining who we are. [...] Gadamer is sometimes criticized for engaging in a sentimental nostalgia for past traditions and epochs. But such a criticism is unwarranted for it misses the primary intention of philosophical hermeneutics. Gadamer has always insisted that we cannot but help to approach past history, traditions, and alien cultures with the questions that arise from our *own* horizon. We never escape from our own linguistic horizon. It is an illusion to think that we can bracket or suspend *all* our current prejudgements. [...] The basic imperative of philosophical hermeneutics is [...] to seek for a *fusion* of horizons in which we expand and deepen our own horizon. In this sense, all hermeneutical understanding involves a *critical* appropriation. [...] It is not a nostalgic return that Gadamer advocates, but rather a critical appropriation for our current situation[98].

---

96 Bernstein 1983, p. 163.
97 Fleury 1993, pp. 358-359. On this topic, see also Ingrid Scheibler's interesting remarks: "Habermas interprets Gadamer's account of tradition as an hypostatization of existing traditions. He believes that Gadamer [...] merely restricts the scope of hermeneutical reflection to the horizon of prevailing conditions and to the prejudiced character of the individual's own situated standpoint. [...] Had Habermas had less of a reflex reaction, the modernist's jerk of the knee when hearing the words authority and tradition, he may have perceived – long before an almost caricatured presentation of Gadamer had taken root – that Gadamer, like himself, upholds the principles of dialogue and communication" (Scheibler 2000, p. 2).
98 Bernstein 2002, pp. 271-273.

In this context, I guess it should also be noticed that, a few years later, Gadamer has openly recognized the provoking nature inherent to the formula "rehabilitation of authority and tradition"[99]. Moreover, on various occasions Gadamer explains that "tradition is not the vindication of what has come down from the past but the further creation of moral and social life"[100], and that the abovementioned formula was not meant at all to legitimate "the stubborn clinging to prejudices or even the blind appeal to authority", which in fact are "nothing but the laziness to think"[101].

By the way, already in *Wahrheit und Methode* tradition was described as an intrinsically dynamic "entity", or better "event", rather than a static, unchanging one. As we read in the section on the hermeneutic significance of temporal distance, tradition is indeed "not simply a permanent precondition", but something that "we produce [...] ourselves inasmuch as we understand, participate in the evolution of tradition, and hence further determine it ourselves"[102]. It is thus "a momentous misunderstanding" when the rehabilitation of tradition and prejudices "is taken to express [...] a defense of the *status quo*"[103]. As he reiterates in his interviews with Carsten Dutt on hermeneutics, aesthetics and practical philosophy:

> The idea that authority and tradition are something one can appeal to for validation is a pure misunderstanding. Whoever appeals to authority and tradition will have no authority. Period. The same thing goes for prejudgments.

---

99 As we read already in the 1966 essay *Die Universalität des hermeneutischen Problems*, that "it is not so much our judgments as it is our prejudices that constitute our being [...] is a provocative formulation", which "certainly does not mean that we are enclosed within a wall of prejudices and let through the narrow portals those things that can produce a pass saying, 'Nothing new will be said here'" (GW 2, p. 224 [GR, p. 82]).
100 GW 2, p. 470 [TM, p. 574]. An interesting and original reading of Gadamer's hermeneutic conception of tradition in the sense of a "phenomenology of the appropriation of tradition (*Phänomenologie der Traditionsaneignung*)" is that provided by Theunissen 2001.
101 Gadamer 1997a, p. 287.
102 GW 1, p. 298 [TM, p. 293].
103 GW 2, p. 470 [TM, p. 574].

Anyone who simply appeals to prejudices is not someone you can talk with. Indeed, a person who is not ready to put his or her own prejudices in question is also someone to whom there is no point in talking[104].

It should also be noticed that Gadamer's concept of *Aufklärung* is probably more complex than is usually acknowledged – something which, in turn, makes the relation or "constellation" of philosophical hermeneutics, science and Enlightenment definitely more complex that is often assumed to be. As a matter of fact, on various occasions he says that beside the "narrower sense of 'Enlightenment' [that] has been used to conceptualize a historical period, the eighteenth century"[105], it is also possible to give this concept a broader meaning. For this reason, he distinguishes two or even three different phases or figures in the whole history of the Western illuminist civilization.

So, for example, in his 1971 review of Jürgen Mittelstrass' book *Neuzeit und Aufklärung*[106] Gadamer makes positive reference to the latter's distinction between a first and a second Enlightenment. Mittelstrass, he explains, "unterscheidet eine erste und eine zweite Aufklärung, die griechische von Thales bis Platon und Aristoteles, und die mit Galilei beginnende Aufklärung der Neuzeit"[107]. In addition to this, Mittelstrass "verficht die These, daß es eine schlechte Aufklärung gewesen sei, die im neuzeitlichen Denken die praxisfremde Theorie und die immanente technische Rationalität absolut gesetzt habe"[108]. And the overall aim of the author – which Gadamer seems to share, although in his review he takes a critical stance to some specific interpretations given by Mittelstrass – is precisely "den

---

104 HÄP, p. 19 [GC, pp. 44].
105 LT, p. 90 [PT, p. 73].
106 See Mittelstrass 1970. In his review Gadamer mostly refers to the first three sections of the first part of Mittelstrass' book, respectively dedicated to the "Ancient (first) Enlightenment (*Antike [erste] Aufklärung*)", "The changed situation (*Die veränderte Lage*)", and the "Modern (second) Enlightenment (*Neuzeitliche [zweite] Aufklärung*)" (Mittelstrass 1970, pp. 15-132).
107 GW 4, p. 60.
108 GW 4, pp. 60-61.

Szientismus als eine falsche Verkürzung der Vernunft auf technische Rationalität [...] hinter sich [zu] lassen"[109].

Now, the very same question is at centre of the 1972 essay *Wissenschaft als Instrument der Aufklärung*. Here Gadamer moves from the claim that "in historical retrospect [...] we distinguish a first and a second Enlightenment", where the first one covers "the entire history of Greek thought stretching from Pythagoras to Hellenistic science", while the second one is obviously "the modern Enlightenment as including the whole, long development that began with the Copernican revolution in astronomy"[110]. He then dwells in particular on the "especially close connection with science" that characterizes "both of these enlightenments", stressing the profound differences between the ancient and modern concept of mathematics, experience and theory, and claiming that while the first Enlightenment (especially with the "leaders of Greek sophistic, such as Protagoras and Gorgias") finally "encouraged skepticism and doubt about all science", the second Enlightenment appealed "wholly to science"[111]. From this point of view, in the modern age "the role of science has been quite different" than what it was before, and this is particularly true of the twentieth century. A century in which, according to Gadamer, "all natural relationships have been fundamentally altered by the technical age's faith in science" that "governs through the society of experts" and is even "behind the global industrialization brought about by the world economy" and "behind the 'electronic war'"[112]. In Gadamer's view, in the twentieth century "the ever-widening movement of Enlightenment" has come to the point that it has become necessary to speak of "something new", i.e. of a "third Enlightenment" characterized by a veritable "faith in science" and a tendency of "technical thinking [...] to expand into a universal view of the world"[113].

109 GW 4, p. 61.
110 LT, pp. 88-89 [PT, pp. 71-72].
111 LT, pp. 89-91 [PT, pp. 72-73].
112 LT, pp. 91-92 [PT, pp. 74-75].
113 LT, pp. 97 and 91-92 [PT, pp. 79 and 74-75].

Finally, in the 1986 essay *Die dreifache Aufklärung* Gadamer resumes the whole question and emphatically claims: "Wir müssen drei Phasen [...] der abendländischen Geschichte der Aufklärung [...] unterscheiden: die griechische Aufklärung, die Aufklärung in der frühen Neuzeit und die Aufklärung unseres Jahrhunderts"[114]. In fact, he says, "mit der Katastrophe der Zweiten Weltkrieges und den ungeheuren Fortschritten der industriellen Technik, die ihr folgten, begann das Bewußtsein einer neuen dritten Aufklärung um sich zu greifen"[115]. This, in turn, has led to

> die Illusionen einer wissenschaftlichen Durchorganisation der menschlichen Gesellschaft [...]. Ich verkenne nicht, daß dies alles wiederum Organisationsformen einer wissenschaftlich-technisch bestimmten Gesellschaft sind, in der eine Denkweise herrscht, die der freien Urteilsbildung nicht günstig ist. [...] Das Schicksal der steigenden Unfreiheit, d.h. der steigenden Abhängigkeit von einer verfestigen Gesellschaftsapparatur, ist unleugbar. Gleichwohl bleibt, wo überhaupt Menschen leben, [...] ein Freiraum des Redens und des Hörens und damit – in noch so beschränktem Maße – die Bildung eigenen Urteils und die Ausbildung echter Solidaritäten. Keine wissenschaftliche Aufklärung in der Zukunft, keine vierte Welle der Aufklärung, wird die Wurzel dieses unseres Menschseins je ganz ausreißen können[116].

---

114 Gadamer 1986a, p. 227.
115 Gadamer 1986a, p. 229.
116 Gadamer 1986a, pp. 229 and 233. Quite interestingly, even another protagonist of contemporary thought, Hilary Putnam, has distinguished three varieties of Enlightenment (see Putnam 2005, pp. 89-108). According to him, indeed, "there was not just one single 'enlightenment', the Enlightenment with a capital 'E' that we associate with the seventeenth and eighteenth centuries, but *three* enlightenments", the first of which "is associated with Plato and Socrates", while the third is associated "with the name of John Dewey" (Putnam 2005, p. 5). Notwithstanding this basic difference in the definition of the three enlightenments, Gadamer and Putnam seem to agree with each other on one point, namely faith in the possibility (not, of course, the inevitability) of certain progress. In the last chapter I will try to show how Gadamer, too, has never surrended to postmodern "drifts" and never abandoned faith in the possibility of progress, reasonableness and freedom.

Now, what emerges from all these passages is the basic idea that, in a somehow paradoxical way, science, which actually represented for many centuries an important antidote to dogmatism and a vehicle for the demythologization of our beliefs, in our epoch has turned into a form of absolute authority, i.e. it has somehow been "dogmatized" and "mythologized". According to Gadamer, indeed, the scientific understanding of reality "compels it unilaterally to lay claim to every place and to leave no place unpossessed outside of itself", and this means that "today not metaphysics but science is dogmatically abused"[117]! As he already claimed in the 1957 essay *Was ist Wahrheit?*:

> Thanks to science we have been liberated from many prejudices and disabused of many illusions. Again and again the truth demands of science are such as to make untested prejudices questionable and in this manner we know better what is the case than we knew before. At the same time, however, it is the case for us that the further the procedures of science extend over everything that is, the more doubtful it becomes from the presuppositions of science whether the question of truth in its full scope will be allowed entry at all. We ask with concern how far it lies directly in the conduct of science that there are so many questions, the answers to which we must know, that it nevertheless forbids us. It forbids them, however, in that it discredits them, i.e. it declares them meaningless. For only that which satisfies its own methods of discovering and testing truth has meaning for science. [...] In fact, science has this in common with the zealot: because it always demands proof and gives proof, it is just as intolerant as he is. No one is as intolerant as he who wants to prove that what he says must be the truth. [...] Is science really, as it claims for itself, the last court of appeal and sole bearer of truth?[118]

To sum up, it thus seems that Gadamer, far from fostering nostalgic and indeed anachronistic hopes of returning to the past and restoring the *ancient* authority of traditions upon *modern* freedom of thought and research, rather aims at encouraging a new balance or equilibrium between science and technology on one side, and what we might call

---

117 VZW, p. 140 [RAS, p. 163].
118 GW 2, pp. 45-46 [Gadamer 1994b, pp. 34-35].

"the varieties of hermeneutic experience"[119] on the other. From this point of view, I think it becomes understandable why he often ascribes to hermeneutics "the truth of a corrective"[120], that is, the truth of a "demythologization of science" itself, and the "warning before all illusions of mastery and domination"[121].

In this context, hermeneutic reflection can play an important role to facilitate the awakening of a new "awareness concerning the limits of objectification in general", including those of "our instrumentally orientated thought" and "our instrumental reason": a question, the latter, that Gadamer considers essential for "the fate of our Western civilization as a whole", since "modern science with its ethos of achievement" has brought our responsibilities "to a critical point", "forcing Western culture towards a critical self-examination"[122]. Not by chance, a famous Gadamerian statement reads: "Philosophy is [always] enlightenment, but precisely also enlightenment with regard to its own dogmatism"[123], and to technological and scientific dogma-

---

119 This last expression is clearly modelled on the title of William James' classic of pragmatism *The Varieties of Religious Experience*.
120 GW 2, p. 448 [TM, p. XXXIV].
121 VZW, p. 124 [RAS, p. 150].
122 ÜVG, pp. 95-98 [EH, pp. 71-72].
123 GW 2, p. 492 [GR, p. 20]. On this basis, I think that it could be intriguing to establish a comparison between Gadamer and other twentieth-century theorists of what we might call "self-critical Enlightenment" – like, for example, Horkheimer and Adorno (2003, pp. 19-60 [2002, pp. 1-34]), the later Foucault of *What is Enlightenment?*, who praises the "critical interrogation on the present and on ourselves which Kant formulated by reflecting on the Enlightenment", and then proposes an ongoing "work on our limits, that is, a patient labor giving form to our impatience for liberty" (Foucault 1984, pp. 49-50), and perhaps even Habermas' concept of Enlightenment as a still uncompleted project of modernity (Habermas 1981a) –, notwithstanding the obvious and sometimes strong differences among them. From this point of view, I consider reasonable and correct Michael Kelly's insight into a possible "dialogue between the ethical theories of Gadamer, Foucault, and Habermas", which would consist "in a plurality of conflicting options concerning [...] the larger question of how to understand modernity. What unifies this plurality and quells the conflict to some degree, however, is the solidarity on the Enlightenment ideal of moral freedom,

tism too. So, I think it should be neither surprising nor shocking to see that Gadamer, in emphasizing the contribution that the Greeks' overall conception of being can still bring to our civilization, explicitly claims: "Im Zeitalter der beginnenden Erdherrschaft kann solches Bewußtsein der dem Menschen als solchen gesetzten Grenzen, wie es die Griechen lehrten, kaum als eine romantische Reaktion – eher als *eine neue Aufklärung* erscheinen"[124].

In the end, I thus argue that the philosophical project of Gadamer's hermeneutics does not consist of a unilateral and radical critique of Enlightenment as such, but rather represents an attempt to emphasize and amend the prejudices which have remained implicit and unthematized in modern Enlightenment itself. Most noticeably, it is the case of "the prejudice against prejudice itself, which denies tradition its power", and which, in Gadamer's view, actually represents the prejudice "that defines [the] essence [...] of the Enlightenment" and that even nineteenth-century "*historicism* [...] *unwittingly shares*"[125]. Hence it should come as no surprise that Gadamer has been defined (correctly, in my opinion) as "an *enlightened* conservative"[126], and that he himself has sometimes relied on the famous Kantian definition of Enlightenment as "*man's emergence from his self-incurred immaturity*", i.e. from "the inability to use one's own understanding without the guidance of another", due to "lack of resolution and courage"[127]. On this basis, Kant then turns the exhortation: "*Sapere aude!* Have courage to use your *own* understanding!", into the veritable "motto of enlightenment"[128], and it is precisely to these famous statements that Gadamer sometimes refers.

So, for example, in his reply to David Detmer's essay *Gadamer's Critique of the Enlightenment* he denies being an anti-illuminist think-

---

which Gadamer calls the highest principle of reason", and which "can only be enhanced by this dialogue" (Kelly 1995, pp. 234-235).
124 HE, p. 107.
125 GW 1, p. 275 [TM, pp. 272-273].
126 Figal 2002b, p. 83 (my italics).
127 Kant 1923, p. 33 [1991, p. 54].
128 Kant 1923, p. 33 [1991, p. 54].

er, and then claims to appeal "with Kant to practical reason and the practice of the faculty of judgment"[129]. In an even more explicit way, in the essay *Wissenschaft als Instrument der Aufklärung* Gadamer directly quotes the abovementioned answer of Kant's to the question: "What is Enlightenment?", and claims that mankind is still "shamefully immature today": in fact, "our prepossession with the technological dream and our obsession with emancipatory utopia [...] represent the prejudices of our time", from which "reflection, as the courage to think, needs to free us"[130]. "Our world is at an end if it keeps going on this way, as if it were always about to 'move forward'"[131], Gadamer pessimistically says. But then he adds that this must not lead us to resignation and defeatism; rather, we must understand that "what we really have to do is alter our consciousness", and it is in such a context that the Enlightenment – which "is still what it always was: it depends on judgment, on thinking for oneself and on cultivating these powers"[132] – can play a decisive role. So, Gadamer concludes: "the present-day sense of the Kantian slogan [...], '*Sapere aude* [...]', can be stated in a new way as the appeal to our social reason to awake from its technological dream"[133].

This is precisely where the contribution of philosophical hermeneutics comes in, with its attempt to restate, in the age of the full-blown domination of science and technology, the value of pre- and non-scientific aspects of human existence. Namely, the value of *all* the unmethodical aspects of our life, apropos of which Gadamer makes an observation which seems to fit perfectly with specific reference to the

---

129 Gadamer 1997a, p. 287. On this occasion, Gadamer says indeed that "it is extremely astonishing to [him] that [his] project of a philosophical hermeneutics [is] being discussed under the title 'critique of enlightenment' and not with reference to the idealist concept of the 'completed enlightenment' [...]. For what matters to us can only be the question whether a completed enlightenment which would dissolve all human predisposition and societal prejudices is an intelligible claim" (Gadamer 1997a, p. 287).
130 LT, p. 98 [PT, p. 79].
131 LT, p. 99 [PT, p. 80].
132 LT, pp. 100 and 102 [PT, pp. 81 and 83].
133 LT, p. 102 [PT, p. 83].

human sciences. At the end of the essay *Geschichtlichkeit und Wahrheit*, he asks indeed: "Wie erscheint es in den historischen Geisteswissenschaften?", and then answers:

> Man bekommt dann, etwa vom Wiener Kreis, zu hören, in den Geisteswissenschaften seien höchstens *zehn Prozent Wissenschaft*, und für den Begriff von Wissenschaftlichkeit, der im Wiener Kreis entwickelt worden ist, ist das wahrscheinlich noch etwas zu freundlich formuliert. Jedenfalls sind es *die anderen neunzig Prozent*, auf die wir für unser gemeinsames Leben und die menschliche Solidarität bauen. Sie eröffnen uns Gesprächsmöglichkeiten auf die Wahrheit hin, die der uns allen gemeinsame *Logos* ist, auch wenn nur zehn Prozent den Normen der Wissenschaftlichkeit genügen[134].

---

134 GW 10, p. 257 (my italics).

9. The Rehabilitation and Universalization of Practical Knowledge and Experience

In the previous chapters I have given an account of what we could define as the *pars destruens* of Gadamer's philosophy, that is, his strong (but, in my opinion, not one-sided or unwarranted) critique of the techno-scientific civilization. This critique is basically aimed at emphasizing the limits of the modern objectifying scientific enterprise, i.e. what Gadamer calls the limits of objectification. In fact, as Jean Grondin expresses it:

> es geht in seiner [*scil.* Gadamers] Hermeneutik [...] um die *Grenzen der Objektivierung* schlechthin. Das menschliche Verstehen, Verhalten, Fühlen hat vielleicht weniger mit Planen, Kontrolle und Bewusstheit zu tun, sondern weit mehr mit einem art-spezifischen Sich-Einfügen in die Ritualität des Lebens, in Traditionsformen, in ein Geschehen, das uns umgreift und das wir nur stammelnd begreifen können[1].

It is now time to analyze the *pars construens* of his philosophical hermeneutics, which basically consists of a rehabilitation of *all* those kinds of experiences and of that knowledge that seem to elude the control of scientific-methodical patterns. In short, such an unmethodical kind of experience consists of the fundamental hermeneutic phenomenon, i.e. understanding (*Verstehen*). This implies that, in Gadamer's view, the two concepts (experience and understanding) are tightly and perhaps even indissolubly linked[2].

---

1 Grondin 2001, p. 125.
2 This close connection has been stressed, among others, by Camera 1991 (p. 196) – according to whom "experiencing (*Erfahren*) develops into 'self-understanding', it becomes *Verstehen*"; by Teichert 1991 (p. 167) – who writes: "Die hermeneutische Wahrheit ist eine Wahrheit der Erfahrung [...]. Der hermeneutische Wahrheitsbegriff erscheint damit weitgehend kongruent mit dem Begriff des Verstehen"; by De Simone 1995 (p. 267) – who notices that "herme-

The starting point for an analysis of this question is the *Introduction* to *Wahrheit und Methode*, in which Gadamer explains that his investigations are focused on the "modes of experience that lie outside science": "modes of experience in which a truth is communicated that cannot be verified by the methodological means proper to science"; "experience[s] of truth" that transcend "the domain of scientific method"[3]. In fact, "the problem of hermeneutics", which is basically the problem of understanding, is "not merely a concern of science", but rather something that "goes beyond the limits of the concept of method as set by modern science", and that "belongs to human experience of the world in general (*menschliche Welterfahrung insgesamt*)"[4]. Gadamer's aim is then "to understand the variety of experiences – whether of aesthetic, historical, religious, or political consciousness", which appear irreducible to the procedures of science and technology: namely, experiences "of a unique kind, certainly different from [...] the knowledge of nature"[5].

Hence, the great ambition of his "universal hermeneutics" seems to be that of unifying, or better, of drawing together, a variety of different phenomena by interpreting them as different modes of hermeneutic experience, i.e. of "the phenomenon of understanding" that "pervades all human relations to the world (*alle menschlichen Weltbezüge*)"[6]. As James Risser has noticed, "the issue of a *philosophical*

---

neutic experience [...] consists precisely of the complex phenomenon of *understanding*"; by Honneth 2000 (pp. 309 and 311) – who claims that, in Gadamer's philosophy, "alles Verstehen die Struktur einer Erfahrung besitzt", his ultimate task being that of "den Erfahrungscharakter des hermeneutischen Verstehens nachzuweisen"; and, more recently, by Deniau 2009 (especially pp. 37-39 and 53-54).

3   GW 1, p. 1 [TM, p. XXI].
4   GW 1, p. 1 [TM, p. XX].
5   GW 1, pp. 104 and 103 [TM, pp. 85 and 84].
6   GW 1, p. 1 [TM, p. XX]. It must be noticed, however, that the universal character of Gadamer's hermeneutics is not to be confused with a claim for "absoluteness", which would contradict Gadamer's constant emphasis on the inescapable *"finitude of our [...] experience"* (GW 1, p. 461 [TM, p. 453]). In fact, "die universalistische Eigenart der Hermeneutik, die man ihre Tendenz zur

hermeneutics", for Gadamer, "is to identify at a fundamental level the operation that unites [...] the experiences of philosophy, art, and history as *experiences of truth* that extend beyond methodological considerations [...] as *experiences of understanding*"[7]. This has obviously led to the question of whether the hermeneutic problem, of which Gadamer confidently claims "the universality"[8], is really universal, despite the heterogeneity of its objects[9].

Anyway, what is important for our specific purposes is precisely the centrality acquired by the concept of experience (*Erfahrung*) in the context of such a philosophical discourse. In order to do justice to what is at stake in our unmethodical understanding – which, although "not concerned primarily with amassing verified knowledge, such as would satisfy the methodological idea of science", is also "concerned with knowledge and truth" – it is necessary indeed "to take the concept of experience more broadly"[10] than modern culture, so strongly influenced by science and technology, has done[11]. It is necessary, in

---

totalen Integration nennen könnte, ist [...] das genaue *Gegenteil* eines erneuerten *Absolutheitsanspruchs der Philosophie*" (Bubner 1971, p. 228). In other words, the hermeneutic claim for universality must not be confused "with totality. This does not concern an encyclopaedic collection of all that is knowable. That would only lead one back to the metaphysical concept of reason and so to the doctrine of the *intellectus infinitus*" (GW 8, p. 401 [Gadamer 2000, p. 152]).

7   Risser 2010, p. 6 (my italics).
8   See his 1966 essay precisely entitled *Die Universalität des hermeneutischen Problems* (GW 2, pp. 219-231 [PH, pp. 3-17]).
9   On this topic, see Weberman 2003 (p. 35), who tries "to elucidate [the] tension between universality and heterogeneity" that characterizes Gadamer's hermeneutics, "and to see if and how it can be resolved". Weberman's conclusion is that ultimately "the universality of hermeneutics is compatible with the heterogeneity of its objects".
10   GW 1, p. 1 and 103 [TM, pp. XX and 84].
11   To be precise, in saying that "it is necessary to take the concept of experience more broadly" than we usually do, Gadamer specifically refers to the Kantian account of knowledge and experience. Nevertheless, I think that Kant is assumed here as the most eminent representative of the basic tendencies which

other words, to understand experience not just as the relation of "an object that stands over against a subject for itself"[12], like the techno-scientific standard attitude somehow forces us to do. In fact, according to Gadamer, understanding and genuine experience are precisely characterized by the fact that "a 'subject' does not stand over against an 'object' or a world of objects. Rather something *plays* back and forth between the human being and that which he or she encounters in the world"[13].

The use of the term "play" is here of strategic significance, I think. Indeed, in the first and third parts of *Wahrheit und Methode* Gadamer adopts the concept of "play" or "game" (*Spiel*) as a clue to the explanation, respectively, of the specificity of aesthetic experience in comparison to aesthetic consciousness[14], and of the peculiarity and universality of language (*Sprache*), or better linguisticality (*Sprachlichkeit*), as the medium of hermeneutic experience and horizon of a hermeneutic ontology[15]. As we read in the second to last page of *Wahrheit und Methode*: "Language games (*Sprachliche Spiele*) exist where we, as learners – and when do we cease to be that? – rise to the understanding of the world (*Verständnis der Welt*)"[16]. Something which, by the way, cannot fail to remind us of the later Wittgenstein's seminal concept of "language-games (*Sprachspiele*)" that notoriously stands for "the whole, consisting of language and the actions into which it is woven"[17].

---

underlie the philosophy of the modern age, so that the meaning of Gadamer's sentence can be "generalized", so to speak.

12 GW 1, p. 108 [TM, p. 103].
13 HÄP, pp. 26-27 [GC, p. 49 (my italics)].
14 See GW 1, pp. 107-116 [TM, pp. 102-110].
15 See GW 1, pp. 387-409 and 442-494 [TM, pp. 385-406 and 436-484]. On the importance of the notion of play in the economy of Gadamer's whole thought, see the contributions of Qualizza 1992, Greisch 2000, Sonderegger 2000 (pp. 19-72), and Marino 2008.
16 GW 1, p. 493 [TM, p. 484].
17 Wittgenstein 1989, p. 241 [2003, p. 4]. On a few, but relevant, occasions Gadamer himself has pointed out the existence of a certain affinity between his own treatment of the notion of *Spiel* and Wittgenstein's concept of *Sprachspiele*

Now, in order to understand Gadamer's basic conception of experience it is necessary first to focus our attention on the section of *Wahrheit und Methode* dealing with the concept of experience and the essence of hermeneutic experience[18]. This section is actually a decisive one: according to Franco Bianco, it represents indeed "the centre of the investigation [...] in Gadamer's vast and many-sided philosophical work"[19], while Damir Barbarić has called it "das höchste Ergebnis von *Wahrheit und Methode* im Ganzen"[20]. By the way, looking back at his 1960 masterpiece Gadamer himself has claimed that "the section on experience takes on a systematic and key position in [his] investigation"[21], going so far as to define that section as "the centerpiece of the whole book"[22]. Now, this section is somehow divided into two parts, the first one concerning "the general structure of experience (*die allgemeine Struktur der Erfahrung*)"[23], and the second one being devoted to what Gadamer calls "hermeneutic experience (*hermeneutische Erfahrung*)"[24]. In my opinion, however, in his following writings, Gadamer has softened this distinction, and has rather focused his attention on the varieties of human experience and the way they all belong to the "hermeneutic" dimension of life, i.e. (as we will see) to the realm of *praxis* and *Lebenswelt*.

(see, for instance, GW 3, pp. 142-146 [PH, pp. 173-177]; GW 2, pp. 4-5, 110, 456 and 507; GW 10, pp. 107, 204 and 347). His use of the concept of *Sprachliche Spiele* already in *Wahrheit und Methode* is also interesting because at that time Gadamer did not yet know Wittgenstein's famous and posthumously published *Philophische Untersuchungen* (1953), which, together with Celan's poems and Derrida's early writings, actually represented the "important things [that] struck [him]" as he "paused to take a look at the world around [him]", after the completion of his "own project in philosophical hermeneutics" (GW 10, p. 149 [GR, p. 377]). For a comparison of Gadamer's and Wittgenstein's philosophies, see Arnswald 2002, Flatscher 2003, and Lawn 2004 (especially pp. 19-40).

18 GW 1, pp. 352-368 [TM, pp. 340-355].
19 Bianco 1992, p. 110.
20 Barbarić 2007, p. 213.
21 GW 2, p. 445 [TM, p. XXXII].
22 HÄP, p. 32 [GC, p. 53].
23 GW 1, pp. 352-363 [TM, pp. 341-352].
24 GW 1, pp. 363-368 [TM, pp. 352-355].

In any case, in the abovementioned section of *Wahrheit und Methode* Gadamer starts by observing that quite paradoxically "the concept of experience", notwithstanding its wide diffusion and its everyday usage, is "one of the most obscure we have"[25]. This situation, according to him, has precise and easily understandable causes, which basically consist in the fact that the concept of experience (as we have already seen in the second chapter) "plays an important role in the natural sciences in the logic of induction"; accordingly, since the seventeenth century this concept "has been subjected to an epistemological schematization that [...] truncates its original meaning"[26]. From this point of view, in Gadamer's opinion, "the main deficiency in theory of experience hitherto [...] is that it is entirely oriented toward science", i.e. it is wholly dominated by its "teleological aspect"[27]. This aspect, however, "is not the only possible"[28].

Gadamer also expresses this idea by saying that the concept of *experience*, in the modern age, was fundamentally reduced to that of the natural sciences' *experiment*: a transformation and a reduction for which he particularly "charges" Francis Bacon's *Novum Organum*, at the very "beginnings of modern scientific theory and logic"[29]. As Gadamer confirms more than thirty years after *Wahrheit und Methode*:

> Experience is, I think, the least well known concept in philosophy as a whole, and this is because the so-called sciences of experience (*Erfahrungswissenschaften*) took the experiment as their starting-point and made it a paradigm for experience. These sciences only grant space to an experience if they can obtain from it methodically guaranteed answers to questions. But on the whole, our life is not like this. Our lives are not lived according to scientifically

---

25 GW 1, p. 352 [TM, p. 341]. On the fact that we somehow live in the age of the "bulimia of experience", but, notwithstanding all this (or, rather, precisely because of this!), we actually ignore the real nature of human experience, see the interesting essay of Cattaneo 2011.
26 GW 1, p. 352 [TM, p. 341].
27 GW 1, pp. 352 and 355 [TM, pp. 341-342 and 344].
28 GW 1, p. 355 [TM, p. 344].
29 GW 1, p. 353 [TM, p. 343].

guaranteed programs and secure from crises; rather, we have to undergo our experiences ourselves[30].

As we also read in the 1994 essay *Hermeneutik auf der Spur*:

> In the sciences, of course, we are fully aware of the superiority of carrying out logically secured demonstration. But we also know about [...] many important human experiences other than those in science [...]. One must grant to all of these their right to be. One simply cannot make everything into an object of knowledge[31].

By the way, it must be said that the dissatisfaction with the modern concept of experience, "dominated by the theory of science and empiricism (*von der Wissenschaftstheorie und vom Empirismus dominiert*)", i.e. the discontent towards a "scientifically narrowed concept of experience (*szientifisch verengten Erfahrungsbegriff*)", and the consequent search for "a wider and more comprehensive concept of experience (*ein weiter gefaßter und umgreifend ansetzender Erfahrungsbegriff*)"[32], is not a prerogative of philosophical hermeneutics alone, but rather a feature of a great part of twentieth-century philosophy. Accordingly, contemporary thought has been defined as characterized on the whole by a veritable "hunger for experience (*Erfahrungshunger*)"[33]. In this respect, Axel Honneth has pointed out that

> Gadamer verfährt bei seiner Analyse im Grunde genommen in derselben Weise, in der schon die amerikanischen Pragmatisten in ihrer Revision des herkömmlichen Erfahrungsbegriffs vorgegangen waren. Auch er kritisiert mithin zunächst, nicht anders als John Dewey, die erkenntnistheoretische Verengung von Erfahrung auf eine nur kognitive Funktion, wie sie in der Idee des Sinnesdatums angelegt ist[34].

Now, ever since Richard Rorty's 1979 groundbreaking work *Philosophy and the Mirror of Nature*, the question of the potential or actual

---

30 HÄP, p. 32 [GC, p. 53].
31 GW 10, p. 172 [GR, p. 404].
32 Früchtl 1996, p. 34.
33 Früchtl 1996, p. 33.
34 Honneth 2000, pp. 309-310.

affinities between hermeneutics and pragmatism has undoubtedly become an issue of great interest for inquiry. In this respect, it has been noticed that, while on one hand, in the Western philosophical tradition "'objectivism' and 'subjectivism' (and 'absolutism' and 'relativism') appear to contradict each other", but ultimately "share a common assumption", which is that "If God is dead, everything is permitted" – so that "there is no middle ground", no recognition "that many of our practices, beliefs, and values are both contingent or historical and rational" –, on the other, philosophical hermeneutics and pragmatism "want to work in this 'middle ground'"[35]. Another similarity between these major trends of contemporary philosophy is "their belief in the finitude and historicity of human life and cultures, and in the rootedness of truth, knowledge, and morality in traditions and social practices"[36].

Notwithstanding these resemblances, there are also, to be sure, radical differences between hermeneutic and pragmatist thinkers, and in my opinion this is probably the case of the concept of experience in Dewey and Gadamer. A concept that Honneth, as we have just seen, pinpoints instead as a point of convergence between them. In fact, while it is certainly true that the claim for a change in the concept of experience lies at the heart of Dewey's ambitious project of "reconstruction in philosophy" (just as it lies at the heart of Gadamer's not less ambitious project of "universal hermeneutics"), it is also true that such a "reconstruction" goes in a different direction to Gadamer's. In fact, Dewey moves from the need of defining "the scopes of experience and [...] its limits", and thus criticizes "traditional philosophy", which has always tried to transcend the contingency of experience through "a power" attaining to "universal, necessary and certain authority and direction"[37]. His aim is thus to propose "another conception of experience", and to show "how and why it is now possible to make claims for experience as a guide" in the whole of our existence "which the older empiricists did not and could not make for

---

35 Hollinger 1985, p. XI.
36 Hollinger 1985, p. XIII.
37 Dewey 2008, p. 124.

it"[38]. At this point, however, Dewey explains that what is desirable is actually "a new conception of experience" that would duly take account of the development of modern biology "which makes possible *a new scientific formulation of the nature of experience*"[39]. In this context, the role of "Bacon and his successors", and "the effect of experimental science", assume an extremely valuable significance, because from that moment on experience became "constructively self-regulative", a "liberating power", an "endeavor for progress"[40]. Experience, Dewey claims, "ceased to be empirical and became experimental", and this represented "something of radical importance"[41]. Hence, for Dewey's "empirical naturalism" or "naturalistic humanism", "everything designated by the word 'experience'" today is "incorporated into scientific procedures and subject-matter"; but

> this was not always so. Before the technique of empirical method was developed and generally adopted, it was necessary to dwell explicitly upon the importance of "experience" [...], and only when the Galilean-Newtonian method had fully triumphed did it cease to be necessary to mention the importance of experience. [...] Now empirical method is the only method which can do justice to [the] inclusive integrity of "experience". [...] The adoption of empirical method thus procures for philosophic reflection something of that cooperative tendency toward consensus which marks inquiry in the natural sciences. [...] The only way to avoid a sharp separation between the mind which is the centre of the processes of experiencing and the natural world which is experienced is to acknowledge that all modes of experiencing are ways in which some genuine traits of nature come to manifest realization[42].

It is not hard to see, I guess, that such philosophical intentions and conclusions are quite distant from those of Gadamer, who surely does not aim to bring philosophy and the humanities into the realm of empirical method, but rather claims their unmethodical status. Moreover, he is in no way interested in wholly naturalizing human

---

38   Dewey 2008, p. 125.
39   Dewey 2008, pp. 127-128 (my italics).
40   Dewey 2008, pp. 133-134.
41   Dewey 2008, pp. 133-134.
42   Dewey 1988, pp. 10, 14-15, 19, 34 and 30-31.

experience and suppressing the distinction between nature and mind/spirit, or better yet between nature and culture – although he explicitly warns us from intending "by the term 'spirit' (*Geist*) [...] anything too elevated", spirit being simply "both the body and that which animates it", i.e. "the spirit of our particular form of life (*die Geistigkeit unserer Lebendigkeit*)"[43]. From this point of view, Gadamer's hermeneutics sometimes seems to represent a renewed version of the somehow classical conflict between "the two cultures" (to use Charles P. Snow's famous expression), as he strongly claims that "a clear boundary [...] separates hermeneutics from the form taken by modern science with its mathematical development"[44].

This is particularly apparent, I think, in those writings where Gadamer speaks of human beings as creatures actually belonging to two worlds: "the world of natural science and the other world represented by human culture in all its riches"[45]. In still other writings, however, he explicitly connects this distinction to "Kant's fundamental notion" that "we are citizens of two worlds (*Bürger zweier Welten*)"[46]: a notion, the latter, that no "reinterpretation by the modern empirical sciences could supersede"[47]. According to Gadamer, indeed,

---

43 ÜVG, p. 128 [EH, pp. 97-98].
44 HÄP, pp. 9-10 [GC, p. 37]. In the essay *Aristoteles und die imperativische Ethik*, Gadamer hints at "the British writer C.P. Snow, who first coined this critical notion, [and] still seriously believed that he needed to decry the deficiency of scientific knowledge in the cultural life of humanity. He was deeply mistaken", Gadamer adds, "if he thought he recognized, as well, a weakness in the education offered by the elite British universities of the time. The question is not whether human facilities, and thus the achievements of science in making our world known, also find sufficient reception in the minds of humanity. The opposite is the real-life question for human beings: whether we will succeed in tying the immense increase in human power to reasonable ends and integrating it into a reasonable system of life" (GW 7, pp. 394-395 [HRE, p. 160]).
45 GW 7, p. 394 [HRE, p. 160].
46 On this concept, see, for instance, Kant 1911b, pp. 452-455 [2011, pp. 135-137].
47 GW 10, p. 233 [EPH, p. 216]. By saying so, Gadamer clearly refers to the fact that Kant excludes the concept of freedom from his epistemology, because of the somehow universal value of its counterpart, namely causality. "The relation of cause and effect", in fact, "forms the condition of the objective validity of our

we humans "live not only in the sensible, we also live from the 'supersensible standpoint' of freedom", and in this regard "one must consider the fact of freedom (*das Faktum der Freiheit*) with Kant as a fact of reason (*Vernunftfaktum*)"[48]. Recognizing this fact leads Gadamer, among other things, to stress the difference between nonhuman and human animals[49]: a difference which precisely consists in that the former, as John McDowell has also noticed, "do not have Kantian freedom"[50].

Worthy of notice, in this context, is finally that Gadamer, following Plato, in some of his later writings clearly distinguishes between "two different concepts of measure and measurement", between "*metron* and *metrion*, between measure and what is measured on the one hand, and what is fitting or appropriate on the other": the first "is

---

empirical judgements with regard to the series of perceptions, and forms therefore the condition of the empirical truth of these judgements, and so of experience. The principle of the causal relation in the succession of appearances is valid, therefore, also for all objects of experience", and "is itself the ground of the possibility of such experience" (Kant 1911a, B 247, p. 175 [2007, p. 221]). At the same time, however, Kant admits freedom into his philosophical system as the very basis of moral philosophy. At the beginning of the *Kritik der praktischen Vernunft* he explains indeed that with the "*practical faculty* [...] transcendental *freedom* is also established, [...] insofar as its reality is proved by an apodictic law of practical reason": "freedom is real, for this idea reveals itself through the moral law" (Kant 1913a, pp. 3-4 [1999, p. 139]).

48 GW 10, p. 233 [EPH, p. 216].
49 See, for instance, GW 8, pp. 409-410 [Gadamer 2000, pp. 26-27], where he introduces the distinction between the two concepts of being "together-with (*Mitsamt*)" and being "with-one-another (*Miteinander*)", in order to account for "the area of animal behavior" and that of human behavior "which, on the basis of natural determination of humans due to human language, supports human being with-one-another".
50 McDowell 1996, p. 182. "That is perfectly compatible", McDowell explains, "with acknowledging that they can be, in their ways, clever, resourceful, inquisitive, friendly, and so forth. I do not suggest that they are somehow 'out of it'. Indeed my whole point, *in appropriating Gadamer's notion of an environment*, is to provide language for saying quite the reverse, even while I deny that, lacking spontaneity as they do, dumb animals can possess the world" (McDowell 1996, p. 182 [my italics]).

that which is used when one wants to take a measurement and the procedure is brought to the object from without", while the second "is the measure which is to be found within the object itself"[51]. Gadamer also draws attention to this distinction in his 1994 essay *Vom Wort zum Begriff*, which actually represents a sort of *summa* of his thought, as testified by its very subtitle: *Die Aufgabe der Hermeneutik als Philosophie*. Here he relies on Plato's presupposition "that two different ways of measuring are possible, and both [...] indispensable"[52], and he goes so far as to identify modern science with *quantitative* thinking, and unmethodical, hermeneutic understanding with *qualitative* experiencing. "In the first form of measuring", Gadamer explains indeed,

> one goes after things with a ruler in order to make them available and controllable [...]. In this case one is clearly concerned with what the Greeks called *poson*, "quantity". The second kind of measuring consists of striking the "right measure", or finding what is appropriate. [...] This concerns what the Greeks called *poion*, "quality". [...] There are [many] cases of this kind that I would claim have an equal right to stand alongside the scientific ideal. [...] This is the reason I have focused on these forms of knowledge [...]. I think it is not

---

51 ÜVG, pp. 166, 168 and 128-129 [EH, pp. 132-133 and 98]. See Plato, *Statesman*, 283d-284e [1997, pp. 326-328]: "Then let's divide it [*scil.* the art of measurement] into two parts; [...] one part will relate to the association of greatness and smallness with each other, the other to what coming into being necessarily is. [...] In that case we must lay it down that the great and the small exist and are objects of judgment in these twin ways. [...] Is it the case then that [...] we must compel the more and less, in their turn, to become measurable not only in relation to each other but also in relation to the coming into being of what is in due measure? [...] This task, Socrates, is even greater than the former one [...]. It's clear that we would divide the art of measurement, cutting it in two in just the way we said, positing as one part of it all those sorts of expertise that measure the number, lengths, depths, breadths and speeds of things in relation to what is opposed to them, and as the other, all those that measure in relation to what is in due measure, what is fitting, the right moment, what is as it ought to be – everything that removes itself from the extremes to the middle".
52 GLB, p. 104 [GR, p. 114].

permissible that one form should try to be the whole answer: one form of measuring is not more important than the other. Rather, both forms are important[53].

I think it is important to understand, however, that this does not lead Gadamer to "resuscitate the old dualisms between nature and spirit (*die alten Dualismen von Natur und Geist*)"[54]. With regard to the abovementioned distinction between animal *Mitsamt* and human *Miteinander*, he specifies indeed that "it is difficult to imagine that one could clearly differentiate together-with and with-one-another in the area of animal behavior", just like "of course we realize that human behavior acquires its form not independent of natural drives"[55]. In other words, in Gadamer's view human beings remain "an interlacing of together-with, to which we are determined as natural beings, and, on the other side, humanity, by which we structure ourselves and our with-one-another"[56]. And the existence of such peculiar living beings as we are, according to him, is not to be explained by means of untenable forms of anti- or super-naturalism. Rather, it must be understood as the result of peculiar tendencies that occur *within* nature itself. As we read indeed in his *Schlußbericht* to the collection in seven volumes *Neue Anthropologie*:

> Daß der Mensch ein Lebewesen unter anderen ist und mit allen Lebewesen Gemeinsamkeiten hat, ist offenkundig. Gerade im Abbau theologisch vererbter Vorurteile haben die moderne Biologie, Abstammungslehre, Verhaltenslehre ihren entscheidenden Durchbruch erzielt. Gleichwohl ist die Stellung des Menschen im Kosmos [...] eine [...] besondere. [...] Es handelt sich hier nicht um theologische oder philosophische Vorurteile zugunsten des Menschen, um eine Art verfeinerter Selbstliebe der Gattung, die sich eine besondere Auszeichnung zusprechen will, sondern um einen tiefen Antagonismus in der Natur

---

53　GLB, pp. 104 and 106 [GR, pp. 114 and 116].
54　Di Cesare 2007, p. 230 [2009, p. 221].
55　GW 8, pp. 409-410 [Gadamer 2000, pp. 26-27].
56　GW 8, p. 410 [Gadamer 2000, p. 27]. On this topic, see also the interesting observations of Gregorio 2011, pp. 33-38.

selbst, der in die natürliche Bestimmtheit des Lebens mit der Entstehung des Menschen eingedrungen ist[57].

In this context, worthy of notice are also Matthias Jung's general observations on what hermeneutics actually is.

> Hermeneutik ist die Lehre vom Verstehen. [...] Verstehen ist ein universales Phänomen, [...] ein menschlicher Grundvollzug mit der elementaren Struktur "etwas als etwas auffassen", eine Sache in ihrem Sinn verstehen. [...] Hermeneutik ist daher Ausdruck einer humanen Binnenperspektive, einer speziesspezifischen Weise, die Welt zu sehen. [...] Die Mannigfaltigkeit und Universalität des Verstehens, vor allem aber seine Kreativität kommen erst in den Blick, wenn es konsequent als Titel für eine spezifisch menschliche Weise der Realitätsaneignung gebraucht wird. [...] In welchem Verhältnis steht das, was wir "Verstehen" nennen und im Alltag ständig praktizieren, zu demjenigen Weltzugang, den die Naturwissenschaften erschließen? [...] Hermeneutisches Denken bezieht sich auf Realität *als* menschlich gedeutete, auf sinnhafte, als Korrelat spezifisch menschlicher Lebenserfahrung angeeignete Wirklichkeit, und nur auf diese. Dadurch unterscheidet es sich von seinem wissenschaftstheoretisch Gegenstück, dem naturalistischen Denken, das methodisch nicht vom Menschen, sondern von der Natur ausgeht. [...] In der Unterscheidung vom naturalistischen Denkstil gewinnt die Hermeneutik Kontur *als Theorie des humanspezifischen Verstehens und Interpretierens*. [...] Wer die Perspektivendifferenz zwischen Hermeneutik und Naturalismus verteidigt, legt sich damit keineswegs auf ein Denken in [...] zwei Welten oder gar – dualistischmetaphysisch – Seinsbereichen (Geist versus Natur) fest. Methodendifferenzen können anders als Gegenstandsbestimmungen komplementär aufgefaßt werden und setzen dann ein inklusives Sowohl-Als-Auch an die Stelle eines exklusiven Entweder-Oder[58].

---

57 Gadamer 1975, p. 380. Similar remarks are to be found in the essay *Die Kunst des Feierns*: "Der Mensch ist ein prometheisches Wesen. [...] Das hebt den Menschen aus der ganzen Reihe der natürlichen Lebewesen heraus, daß er Abstand zu sich selbst besitzt, Freiheit gegenüber der Unmittelbarkeit der Naturzwänge, aber auch Freiheit gegenüber den Zwängen seiner eigenen Triebe. Darin besteht seine Exzentrizität, wie Hellmut Plessner es genannt hat" (Gadamer 1981, p. 68).

58 Jung 2001, pp. 7-8, 17, 10-11 and 23-24. A strong attempt to reduce hermeneutic thinking to a naturalistic framework has been recently made by Chrysostomos Mantzavinos, who has criticized the "hermeneutic dead ends" of Dilthey's,

Anyway, let us return now to the main question at the beginning of this chapter, namely that of hermeneutic experience. On the basis of what we have seen up to now, it is clear that Gadamer's account of experience will not let itself be guided by what he calls the teleological model. A model which tries to "purify" experience by means of methodical procedures, and to "objectify" it, until it no longer contains any hermeneutical, i.e. historical, practical and life-wordly elements.

In order to adjust the notion of experience that is currently taken for granted, and in order to show that experience also contains aspects other than those grasped by scientific experiment – which, in Gadamer's opinion, correctly grasps "a true element in the structure of experience", namely "the fact that experience is valid so long as it is not contradicted by new experience"[59], but fails to do justice to the whole of experience –, he thus turns to three great masters or "classics" of the Western philosophical and cultural tradition: Aristotle, Hegel and Aeschylus[60].

Without entering into details about Gadamer's interpretation of these three authors, we may simply notice that he pays attention only

---

Heidegger's and Gadamer's philosophies (Mantzavinos 2006, pp. 5-61 [2005, pp. 3-69]), and has consequently proposed "hermeneutic ways out" based on a veritable universalization of the "hypothetico-deductive method": "a methodological procedure that", according to him, "is in principle applicable to every subject matter (*Sachverhalte*), whether it is meaningful or not" (Mantzavinos 2006, p. 2 [2005, p. X]).

59 GW 1, p. 356 [TM, p. 345].
60 To be precise, Gadamer emphasizes not only Aristotle's and Hegel's achievements, but also some limits or deficiencies in their conceptions. In short, he charges them both of having finally conceived of the essence of experience only in regard to "science", which is obviously not Cartesian-Galileian-Baconian science, but rather "knowledge (*Wissen*)" for the former, and "self-knowledge (*Sichwissen*)" for the latter (GW 1, pp. 358 and 361 [TM, pp. 347 and 349]). In other words, according to Gadamer, both thinkers "regard experience [only] in terms of its result", thus ignoring "the fact that experience is a process", in Aristotle's case, and aiming at the "overcoming of all experience [...] in absolute knowledge", in Hegel's case (GW 1, pp. 358-359 and 361 [TM, pp. 347 and 349]).

to some particular features of their works: namely, those features that can help him give an account of what genuine experience is. This is the case, in particular, with Aristotle's concepts of induction and experience[61], Hegel's dialectical theory of experience as a reversal of consciousness (presented in the *Preface* to the *Phänomenologie des Geistes*)[62], and Aeschylus' idea that "wisdom comes through suffering *(ton pathei mathos)*" as expressed in the *Hymn to Zeus* of the *Agamemnon* tragedy[63]. In short, what Gadamer derives from such different philosophical and poetical perspectives are three basic features of human experience: its radical finiteness (Aeschylus), its dialectical negativity (Hegel), and its openness and unpredictability (Aristotle)[64].

---

61 See Aristotle, *Posterior Analytics* II 19, 99b 35 ff. [1991, pp. 165-166], and *Metaphysics* I 1, 980a 21 – 982a 2 [1991, pp. 1552-1553], where he notoriously presents a progression of knowledge-levels consisting of sensation or perception *(aisthesis)*, memory *(mneme)*, experience *(empeiria)*, art or skill *(techne)*, science *(episteme)*, and finally wisdom *(sophia)*.

62 Hegel 1970a, pp. 11-67 [1977, pp. 1-45]. *Phenomenology of Spirit* occupies a special place in Gadamer's philosophical confrontation with Hegel, since, according to him, "Hegel hat nur zwei Bücher geschrieben: Die 'Phänomenologie des Geistes' und die 'Logik'. Alles andere, was wir in der gewaltigen Masse seines Werkes vor uns haben, sind Handbücher zu Vorlesungen oder Nachschriften von Vorlesungen. Auch die berühmte Rechtsphilosophie [...] war ja kein Buch, sondern ein in Paragraphen eingeteilter Grundriß zu Hegels Berliner Vorlesungen" (Gadamer 1971b, p. 12).

63 Aeschylus, *Agamemnon*, vv. 178 and 250 [2007, pp. 13 and 15]. Aeschylus is always praised by Gadamer for "showing us our finitude" with his "*pathei-mathos* maxim" (HÄP, p. 32 [GC, p. 53]). He translates the maxim "*pathei-mathos*" as: "*Durch Leiden Lernen*", which, in turn, is translated in the English edition of *Wahrheit und Methode* as "learning through suffering" (GW 1, p. 362 [TM, p. 351]).

64 In *Wahrheit und Methode*, Gadamer recalls indeed a fine image that Aristotle uses in *Posterior Analytics* (II 19, 100a 10 ff. [1991a, p. 166]) to describe "how various perceptions unite to form the unity of experience", which is clearly "the unity of a universal", although "not yet the universality of science". To this end, Aristotle uses indeed the image of "a fleeing army" that, like "the many observations someone makes", hurry away, until "in this general flight an observation is confirmed by its being experienced repeatedly [...]. At this point the general flight begins to stop. If others join it, then finally the whole fleeing host stops

At this point in the chapter, having outlined the general structure of experience, Gadamer turns to the properly "hermeneutic" experience, and begins his analysis with the somehow surprising claim that this kind of experience "is concerned with *tradition (Überlieferung)*. This is what is to be experienced"[65]. The final pages of the chapter are devoted to a parallel between three different ways of interpreting texts and understanding the tradition, and three different forms of intersubjective relation. Gadamer's presupposition is indeed that "tradition [...] expresses itself like a Thou", and thus "the relationship to the Thou and the meaning of experience implicit in that relation must be capable of teaching us something about hermeneutical experience"[66].

Now, when Gadamer compares tradition to a person relating themselves to us, rather than to an object standing across from us, or, even more so, when he outlines three varieties of intersubjective relations (in which the third one, consisting in "historically effected consciousness", is seen as the most comprehensive and the highest one), he is introducing ideas fascinating and rich in consequences[67]. Nonetheless, if I said that the equation "hermeneutic experience = encounter with tradition" may appear surprising to the reader of *Wahrheit und Methode*, it is because, once one arrives at the end of the first part of this section, one would expect Gadamer to turn to a phenomenology of life-world and pre-scientific experience. Hence, when he suddenly turns to the understanding of tradition alone, it may appear as an unjustified restriction of the whole realm of problems

---

and again obeys a single command. The whole army under unified control is an image of science" (GW 1, pp. 357-358 [TM, p. 346]). The same image is also recalled by Gadamer in other essays: see, for instance, GW 2, pp. 149-150, 200-201 and 228-229.

65   GW 1, p. 363 [TM, p. 352].
66   GW 1, p. 364 [TM, p. 352].
67   For an intriguing analysis of this specific part of the experience-section of *Wahrheit und Methode*, see Honneth 2000 (especially pp. 309-315). On the same question, see also the original contribution of Elm 2007 (especially pp. 153-168), who compares Gadamer's conception of experience and historically effected consciousness with the later Merleau-Ponty's concept of chiasm (see Merleau-Ponty 1964, pp. 172-204 [1968, pp. 130-155]).

concerning unmethodical experience[68]. And even if Gadamer, in the subsequent sections, broadens again the horizon of his philosophical hermeneutics by taking into account such "universal" issues like those of the "linguisticality of understanding" and of "language [which] characterizes our human experience of the world in general"[69], it is nevertheless true that he ambiguously persists in claiming that hermeneutics is only "concerned with *understanding texts*", and that "historically effected consciousness" (which, according to him, "has the structure of *experience*") is limited by him to the "hermeneutical activity [...] of philologist as well as of the historian"[70]. That is, it is limited to the actual procedure of the *Geisteswissenschaften*. So, even in the most systematic section of *Wahrheit und Methode*, namely the third, in which Gadamer gives his hermeneutics a decisive ontological turn guided by language, one reads that "the significance of the *hermeneutical experience*" is that "*language* opens up a completely new dimension, the profound dimension from which *tradition* comes down to those now living"[71].

Furthermore, given the basic dichotomy "consciousness versus experience" that seems to underlie *Wahrheit und Methode*, on the whole[72], it may appear surprising that Gadamer's account of experience culminates in the notion of "historically effected consciousness (*wirkungsgeschichtliches Bewußtsein*)", i.e. in a notion that

---

68 I borrow these considerations on the "sudden and unjustified turn" that takes place in the second part of the experience-section of *Wahrheit und Methode* from Bonanni 2004, p. 39.
69 GW 1, pp. 393 and 460 [TM, pp. 391 and 452]. On the "historicity of understanding (*Geschichtlichkeit des Verstehens*)" and the "linguisticality of understanding (*Sprachlichkeit des Verstehens*)" as "the basic structure and essential foundation of the hermeneutic experience (*die Wesensstruktur und die wesentliche Grundlage der hermeneneutischen Erfahrung*)", see Lee 2004.
70 GW 1, pp. 389, 352 and 346 [TM, pp. 387, 341 and 336].
71 GW 1, pp. 466-467 [TM, p. 458 (my italics)].
72 I owe this insight into the basic framework, so to speak, of Gadamer's *magnum opus*, to Matteucci 2004, p. 140 – who notices that "the scheme according to which experience is opposed to consciousness [...] permeates the entire structure of *Wahrheit und Methode*".

still makes use of the term "consciousness". Not by chance, this was precisely one of the most striking objections Heidegger raised against Gadamer's philosophy – the other most relevant ones probably being that of secretly aiming to "sublate (*aufheben*)" everything in hermeneutics[73], and that of remaining "trapped" inside a traditional metaphysical framework[74]. In fact, as two distinguished scholars like Richard E. Palmer and Riccardo Dottori have recalled, relying on their memories of personal encounters with Heidegger and Gadamer, in 1965, when asked if he was proud of his student's philosophical hermeneutics, Heidegger replied: "Perhaps, but do you know his term *wirkungsgeschichtliches Bewußtsein*? [...] It is straight out of Dilthey!"[75]. Then, in a 1970 Heidelberg Seminar organized by Gadamer, Heidegger raised the objection that Gadamer's philosophy, on the

---

[73] This critique of Heidegger is recalled by Silvio Vietta in his 2001 interviews with Gadamer, where he says: "ich erinnere mich an eine Bemerkung von Heidegger, in Freiburg, da sagte er einmal: 'In Heidelberg sitzt Gadamer, und der glaubt alles in die Hermeneutik aufheben zu können'. So hat Heidegger gesprochen". Then, Gadamer asks to Vietta: "Sie haben das selbst gehört?", and Vietta confirms: "Ich hab es selbst gehört". At this point, Gadamer comments on this "revelation" with the following words: "Da hat er natürlich auch die Hermeneutik der Faktizität wiederum etwas zu dünn gedacht. Nein, nein. [...] Heidegger war ja mir gegenüber, [...] wahnsinnig streng. [...] Heidegger war wahnsinnig streng" (IG, pp. 54-55).

[74] In a still unpublished letter to Otto Pöggeler dated January 11, 1962, Heidegger comments on *Wahrheit und Methode* with the following words: "It is indeed curious (*merkwürdig*) to see how Gadamer takes up the metaphysics of Being (*Seinsmetaphysik*) at the end of his book without further examination and understands language as a transcendental determination of Being". I borrow this information about Heidegger's letter to Pöggeler, as well as the quotation taken from the same letter, from Grondin 2010b (pp. 200 and 201 note).

[75] Palmer 2010, pp. 122-123. Palmer also mentions that he "asked Gadamer himself about Heidegger's remark. Gadamer replied that Heidegger had already expressed to him that he did not like the implications of Gadamer's use of the term (consciousness). The term suggested that Gadamer was falling back into thinking about the human subject within a world of objects. Gadamer had apologized to Heidegger and now to me: he did not like the term 'consciousness' either – but 'I could not find a better term!'" (Palmer 2010, p. 123).

whole, would have failed to avoid a "fall back into consciousness (*Rückfall in das Bewußtsein*)"[76].

To be sure, I am neither trying to "accuse" Gadamer of having misunderstood his teacher's philosophy, nor claiming that Heidegger had a low opinion, so to speak, of his former pupil, which would be obviously absurd. In fact, if it is true that Heidegger sometimes distanced himself from Gadamer, it is also true that he suggested Gadamer as his most gifted student[77], and even recognized that Gadamer had given excellent interpretations of his thought, for instance with regard to the philosophy of art[78]. Rather, I think that the real point is represented by the effective consequences of the two thinkers' disagreement on various fundamental doctrines: consequences which, in my opinion, are wider and more radical than usually recognized[79].

Anyway, all these "limitations" or "restrictions" of the universal significance of hermeneutics have been later recognized, clarified and in a sense "overcome" by Gadamer himself. So, with regard to the question concerning the use of the term "consciousness" in shaping the concept of "historically effected consciousness", he discussed and clarified his particular use of the notion of *Bewußtsein*[80], explaining

---

76 Dottori 1996, p. 201.
77 See Heidegger's letter to Stadelmann dated September 1, 1945 (now in Heidegger 2000c, p. 395).
78 See Heidegger's letter to Gadamer dated September 3, 1960 (now in Heidegger 2005-2006, p. 37).
79 In this context, it is surely worth mentioning Gadamer's letter to Heidegger dated June 28, 1957, in which he optimistically states that he reckons to conclude his *opus* in a few weeks, but then adds that Heidegger will probably consider it as an insufficiently radical radical philosophical effort. "Ich hoffe sehr, in diesen Wochen mein eigenes Manuskript abzuschließen, das Ihnen viel zu wenig radikal im Fragen erscheinen wird, aber wenigstens ehrliche und offene Arbeitsweise bekunden wird" (ABMH, pp. 26-27). The idea that Gadamer's hermeneutics is insufficiently radical and fails to recognize the "negatively absolute situation", the "radical crisis", the "unprecedented crisis" of our age – that "Heidegger means by the approach of the world night" – lies also at the heart of Leo Strauss' critical observations on *Wahrheit und Methode* (Gadamer and Strauss 1978, pp. 7 and 11).
80 See, for instance, GW 2, pp. 10-11 and 495-496.

that "the effective historical consciousness [...] has more Being than being conscious; that is, more is historically affected and determined than we are conscious of as having been effected and determined"[81]. Instead, apropos of his reduction of hermeneutic experience, in *Wahrheit und Methode*, to the sole aspects of historical tradition and textual interpretation[82], he claims: "The problem is really universal. The hermeneutical question, as I have characterized it, is not restricted to the areas from which I began in my own investtigations"[83]. Hermeneutic consciousness, that is, "the consciousness that is effected by history", has to do indeed

> not only [with] the artistic tradition of a people, or historical tradition, or the principle of modern science in its hermeneutical preconditions, bur rather [with] the whole of our experience (*das Ganze unseres Erfahrungslebens*), [with] our own universal and human experience of life. [...] What I am describing is the mode of the whole human experience of the world. I call this experience hermeneutical for the process we are describing is repeated continually throughout our familiar experiences[84].

The reason for such ambiguities and partial restrictions, in *Wahrheit und Methode*, of the breadth of the hermeneutic problem – which, as we read at the very beginning of the book, "is not a problem specific to the methodology of the human sciences alone"[85] – probably lies in a

---

81 GW 3, p. 221 [HW, p. 58].
82 This reduction has given Odo Marquard cause to ironically define Gadamer's philosophical hermeneutics as a theory of "Being toward the text (*Sein zum Text*), [...] Being toward the literary text", in contrast to Heidegger's definition of existence, "specifically in *Being and Time*", as "Being toward death (*Sein zum Tode*)" (Marquard 1991, pp. 130 and 121 [1989, pp. 123 and 115]).
83 GW 2, p. 226 [PH, p. 10].
84 GW 2, pp. 228 and 230 [PH, pp. 13 and 15].
85 GW 1, p. 1 [TM, p. XXI]. Gadamer particularly insists on this point in answering the objections of Emilio Betti, an Italian legal historian and theorist of *methodical* hermeneutics. In a letter dated February 18, 1961 he explains indeed: "Fundamentally I am *not proposing a method*; I am describing *what is the case*. That it is as I describe it cannot, I think, be seriously questioned. [...] I am trying to go beyond the concept of method held by modern science (which retains its limited justification) and to envisage in a fundamentally universal way what

sort of "indecision" or "hesitation" felt by Gadamer in presenting "the hermeneutic phenomenon in its full extent"[86]. Indeed, as Jean Grondin has noticed, "the theme [of] the humanities [...] dominated in *Truth and Method*": "the self-understanding of the humanities" was "the *guiding concept*"[87] of the book, or at least of its second part. Although "the development toward a *philosophical* hermeneutics, which leaves the 'bounded' problem of the humanities behind it, is already present in 1960", it is apparent that Gadamer continually presents his project "as one of a 'hermeneutics of the humanities' (*geisteswissenschaftliche Hermeneutik*)"[88]. "This must be emphasized", Grondin concludes, "because *after Truth and Method* the problem of hermeneutics was considered to be one of a general theory of historicity, facticity, the lifeworld, and dialogue"[89].

Analogous remarks have been made by Günter Figal, who has noticed that

> The formulation of the question of philosophical hermeneutics may be understood from its historical context. It arises from the nineteenth century and achieves its particular profile with the development of the human sciences. [...] Gadamer's project of a philosophical hermeneutics may be understood as the most distinguished of its kind. Although it is quite removed from the founda-

---

always happens" (Gadamer 1961). Gadamer himself reports this passage of his letter to Betti in the 1965 essay *Hermeneutik und Historismus* (GW 2, p. 394 [TM, pp. 512-513]).

86 GW 1, p. 3 [TM, p. XXII].
87 Grondin 1992-93, pp. 72 and 64 [1995, pp. 37 and 29-30].
88 Grondin 1992-93, pp. 66-67 [1995, pp. 31-32].
89 Grondin 1992-93, pp. 66-67 [1995, p. 31]. This has been later recognized by Gadamer himself, who has observed: "I have altered some of the emphasis which I had previously given to the work. I used to think from the perspective of the *Geisteswissenschaften* as the central problem, more so than I do now. [...] Now, when I lecture on hermeneutics, I can raise this entire debate to a more adequate level. I begin from the opposite end, so to speak. I now begin [...] with language, the linguistic structure of experience [...]. I hardly mention the human sciences. [...] Insofar as hermeneutics is more than a theory of the human sciences, it also has the human situation in the world in its entirety in view. [...] That is the essence, the soul of my hermeneutics" (Gadamer 1992e, pp. 150 and 152).

tional phase of philosophical hermeneutics, it nevertheless remains marked by the problems posed in this phase. [...] Gadamer, and in this he takes up the bequest of Dilthey, wants to make a contribution to "self-reflection" in the human sciences[90].

Having said this, let us return now to Gadamer's account of experience in *Wahrheit und Methode*. Here, Gadamer confidently claims that "experience itself can never be science", and even that the "structure of the hermeneutical experience [...] totally contradicts the idea of scientific methodology"[91]. Nonetheless, experience "also has its own rigor", and "the hermeneutic phenomenon", i.e. understanding, is also "concerned with knowledge and with truth"[92]. So, the question is: "what kind of knowledge and what kind of truth?"[93].

Now, in general, with regard to this question, what Gadamer highlights is the difference (or, sometimes, the opposition) between the scientific ideal of full objectivity and the hermeneutic consciousness of the fundamental belonging (*Zugehörigkeit*) of the knowing subject to the knowledge object[94]. As far as I can see, however, in *Wahrheit und Methode* Gadamer does not give an explicit, univocal and resolving answer to the former questions. This, together with the somehow "exaggerated" attention paid to the question of the humanities, can perhaps transmit a sensation of vagueness or insufficiency to

---

90 Figal 2006, pp. 5-6 [2010, pp. 5-6].
91 GW 1, pp. 361 and 467 [TM, pp. 349 and 459].
92 GW 1, pp. 469 and 1 [TM, pp. 461 and XX].
93 GW 1, p. 1 [TM, p. XX].
94 See GW 1, pp. 462-467 [TM, pp. 454-459]. In the essays *Wahrheit in den Geisteswissenschaften* and *Die Kontinuität der Geschichte und der Augenblick der Existenz*, Gadamer defines the specific "truth-criterion" of the humanities and of "historical experience (*geschichtliche Erfahrung*)" as "auf Überlieferung hören und in Überlieferung stehen", and as "erinnerte Wirklichkeit [...]. [Diese] Erfahrung", he explains, "scheint mir eine Art Erkenntnis zu sein. Was da he rauskommt, ist Wahrheit" (GW 2, pp. 40 and 141-142). In general, what he seems to suggest is that "the ideal of objective knowledge which dominates our concepts of knowledge, science, and truth, needs to be supplemented by the ideal of sharing (*Teilhabe*), of participation (*Partizipation*)" (HÄP, pp. 14-15 [GC, p. 40]).

the reader. Gadamer, however, seems to hand us a clue when he says that understanding and experience stand "in an ineluctable opposition [...] to the kind of instruction that follows from general *theoretical* or *technical* knowledge"[95]. In fact, if we pay heed to Aristotle's basic distinctions of human activities and virtues (*theoria, praxis* and *poiesis; episteme, phronesis* and *techne*)[96], which have been so influential in the development of Gadamer's thought, then we realize, I think, that what he has in mind must be a concept of hermeneutic understanding and experience as practical knowledge[97].

The question concerning practical knowledge surely represents one of the leading questions of Gadamer's entire path of thought. As a matter of fact, this question is already at the core of his first research and publications, as testified by his 1930 essay *Praktisches Wissen*[98]. Thirty years later, we encounter the same question in one of the most interesting and influential sections of *Wahrheit und Methode*, namely that on the hermeneutic relevance of Aristotle, in which he lingers on "the problem of *application*, which is to be found in all understanding", i.e. the problem of "applying something universal to a par-

---

95 GW 1, p. 361 [TM, p. 350 (my italics)].
96 See, for instance, Aristotle, *Topics* VI 6, 145a 15 [1991, p. 244], *Metaphysics* VI 1, 1025b 25 [1991, p. 1619], and *Nicomachean Ethics* VI 2, 1139a 27-28 [1991, p. 1798], where Aristotle clearly presents his conception of all thought or knowledge as *either* theoretical-contemplative *or* practical *or* productive-technical.
97 On this particular aspect, see Jean Grondin's sharp observations on one of the basic meanings that understanding has to Gadamer, namely "understanding as practical know-how", the other ones being "understanding as an intellectual grasp" (which, however, plays a secondary role in *Wahrheit und Methode*) and "understanding as agreement". "Gadamer", Grondin notices indeed, "uses [a] 'practical' notion of understanding to shake up the epistemological notion that prevailed in the tradition of Dilthey and the methodology of the human sciences. To understand, even in these sciences, is [...] to apply [...]. A very important source for this Gadamerian notion of practical or applicative understanding, perhaps more so than for Heidegger" (who first undermined in *Sein und Zeit* the "epistemological understanding of understanding as an intellectual grasp"), "was Aristotle's notion of practical understanding (*phronesis*)" (Grondin 2002, pp. 36-41).
98 GW 5, pp. 230-248.

ticular situation"[99]. The question of practical knowledge becomes then a question of the greatest importance in the 1970s and 1980s, when Gadamer makes explicit what had been somewhat left implicit, that is, he "reveals" the real nature of his philosophical hermeneutics as a form of practical philosophy[100]. At the end of the 1990s this question finally leads to Gadamer's own translation of the sixth book of the *Nicomachean Ethics*, which he had first studied in Freiburg under Heidegger's guidance back in the early 1920s.

On many occasions, Gadamer has emphasized the relevance of his teacher's early "hermeneutics of facticity" for the development of his own philosophical project[101], saying that the "problem of herme-

---

99 GW 1, pp. 312 and 317 [TM, pp. 306 and 310]. As Günter Figal has noticed: "Verstehen, so müßte man mit Gadamer sagen, ist die geschichtliche Variante des praktischen Wissens. Und Hermeneutik müßte dann die philosophische Artikulation des praktischen-geschichtlichen Wissens sein. [...] Die historischen Geisteswissenschaften müssen letzlich als Artikulationen der geschichtlichen Phronesis begriffen werden. In *Wahrheit und Methode* werden die Geisteswissenschaften zwar nur zusammen mit 'Erfahrungsweisen' wie der Philosophie, der Kunst und der Geschichte zusammen genannt; doch in den späteren Arbeiten Gadamers tritt die Bezogenheit der Geisteswissenschaften auf das 'sittliche' oder 'praktische' Wissen im Sinne des Aristoteles immer mehr in den Vordergrund" (Figal 1992, p. 26). On practical knowledge, i.e. *phronesis*, as a model for hermeneutic understanding, see also the accurate analyses provided by Rese 2007 and Dottori 2008.

100 On this topic, see his many essays on the problems of practical reason and hermeneutics as practical philosophy: for instance, GW 2, pp. 301-318 [RAS, pp. 113-138]; GW 4, pp. 175-188 [HRE, pp. 18-36]; GW 4, pp. 216-228 [RAS, pp. 69-87]; GW 10, pp. 238-246 and 259-266; LT, pp. 67-76 [PT, pp. 50-61]; VZW, pp. 78-109 [RAS, pp. 88-112]. According to Franco Volpi, however, one should more precisely speak of a *"Rehabilitierung der Phronesis"* in Gadamer's case, and of a specific *"Rehabilitierung der Praxis"* in Hannah Arendt's case (Volpi 1992, pp. 15 and 13).

101 It is worth noticing that Gadamer has later indicated his first encounter with Heidegger's phenomenological interpretations of Aristotle as the original source of his whole philosophy. So, in his introduction to Heidegger's *Natorp-Bericht*, first published in 1989 after the text had been considered lost for decades, he writes: "Wenn ich diesen ersten Teil der Einleitung zu den Aristoteles-Studien Heideggers, die Anzeige der hermeneutischen Situation, heute wieder lese, so ist

neutics [became] universal in scope, even attaining a new dimension", only through Heidegger's "transcendental interpretation of understanding"[102]. In his own words: "I received impetuses for thinking from Heidegger very early on, and I attempted from the very beginning to follow such impetuses within the limits of my capabilities and to the extent that I could concur"[103]. It is important to notice that such impetuses came from Heidegger's both early and late philosophy. Gadamer, for example, claims that his hermeneutics "follows the intentions of Heidegger's late philosophy"[104], and that the basis of his own "treatment of the universal hermeneutic problem" are precisely formed by the latter's "thinking of 'the turn'"[105]. For our specific purposes, however, it is, above all, important to notice how he compared his 1922 reading of the so-called *Natorp-Bericht* to "being hit by a charge of electricity"[106], and also pointed out the decisive importance of his 1923 attendance at Heidegger's lecture course *Ontologie (Hermeneutik der Faktizität)* and seminar on Aristotle's ethics[107].

Given all this, it is thus understandable why some distinguished scholars of hermeneutics have indicated the Aristotelian question of practical knowledge as "Gadamer's original conception (*ursprüngliche Konzeption*)"[108], or his "interpretation of Heidegger's inter-

---

es, als ob ich darin den Leitfaden meines eigenen philosophischen Werdegangs wiederfände und meine schließliche Ausarbeitung der philosophischen Hermeneutik wiederholen sollte" (Gadamer 1989b, p. 229).
102 GW 1, p. 268 [TM, p. 254].
103 GW 3, p. VI [HW, p. VII].
104 GW 3, p. 220 [HW, p. 58].
105 GW 2, p. 446 [TM, pp. XXXII-XXXIII].
106 GW 3, p. 263 [HW, p. 113].
107 On this specific question, see, for instance, GW 2, p. 485; GW 10, pp. 4-5, 21, 32, 61 and 66. Quite interestingly, in 1929 Gadamer himself held a seminar on Aristotle's *Nicomachean Ethics*, of which he informed Heidegger in a letter dated April 17, 1929 (SBMH, p. 28). For a complete list of his lectures and seminars held at the universities of Marburg, Kiel, Leipzig, Frankfurt and Heidelberg, see Grondin 1999, pp. 390-399 [2003, pp. 366-380].
108 See Chang 1994, pp. 95-104.

pretation of Aristotle (*Gadamers Interpretation von Heideggers Aristoteles-Interpretation*)" as the "key for comprehending his own hermeneutic theory (*Schlüssel für das Verständnis seiner eigenen hermeneutischen Theorie*)"[109]. To sum up the whole question, in Günter Figal's words:

> Whoever wants to understand Gadamer's conception of philosophical hermeneutics must go back to the year 1923. In the summer semester of this year in Freiburg, the later author of *Wahrheit und Methode* attends Heidegger's lecture course on "Ontology", which comprises, at its core, the development of a philosophically understood hermeneutics. What the young Gadamer takes in is intensified by his reading of Heidegger's early, programmatic piece: the so-called *Natorp-Berichts*[110].

Now, it is my opinion that the concept of practical knowledge, as assumed and developed by Gadamer, presents at least to some extent an ambiguity: namely, that of being interpretable in two partially different ways, or better, on two different levels. On the one side, *praxis* and *phronesis* are strictly and exclusively related to ethics and politics, i.e. with what Aristotelian practical philosophy properly consists of. On the other side, however, I argue that Gadamer sometimes adopts the concepts of *praxis* and *phronesis* in a wider and more comprehensive sense: that is, as concepts indicating an all-encompassing dimension of human existence, of which ethics and politics are only a part.

---

109 Stolzenberg 2005, p. 135. On this last point, see Donatella Di Cesare's sharp observations: "[Gadamers] Rehabilitierung der praktischen Philosophie, auch wenn sie zweifellos von Heideggers Ansatz beeinflußt ist, folgt jedoch einem anderen Weg [...]. Heidegger läßt Platon hinter sich, um sich Aristoteles zuzuwenden, wobei er nicht so sehr die *phrónesis* als vielmehr die *sophía* im Auge hat [...]. Umgekehrt liest Gadamer die aristotelische Ethik im Licht von Platons Dialektik, und Aristoteles interessiert ihn nur, sofern er sokratischer als Sokrates selbst sein kann" (Di Cesare 2007, pp. 153-154 [2009, p. 141]). On the resemblances and divergences between Heidegger's and Gadamer's appropriations of Aristotle, see Coltman 1998 (pp. 11-24), Risser 2000 and Smith 2003.
110 Figal 2006, p. 9 [2010, p. 8].

It is precisely in such a broader sense of practical knowledge that this concept seems to become synonymous with hermeneutic experience, which, in turn, after *Wahrheit und Methode* ceases to be identified with our sole relation to, and understanding of, texts and tradition, and is rather intended as "the way experience in the *lifeworld* is lived"[111]. From this point of view, I think that, in Gadamer's case, one can correctly speak of an actual "universalization" of *praxis*, whereas in Heidegger's case one should probably speak of an "ontologization" of *praxis*[112]. This point clearly emerges, I think, in the *Nachwort* to the third edition of *Wahrheit und Methode*, where we read:

> Philosophically regarded, what emerges from the background of the great tradition of practical (and political) philosophy reaching from Aristotle to the turn of the nineteenth century is that practice (*praxis*) represents an independent contribution to knowledge. [...] Relying on the tradition of practical knowledge helps guard us against the technological self-understanding of the modern concept of science. [...] I can appeal to the fact that the *fore-knowledge* [or] *pre-scientific knowledge* [...] stemming from the way *language* orients us in the

---

[111] HÄP, p. 31 [GC, p. 52].

[112] I owe this clear and sharp distinction between Heidegger's and Gadamer's different appropriations of practical philosophy (*Ontologisierung der Praxis* versus *Universalisierung der Praxis*) to a private conversation with Prof. Günter Figal at the University of Freiburg in February 2011. According to him, however, such an ontologization/universalization of practice is problematic, inasmuch as it undervalues the enduring significance and relevance of its counterpart, that is, theory. "The hermeneutics of facticity is not to be understood without this fundamental critique of the theoretical. It lives from the fact that it radically brings into question the possibility of a theoretical philosophy. [...] Compared with Heidegger's hermeneutical conception, Gadamer's is more convincing in one respect: Whereas Heidegger overburdens practical philosophy through the elevation of its status as ontological, Gadamer simply allows it to stand on its own. [...] The fundamental difficulty that had shown itself in Heidegger is admittedly also here: Gadamer leaves open how a practical philosophy, without its relation to the theoretical, which was essential for Aristotle, is supposed to be possible. Theory appears in his considerations solely as a counter-model. It is *scientific theory*", that is, nothing more than "cold, indifferent observation" (Figal 2006, pp. 21 and 28-30 [2010, pp. 17 and 23]).

world [...] comes into play *wherever the experience of life is assimilated*, linguistic tradition is understood, and social life goes on. Such fore-knowledge is certainly no higher court where science is tried; it is itself exposed to every critical objection that science raises, but it is and remains the vehicle of *all understanding*. [...] Philosophy [...] does pertain to *the whole of our experience of life and our world*, but like no other science – rather like *our very experience, articulated in language, of life and the world*. I hardly want to assert that the knowledge of this *totality* is certain or that it does not need to be thoughtfully submitted to constant critique. But still, one cannot ignore such "knowledge", *in whatever form it expresses itself*: in religious or proverbial wisdom, in works of art or philosophical thought[113].

What emerges is consequently that, in Gadamer's view, art, history, philosophy, ethics, law, language and religion, as well as our everyday-life relationships, all somehow belong to the "forms of inner self-enlightenment and to the intersubjective representation of human experience"[114]. In this respect, it is probably correct to interpret Gadamer's philosophical project, on the whole, as the project of a hermeneutics which "embraces the whole of the human life-world as its practical understanding of itself in all of its dimensions"[115]. This seems to lead in the direction of an extremely complex and stimulating phenomenology of cultural mediations, which accounts for various kinds of non-scientific experience by including them in the universal dimension of understanding (*Verstehen*) and practical knowledge (*praktisches Wissen*)[116].

---

113 GW 2, pp. 455, 459 and 461 [TM, pp. 560-561 and 564-566 (my italics)].
114 GW 2, p. 461 [TM, p. 566].
115 Bruns 2004, p. 44. According to Robert Sokolowski, Gadamer "builds up a philosophical position, a 'universal hermeneutics', a theory about being and the human condition. This theory [...] is developed on the margins of his commentaries and analyses, and for that reason it is fragmentary" (Sokolowski 1997, p. 224).
116 That the universality of hermeneutics is actually a practical universality is claimed, for example, in the 1980 essay *Probleme der praktischen Vernunft*, in which we read: "Es ist dieses Ideal der praktischen Vernunft, das mir für unsere Geisteswissenschaften, auch wenn sie es nicht wahrhaben wollen, gültig scheint. [...] Was hier gewußt wird, ist nicht ein bestimmter Bereich von Objekten, sondern der Inbegriff dessen, worin sich die Menschheit selber objektiviert, ihre

In this respect, however, one can ask whether such a "reduction" of all forms of unmethodical experience to the realm of practice does full justice to the richness and variety of human world-experience, or whether this ambitious task actually requires a more sophisticated, nuanced and subtly differentiated concept of understanding. In recent times, this objection has been raised by Günter Figal, according to whom

> wenn Geschichte, Kunst, Religion und Philosophie sich angemessen nur im Verstehen erschließen, ist das Verstehen nicht die Aufgabe besonderer Wissenschaften, sondern ein Grundzug der Kultur überhaupt. Und wenn aufgrund seiner wesentlichen Zugänglichkeit in der Sprache *alles*, was zugänglich sein kann, verstanden werden muß, hat es die hermeneutische Reflexion mit einem Grundsachverhalt des menschlichen Lebens zu tun. Dann löst sich die Aufgabe dieser Reflexion nur auf philosophische, diesem Grundsachverhalt Rechnung tragende Weise ein. [...] Gleichwohl [...] findet das Verstehen in ihnen [*scil.* Reflexion und Kritik] Ausprägungen, die eine Differenzierung des Verstehensbegriff erforderlich machen. Auch wenn es einen einheitlichen Begriff des Verstehens gibt, ist das Verstehen je nach Ausprägung anders. Die Vielfalt seiner Möglichkeiten wird nur in deren genauer Beschreibung erfaßt. Darin läßt es Gadamer in *Wahrheit und Methode* fehlen. [...] [Die] Universalität des Hermeneutischen [...] läßt sich [...] sehr viel überzeugungskräftiger vertreten, wenn man den Begriff des Verstehens differenzierter entwickelt, als es bei Gadamer geschieht[117].

Taten und Leiden so gut wie ihre dauerhaften Schöpfungen. Die *praktische Universalität*, die im Begriff der *Vernünftigkeit* [...] impliziert ist, *umfaßt uns allesamt* und ganz und gar" (GW 2, p. 327 [my italics]).

117 Figal 2007b, pp. 299-230. On the same problem, see also Figal 2006, pp. 28-29 [2010, p. 23], according to whom, in Gadamer's case, "hermeneutical consciousness is to be demonstrated as a variation of practical knowledge", so that "philosophical hermeneutics is consequently able to be understood on the model of ethics as 'practical philosophoy'"; accordingly, hermeneutic experience, "even if it encompasses 'aesthetic' phenomena, is conceived on the model of practical philosophy. This answer does not put the matter to rest, however". In order to clarify this point, Figal cunningly quotes a long sentence from *Wahrheit und Methode* concerning "ethical consciousness" (GW 1, p. 318 [TM, p. 311]), and then comments: "One needs only to put hermeneutical consciousness in the place of ethical consciousness here in order to find this statement a program-

In this context, moreover, it might be intriguing to draw a comparison between Gadamer's hermeneutic phenomenology of "practical" knowledge-forms and, for example, Cassirer's transcendental (and later anthropological)[118] phenomenology of such "symbolic" forms of knowledge as language, art, myth, history and religion. However, it is not possible to undertake here such comparisons or to open new parentheses in our general discourse on practical knowledge and hermeneutic experience[119]. So, let me simply remind the reader of the following, fitting description of Gadamer's philosophical hermeneutics as a *phenomenology of culture*:

---

matic self-description of Gadamer's philosophy" (Figal 2006, p. 27 [2010, p. 21]).

118 By saying so, I basically refer to Cassirer's 1944 *Essay on Man*, which somehow represents a transposition, so to speak, of his early *Philosophy of Symbolic Forms* (1923-29) on an anthropological level, or better yet on the level of a philosophy of culture. Cassirer's systematic and all-encompassing approach is well expressed by such statements as: "Man's outstanding characteristic, his distinguishing mark, is not his metaphysical or physical nature – but his work. It is this work, it is the system of human activities, which defines and determines the circle of 'humanity'. Language, myth, religion, art, science, history are the constituens, the various sectors of this circle. A 'philosophy of man' would therefore be a philosophy which would give us insight into the fundamental structure of each of these human activities, and which at the same time would enable us to understand them as an organic whole. Language, art, myth, religion are no isolated, random creations. They are held together by a common bond" and "a common origin" (Cassirer 1972, p. 68).

119 Gadamer hints at Cassirer on various occasions. For example, in GW 10, p. 350 [Gadamer 1997b, p. 23] he recalls that in the 1920s "Cassirer represented something quite individual and special in Neo-Kantianism", due to his "enormous flexibility, [...] astonishing familiarity with literature, and apparently [...] good bit of natural historical sense", which made him capable of fruitfully applying "transcendental philosophy to the historical world". In the essay *Mythos und Vernunft* Gadamer then praises Cassirer's ability to recognize the peculiar non-scientific truth that pertains to art and myth (GW 8, p. 162). On other occasions, however, he also criticizes Cassirer for his incapacity to break with the transcendental-subjectivistic attitude of Neo-Kantian philosophy (see, for example, GW 2, pp. 72 and 111; GW 8, p. 401).

eine Phänomenologie der Vermittlungen, des vermittelten, nur in der Vermittlung erfahrbaren Sinns von Welt- und Lebenszusammenhänge. [...] Phänomenologie der Sinnvermittlung und des vermittelten Sinns [ist] die eigentliche Aufgabe von *Wahrheit und Methode* [...]. Das Verstehen von Rede und Text, ob es geisteswissenschaftlich betrieben wird oder nicht, ist nur eine Ausprägung des hermeneutischen Phänomens, und zwar, wenn man Gadamer folgt, noch nicht einmal die maßgebliche. Maßgeblich sind vielmehr drei "Erfahrungen" [...]: die Erfahrung der Kunst, der Geschichte und der Philosophie. [...] Philosophische Hermeneutik im Sinne Gadamer ist mehr als eine Philosophie des Verstehens. Sie ist, als Phänomenologie der Kultur, Aufklärung über die reicheren Möglichkeiten des menschlichen Daseins, Erinnerungshilfe in Situationen, wo diese Möglichkeiten marginal zu werden drohen[120].

In light of what we have seen up to now, I thus think we might say that Gadamer's concept of "understanding knowledge (*verstehendes Wissen*)", which he intends as "a totally different kind of knowledge (*eine ganz andere Art von Wissen*)" in comparison to modern technoscientific knowledge, basically consists

in der hinter allem Wissen versteckten praktischen Orientierung, die immer vorläufig zum erreichbaren Ziel eine Voraussicht auf das Ganze besitzt. Phänomenologisch in Anlehnung an Husserl bezeichnet Gadamer dieses Wissen auch als "Wissen von der Lebenswelt". [...] Die hermeneutische Erfahrung manifestiert sich produktiv in der gesamten menschlichen Praxisdimension der Lebenswelt. [...] Gadamer [...] unterstreicht das für uns wirklich wesentliche, entscheidende Wissen, das nicht von der Erfahrung im weitesten Sinne zu unterscheiden ist. [...] Lebenswelt ist die sich abwechslungsreich gestaltende und nicht getrennt vom alltäglichen Leben liegende Welt. Sie schließt in sich nicht nur die vor- und außerwissenschaftliche Welt ein, sondern stellt den größtmöglichen Umkreis der Lebenserfahrung dar. [...] Es ist die geordnete Lebenswelt selbst, in der wir uns alle als Lebende befinden, und in die wir immer schon verstehend und handelnd einbezogen sind [...]. Es muß einen letzten Horizont geben, der uns alle umschließt, in dem wir alle schon gelebt haben und leben werde. Dieser Horizont ist eben die Lebenswelt der menschlichen Praxis[121].

---

120 Figal 2001, pp. 103-104 and 106.
121 Chang 1994, pp. 101-102, 104 and 114.

To sum up, philosophical hermeneutics is presented by Gadamer both as a philosophy of *praxis* and as a hermeneutics of *Faktizität*: a concept, the latter, that he openly borrows from Heidegger's philosophy of the 1920s, although reinterpreting it and "adapting" it to his own philosophical preoccupations. So, for example, in the section of his 1960 masterpiece dedicated to his teacher's early project of a hermeneutic phenomenology, Gadamer explains that "what constituted the significance of Heidegger's *fundamental ontology* was not that it was the solution to the problem of historicism"[122], namely the problem with which Gadamer copes in the second part of *Wahrheit und Methode*. Although conceding that Heidegger's "revolutionary and polemical beginning" aimed at "renewing the question of being in general and not producing a theory of the human sciences", he then interprets it in light of his own theoretical interests[123], and thus emphasizes how "this new aspect of the hermeneutical problem" – namely, that of understanding, no more conceived as "a resigned ideal of human experience", but as "the *original form of the realization of*

---

122 GW 1, p. 261 [TM, p. 247].
123 In this context, Günter Figal has pinpointed that Gadamer, with his "discrete radicality "(*diskrete Radikalität*)" and "philosophical diplomacy (*philosophische Diplomatie*)", has carried out since the very beginning a "reinterpretation (*Umdeutung*)" of Heidegger's early phenomenological-hermeneutical project, whose concept of *Faktizität* stood neither for "ungroundability or underivability of *Dasein*", nor for "the 'immemorial' that withdraws from conception (*sich entziehende 'Unvordenklichkeit'*), an idea made use of by Schelling against Hegel [...]. Facticity, as it is identified in Heidegger, 'is the signification of 'our' 'own' *Dasein* (*die Bezeichnung 'unseres' 'eigenen' Daseins*)'. [...] Life, then, is factical insofar as it is lived. [...] That this reinterpretation could not be more radical becomes clear when one considers its philosophical consequences. [...] Heidegger concerns himself, in a word, with the fact of the hermeneutical (*das Faktum des Hermeneutischen*), Gadamer with the hermeneutics of the factical (*die Hermeneutik des Faktischen*)" (Figal 2006, pp. 2, 13, 11 and 14 [2010, pp. 1, 13, 10 and 12]). Analogous remarks in Figal 2005 (especially pp. 137 and 146-152), and Figal 2003 (p. 146), according to whom: "So gibt es die Hermeneutik der Faktizität zwei Mal – in einer Verdoppelung, die als Verschiebung aufschlussreich ist. Das spätere profiliert sich am Früheren, und ebenso gewinnt das Frühere im Vergleich mit dem Späteren größere Prägnanz".

Dasein" – attains "a fundamentally new position with regard to the aporias of historicism"[124].

In his subsequent writings, Gadamer also interprets facticity as "that which could not be thought of in advance (*das Unvordenkliche*)", as the "unanticipability (*Unvordenklichkeit*)" – to put it in Schelling's words – of the ground upon which human existence rests: "In this situation", Gadamer explains, "hermeneutics [as a hermeneutics of facticity] is focused on something that is *not understandable*"[125], i.e. on life as such. As we read in still another writing, "in his early thinking, Heidegger fashioned the concept of a 'hermeneutics of facticity', and in so doing [...] he formulated the paradoxical task of explicating the *Unvordenkliche* [Schelling: 'unthinkable'] dimension of *Existenz*"[126]. In the 1986 essay *Vernunft und praktische Philosophie* Gadamer even speaks of facticity as practice[127], thus drawing these two keywords of his philosophical

---

124 GW 1, pp. [TM, pp. 246 and 249-250].
125 GW 10, p. 63 [GR, p. 363].
126 GW 2, p. 103 [GR, p. 56]. To be true, in his 1923 lecture course Heidegger defines facticity as "the character of the being of 'our' 'own' *Dasein*", while (phenomenological) hermeneutics stands for the philosophical approach which shows that *Dasein* "has its being as something capable of interpretation and in need of interpretation and that to be in some state of having-been-interpreted belongs to its being. [...] In hermeneutics what is developed for *Dasein* is a possibility for its becoming and being for itself in the manner of an *understanding* of itself" (Heidegger 1988, pp. 7 and 15 [1999, pp. 5 and 11]). As is well known, however, in his works following the famous and much discussed "turn (*Kehre*)" of the early 1930s, Heidegger abandoned philosophical hermeneutics in favour of new paths of thought: "in my later writings I no longer employ the term 'hermeneutics'", he explains indeed in his dialogue on language with a Japanese (Heidegger 1982, p. 98 [1982, p. 12]). In a famous letter to Otto Pöggeler, dated January 5, 1973, he takes a strong critical stance to Gadamer's hermeneutics, and unswervingly states: "Die 'hermeneutische Philosophie' ist die Sache von Gadamer" (quoted in Pöggeler 1983, p. 395).
127 "Die Rationalität der menschlichen Praxis und die Rationalität der praktischen Philosophie stoßen nicht auf das Kontingente als auf ein anderes ihrer selbst. Sie sind auf die Faktizität der Praxis, die unsere Lebenswirklichkeit ist, gegründet" (GW 10, pp. 265-266).

dictionary close to each other, while in the 1987 essay *Die deutsche Philosophie zwischen den beiden Weltkriegen* he speaks of language as "something unthinkable (*ein Unvordenkliches*)". "Was das Element ist, in dem man lebt", Gadamer explains indeed,

> ist etwas, das man nicht zum Gegenstand macht. Das Element, die Luft, die wir atmen, ist [...] das, worin wir leben und was wir nicht zum Gegenstand unserer Aufmerksamkeit machen, wenn wir sie atmen. So ist es auch mit der Sprache. Sie ist sozusagen das, worin wir zu Hause sind, was uns so heimisch sein läßt auf diesem merkwürdig bevorzugten Planeten eines riesigen Universum. [...] Sie bleibt für uns alle ein letztes Daheim- und Zuhausesein, ein Unvordenkliches, das eine entfremdete Welt, die alles auf das Machbare allein anzusehen gewohnt ist, uns gelassen hat; und dieses ist die ganze Welt noch einmal – als die unsere[128].

In addition to this, in some of his works, Gadamer also hints at the conceptual proximity of the notions of facticity, practice and lifeworld. In fact, he explains that his own "step toward hermeneutic philosophy" was actually a process towards "validating hermeneutics [...] as referring to the actual performance of life", and defines his "hermeneutic philosophy" as a "phenomenologically grounded hermeneutics"[129]. On this basis, I think it is correct to speak of a "life-wordly shift of hermeneutics (*lebensweltliche Wende der Hermeneutik*)" as an appendix to its turn to the all-encompassing dimension of the "lifeworld of human practice (*Lebenswelt der menschlichen Praxis*)"[130].

Now, it is a well known fact that the concept of *Lebenswelt* represents a somehow original coinage of the later Husserl. "Prior to 1920 Husserl can already be found making sporadic use of the expression 'lifeworld'"[131], for example in the second book of his *Ideen zu einer reinen Phänomenologie und phänomenologischen Philosophie*[132]. "It is not until the 1920s, however, that it enters Husserl's

---

128 GW 10, p. 369.
129 Gadamer 1997a, p. 235.
130 Chang 1994, pp. 114-115.
131 Bernet, Kern and Marbach 1989, p. 199 [1999, p. 217].
132 See Husserl 1969, pp. 374-375 [1989, pp. 384-385]: "The life-world of persons escapes natural science, even though the latter investigates the totality of

philosophy as a technical term for a fundamental problem": namely, "the question concerning the unity and inner structure of the *world* to which all of [the] different sciences refer"[133]. But "what at first was for Husserl a foundational problem in the theory of science, developed [...] in his last work", the *Krisis der europäischen Wissenschaften*, "into a 'universal problem'"[134]. In fact,

> during the 1920s, the regress from the sciences to the experiential foundation signified for Husserl the return to "simple" or "pure" experience. At the time, this meant for him a return to *preconceptual* (prelinguistic, pre-predicative) experience. [...] It is the world of bare, preconceptual perception and memory, the world of bare intuition. [...] During the 1920s Husserl also called this unhistorical "world of intuition" the "lifeworld". [...] In the course of time, however, Husserl's definition of the kind of experience that could furnish a foundation for the sciences changed, and, with this change, the concept of the "lifeworld" changed as well. [...] The experience which ultimately supports the sciences is thus no longer a mute, preconceptual intuition, but rather the experience of the actually present (*aktuell*), concrete, historical world, together with its cultural products and, hence, its concepts and sciences. This thought, initially expressed hesitantly by Husserl during the 1920s, was clearly conveyed in the *Crisis*. There Husserl maintains that objective science has its foundation in the lifeworld and, as a human achievement, belongs, like all other human achievements, in the concrete lifeworld[135].

It is precisely here, I think, that Husserl's account of the life-world meets Gadamer's attempt to develop a philosophical hermeneutics of facticity which, *at the same time*, aims to include the traditional hermeneutic question of the humanities, and conceives itself as the heir of Platonic-Aristotelian practical philosophy. Not by chance, already in *Wahrheit und Methode* Gadamer devotes a specific section

---

> realities, for even the most subtle theory in natural science does not touch the life-world [...]. The basic relationship in this life-world, which predelineates the point of view of the method, is not causality but motivation. [...] The life-world is the natural world – in the attitude of natural life we are living functioning subjects together in an open circle of other functioning subjects".

133 Bernet, Kern and Marbach 1989, pp. 199-200 [1999, pp. 217-218].
134 Bernet, Kern and Marbach 1989, p. 201 [1999, p. 220].
135 Bernet, Kern e Marbach 1989, pp. 202-203 [1999, pp. 220-222].

to the concept of life in Husserl's phenomenology[136]. Here, although emphasizing the limits of Husserl's approach – namely, that of being "everywhere concerned with the 'achievements' of transcendental subjectivity" and remaining trapped in "the epistemological schema"[137], rather than overcoming it, as Heidegger's ontological radicalization of phenomenology did – he points out the invaluable merits of the Husserlian decisive break with scientific objectivism. This break and radical critique of objecttivism is already present in the *Logische Untersuchungen* (1900-1901). It gets even stronger in the *Ideen* (1913), and finally culminates in the *Krisis* (1936), at the centre of which is the concept of *Lebenswelt*[138], a concept that, according to Gadamer, "is the antithesis of all objectivism" and refers to "the whole in which we live as historical creatures. [...] The concept of the *life-world*", he writes, "is an essentially historical concept", that includes "the world in which we are immersed in the natural attitude that never becomes an object as such for us, but that represents the pregiven basis of all experience", and involves at the same time the "communal world", the "world of persons [which] is always assumed [...] in the natural attitude"[139].

In any case, with regard to the key concept of this chapter, namely that of practice, it must be said that Gadamer intends it in the widest possible meaning, as "the all-inclusive, distinctive characteristic of the human being"[140]. It is in particular in the seminal essay *Hermeneutik als praktische Philosophie* that Gadamer gives decisive elucidations on this point. Here we read indeed:

> practice formulates [...] the mode of behavior of that which is living in the broadest sense. Practice, as the character of being alive, stands between activity and situatedness. As such it is not confined to human beings, who alone are active on the basis of free choice (*prohairesis*). Practice means instead the actuation of life (*energeia*) of anything alive, to which corresponds a life, a way

---

136 See GW 1, pp. 246-258 [TM, pp. 235-245].
137 GW 1, pp. 251 and 254 [TM, pp. 238 and 241].
138 See Husserl 1976, pp. 105-193 and 459-462 [1970, pp. 103-189 and 379-384].
139 GW 1, pp. 251-252 [TM, p. 239].
140 GW 7, p. 226 [IGPAP, p. 175].

of life, a life that is led in a certain way (*bios*). Animals too have *praxis* and *bios*, which means a way of life. Of course there is a decisive difference between animal and human being. The way of life of human beings is not so fixed by nature as is that of other living beings. This is expressed by the concept of *prohairesis*, which [...] means "preference" and "prior choice" [and] which can be predicated only of human beings[141].

Now, one of the most dangerous tendencies that Gadamer sees in the modern age is precisely the loss of the original meaning and importance of practice. As we read indeed in the essay *Was ist Praxis?*: "we are no longer aware" of what *praxis* really is, "because in starting from the modern notion of science when we talk about practice, we have been forced in the direction of thinking of the application of science"[142]. What Gadamer denounces is the present-day tendency to immediately identify practice and technology, without understanding that the former, as Aristotle carefully explained, actually represents an autonomous and indeed universal, all-encompassing aspect of human existence. So, in the essay *Theorie, Technik, Praxis* we read:

> it is apparent that the conceptions both of theory and practice have fundamentally changed. Naturally there was always application of knowledge to practice, as indicated by the very terms "sciences" and "arts" (*epistemai* and *technai*). "Science" [...] understood itself, however, as pure *theoria*, that is, as knowledge sought for its own sake and not for its practical significance. It was in the Greek idea of science that the relation between theory in this precise sense and practice first came to a critical point as a problem. [...] Yet this divergence can hardly be compared to the modern relation between theory and practice, which was formed by the seventeenth-century idea of science. For science is no longer the totality of the knowledge of the world and of humankind [...]. The foundation of modern science is experience in a wholly new sense. [...] It is thus not altogether wrong to say that modern natural science – without detracting from the purely theoretical interest that animates it – means not so much knowledge as know-how. This means that it is practice. It would appear to me more

---

141 VZW, p. 81 [RAS, pp. 90-91].
142 GW 4, p. 216 [RAS, p. 69].

correct, however, to say that science makes possible knowledge directed to the power of making, a knowing mastery of nature. This is technology[143].

---

143 GW 4, pp. 245-247 [EH, pp. 4-6].

10. Reasonableness, Dialogue and Freedom: Ethical-Political Consequences of Hermeneutics

As we have seen in the previous chapter, from the early 1970s onwards Gadamer has explicitly "converted" philosophical hermeneutics into practical philosophy, giving a very broad interpretation to the concept of *praxis*, which he has taken for "the whole original situatedness of humans in their natural and social environment"[1]. In this respect, *praxis* becomes a synonym, so to speak, for the entire life-wordly, "factic" and hermeneutic dimension of life. The word itself, "practice", according to Gadamer, points indeed to "the *totality* of our practical life, *all* our human action and behavior; the self-adaptation of the human being *as a whole* in this world. [...] Our *praxis*, in short, is our 'form of life' (*unsere Lebensform*)"[2].

Besides this wide and all-encompassing meaning, however, there is also a narrower sense in which Gadamer understands the concept of practice. As a matter of fact, *praxis* originally meant "action", which for Aristotle, as I said, differs from both theory (*theoria*) and production or making (*poiesis*). Accordingly, the virtue of practical wisdom (*phronesis*) – intended as "a true and reasoned state of capacity to act with regard to the things that are good or bad for man"[3] – is essentially "concerned with action"[4], and is accurately distinguished by Aristotle from knowledge (*episteme*) and art (*techne*)[5]. Strictly speaking, the

---

1 GW 10, p. 234 [EPH, p. 217].
2 HÄP, p. 65 [GC, pp. 78 79 (my italics)].
3 Aristotle, *Nicomachean Ethics* VI 5, 1140b 4-6 [1991, p. 1800].
4 Aristotle, *Nicomachean Ethics* VI 7, 1141b 21 [1991, p. 1802].
5 To be precise, in the sixth book of the *Nicomachean Ethics* he distinguishes five "states by virtue of which the soul possesses truth by way of affirmation or denial": besides art, knowledge and practical wisdom, Aristotle also mentions

realm of *praxis* is that of "moral action", and so it is not by chance if practical philosophy, from Aristotle onwards, has always been identified with philosophical ethics.

Now, even in Gadamer's case, practical philosophy – at least in what I have previously called its narrower sense – has basically to do with philosophical ethics. This obviously confers to ethics, i.e. moral philosophy, a decisive importance within Gadamer's entire philosophy. So, on the one side, ethics represents only a part of his universal hermeneutics: namely, a hermeneutics whose ambitious aim is that of embracing all forms of life-worldly and practical understanding (first of all, those of art, history and language, with which he deals in the three parts of *Wahrheit und Methode*). On the other side, however, given these basic assumptions, it is understandable that ethics plays a somehow special role in comparison to other forms of hermeneutic experience. As Richard J. Bernstein has claimed, indeed, it is precisely the "practical-moral orientation" that represents "the approach that pervades so much of Gadamer's thinking and helps to give it unified perspective"[6]. In fact,

> it is important to remember that in *Truth and Method* Gadamer's primary concern is with the understanding and interpretation of works of art, texts, and traditions, with "what is handed down to us". Ethics and politics are not in the foreground of his investigations. [...] But it is also clear that if we pay close attention to Gadamer's writings before and after the publication of *Truth and Method*, we will see that from his very earliest to his most recent writings he has consistently shown a concern with ethics and politics, [returning] again and again to the dialectical interplay of hermeneutics and *praxis*[7]

From this point of view, Gadamer's hermeneutics can probably be contextualized in the so-called "need for ethics" which is so characteristic of our time.

---

philosophic wisdom (*sophia*) and comprehension (*nous*) (see *Nicomachean Ethics* VI 3, 1139b 15-18). For Gadamer's comment on these Aristotelian distinctions, see ANE, pp. 4-12.
6   Bernstein 1983, p. 166.
7   Bernstein 1983, pp. 150-151.

Anyway, in order to prevent possible misunderstandings, it must be noticed that Gadamer has always been quite suspicious of all attempts to start a new ethics, or at least to lay the foundations for it, by means of philosophical theories. In his opinion, such an ambitious purpose – which, by the way, has been and is common to many philosophers of the past and present ages – collides indeed with the basic and inescapable fact of our finitude, limitedness and situatedness. That is, it collides with the fact that we constantly belong to, and participate in, a broad network of relationships, "prejudices" and values, which one cannot simply overcome by proposing new methods, approaches or theories. This basic conviction about the impossibility of philosophically founding a new ethics emerges from many of Gadamer's essays on practical philosophy, and it is tightly connected to the fundamental concept of *ethos*. For example, in the essay *Vernunft und praktische Philosophie* he emphasizes the insurmountable importance of "the diversity of ethical formations (*Vielfalt von Ausformungen des Ethos*)"[8] in the field of moral philosophy. While in the essay *Probleme der praktischen Philosophie* he puts stress on the actual meaning of the Greek word *ethos*, claiming that it stands for

> the factuality (*Tatsächlichkeit*) of the convictions, values, and habits that we all share with the deepest inner clarity and the most profound communality, the quintessence of all that goes to make up our way of life. The Greek word for this

---

[8] GW 10, p. 265. Here he claims indeed: "jede Möglichkeit der praktischen Philosophie […] beruht […] auf einer solchen vorgängigen Raumschaffung des philosophischen Gedankens […], die auf die Existenz von Ethos, von Solidarität, von fragloser und begründungsunbedürftiger Gemeinsamkeit gegründet ist" (GW 10, p. 265). Similar remarks can also be found in the essay *Geschichte des Universums und Geschichtlichkeit des Menschen*, in which we read: "Dieses Wort [*scil.* 'Ethik'] hängt zusammen mit 'Ethos' und am Ende mit der Gewohnheit, die man angenommen hat und die zum gedankenlosen Weitermachen führt. Das ist oft nichts, was wir nach Regeln rekonstruieren und kontrollieren können, sondern wir folgen früh einsetzenden Anpassungsprozessen, die man heute 'Sozialisation' nennt. Da mögen Sitten, Ordnungen und Herkommen noch so zerfallen, vieldeutig und fragwürdig geworden sein, so daß *manche sogar so naiv sein mögen, nach einer neuen Ethik zu rufen, als ob das die Aufgabe von Professoren der Philosophie wäre*" (GW 10, p. 221 [my italics]).

quintessential factuality is the well known concept of *ethos*, the being that comes about through practice and habituation. Aristotle is the founder of ethics because he privileged this factuality as the definitive kind[9].

Even more clearly and strongly, in the essay *Über die politische Inkompetenz der Philosophie* he writes:

> we must ask ourselves why those who feel themselves drawn toward [those] philosophical questions to which no science can offer answers should, because they are professors of philosophy, have a particular aptitude to comprehend and even resolve the problems of the day. I am always amazed that the philosopher, in the academic sense of the word, is supposed to have a particular competence denied to others, by virtue of which he ought even perhaps be invested with a particular responsibility, something that is frequently expected of us. [...] It will be recalled that Heidegger was once asked (by a young Frenchman, Beaufret, after the war) when he was going to write an ethics, and he tried to give a detailed answer. The burden of his reply was that the question cannot be put like that, as if it was the philosopher's job to "teach" someone an *ethos*, that is to propose or justify a social order, or recommend this or that moral order, this or that manner of influencing widely held convictions[10].

---

9   GW 2, p. 325 [PT, p. 58].
10 HE, p. 37 [Gadamer 1998d, pp. 5-6]. By saying so, Gadamer refers to a famous passage of Heidegger's *Humanismusbrief*, where we read: "Soon after *Being and Time* appeared a young friend asked me, 'When are you going to write an ethics?'. [...] The desire for an ethics presses ever more ardently for fulfillment as the obvious no less than the hidden perplexity of human beings soars to immeasurable heights. The greatest care must be fostered upon the ethical bond" in the age of technology (Heidegger 1976, p. 353 [1998, p. 268]). In my opinion, however, on this and other occasions Gadamer strongly (and perhaps consciously) "urbanizes" Heidegger's radical and provocative thought, to use the famous expression coined by Jürgen Habermas (1981b). In fact, Gadamer's aim is simply to emphasize the "educational processes which had clearly been undertaken on for a long time and had conditioned all and sundry before humankind began to raise the radical questions customarily ascribed to philosophy" (HE, p. 37 [Gadamer 1998d, p. 6]). Whereas Heidegger's aim is more ambitious, and rather points in direction of a (quite unclear, in my opinion) "originary ethics" that would actually coincide with "thinking which thinks the truth of being as the primordial element of the human being" (Heidegger 1976, p. 356 [1998, p. 271]).

Now, such observations on what we might define, with Gadamer, as the ethical and political "incompetence" of philosophy, are obviously not unquestionable or beyond all doubt. His view on the inexistence of moral experts seems to be at odds with such typical institutions of modern, secularized and pluralistic societies as, for example, bioethics commissions, which usually group various scholars and professional experts on a specific subject[11]. Furthermore, Gadamer's opinions sharply contrast with those of other thinkers, who somehow consider moral philosophers as potential moral experts. To my knowledge, one of the strongest versions of this claim has been made by the Australian philosopher Peter Singer, who in a seminal 1972 article wrote:

> The role of the moral philosopher is not the role of the preacher, we are told. But why not? The reason surely cannot be [...] that the preacher is doing the job "so adequately". It is because those people who are regarded by the public as "moral leaders of the community" have done so badly that "morality", in the public mind, has come to mean a system of prohibitions against certain forms of sexual enjoyment. [...] Someone familiar with moral concepts and moral arguments, who has ample time to gather information and think about it, may reasonably be expected to reach a soundly based conclusion more often than someone who is unfamiliar with moral concepts and moral arguments and has little time. So moral expertise would seem to be possible. [...] If moral expertise is possible, have moral philosophers been right to disclaim it? Is the ordinary man just as likely to be expert in moral matters as the moral philosopher? On the basis of what has just been said, it would seem that the moral philosopher does have some important advantages over the ordinary man. First, his general training as a philosopher should make him more than ordinarily competent in argument and in the detection of invalid inferences. [...] Next, his specific experience in moral philosophy gives him an understanding of moral concepts and of the logic of moral argument. [...] Clarity is not an end in itself, but it is an aid to sound

---

11   Not by chance, on some occasions Gadamer has taken a critical stand on the existence itself of such institutions, claiming that "we in the West should go back once again to see the fateful way in which from a great beginning we find ourselves now driven to a point that is dangerously one-sided. [...] I am no prophet, but I would think that by means of language and its possibility of creating solidarity in our mobile world, we will again and again discover points of solidarity. And then we will no longer need an ethics commission" (Gadamer 1994a, p. 149 [GC, p. 101])!

argument [...]. Finally, there is the simple fact that the moral philosopher can, if he wants, think full-time about moral issues, while most other people have some occupation to pursue which interferes with such reflection. [...] If we are to make moral judgments on some basis other than our unreflective intuitions, we need time, both for collecting facts and for thinking about them[12].

Anyway, for our specific purposes what matters is not establishing once and for all whether Gadamer is right and Singer and those philosophers who share opinions like his are wrong, or vice versa. This would require taking into account not only their different concepts and arguments, but also their different backgrounds: in Gadamer's case, Platonic-Aristotelian ethics and, in general, twentieth-century Continental philosophy; in Singer's case, Benthamian utilitarianism and, in general, twentieth-century analytic philosophy. Undertaking such long and well-structured analyses, however, is something that goes far beyond the scope of this research. Rather, what is important to understand in the present context is what Gadamer's hermeneutic ethics really aims at, that is, his actual philosophical scopes and purposes.

As has been noted, "Gadamer's ethical thought" consists neither of "moral precepts", nor of "a theory of values", but rather represents "an attempt to properly understand ethics as practical knowledge, by giving a general outline of it and locating its foundations in the very historicity of human beings"[13]. Regarding this, I think that the centre of Gadamer's ethics is actually constituted with the two abovementioned concepts of *ethos* and *phronesis*, or better, with the particular "interplay" he theorizes between such concepts.

First of all, Gadamer praises Aristotle for having "placed the conditionedness of human life at the center and singled out concretizing the universal, by applying it to the given situation, as the central task of philosophical ethics and moral conduct alike"[14]. This "conditionedness (*Bedingtheit*)", in Gadamer's opinion, represents indeed "no deficiency and no obstacle", and has actually "the social and political de-

---

12 Singer 2000, pp. 3-6.
13 Ripanti 1999, p. 131.
14 GW 4, p. 187 [HRE, p. 34].

terminacy (*Bestimmtheit*) of the individual as its positive content", which, in turn, "is more than dependence on the changing conditions of social and historical life"[15]. By doing so, Aristotle did full justice to "family, society, and state [that] determine the essential constitution of the human being": that is, he did full justice to "the '*ethos*' of humankind prior to all appeals to reason", which makes "such appeals possible in the first place"[16]. According to Gadamer, we thus owe Aristotle our unending thanks for having appropriately accounted for the decisive importance of the *ethos*, and that is one of the reasons why he actually prefers the Stagirian to Kant himself, notwithstanding the latter's discovery of "what is perhaps the most enduring definition of morality": namely, "that one ought never to use another person as a means, but always acknowledge as well that he is an end in himself"[17]. Hence, it is the binding value of the *ethos* in the development of all human relationships that is the first relevant element in Gadamer's conception of ethics. As we read in the essay *Zur Phänomenologie von Ritual und Sprache*:

> The rationality of practical reason receives its normative power not so much from arguments as from what Aristotle called "*ethos*", that means from the determination of one's emotional life that shows practical reason at work in education and moral training. [...] So here one is not concerned with a boundary of rationality, but rather it is a very different rationality than the one consisting of knowledge of true propositions. As another type of knowledge (*allo eidos gnoseos*), this rationality is at work in practical life. This I recognize as the decisive insight of Aristotle, to think *ethos* and *logos* as two sides of the same one[18].

However, in defining this key concept of Gadamer's ethics, besides the self-evident Aristotelian elements that are present in it, some Hegelian elements concur as well. I refer, above all, to Hegel's doctrine of the "objective mind" or "spirit" (*objektiver Geist*), and especially to

---

15   GW 4, p. 188 [HRE, p. 35].
16   GW 4, pp. 187-188 [HRE, pp. 34-35].
17   GW 7, p. 393 [HRE, p. 158].
18   GW 8, p. 437 [Gadamer 2000, pp. 48-49].

his concept of "ethical life (*Sittlichkeit*)". Not by chance, Gadamer defines the philosophy of the objective spirit, i.e. the second subdivision of the third part of Hegel's entire system[19], as "the point with regard to which the indispensability of Hegel for philosophic thought is made most starkly manifest and where one can be sure that those who damn all philosophy, especially that of Hegel, actually live out of it, especially the sociologists"[20]! Gadamer, in particular, praises Hegel's strong critique of "moralism in social life" and of "a purely inward morality that is not made manifest in the objective structures of life that hold human beings together"[21]. So, in the essay *Hegels Philosophie und ihre Nachwirkungen bis heute* we read:

> Hegel became a critic of Kantian moral philosophy. He criticized the extent to which this moral philosophy is perched upon moral self-certitude and thinks itself independent in its knowledge of its own duty from all external conditions, whether natural or social [...]. This Kantian impulse is great in itself, but Hegel treated it critically, especially at the point where as a morality of inwardness it amounts to a moralistic attitude over against the reality of state and society. The thrust of the theory of the objective spirit is that not the consciousness of the individual but a common and normative reality that surpasses the awareness of the individual is the foundation of our life in state and society. [...] It was one of the greatest merits of Hegel that he made the emergence of family, society, and state from this one root convincing for thought: They each arise from the overcoming and surpassing of the subjective spirit, of the individual consciousness, in the direction of a common consciousness[22].

Closely connected to this discourse about the importance of such "objective", i.e. super-individual and communal institutions, is also Gadamer's concern for the loss of genuine solidarity he envisages in the present age. As a matter of fact, concepts like those of *Solidarität, Gemeinsamkeit* and even *Freundschaft*, play a decisive role in Gadamer's so-called political writings, in which he explains that "life together can be established on no other basis than binding solidarities", and

19 See Hegel 1970b, pp. 303-365 [1971, pp. 241-291].
20 VZW, p. 43 [RAS, pp. 29-30].
21 VZW, p. 44 [RAS, p. 30].
22 VZW, pp. 44-45 and 48 [RAS, pp. 31 and 33].

complains about "all loss of solidarity [that] signifies the suffering of isolation"[23]. Faced with circumstances and events that are "a matter of the destiny of everyone on this earth", such as those we have taken into account in the fourth and fifth chapters of this book, "humanity in the course of one or perhaps many, many crises, and in virtue of a history involving many, many sufferings", must necessarily

> learn to rediscover out of need a new solidarity. [...] Even a solidarity out of necessity can uncover other solidarities. Just as we, in our overstimulated process of progress of our technological civilization, are blind to stable, unchanging elements of our social life together, so it could be with the reawakening consciousness of solidarity of a humanity that slowly begins to know itself as humanity [...]. Practice is conducting and acting in solidarity. Solidarity, however, is the decisive condition and basis of all social reason[24].

Anyway, besides this first element of moral philosophy, namely that of the *ethos* (Aristotle) or "ethical life" (Hegel), Gadamer always emphasizes the relevance of a second key concept. This is the concept of *phronesis*, which forms an indissoluble unity with that of *ethos*, and which, according to him, does not stand for mere prudence or astuteness (*Klugheit*), as it has sometimes been interpreted. Rather, this concept defines to Gadamer human wisdom or reasonableness (*Vernünftigkeit*), "the reasonableness of practical knowing"[25], i.e. our capacity to reasonably judge in practical situations. "*Phronesis*, or reasonableness", he explains indeed in his extended interview with Riccardo Dottori, "is nothing other than the conscious side of action", and this

---

23 LT, p. 135 [PT, p. 110].
24 GW 4, pp. 227-228 [RAS, pp. 85-87]. On this topic, see also Gadamer's observations in the 1999 essay *Freundschaft und Solidarität*: "Unsere repräsentative Demokratie macht uns heutzutage viele Sorgen, weil es unserer Wählerschaft an Solidarität fehlt. [...] Wir selber leben freilich in diesem Zeitalter der anonymen Verantwortlichkeit, das dank seiner eigenen Organisations kunst eine Welt gegenseitiger Fremdheit heraufgeführt hat. [...] In dieser Situation müssen wir uns fragen, was Solidarität anmahnt [...]. Wir müssen erkennen, wie im Leben unserer Gesellschaft die Gruppierung zu Solidaritäten führt und uns damit anderen gegenüber verpflichtet" (HE, pp. 64 and 57).
25 UD, p. 23 [CP, p. 21].

is something that "cannot be gauged with a scientific concept like mathematics; it's something quite different – it's rhetoric"[26]. Not only "*phronesis* is rhetoric", Gadamer continues, but "the whole of ethics is rhetoric"[27], whereas the concept of rhetoric is understood by him in such a broad and universal sense that it becomes virtually synonymous with the whole of our "everyday situation of communication, where we do have to defend our *raisons*, our good reasons [...], reasons that are just not as evident to the other person"[28].

In this context, Gadamer goes so far as to define his "whole philosophy [as] nothing but *phronesis*"[29]. But what matters the most, for our specific purposes, is the strong emphasis he puts on the fact that *phronesis* actually constitutes an autonomous and indeed valid kind of rationality, if compared to scientific-technological reason. So, in the *Introduction* to his own translation of the sixth book of Aristotle's *Nicomachean Ethics* Gadamer writes:

> Das Wissendsein der *Phronesis* ist also nicht so sehr ein bestimmtes Wissen, sondern zunächst ein Erwägen – nämlich was das Rechte in Bezug auf das Verhalten im praktischen Leben ist. Damit ist die Abgrenzung zur *Episteme*, zur Wissenschaft, einfach. [...] Für das in der *Praxis* stehende Wissen bedarf es offenkundig der Erfahrung. Es handelt sich hierbei also wirklich um ein *állo eídos gnóseos* eine andere Art, um sich selber zu wissen, als das theoretische Wissen ist, das man im weitesten Sinne *Episteme* nennen mag und das der Er-

---

26 UD, pp. 57-58 [CP, pp. 53-54].
27 UD, p. 57 [CP, p. 53].
28 UD, pp. 55-56 [CP, p. 52]. According to Gadamer, indeed, we usually misunderstand "the true sense of Platonic-Aristotelian rhetoric because we remain trapped in a false estimation of rhetoric that we have dragged along with us through the intervening centuries in which the schools of rhetoric have dominated. The rhetoric that we can call the art of speech or persuasion does not, as we have believed for centuries, consist in a body of rules according to whose application and adherence we can achieve victory over our opponent or our partner in public debates or simply in conversation with one another. [It] consists, rather, in the innate ability – which we can also, of course, develop and perfect – of being able to actually communicate with others and even persuade them of the true without being able to prove it" (UD, pp. 55-56 [CP, pp. 51-52]). On the relationship of rhetoric and hermeneutics, see GW 2, pp. 276-291 and 292-300.
29 UD, p. 58 [CP, p. 54].

fahrung nicht bedarf. [...] Es ist nicht nur die Vernünftigkeit, es ist auch eine Art politischer und sozialer Verantwortlichkeit, die hier gemeint ist, und das ist der Grund, warum ich für *Phronesis* öfters zwei Worte gebrauche, Vernünftigkeit oder Gewissenhaftigkeit. [...] Die praktische Vernünftigkeit, die *Phronesis* heißt, umgreift sowohl die praktischen Normen, die das *Ethos* bilden, als auch das rechte Vorgehen von Schritt zu Schritt bei allen Entscheidungen. [...] Es war eine durch die Jahrhunderte gehende Fehlinterpretation, die *Phronesis* nur als ein Mittel zum Zweck, als eine Art von Klugheit anzusehen, als ob die sittliche Ausrichtung der Person allein vom *Ethos* abhinge. In Wahrheit *sieht Aristoteles beides als untrennbar an*. [...] Offenbar lag Aristoteles daran, daß das praktische Wissen der *Phronesis* vor allem die Urteilsfähigkeit im konkreten Fall meint, auch wenn man normative und begriffliche Gesichtspunkte der Erziehung und des *Ethos* auf diese Weise verwirklicht[30].

Gadamer's aim is thus to show the inseparability of *ethos* and *phronesis*. This point is so relevant for the development of his hermeneutic ethics, I think, that one could probably detect the latter's essence in the principle that "there is no *phronesis* without *ethos* and no *ethos* without *phronesis*"[31] – just like, according to him, one of the "fundamental moral-anthropological facts" of our life is represented by the "deep inner interconnection [...] between authority and critical

---

30 ANE, pp. 8, 13-14 and 19 (my italics). On Gadamer's interpretation of the Aristotelian virtue of *phronesis* as reasonableness, see also GW 10, p. 18 – where he defines it as "[die] sittliche Vernünftigkeit und Besonnenheit, [...] Wachsamkeit und Achtsamkeit, die offenbar die eigentliche Auszeichnung des Menschen ist, die es ihm möglich macht, sein Leben zu 'führen'". Then, in GW 10, p. 367, Gadamer explains: "Ich würde vorziehen, 'Phronesis' durch 'Vernünftigkeit' [und nicht durch] 'Klugheit' [...] wiederzugeben. Vernünftigkeit ist ja nicht einfach Ausstattung mit Vernunft, sondern Vernünftigkeit ist eine positive 'Eigenschaft', die ein Mensch hat und die ihn zu vernünftigen und verantwortlichen Entscheidungen betähigt. Vernünftigkeit ist also nicht bloß eine Fähigkeit, etwas zu denken, zu sehen und zu erkennen, sondern eine Grundhaltung des eigenen Seins". In GW 10, p. 278, he intriguingly puts side by side the Aristotelian virtue of *phronesis* and the Kantian concept of judgement (*Urteilskraft*), claiming that "Aristoteles hatte noch den Begriff der Phronesis als eine 'andere Art von Erkenntnis' neben der Episteme [...] ausgezeichnet. [...] In der Tat, diese andere Art der Erkenntnis ist Urteilskraft".
31 GW 7, p. 390 [HRE, p. 155].

freedom"[32], i.e. by the fact that there is no genuine freedom without genuine authority, and vice versa. The last quotation was taken from the 1983 essay *Autorität und kritische Freiheit*, in which Gadamer first distinguishes being "authoritative (*autoritativ*)" from being "authoritarian (*autoritär*)". He then criticizes the tendency he sees in our age to equate the two concepts. Finally, he concludes by detecting "the foundation of all genuine authority" in "critical freedom": that is, in "the capacity to criticize", which "includes and is a precondition both of our own recognition of the superior authority of others" – genuine authority, according to him, being "recognized as involving superior knowledge, ability and insight", rather than just power – "and of others' recognition of our own authority"[33].

Such considerations, I think, are actually of great importance in order to "save" Gadamer's hermeneutics from the somehow habitual, but erroneous, charge of being a mere plea for blind authority, tradition and prejudices. Hence Gadamer, responding to those who accuse him of reducing philosophy to an uncritical defence of the *status quo* and existing institutions, explains:

> *Phronesis*, answerable rationality, can ensure that [the] *ethos* is not mere indoctrination or accession to custom and has nothing to do with the conformism of a half-guilty conscience [...]. Anyone who is not "asocial" has always already accepted others, the exchange of ideas and the construction of a common world of convention. "Convention" is something better than the world's contemporary connotations might suggest. It means agreement that has currency – not a mere externally prescribed system of rules but the identity between an individual's consciousness and convictions represented in other people's consciousness, between the various ways we organize our lives. In one sense, this is a question of rationality, but not just in the sense of pragmatic and technological reason [...]. That is Max Weber's famous means-end rationality. [...] But rationality, in the great moral and political sense of Aristotelian *phronesis*, without doubt goes beyond knowing how to use the right means for given ends. In human society, everything depends on how that society sets its goals or, better still, on how it

---

32 ÜVG, p. 157 [EH, p. 123].
33 ÜVG, pp. 157 and 154 [EH, pp. 123 and 121].

gets everybody to agree on the goals that they affirm and finds the right means to achieve them[34].

Although the question of the real nature of *phronesis* – i.e. whether it is a rationality of the right means for given ends, or, rather, a rationality of the right ends as such – has been and still is much debated and controversial[35], Gadamer appears quite confident on this point. In fact, in his writings he repeatedly insists on the "alternative" meaning of practical reasonableness, compared to techno-scientific, "instrumental" or "calculating" reason. So, for example, in the essay *Philosophische Bemerkungen zum Problem der Intelligenz* he claims that "the concept of *phronesis*", in Aristotle's practical philosophy, stands not only for "the clever, skilful discovery of means for meeting specific tasks", and not only for "an awareness of what is practical, of how to realize incidental goals", but also for "the sense for setting the goals themselves (*Sinn für die Setzung der Zwecke selber*) and taking responsibility for them"[36]. Again, in the final chapter of his important study on the idea of the good in Plato and Aristotle, we read that, while "in the technical realm the only concern is with the right choice of means for pre-given ends or purposes", *phronesis* "is displayed not only in knowing how to find the right means", but also (and, perhaps,

---

34 GW 2, pp. 325-326 [PT, pp. 58-59]. The same thing, according to Gadamer, holds true also for Hegel's "doctrine of the spirit objectified in institutions", which "is not concerned with defending the existing institutions in their unchangeable correctness. Hegel defended institutions not in a wholesale fashion but against the pretense of knowing better on the part of the individual" (VZW, p. 44 [RAS, p. 30]).
35 I borrow this observation from Natali 2007 (pp. 268-276), who stresses the fact that it is difficult to assume a univocal and unambiguous position on this point, since Aristotle himself has disseminated his writings with passages that seem to go in both directions. Natali, for instance, refers to *Nicomachean Ethics* VI 12, 1144a 6-9, and VI 13, 1145a 4-6 [1991, pp. 1807-1808]), on the one side; and *Nicomachean Ethics* VI 5, 1140a 25-28 and VI 7, 1141b 18-20 [1991, pp. 1800 and 1802]), on the other side.
36 GW 4, p. 278 [EH, pp. 47-48].

most of all) "in holding to the right ends"[37]. Finally, in the essay *Die Grenzen des Experten*, Gadamer explains:

> When Aristotle described [the] rational element in all decision making in human action, he evidently considered both aspects in their indivisible unity in the concept of *phronesis*. One is that rationality which is used in discovering the correct means for a given end. The other is used in discovering the end, becoming conscious of it and retaining it, in other words the rationality in the choice of ends and not only in the choice of means[38].

Now, it is not my aim to enter anymore into details about Gadamer's interpretation/appropriation of Aristotle's ethics, especially with regard to the question of its exact degree of philological correctness. With regard to this issue, let me just remind the reader of the objections that an outstanding Italian scholar of ancient philosophy, Enrico Berti, has raised against Gadamer's reading of the *Nicomachean Ethics*. According to Berti, indeed, Gadamer would have ignored, or at least undervalued, a fundamental distinction made by Aristotle: namely, the distinction between *phronesis* and *episteme praktike*, i.e. between *practical* wisdom in itself, as it is experienced and practiced by reasonable men and women in their everyday life, on the one side, and the philosopher's *theoretical* reflection on practical reasonableness, on the other side. To be sure, Berti acknowledges that it would be absurd to accuse a distinguished classical philologist like Gadamer of having confused *phronesis* and *episteme praktike*. Rather, he thinks that, in Gadamer's case, we are faced with "a conscious and deliberate reduction of the latter to the former"[39].

---

37 GW 7, pp. 220-221 [IGPAP, p. 165].
38 EE, p. 142 [EPH, p. 184].
39 Berti 1992, p. 205. As Berti notes in another writing, "Gadamer is surely aware of the difference between practical philosophy, on the one side, which falls within to Aristotle's conception of all sciences as either theoretical or practical or productive (*Metaph.* VI I), and *phronesis*, on the other side, which is one of the dianoetic virtues presented in *Eth. Nic.* VI". Nevertheless, Gadamer often "tends to identify them", or better, "we observe in Gadamer a particularly strong tendency to reduce all practical knowledge to *phronesis*, and thus to exclude the

In any case, such philological-philosophical remarks, although surely interesting and worthy of mention, are not of immediate relevance for the scope of this research. Rather, what is important to notice in this context is that, among Gadamer's strongest philosophical anxieties, one must surely mention his concern for the loss of practical wisdom and reasonableness in the present age. According to him, indeed,

> Vernunft [ist] im Zeitalter der Wissenschaft in eine schwierige Lage geraten. Die moderne Wissenschaft trägt in einem solchen Grade zum allgemeinen Wohlstand bei, daß ihre Stimme, die Stimme der Experten, kaum noch einen Raum für freie Entscheidungen aus vernünftiger Besinnung offen läßt. [...] Es sieht so aus, als ob ein unerbittliches Schrittgesetz die wissenschaftliche Forschung beherrscht, so daß sie unbeirrbar ihren Weg geht. Auch wenn sie die Menschheit zur Verfremdung von ihrer Umwelt zwingt oder gar zur Verwüstung der heimatlichen Erde führt, muß sie voranschreiten[40].

From this point of view, Gadamer's demand for a rehabilitation of practical philosophy seems to converge with his overall demand to revaluate "the *humanistic tradition*", whose "resistance to the claims of modern science" confers it "a new significance"[41]. As is well-known, in *Wahrheit und Methode* Gadamer develops a long and complex reconstruction/interpretation of the history of some guiding concepts of humanism: culture (*Bildung*), taste (*Geschmack*), judgement (*Urteilskraft*)[42] and common sense (*sensus communis*)[43]. All concepts

---

very possibility of a practical science (*episteme praktike*)" (Berti 2001, pp. 376 and 380).

40   GW 7, p. 429.
41   GW 1, p. 23 [TM, p. 16].
42   As Gadamer emphatically declares in the essay *Europa und die Oikoumene*: "Wir brauchen eine neue Legitimation der Urteilskraft. [...] Dafür die Augen zu öffnen, ist die Hauptaufgabe der hermeneutischen Philosophie" (GW 10, p. 278).
43   On Gadamer's rehabilitation of common sense in the age of science, technology and "technocracy", see, in particular, his interview with Claus Grossner, where he says: "Ich habe in meinen eigenen Untersuchungen deswegen dem *sensus communis* [...] seine Legitimität zurückzugeben versucht. Ich bin in der Tat überzeugt, daß wir in einem höchst kritischen Weltaugenblick stehen [...]. *Sensus communis* heißt [...] ein gesellschaftlich integriertes Bewußtsein spre-

which, according to him, have unfortunately lost a great part of their significance in the modern age.

In the context of the present inquiry into Gadamer's critique of the modern techno-scientific civilization, the latter two concepts appear of particular importance. As a matter of fact, in some of his later writings and interviews he emphasizes the need, in such a "bureaucratic democracy (*bürokratische Demokratie*)"[44] like ours, for a rediscovery of common sense and a capacity for independent judging. In the age of mass-media invasion, social engineering and incapacity for genuine personal communication, it has become a huge but unavoidable task for us to "incentivize" the assumption of personal responsibility and autonomous decision making. That is, we must learn to rely, more than we are used to, "on our faculty of judgment, [...] on the possibility of our taking a critical stance with regard to every convention"[45]. In fact,

> while the virtues of accomodation and adjustment to [our] rational forms of organization are correspondingly cultivated, the autonomy of the formation of judgement and of action according to one's own judgement are correspondingly neglected. That has its basis in the character of modern civilization and permits the following to be pronounced as a general rule: the more rationally the organizational forms of life are shaped, the less is rational judgement exercised and trained among individuals[46].

This obviously has noteworthy repercussions for the ethical and political implications of Gadamer's philosophy, which are actually the subject of this chapter. The emergence of this kind of "illuminist" aspect in Gadamer's hermeneutics, consisting, as we have seen, of his emphasis on the importance of "judgement-training (*Urteilsschulung*)

---

chen lassen. [...] *Sensus communis* meine ich mit 'Verstand'. [...] [D]er Selbstkritik seiner Interessen fähig [zu] sein – [...] das nennt man *sensus communis*! [...] *Sensus communis* heißt auf Deutsch Gemeinsinn, also nicht nur allgemeine Vernunft, sonder Verantwortung für das Ganze der Gemeinschaft, der Gesellschaft" (Gadamer 1971a, pp. 221-224).

44   Gadamer 1998a, p. 41.
45   GW 2, p. 204 [TM, p. 551].
46   GW 4, p. 256 [EH, p. 17].

and courage for one's own judgement (*Mut zum eigenen Urteil*)"[47], together with his well-known dialogical-conversational attitude[48], seems to lead indeed in a liberal and democratic direction. Despite "the restoring, not to say 'reactionary', prejudice against hermeneutics (*das restaurative, um nicht zu sagen 'reaktionäre' Vorurteil gegen die Hermeneutik*)"[49], I thus think one should not be surprised if some distinguished scholars have claimed that "Gadamer's position is deeply, even if prudently, critical and reformist"[50]. He is "fundamentally a liberal", "both less conservative and less relativistic than Habermas" – and those who, today, still follow the "hermeneutics *versus* ideology critique" line of thought – "charges"[51].

By the way, this interpretation seems to correspond entirely to Gadamer's political self-interpretation. As a matter of fact, on many

---

47 HE, p. 174. Gadamer writes indeed in the essay *Die Kunst und die Medien*: "da man ein Rad nicht zurückdrehen kann, das die ganze Zivilisationsbewegung erst möglich macht, wird *die Aufgabe* immer deutlicher, *die Kräfte des selbstständigen Denkens und des eigenen Urteilens zu entwickeln*, die in uns nicht fehlen, aber durch die Strukturen einer durchrationalisierten Gesellschaft bedroht sind. Dazu gehört, daß wir die Anpassungsqualitäten nicht allzu sehr privilegieren dürfen. [...] Es sollte die Aufgabe unserer Besinnung über die Kultur und die Massenmedien sein, daß wir uns erneut erinnern, daß Kultur nicht nur eine bloße Einrichtung ist, sondern der Pflege bedarf. Was Kultivierung ist und der Pflege bedarf, das ist, *die Freiheit zum eigenen Urteil zu lernen*" (HE, pp. 173 and 175 [my italics]).

48 "*Being that can be understood is language*", reads Gadamer's most famous statement; at the same time, however, it must be recalled that, for him, "language has its true being only in dialogue, in *coming to an understanding*. [...] For language is by nature the language of conversation" (GW 1, pp. 478 and 449-450 [TM, pp. 470 and 443]). "Yes, we live constantly in dialogue", he explains: "we could even say that we are a living dialogue" (UD, p. 52 [CP, p. 48]).

49 Grondin 2000b, pp. 154-155.

50 Madison 1995.

51 Zuckert 1996, pp. 102-103. For example, Richard Wolin unhesitatingly speaks of an "endemically 'conservative' nature of the hermeneutic standpoint", which "came across vividly in Gadamer's well-known debate with Habermas". "Gadamer's hermeneutics", Wolin adds, "has never sought to conceal its fundamentally 'conservative' bearing" (Wolin 2004, p. 118).

occasions he has explicitly declared to see himself "not as a right-wing conservative but rather as a liberal"[52]. "I never thought of myself as a conservative", he declares in the interview *The 1920s, the 1930s, and the Present*; "I have always been a liberal, from early times to today, and I have always voted for the FDP"[53]. "So", he concludes, "the kind of conservativism that Habermas is thinking of is utterly alien to me"[54]. Not by chance, in his 1990 Aristotle-lectures given at the Institute for Philosophical Studies in Naples, referring to the surprising and "revolutionary" historical-political changes of the time, Gadamer observed:

> In these months we are witnessing the fall of the communist regimes in East Europe, which is due to their lack of consensus by the citizens. [...] It is without doubt that governments can last, in the long term, only if supported by the citizens' approval. And this happens only in Western democracies[55].

On this basis, István M. Fehér has correctly noticed that

> Hermeneutik und Demokratie schließen sich nicht, wie oft behauptet wird, aus, vielmehr gibt es gute Gründe, die philosophische Hermeneutik als eine Philosophie der Demokratie und des Pluralismus auszuzeichnen. [...] [Den] Charakter von Pluralität und Gemeinschaftsbildung weist [...] Gadamers Hermeneutik auf, besonders im Sinne des Prinzips der Offenheit und d.h., auf der Ebene der politischen Philosophie, der Toleranz [...]. Die Offenheit – sowohl die für die Über-

---

52 Gadamer 1990, p. 546 [GC, p. 120].
53 Gadamer 1992e, p. 140.
54 UD, p. 101 [CP, p. 99].
55 MET, p. 72. In the light of such explicit statements, I think that considerations like the following are actually untenable: "Political wisdom consists [*scil.* for Gadamer] in the prudent acceptance of the relevant differences and inequalities. [...] Therefore, he concedes that differences between 'Western' democracy (such as that found in Europe and North America) and democracy in primarily one-party states (such as the Soviet Union) are not absolute. As with other conservative Germans of his generation, Gadamer fails to be impressed by the Enlightenment pathos of liberal democracy and its advocates, and [...] fails to perceive the difference between emancipatory and technocratic politics" (Misgeld 1990, pp. 172-173).

lieferung als auch für die Zeitgenössen – bildet [...] die Grundlage einer im Popperschen Sinne "offenen Gesellschaft"[56].

On the same topic, let me also remind the reader of the interesting and appropriate remarks of Robert R. Sullivan (one of the few interpreters of Gadamer's hermeneutics who has paid close and specific attention to its political aspects), who asks himself whether "Gadamer's vision of a binding political *ethos*" is really "hostile to [...] liberalism", and then confidently and convincingly answers that it is not at all hostile to "*liberal* society"[57]. In fact, Sullivan notices that

> the kind of liberalism with which we are most familiar in the English-speaking world is Anglo-Saxon liberalism, and from Locke through Mill and up to Rawls this liberalism has privileged or at least accepted the pursuit of individual interest as being central to modernity. [...] This liberalism has become a kind of civic religion in the United States. But it does not follow from this that [...] Gadamer's program for reconstituting a "binding political *ethos*" is illiberal. Ever since Wilhelm von Humboldt was Prussian Minister of Education, there has been a kind of distinctly German liberalism which has focused on the educational development of the individual and devalued the distinctly Anglo-Saxon development of property. [...] Gadamer is very much in harmony with this distinctly German liberalism when he conceives his "binding political *ethos*" in terms of an educational state which does not impose a predefined ideal of the good citizen but rather uses language to enter into a play with the conflicting elements of the human soul, one that is designed to build a real political man[58].

In my opinion, emphasizing the liberal and democratic implications of Gadamer's hermeneutics is highly important, today more than ever. In

---

56 Fehér 1996, pp. 252, 256 and 258.
57 Sullivan 1997, p. 252.
58 Sullivan 1997, pp. 252-253. Another attracting interpretation is that provided by Thomas M. Alexander, who explores in detail "the similarities between Gadamer's philosophy and Dewey's", saying that "they are surprisingly many", and concluding that "the question of hermeneutics as conceived by Gadamer has great bearing, then, upon the possibility for a democracy. The democratic society is engaged in the project of mutual interpretation [...]. Hence, then, we may discover the meeting place of hermeneutics and pragmatics, interlocutors in the democratic community with all its traditions and future projects" (Alexander 1997, pp. 323 and 343).

recent times, the question concerning the political consequences of hermeneutic philosophy has acquired indeed new importance and significance, since some scholars raised the question of whether Gadamer's writings (especially those he wrote in Germany under the Nazi regime) contained some secret "fascist" allusions[59].

This question has been raised, in particular, by Richard Wolin and Teresa Orozco, according to whom Gadamer's 1934 lecture *Plato und die Dichter*[60] and 1942 essay *Platos Staat der Erziehung*[61] "are rich with interdiscursive implications and allusions", and "provide a hermeneutic horizon that is congruent with the ideal self-understanding of National Socialism as a political decision to 'renew' the state after the 'decay' of the Weimar Republic"[62]. Orozco argues that "Gadamer was able to identify with the national conservative faction of National Socialism without, however, publicly declaring his opposition to its most popular forms. The contemporary relevance of his interpretations of Plato" – which Orozco, at least in her paper *The Art of Allusion*, actually interprets in a bizarre and problematic way, taking a few sentences out of context and interpreting them as a plea for "an ideal fascism" or "an authoritarian state with a highly centralized concentration of power" – "enabled him to construct bridges that allowed various connections to be drawn without the need to state them explicitly"[63].

Wolin, for his part, unhesitatingly includes Gadamer's hermeneutics in a wide philosophical discourse of the twentieth century concerning "indictments of Western humanism", from Nietzsche to postmodernism, and "Counter-Enlightenment arguments", in both "the

---

59 On the whole question, let me remind the reader of the special issue of the *Internationale Zeitschrift für Philosophie* (n. 1/2001) entirely dedicated to the question of hermeneutics and politics in Germany before and after 1933 – with contributions from M. Brumlik, A. Graeser, F.-R. Hausmann, G. Motzkin, R.R. Sullivan, G. Warnke and R. Wolin.
60 See GW 5, pp. 187-211.
61 See GW 5, pp. 249-262.
62 Orozco 2004, p. 219.
63 Orozco 2004, pp. 222-223.

political right [and] the cultural left"[64]. Then, Wolin focuses his attention on Gadamer's 1941 lecture *Volk und Geschichte im Denken Herders*[65], and claims that this text – "although it is, strictly speaking, a non-Nazi text", and although "Gadamer never was [...] an ardent Nazi" – undeniably "exhibits the salient features of the German *Sonderweg mentalité*"[66]. In short, Gadamer would have believed that "the Nazi victory testified to the supremacy of the German 'way' and to the inferiority of French 'civilization'", and even his following writings, according to Wolin, give us no reason to presume that he later abandoned his "basic antipathy to Western liberalism"[67], which he presumably shared with other German intellectuals of the time.

What Wolin erroneously takes for granted, however, is that Gadamer's hermeneutics fully belongs to the horizon of what he describes as post-Nietzschean, post-Heideggerian and poststructuralist Counter-Enlightenment. As a matter of fact, if it is true that one of the basic features of this supposed current of contemporary thought is represented by its "assault on humanism"[68], then one should remind Wolin that Gadamer precisely intended his own philosophy, from the beginning to the end, to be an attempt to rehabilitate the humanist tradition. This, by the way, evidently marks his distance from Heidegger's "destruction" of humanism[69] and, for example, from

64 Wolin 2004, pp. 9 and 3.
65 See GW 4, pp. 318-335. To be precise, the essay included in Gadamer's collected works is entitled *Herder und die geschichtliche Welt*, and was first published in 1967, after a revision of the 1941 lecture which deleted some passages of the original text. This is one of the points on which Gadamer's critics insist the most, because of the content of the missing passages, and because of the peculiar circumstances in which the Herder-lecture was held: namely, at the German Institute in Paris occupied by the Nazis. For a comparison of the two versions of Gadamer's Herder-essay, see Orozco 1995, pp. 235-240.
66 Wolin 2004, pp. 122-123.
67 Wolin 2004, p. 122.
68 Wolin 2004, p. 5.
69 I obviously refer here to Heidegger's famous observations on humanism, interpreted as a form of "metaphysical" thought, in *Wegmarken* (Heidegger 1976, pp. 236, 315-322, 330-335 and 344-352 [1998, pp. 181, 241-246, 251-255 and 262-

Foucault's controversial and radically anti-humanistic idea of "the end of man"[70]. Nor is Gadamer chargeable for the kind of "anti-Americanism" that Wolin (not wrongly, I think) considers as "an enduring component of Counter-Enlightenment and postmodernist discourse", and that he sees in various German and French thinkers of the last century, from Oswald Spengler to Jean Baudrillard[71]. As is well-known, indeed, Gadamer never debunked American philosophy and culture (as even his teacher Martin Heidegger, for instance, openly did)[72], and in the 1999 interview *Was bleibt?*, after having

---

268]). The essential difference between Heidegger's and Gadamer's evaluations of humanism has been correctly stressed by Grondin 1997.

70 See IFO, p. 22 [BP, p. 17]. As is well-known, Foucault's influential idea of the end of man is presented in *Les mots et les choses*, where we read: "As the archaeology of our thought easily shows, man is an invention of recent date. And one perhaps nearing its end. [...] In our day, [...] it is not so much the absence or the death of God that is affirmed as the end of man" (Foucault 1966, pp. 398 and 396 [1994, pp. 387 and 385]).

71 Wolin (2004, p. 23) refers here to some highly controversial and, I think, even shameful considerations that Baudrillard made soon after the terrorist attacks of the 11th September, 2001: "All the speeches and commentaries betray a gigantic abreaction to the event itself and to *the fascination that it exerts*. Moral condemnation and the sacred union against terrorism are equal to *the prodigious jubilation* engendered by witnessing this global superpower being destroyed [...]. Though it is (this superpower) that has, through its unbearable power, engendered all that violence brewing around the world, and therefore this *terrorist imagination which – unknowingly – inhabits us all*. [...] That *we have dreamed of this event,* that *everybody without exception has dreamt of it* [...] – this is unacceptable for Western moral conscience, but it is still a fact [...]. *It is almost they who did it, but we who wanted it*" (Baudrillard 2001 [my italics]).

72 I refer, for example, to his famous definition of American pragmatism as a philosophy that "still remains outside the realm of metaphysics" (Heidegger 1977b, p. 112 [2002, p. 85]). Worthy of notice is Richard Rorty's comment to this remark, halfway between irony and sobriety, that reads: "It is unlikely that Heidegger meant that cryptic sentence as a compliment", and he "probably meant that Americans are so primitive that their understanding of their own technological frenzy does not even take a respectably philosophical form. But one *could* take Heidegger to be paying pragmatism a compliment. One might read him as saying that America is still, happily, innocent of metaphysics" (Rorty 1990, pp. 1-2)!

noticed that "die Wirtschaft nicht allein eine staatsbildende Kraft ist, sondern zugleich staatsunterhöhlend wirkt", he even pointed to the U.S.A. as a model:

> Wir müssten uns, um solche falschen Entwicklungen einzudämmen, mehr an Amerika orientieren. Die sind uns im ökonomischen Kampf weit voraus. Aber auch in der Ausbildung ihrer kulturellen Identität sind die Amerikaner für uns vorbildlich. [...] Was dort an Kultur entwickelt wird, ist enorm. [...] Sehen Sie sich Amerika an! Die Atomisierung der Gesellschaft und die Auflösung der Familie wurden dort von einer neuen religiösen Bewegung konterkariert. Auf der einen Seite ist es der Atheismus der triumphiert, auf der anderen Seite werden die alten Werte verteidigt[73].

Finally, I think that both Orozco and Wolin fail to explain why a supporter, or at least sympathizer, of the Nazi regime, had to make recourse to subtle and almost unperceivable "allusions" (as they say Gadamer did) in the few texts he published in those years. As Jean Grondin has pointed out, "if Gadamer had really sympathized with them [*scil.* the Nazis], wouldn't it have more readily occurred to him and been smarter tactically to have publicly acknowledged the fact?"[74]. In fact, "the 'art of intimation' tends in just the opposite direction in a totalitarian state", where "anyone who is in agreement with official ideology does not need to hide it", and it is rather "those who dissent and want it known" who "need to resort to 'intimation', since open resistance would be suicidal"[75]! In my opinion, the definitive word on this question has been said by Donatella Di Cesare, who has shown why the whole "prosecution framewok" against Gadamer, in the absence of any evidence, must fall down. As Di Cesare notes, indeed,

> Wenigstens drei Klarstellungen sind zu Beginn notwendig. Erstens war Gadamer kein Nationalsozialist – im Gegensatz zu Heidegger und anderen "zum Waffendienst einberufenen Musen". Er ist nie Mitglied der NSDAP (Nationalsozialistische Deutsche Arbeiterpartei) und nie Anhänger von national-

---

73 Gadamer 1999.
74 Grondin 1999, p. 190 [2003, p. 165].
75 Grondin 1999, p. 190 [2003, p. 165].

sozialistischen Ideen gewesen. [...] Kein Parteimitglied zu sein war im übrigen keine Bagatelle. Damit riskierte man sein Leben. Gadamer war kein Antisemit. Dies war in jenen Jahren alles andere als selbstverständlich, hatte der Antisemitismus doch tiefe und weitverbreitete Wurzeln. [...] Doch viel wichtiger ist, daß seine Freundschaft zu den Juden, mit denen die meisten jede Beziehung abgebrochen hatten, unverändert blieb. [...] [S]o ist es nicht nur, daß Gadamer nie in der NSDAP eingeschrieben war; darüber hinaus gibt es auch nirgendwo ein Dokument, aus dem seine Mitwirkung, am Nationalsozialismus abgeleitet werden könnte. [...] Schließlich war Gadamer keineswegs "unpolitisch" – und sicherlich nicht nach 1933. [...] Gadamer gehörte zu der Kulturelite, die sich Hitler niemals angeschlossen hatte und die auch nach dem ersten "schrecklichen Erwachen" unbeirrt meinte, die Nazis würden sich nur für wenige Monate an der Macht halten. Seine Position unterschied sich hierin nicht von derjenigen, die etwa Löwith vertrat. [...] Um [den] Unterschied [*scil.* zu Heidegger] noch klarer zu machen, muß man hinzufügen, daß Gadamer nie der Faszination erlag, die der Nationalsozialismus auf die zweite Generation des europäischen Nihilismus ausübte [...]. Außerdem war er allergisch gegen die mystische Exaltiertheit, mit der Ernst Jünger schon im Ersten Weltkrieg die "Stahlgewitter" beschrieben hatte, so wie er unberührt von der faschistischen Ideologie blieb, die im Hitlerregime den Triumph vitalistischer Impulse, den Siegeszug von Natur und Technik, von Kraft und Mythologie feierte[76].

Having clarified these delicate and controversial issues, let us now return to our analysis of the key concepts of Gadamer's political philos-

---

[76] Di Cesare 2007, pp. 27-28, 33 and 28-29 [2009, pp. 19-20, 25 and 21-22]. On the same question, see also Chris Lawn's brief but fitting remarks: "whereas Heidegger's shameful tangle with National Socialism is well documented Gadamer's relationship to the Nazis is much more sketchy and vague. [...] Against [the] generally accepted picture of Gadamer's non-involvement with the Nazis during the war years, recent controversial studies – of questionable academic worth it has to be said – suggest a murkier past. [...] When quizzed about this period Gadamer responded that as a liberal he disliked the regime, stood by his Jewish colleagues and friends, and was left alone by the Nazis for he was not a threat and after all they had no use for philosophers. At the same time Gadamer claims to have followed the familiar path of 'inner emigration' [...]. This last point rings true. Of the works on Herder and Plato, the Herder essay is not a glorification of the German people and the Plato essay if anything is a warning against the dangers of too powerful a state and thus is, if anything, subversive of Nazism rather than supportive of it". In the end, "those attacking Gadamer rely more on conjecture than hard evidence" (Lawn 2006, pp. 20-22).

ophy: namely, those of *ethos* and *phronesis*, tradition and practical reasonableness, authority and critical freedom, dialogue and judgment. Now, I think that in a world like ours, characterized by strong contrasts between different cultural schemes and thought-paradigms, a hermeneutic perspective like Gadamer's – which aims "to make possible that situation of mutual understanding and solidarity that is a dialogue", and which is based on the "good will to come to an agreement"[77] – may appear very promising and challenging. In order to prevent the potential degeneration of the encounter of divergent worldviews into political struggle or clash of civilizations, what is required, indeed, is first and foremost a hermeneutic openness to the other's viewpoint, and a capacity for reasonable thinking and acting, "which is meant to bring us to consensus and mutual understanding"[78].

On the basis of what we have seen up to now, however, it might still be questioned whether Gadamer's confident reliance on dialogue and practical wisdom is really appropriate to a world-situation like that of the present age. From a certain point of view, it might be argued that the way he takes human reasonableness for granted leads him to an optimistic or perhaps even naïve faith in the good will of mutual understanding. Furthermore, we have already noticed that *phronesis* "is inevitably linked to an already existing *ethos*", so that "the (wise) choice of the good is only possible under the presupposition of a deeply-rooted and well-practiced set of virtues"[79]. In order words, *phronesis* is a context-bound and "*ethos*-relative reason (*ethosrelative Vernunft*)"[80]. But such an emphasis on the tradition-dependent nature of practical rationality risks being led to complete

---

77 UD, pp. 62 and 39 [CP, pp. 60 and 36].
78 UD, p. 64 [CP, p. 62]. In his interview with Jean Grondin on his collected papers and their effective history, Gadamer claims that "the multiplicity of languages does not represent an insurmountable barrier to the hermeneutical task": "a person is always capable of overcoming all boundaries [represented by language], when that person seeks to reach an understanding with the other person" (GLB, p. 287 [GR, p. 418]).
79 Da Re 2001, pp. 15-16.
80 Tietz 1999, p. 113.

(and, as such, untenable) relativism, i.e. to the uncritical acceptance of the plurality of moral and political traditions, in their mutual irreducibility and incommensurability. What Gadamer's political hermeneutics seems to lack is thus a stable and, so to speak, "cross-cultural" principle, through which to orient the conversation between different ethical conceptions.

Now, it is surely true that, "from a hermeneutic point of view, the attempt to find some unconditioned 'Archimedean point' for assessing the norms and principles of a given society fails to account for the limits of its own historical perspective"[81]. At the same time, however, in some of his writings, Gadamer prudently but confidently hints at a concept that, in his view, has something like an "absolute" and unconditioned validity. Hence, a concept that might prove useful in order to get to a genuine "fusion of horizons", based on the practice of giving and asking for good reasons[82] and persuasive arguments, rather than on the acceptance of mere compromise solutions. Such a principle, in short, is that of freedom, of freedom for all, and Gadamer openly borrows it from Hegel.

According to him, indeed, Hegel understood the absolute and indubitable value of freedom better than any other thinker (even better than Kant, whose concept of freedom, as we saw, Gadamer holds in high esteem). More precisely, what Hegel recognized, in contrast to Kant, was the objective, and not merely subjective meaning of freedom: that is, its being concretely embodied in social practices and institutions. One of the interpreters who paid the greatest attention to

---

81 Warnke 1990, p. 136.
82 I freely borrow the expression "practice of giving and asking for reasons" – adapting it to the present context of moral and political philosophy – from Robert B. Brandom's "inferentialism" and *rationalist* pragmatism" (Brandom 2000, p. 11). In his work *Tales of the Mighty Dead*, Brandom has also paid attention to Gadamer's "hermeneutic platitudes" (Brandom 2002, pp. 92-94). "By calling them that", however, Brandom does not mean "to impugn their originality, but rather to mark that they have, thanks to Gadamer's work, *become* platitudes expressing a select set of the framework attunements of hermeneutic theory. Calling them 'platitudes' suggests that I think we should believe them" (Brandom 2002, p. 94).

this particular feature of Hegel's thought is probably Charles Taylor, who noticed that "Hegel laid bare the emptiness of the free self and the pure rational will, in his critique of Kant's morality and the politics of absolute freedom"[83]. He sought to overcome this emptiness by "situating freedom"[84], i.e. by proposing a concept of situated, rather than abstract and decontextualized freedom.

"No higher principle is thinkable than that of the freedom of all", and "there is no higher principle of reason than that of freedom", Gadamer emphatically claims: "Thus the opinion of Hegel and thus our own opinion as well"[85]. Furthermore, it is precisely "from the perspective of this principle" that we understand "actual history [...] as the ever-to-be-renewed and the never-ending struggle for this freedom"[86]. Gadamer obviously refers here to Hegel's application of the concept of freedom to the philosophy of world history, which makes him capable of reading "history as a progress of freedom":

> If in the Orient one was free and all others unfree; and in Greece only those who were citizens of a city were free while the others were slaves; so in the end it is through Christianity and modern history, especially the emancipation of the third estate and the liberation of the peasants, that we have arrived at the point where all are free. [...] As a matter of fact, since then history is not to be based upon a new principle. The principle of freedom is unimpugnable and irrevocable. It is no longer possible for anyone still to affirm the unfreedom of humanity[87].

---

83 Taylor 1979, p. 158.
84 Taylor 1979, pp. 154-165.
85 VZW, pp. 17-18 [RAS, p. 9].
86 VZW, p. 18 [RAS, p. 9].
87 VZW, p. 52 [RAS, p. 37]. As we read in the § 549 of Hegel's *Enzyklopädie*: "It is the spirit which not merely broods over history as over the waters but lives in it and is alone its principle of movement: and in the path of that spirit, liberty, i.e. a development determined by the notion of spirit, is the guiding principle and only its notion its final aim, i.e. truth. For Spirit is consciousness. Such a doctrine – or in other words that Reason is in history – will be partly at least a plausible faith, partly it is a cognition of philosophy" (Hegel 1970b, p. 352 [1971, p. 281]).

This, however, does not lead Gadamer to subscribe to Hegel's philosophy of history on the whole. Disregarding the vastness and depth of his philosophical confrontation with Hegel, what we know for sure is that while he considers Hegel's doctrine of the objective spirit absolutely fundamental and still topical, the so-called "Absolute" viewpoint of the philosophy of history is definitely less relevant for him, rather, it constitutes a point of discrepancy.

This is implicitly confirmed by those important sections of *Wahrheit und Methode* in which he considers "how the 'historical school' tries to deal with [the] problem of universal history", and claims that "representatives of the historical worldview [like] Ranke, Droysen, and Dilthey", despite their "rejection of the aprioristic construction of world history" and their criticism of Hegel, in the end are not "free from metaphysical assumptions"[88]. Rather, they are closer to Hegel than they believe themselves to be, since they somehow share with him the idea of a "teleological [...] ontological structure of history", and the "basic viewpoint [...] that continuity is the essence of history"[89]. Hence they simply replace the "full transparency of being, which Hegel saw as realized in the absolute knowledge of philosophy", with the idea of a perfect culmination of knowledge in the "historical consciousness", which similarly represents "transparency, the complete dissolution of all alienness, of all difference"[90]. But one of Gadamer's fundamental beliefs is that the historically conditioned character of consciousness constitutes "an insuperable barrier to its reaching perfect fulfilment in historical knowledge", which evidently questions every effort to reach an "historical viewpoint on everything" and understand history as "a structured whole"[91].

Here Gadamer's criticism towards Hegel explicitly emerges, since the ambition of the latter's philosophy of history – namely, to develop a *"thoughtful consideration of it"*, to penetrate *"the infinite complex of things"* that "reveals itself in the world", and to understand

---

[88] GW 1, pp. 204-205 [TM, pp. 197-199].
[89] GW 1, pp. 207 and 213 [TM, pp. 201 and 206].
[90] GW 1, pp. 215 and 233 [TM, pp. 208 and 223].
[91] GW 1, p. 235 [TM, p. 225].

that "the history of the world, therefore, presents us with a rational process", "the rational necessary course of the world-spirit"[92] – appears to him quite illegitimate. As a matter of fact, such an ambition seems to presuppose the possibility of elevating oneself to the unhistorical, universal standpoint of the *"Divine* Providence" that "presides over the events of the world" and "leads into truth, knows all things, penetrates even into the deep things of the Godhead", thus realizing the aim of an "absolute rational design of the world"[93]. According to Gadamer, however, "being historical" means precisely "never being able to pull everything out of an event such that everything that has happened lies before me": thus, "that which Hegel named the *bad infinity* is a structural element of the historical experience as such"[94]. Not by chance, Gadamer explicitly affirms that "*the structure of historically effected consciousness*" must be defined "with an eye to Hegel, setting it against his own approach"[95]. And he constantly warns "the interpreter of history" from "the risk of hypostasizing the connectedness of events", since unless "Hegel's conditions hold true" (that is, unless "the philosophy of history is made party to the plans of the world spirit and on the basis of this esoteric knowledge is able to mark out certain individuals as having world-historical importance"[96]), then the development of such grandiose narratives can only appear as a sort of philosophical-historical *hubris*.

Moreover, sometimes Gadamer hints at Karl Löwith's relevant discovery of the affinities between theological and philosophical views of history[97], respectively aiming "to understand the plan for salvation" and "to understand the coming to pass of history and to recognize its order"[98]. According to him, however, "such a philosophy

---

92   Hegel 1970c, pp. 20 22 [1952, pp. 156-157].
93   Hegel 1970c, pp. 25 and 27 [1952, pp. 158-159].
94   GW 3, p. 221 [HW, pp. 58-59].
95   GW 1, pp. 351-352 [TM, p. 341].
96   GW 1, p. 377 [TM, pp. 364-365].
97   I obviously refer here to his famous book *Meaning in History: The Theological Implications of the Philosophy of History*.
98   GW 2, pp. 139-140 [Gadamer 1972, pp. 235-236].

of history [cannot] gain access to the reality of history", because "it stands in complete contradiction to the finitude of man's existence"[99]. Gadamer's own version of the criticism of the "poverty of historicism" – understanding here this term in its peculiar Popperian meaning[100] – thus relies on his objection to "the idea of [...] totality as a *completion*", because "any claim for an inner teleology and the completion of a development would have to be made from some position external to historical forms of life"[101]. Hence a "magnificent and yet violently construing philosophy of world history"[102] like Hegel's runs the risk not to do justice to

> the actual reality of the event, especially its absurdity and contingency [...]. The finite nature of one's own understanding is the manner in which reality, resistance, the absurd, and the unintelligible assert themselves. If one takes this finitude seriously, one must take the reality of history seriously as well[103].

From this point of view, the fact that Gadamer has often distanced himself from such all-encompassing philosophical-historical views as those provided by Hegel, Spengler – whom he sometimes defines as an outsider with a "colossal imagination (*überdimensionierte Phantasie*)", and a mere "ingenious dilettante (*genialer Dilettant*)"[104] – or

---

99 GW 2, p. 140 [Gadamer 1972, p. 236].
100 As is well known, Poppers subsumes under "historicism" every kind of philosophical "belief in historical destiny" and "prediction of the course of human history", which for him is just "sheer superstition" (Popper 2002, p. IX). In other words, "historicism" is "a label" that Popper "introduced as a convenient way of talking about various connected theories", and that he intended as something different from "historical relativism, which [he] referred to as 'historism'" (Popper 1994, p. 131). In its peculiar Popperian meaning, "historicism" has to do with the very "idea of a plot in history", as it is presented, for example, by "theories of intrinsic historical progress or regress" (Popper 1994, p. 132).
101 Pippin 2002, p. 229.
102 GW 3, p. 214 [HW, p. 50].
103 GW 2, p. 445 [TM, pp. XXXI-XXXII].
104 GW 10, pp. 49 and 209.

even Heidegger[105], might suggest that he was at odds with the very idea of "metanarratives" or *grands récits*[106].

Far from being just a digression on the relationship of philosophical hermeneutics to modern and postmodern conceptions of history, this has precise and relevant repercussions for the ethical and political issues we are debating in this chapter. In fact, the philosophical-historical and political discourse of the twentieth century has been characterized, among other things, by a "long line of *deterministic doctrines* about social development" and by various "discourses about the *fate* of modernity", that one might summarize

---

105 Gadamer claims indeed that "Heidegger's description of the history of Being" undeniably involves "a similarly comprehensive claim" as Hegel's attempt "to penetrate the history of philosophy philosophically from the standpoint of absolute knowledge [...]. For Heidegger [...] it is fate, not history (remembered and penetrable by understanding), that originated in the conception of Being in Greek metaphysics and that in modern science and technology carries the forgetfulness of Being to the extreme. [...] And so Heidegger too appears to claim a genuinely historical self-consciousness for himself, indeed, even an eschatological self-consciousness" (GW 3, pp. 230-231 [HW, p. 71]). Accordingly, even though Heidegger "never speaks of an historical necessity anything like the one which Hegel claims as the basis of his construing of world history", nonetheless "in conceiving of metaphysical thought as a history unified by the forgetfulness of being which pervades it" he cannot avoid attributing "a kind of inner consequentiality to history". Furthermore, Gadamer argues that "it is made evident by certain of Heidegger's phrases [...] that there is even a connection between increasing forgetfulness of being and the expectation of this coming or epiphany of being – a connection quite similar to that of a dialectical reversal". The very idea of a "radical deepening of forgetfulness of being in the age of technology" leads indeed to a sort of "eschatological expectation in thought of a turnabout", and in Gadamer's eye "such an historical self-consciousness as this is no less all-inclusive than Hegel's philosophy of the Absolute" (GW 3, pp. 95-96 [HD, pp. 109-110]).
106 I obviously refer here to Jean-François Lyotard's influential interpretation of the so-called postmodern condition as characterized by the "breaking up of the grand narratives", i.e. by the fact that today "the grand narrative has lost its credibility" (Lyotard 1979, pp. 31 and 63 [1999, pp. 15 and 37]).

with the concept of "endism"[107]. As has been noted, "fatalism is one of the principal orientations towards social change in social and political thought, and the writing on endism is only the latest example of it"[108]. The "avalanche of books and articles" published at the end of the twentieth century, "proclaiming the end of history, the end of the nation-state, the end of politics", actually sought "to reveal the fate of the modern world and modern civilization"[109]. By the way, to be fatalistic does not imply to believe "that the outcomes are always necessarily bad": in fact, although "it is more usual [...] to find fatalism linked to pessimism", it is also possible "to be a fatalist and an optimist"[110].

Among the most famous and influent (also on a geopolitical level, I think) "fatalistic" meta-narratives that have been proposed in the last decades, one must surely mention Francis Fukuyama's reinterpretation of nineteenth-century *Geschichtsphilosophie*. A concept, the latter, centred on the respectively Hegelian and Nietzschean concepts of "the end of history" and "the last man", and explicitly aimed at renewing the ambitious search for "what drives the *whole* historical process"[111]. Following Hegel, and greatly relying on the interpretation of his philosophy provided by Alexandre Kojève, Fukuyama feels urged by "the need to look again at the question of whether there is some deeper connecting thread underlying" all historical developments, "or whether they are merely accidental instances of good [or bad] luck"[112]. Accordingly, he poses the question of "whether there is such a thing as progress, and whether we can construct a coherent and directional Universal History of mankind"[113]. Fukuyama is confident that a large

---

107 Gamble 2000, pp. 12-13 (my italics). By "endism" Gamble refers to such modern and especially postmodern theories as those concerning "the end of history, the end of the nation-state or the end of politics": all events that "are presented as the fate of modernity" (Gamble 2000, p. 12).
108 Gamble 2000, p. 12.
109 Gamble 2000, p. 10.
110 Gamble 2000, p. 12.
111 Fukuyama 1998, p. XVII (my italics).
112 Fukuyama 1998, p. XIV.
113 Fukuyama 1998, p. XXIII.

"pattern [...] is emerging in world history", and that it consists of "a pronounced secular trend in a democratic direction": in fact, "there is a fundamental process at work that dictates a common evolutionary pattern for *all* human societies – in short, something like a Universal History of mankind in the direction of liberal democracy"[114]. On this basis, he enthusiastically claims: "we cannot picture to ourselves a world that is *essentially* different from the present one, and at the same time better":

> History [is] not a blind concatenation of events, but a meaningful whole [...]. A Universal History of mankind is [...] an attempt to find a meaningful pattern in the overall development of human societies generally. [...] The notion that history is directional, meaningful, progressive, or even comprehensible is very foreign to the main currents of thought of our time. [...] To [the] question, Is it possible to write a Universal History from a cosmopolitan point of view?, our [...] answer is yes[115].

Now, having mentioned the case of Francis Fukuyama's neo-Hegelian construction of a universal history – Hegel being for him *"the* philosopher of freedom, who saw the entire historical process culminating in the realization of freedom in concrete political and social institutions"[116] – it is just because it probably represents the most famous embodiment, in recent times, of what we previously defined as a "fatalistic" attitude. Notwithstanding his admission that "we have no guarantee and cannot assure future generations that there will be no

---

114 Fukuyama 1998, pp. 45 and 48. It must be said, however, that Fukuyama's construction of a universal history directed to the affirmation, in the whole world, of democracy and freedom, does not aim to represent "a kind of secular theodicy, that is, a justification of all that exists in terms of history's final end. This no Universal History can reasonably be expected to do. [...] A Universal History is simply an intellectual tool" (Fukuyama 1998, p. 130).
115 Fukuyama 1998, pp. 46, 51, 55, 69 and 126. To be precise, the last sentence reads: "our provisional answer is yes". However, I have chosen to suppress the adjective "provisional" because Fukuyama says this in the eleventh chapter of the book (which is made up of thirty-one chapters): that is, at a *provisional* stage of his "demonstration" of the possibility of a universal history of mankind.
116 Fukuyama 1998, p. 60.

future Hitlers or Pol Pots", it is indeed the very idea of a "locomotive of History"[117], i.e. of a development secretly guided by some sort of rational principle, that implicates concepts like that of historical necessity and, ultimately, of fate.

As a general rule, according to "fatalistic" philosophical-political views, historical events are somehow "determined in advance, rendering any notion of free will or choice irrelevant"[118]. This means, however, that both optimistic and pessimistic fatalists "believe that events are unfolding in such a way that no other outcome is possible": to be fatalistic, in the final analysis and in its most radical conesquences, implies to refuse the very idea "that any change could be brought about by human agency"[119].

Now, although Gadamer embraces the idea of the possibility of progress and, indeed, of a progress of freedom, he nevertheless never goes so far as to believe in an intrinsic and fateful rationality of historical changes. According to him, "universal history is indisputably an aspect of the experience of our being in history" and "a legitimate need in a human reason that is explicitly conscious of its historical character":

> Like all other history, however, universal history too must always be rewritten [...]; and each projection of writing a universal history has a validity that does not last much longer than the appearance of a flash momentarily cutting across the darkness of the future as well as of the past as it gets lost in the twilight. This finitude is a point of hermeneutical philosophy that I have dared to defend against Hegel[120].

At the same time, however, it is precisely Gadamer's reliance on the Hegelian concept of history as a progress of freedom, I think, that makes him look with suspicion at the widespread tendency, in twentieth-century thought, to radically question the ideas of modern Enlightenment and claim that "the hope that things could improve and

---

117 Fukuyama 1998, pp. 128-129.
118 Gamble 2000, pp. 12 and 9.
119 Gamble 2000, p. 12.
120 GW 4, p. 481 [GR, p. 342].

would improve", i.e. "the idea of the progress", has "now proved baseless"[121]. From this point of view, I guess that Gadamer could have endorsed the reasonable words with which Hilary Putnam concludes his lecture *The Three Enlightenments*[122] – and this is perhaps one of the reasons why a certain "postmodern" thought has interpreted Gadamer's hermeneutics as too naïve, "old-fashioned" or still "metaphysical". As Putnam expresses it:

> There are many thinkers to whom my talk of three enlightenments will seem naïve. "Poststructuralists", positivists, and a host of others will react with horror. But I have chosen to speak in this way to make clear that I am an unreconstructed believer in progress, though not, indeed, progress in the stupid sense of [...] a secular version of eschatology. But what I do believe in is the *possibility* of progress. Such a belief can indeed be abused – what belief can't be? But to abandon the idea of progress and the enterprise of enlightenment – when that abandonment is more than just fashionable "postmodern" posturing – is to trust oneself to the open sea while throwing away the navigation instruments. I hope we shall not be so unwise[123].

Gadamer's anti-fatalistic hermeneutics, if I may define it so, thus reinterprets Hegel's concept of history and freedom as articulating "a task for each individual rather than a legitimation for the inactivity of us all"[124]. "The principle that all are free never again can be shaken.

---

121 Gamble 2000, p. 14.
122 In this respect, it is not by accident if, notwithstanding all differences and divergences between them, "critical theorists agree with Gadamer when he says [...] that 'the principle that all are free can never again be shaken'. It is the 'new world-historical principle'. [...] [C]ritical theorists, certainly since Habermas and just like Gadamer, have given expression to the hope that the spirit of dialogue and open communication can actually prevail in society" (Misgeld 1991, pp. 173 and 177).
123 Putnam 2005, p. 108.
124 VZW, p. 52 [RAS, p. 36]. Gadamer's anti-fatalistic and anti-deterministic attitude towards history is well exemplified, I think, from the essay *Kausalität in der Geschichte?*, where we read: "Geschichte ist ein Ablauf der Dinge, ein Zusammenhang von Ereignissen, der nicht primär in der Weise des Planens und des Erwartens und des noch so unsicheren Vorauswissens erfahren wird, sondern grundsätzlich immer als ein schon geschehener. Damit gehört er aber einer

But does this mean that on account of this, history has come to an end?"[125]. According to Gadamer, it is definitely not so. Rather, this means that "the historical conduct of man has to translate the principle of freedom into reality": far from giving "becalming assurance that everything is already in order", "this points to the unending march of world history into the openness of its future tasks"[126]. From a specifically political point of view, this leads Gadamer to be "in favor of a government and politics that would allow for mutual understanding and the freedom of all": something which, he adds, "has been self-evident to any European since the French Revolution, since Hegel and Kant"[127].

In the context of the present inquiry into Gadamer's hermeneutics, in the light of his critique of the modern, techno-scientific civilization, the specific attention he pays to the concept of freedom acquires a special significance. So, at the end of the essay *Die Dialektik des Selbstbewußtseins*, referring this time to Hegel's famous description of the relationship between master and servant, he writes:

---

ganz anderen Dimension an. [...] Es sind 'Szenen der Freiheit', aus denen Ranke zufolge die Weltgeschichte besteht. [...] [Der] Zusammenhang, zu dem sich die Weltgeschichte fügt, ist alles andere als in seiner Notwendigkeit erkennbar oder gar voraussehbar. Er hat nicht den Charakter des Zusammenhangs von Ursache und Wirkung [...]. Was in Wahrheit ist, erkennt niemand recht. Es sind die unscheinbaren Anfänge, aus denen das wird, was die Zukunft beherrschen wird" (GW 4, pp. 107-108).

125 VZW, p. 52 [RAS, p. 37].
126 VZW, pp. 52-53 [RAS, p. 37]. On the controversial question of the so-called "end of history", see also Gadamer's following observation at the end of the essay *Was ist Geschichte?*: "Die technologische Gesinnung des industriellen Zeitalters, in dem wir stehen, unternimmt inzwischen alle Anstrengungen, die geschichtliche Überlieferung und die Überlieferung des geschichtlichen Denkens abzubauen und im Ideal des Planens, Konstruierens und Machens die neuen Illusionen eines sich souverän dünkenden Bewußtseins zu hegen. Sie nennt das Emanzipation, die nicht zuletzt die vom Druck der Geschichtlichkeit sein will und ein *Zeitalter der post-histoire* heraufführen möchte" (Gadamer 1980b, p. 456 [my italics]).
127 Gadamer 1983, p. 264.

the question necessarily arises who could be really free in the industrial society of today with its ubiquitous coercion of things and pressure to consume. Precisely in regard to this question Hegel's dialectic of master and servant seems to delineate a valid truth: if there is to be freedom, then first of all the chain attaching us to things must be broken. The path of mankind to universal prosperity is not as such the path to the freedom of all. Just as easily, it could be a path to the unfreedom of all[128].

The awareness of this and other dangers of our civilization, together with the intention to contrast them by appealing to the unnegotiable principles of reasonableness, solidarity, dialogue, autonomous judgment and freedom, represent in my opinion one of the most important and interesting aspects of Gadamer's hermeneutic philosophy.

---

128 GW 3, p. 64 [HD, pp. 73-74].

Bibliography

1. Works of Hans-Georg Gadamer

1.1. Books and Collections of Papers (Original Editions)

(GW) *Gesammelte Werke*, Mohr Siebeck (UTB), Tübingen 1999
(GW 1) *Hermeneutik I: Wahrheit und Methode. Grundzüge einer philosophischen Hermeneutik* (1986)
(GW 2) *Hermeneutik II: Wahrheit und Methode. Ergänzungen – Register* (1986)
(GW 3) *Neuere Philosophie I: Hegel, Husserl, Heidegger* (1987)
(GW 4) *Neuere Philosophie II: Probleme – Gestalten* (1987)
(GW 5) *Griechische Philosophie I* (1985)
(GW 6) *Griechische Philosophie II* (1985)
(GW 7) *Griechische Philosophie III: Platon im Dialog* (1987)
(GW 8) *Ästhetik und Poetik I: Kunst als Aussage* (1993)
(GW 9) *Ästhetik und Poetik II: Hermeneutik im Vollzug* (1993)
(GW 10) *Hermeneutik im Rückblick* (1995)

(ABMH) "Ausgewählte Briefe an Martin Heidegger", in *Jahresgabe der Martin-Heidegger-Gesellschaft*, 2002
(ANE) *Aristoteles. Nikomachische Ethik VI*, tr. and ed. H.-G. Gadamer, Klostermann, Frankfurt a.M. 1998
(EE) *Das Erbe Europas. Beiträge*, Suhrkamp, Frankfurt a.M. 1989
(ESE) *Erziehung ist sich erziehen*, Kurpfälzischer Verlag, Heidelberg 2000
(GLB) *Gadamer Lesebuch*, ed. J. Grondin, Mohr Siebeck (UTB), Tübingen 1997
(HÄP) *Hermeneutik – Ästhetik – Praktische Philosophie. Hans Georg Gadamer im Gespräch*, ed. C. Dutt, Winter, Heidelberg 1993
(HE) *Hermeneutische Entwürfe*, Mohr Siebeck, Tübingen 2000
(IFO) *L'inizio della filosofia occidentale*, ed. V. De Cesare, Guerini, Milano 1993
(IG) *Im Gespräch: Hans-Georg Gadamer und Silvio Vietta*, Fink, München 2002

(KS 1) *Kleine Schriften 1: Philosophie, Hermeneutik*, Mohr Siebeck, Tübingen 1967
(LT) *Lob der Theorie. Reden und Aufsätze*, Suhrkamp, Frankfurt a.M. 1983
(MET) *Metafisica e filosofia pratica in Aristotele*, ed. V. De Cesare, Guerini, Milano 2000
(PCH) *Le problème de la conscience historique*, Nauwelaerts, Louvain-Paris 1963
(PL) *Philosophische Lehrjahre. Eine Rückschau*, Klostermann, Frankfurt a.M. 1977
(PTI) *Plato. Texte zur Ideenlehre*, tr. and ed. H.-G. Gadamer, Klostermann, Frankfurt a.M. 1986
(SBMH) "Sechs Briefe an Martin Heidegger aus der Marburger Zeit", in *Jahresgabe der Martin-Heidegger-Gesellschaft*, 1999
(SCH) *Schmerz. Einschätzungen aus medizinischer, philosophischer und therapeutischer Sicht*, Winter, Heidelberg 2003
(UD) *L'ultimo Dio. Un dialogo filosofico con Riccardo Dottori*, Meltemi, Roma 2002
(ÜVG) *Über die Verborgenheit der Gesundheit. Aufsätze und Vorträge*, Suhrkamp, Frankfurt a.M. 1993
(VZW) *Vernunft im Zeitalter der Wissenschaft. Aufsätze*, Suhrkamp, Frankfurt a.M. 1976

1.2. Books and Collections of Papers (English Translations)

(BP) *The Beginning of Philosophy*, tr. R. Coltman, Continuum, London-New York 1998
(CP) *A Century of Philosophy: Hans-Georg Gadamer in Conversation with Riccardo Dottori*, tr. R. Coltman and S. Koepke, Continuum, London-New York 2003
(DD) *Dialogue and Dialectic: Eight Hermeneutical Studies on Plato*, tr. P. C. Smith, Yale University Press, New Haven-London 1980
(DDGD) *Dialogue and Deconstruction: The Gadamer-Derrida Encounter*, tr. and ed. D. P. Michelfelder and R. E. Palmer, SUNY Press, Albany 1989
(EH) *The Enigma of Health: The Art of Healing in a Scientific Age*, tr. J. Gaiger and N. Walker, Stanford University Press, Stanford 1996
(EPH) *Hans-Georg Gadamer on Education, Poetry, and History: Applied Hermeneutics*, tr. L. Schmidt and M. Reuss, ed. D. Misgeld and G. Nicholson, SUNY Press, Albany 1992

(GC) *Gadamer in Conversation: Reflections and Commentary*, tr. and ed. R. E. Palmer, Yale University Press, New Haven-London 2001

(GOC) *Gadamer on Celan: "Who Am I and Who Are You?" and Other Essays*, tr. and ed. R. Heinemann and B. Krajewski, SUNY Press, Albany 1997

(GR) *The Gadamer Reader: A Bouquet of the Later Writings*, tr. and ed. R. E. Palmer, Northwestern University Press, Evanston 2007

(HD) *Hegel's Dialectic: Five Hermeneutical Studies*, tr. P. C. Smith, Yale University Press, New Haven-London 1976

(HRE) *Hermeneutics, Religion, and Ethics*, tr. J. Weinsheimer, Yale University Press, New Haven-London 1999

(HW) *Heidegger's Ways*, tr. J. W. Stanley, SUNY Press, Albany 1994

(IGPAP) *The Idea of the Good in Platonic-Aristotelian Philosophy*, tr. P. C. Smith, Yale University Press, New Haven-London 1986

(PA) *Philosophical Apprenticeships*, tr. R. R. Sullivan, MIT Press, Cambridge 1985

(PDE) *Plato's Dialectical Ethics: Phenomenological Interpretations Relating to the "Philebus"*, tr. and ed. R. M. Wallace, Yale University Press, New Haven-London 1991

(PH) *Philosophical Hermeneutics*, tr. and ed. D. E. Linge, University of California Press, Berkeley-Los Angeles-London 1976

(PT) *Praise of Theory: Speeches and Essays*, tr. C. Dawson, Yale University Press, New Haven-London 1998

(RAS) *Reason in the Age of Science*, tr. F. G. Lawrence, MIT Press, Cambridge-London 1983

(RB) *The Relevance of the Beautiful and Other Essays*, tr. N. Walker, ed. R. Bernasconi, Cambridge University Press, Cambridge 1986

(TM) *Truth and Method*, second, revised edition, tr. J. Weinsheimer and D. G. Marshall, Continuum, London-New York 2004

1.3. Articles, Interviews, Lectures and Reviews

1923-24: "Metaphysik der Erkenntnis. Zu dem gleichnamigen Buch von Nicolai Hartmann", in *Logos*, 12, pp. 340-359

1924: "Zur Systemidee in der Philosophie", in AA.VV. *Festschrift für Paul Natorp zum siebzigsten Geburtstage*, De Gruyter, Berlin-Leipzig, pp. 55-75

1939: "Zu Kants Begründung der Ästhetik und dem Sinn der Kunst", in AA.VV. *Festschrift Richard Hamann zum sechzigen Geburtstage am 29. Mai 1939*, Hopfer, Burg bei Magdeburg, pp. 31-39

1961: "Letter to Emilio Betti" (excerpts), in E. Betti, *L'ermeneutica come metodica generale delle scienze dello spirito*, ed. G. Mura, Città Nuova, Roma 1990, p. 201 note

1971a: *"Sensus communis* gegen Technokratie. Gespräch mit Hans-Georg Gadamer", in C. Grossner (ed.) *Verfall der Philosophie. Politk deutscher Philosophen*, Wegner, Reinbeck bei Hamburg, pp. 219-233

1971b: "Hegel – Vollendung der abendländischen Philosophie?", in H. Gehrig (ed.) *Hegel. Hölderlin. Heidegger*, Badenia, Karlsruhe, pp. 11-23

1972: "The Continuity of History and the Existential Moment", in *Philosophy Today*, 16/3, pp. 230-240

1975: "Schlußbericht", in H.-G. Gadamer and P. Vogler (ed.) *Neue Anthropologie*, 7 voll., Thieme, Stuttgart 1972-1975, vol. 7, pp. 374-392

1977: "Herméneutique et théologie", in *Revue des sciences religieuses*, 51/4, pp. 384-397

1978: "Gadamer-Strauss. Correspondence Concerning *Wahrheit und Methode"*, in *The Independent Journal of Philosophy*, 2, pp. 5-12

1979: "Historical Transformations of Reason", in T. F. Geraets (ed.) *Rationality Today. La rationalité aujourd'hui. Proceedings of the International Symposium*, University of Ottawa Press, Ottawa, pp. 3-14

1980a: "Religious and Poetical Speaking", in A. M. Olson (ed.) *Myth, Symbol, and Reality*, University of Notre Dame Press, Notre Dame-London, pp. 86-98

1980b: "Was ist Geschichte? Anmerkungen zu ihrer Bestimmung", in *Neue Deutsche Hefte*, 167/3, pp. 451-456

1981: "Die Kunst des Feierns", in H. J. Schultz (ed.) *Was der Mensch braucht. Anregungen für eine neue Kunst zu leben*, Kreuz, Stuttgart-Berlin, pp. 61-70

1982a: "The Conflict of Interpretations", in R. Bruzina and B. Wilshire (ed.) *Phenomenology: Dialogues and Bridges*, SUNY Press, Albany, pp. 299-304

1982b: "On the Problematic Character of Aesthetic Consciousness", in *Graduate Faculty Philosophy Journal*, 9, pp. 31-40

1983: "A Letter by Professor Hans-Georg Gadamer", Appendix to R. J. Bernstein, *Beyond Objectivism and Relativism: Science, Hermeneutics and Praxis*, University of Pennsylvania Press, Philadelphia, pp. 261-265

1984a: "The Hermeneutics of Suspicion", in G. Shapiro and A. Sica (ed.) *Hermeneutics: Questions and Prospects*, University of Massachusetts Press, Amherst, pp. 54-65

1984b: "Hans-Georg Gadamer et le pouvoir de la philosophie", in AA.VV. *Les Entretiens avec "Le Monde". Vol. 1*, Editions la Découverte, Paris, pp. 231-239

1984c: "Gadamer on Strauss. An Interview", in *Interpretation. A Journal of Political Philosophy*, 12/1, pp. 1-13

1984d: "Articulating Transcendence", in F. Lawrence (ed.) *The Beginning and the Beyond. Papers from the Gadamer and Voegelin Conferences*, Scholars Press, Chico, pp. 3-9

1984e: "Und dennoch: Macht des guten Willens", in P. Forget (ed.) *Text und Interpretation. Eine deutsch-französische Debatte*, Fink, München, pp. 59-61

1985: "A New Epoch in the History of the World Begins Here and Now", in J. Donovan and R. Kennington (ed.) *The Philosophy of Immanuel Kant*, Catholic University Press, Washington, pp. 1-14

1986a: "Die dreifache Aufklärung", in *Neue Deutsche Hefte*, 33/2, pp. 227-233

1986b: "Freiheit und Verantwortung der Wissenschaft", in E. Teufel (ed.) *Schriftenreihe der CDU-Fraktion im Landtag von Baden-Württenberg. Vol. 16*, Stuttgart, pp. 18-30

1986c: "Interview. Cold Barkhausen spricht mit Hans-Georg Gadamer", in *Sprache und Literatur im Wissenschaft und Unterricht*, 17/57, pp. 90-100

1986d: "'Traditionen sind der Wissenschaft oftmals weit überlegen'. Ein Gespräch mit dem Heidelberger Philosophen Hans-Georg Gadamer", in *Bild der Wissenschaft*, 23/6, pp. 80-88

1986e: "Natural Science and Hermeneutics: The Concept of Nature in Ancient Philosophy", in J. Cleary (ed.) *Proceedings of the Boston Area Colloquium in Ancient Philosophy*, University Press of America, Lanham, pp. 39-52

1986f: "Religion and Religiosity in Socrates", in J. Cleary (ed.) *Proceedings of the Boston Area Colloquium in Ancient Philosophy*, University Press of America, Lanham, pp. 53-75

1987: "The Relevance of Greek Philosophy for Modern Thought", in *South African Journal of Philosophy*, 6/2, pp. 39-42

1988a: "Interview with Hans-Georg Gadamer", in *Theory, Culture, & Society*, 5/1, pp. 25-34

1988b: "Die Menschenwürde auf ihrem Weg von der Antike bis heute", in *Humanistische Bildung*, 12, pp. 95-107

1988c: "Zurück von Syrakus?", in J. Altwegg (ed.) *Die Heidegger Kontroverse*, Athenäum, Frankfurt a.M., pp. 176-179

1989a: "Back From Syracuse?", in *Critical Inquiry*, 15/2 1989, pp. 427-430

1989b: "Heideggers 'theologische' Jugendschrift", in *Dilthey-Jahrbuch*, 6, pp. 228-234

1990: "'...die wirklichen Nazis hatten doch überhaupt kein Interesse an uns'. Hans-Georg Gadamer spricht mit Dörte von Westernhagen", in *Das Argument*, 182, pp. 543-555

1991a: "Gespräch mit Hans-Georg Gadamer", in *Sinn und Form*, 43/3, pp. 487-500

1991b: "Il filosofo e la morte" (Extract of the Interview of the 10th April, 1991). Available at: www.emsf.rai.it/interviste

1991c: "Il metodo dell'ermeneutica" (Extract of the Interview of the 27th November, 1991). Available at: www.emsf.rai.it/interviste

1991d: "Gadamer on Gadamer", in Silverman (ed.) 1991, pp. 13-19

1991e: "Hegel und die Sprache der Metaphysik", in H.-G. Gadamer, H. Jonas, U. Beck and W. Ch. Zimmerli, *Sprache und Ethik im technologischen Zeitalter*, Fränkischer Tag, Bamberg, pp. 11-38

1992a: "Humanismus heute?", in *Humanistische Bildung*, 15, pp. 57-70

1992b: "The Beginning and the End of Philosophy", in C. Macann (ed.) *Martin Heidegger: Critical Assessments. Vol. 1*, Routledge, London-New York, pp. 16-28

1992c: "Interview. The German University and German Politics. The Case of Heidegger", in EPH, pp. 5-14

1992d: "Interview: Historicism and Romanticism", in EPH, pp. 125-131

1992e: "Interview: The 1920s, the 1930s, and the Present: National Socialism, German History, and German Culture", in EPH, pp. 135-153

1992-93: "*Wahrheit und Methode. Der Anfang der Urfassung (ca. 1956)*", ed. J. Grondin and H.-U. Lessing, in *Dilthey-Jahrbuch*, 8, pp. 131-141

1993a: "'Im Alter wacht die Kindheit auf'. Ein Gespräch mit dem Philosophen Hans-Georg Gadamer über den Humor der alten Tage, den Tod und den Schatz der Erfahrung", in *Die Zeit*, 26 March 1993, pp. 22-23

1993b: "Gadamer: 'El alma de la politica es el compromiso'", in *Diario 16*, 27 February 1993, pp. II-IV

1994a: "Hans-Georg Gadamer: 'Die Griechen, unsere Lehrer'. Ein Gespräch mit Glenn W. Most", in *Internationale Zeitschrift für Philosophie*, 1, pp. 139-149

1994b: "What is Truth?", in Wachterhauser (ed.) 1994, pp. 33-46

1994c: "Heidegger und Nietzsche: 'Nietzsche hat mich kaputtgemacht!'. Gespräch mit Prof. Dr. Hans-Georg Gadamer am 3.11.1993 in Heidelberg", in *Aletheia. Neues Kritisches Journal der Philosophie, Theologie, Geschichte und Politik*, 5, pp. 6-8

1995a: "La religione e le religioni", in J. Derrida and G. Vattimo (ed.) *La religione*, Laterza, Roma-Bari, pp. 197-207

1995b: "An der Sklavenkette. Hans-Georg Gadamer, Nestor der deutschen Philosophie, über die Gefahren der Fernsehgesellschaft", in *Die Woche*, 11 Februar 1995, p. 33

1995c: "A Conversation with Hans-Georg Gadamer", in *The Journal of the British Society for Phenomenology*, 26/2, 1995, pp. 116-126

1997a: "Replies (to R. Sokolowski, R. R. Sullivan, D. Detmer and T. M. Alexander)", in Hahn (ed.) 1997, pp. 235-236, 256-258, 287 and 346-347

1997b: "Reflections on my Philosophical Journey", in Hahn (ed.) 1997, pp. 3-63

1997c: "Bildende und sprachliche Kunst am Ende des XX. Jahrhuderts", in K. Manger (ed.) *"Zukunft ist Herkunft". Hans-Georg Gadamer und Emil Schumacher Ehrenbürger der Universität*, Friedrich Schiller Universität, Jena, pp. 55-63

1997d: "Was den Menschen fehlt: Fragen und Antworten der Philosophie. Ein Gespräch zwischen Hans-Georg Gadamer und Dieter Henrich", in U. Boehm (ed.) *Philosophie heute*, Campus, Frankfurt a.M.-New York, pp. 177-193

1997-98: "Die Logik des verbum interius. Gespräch mit Hans-Georg Gadamer", in *Dilthey-Jahrbuch*, 11, pp. 19-30

1998a: "Über den Ernst des Fehlens von Festen. Hans-Georg Gadamer im Gespräch mit Rainer Buland", in *Homo Ludens*, 8, pp. 20-41

1998b: "The Drama of Zarathustra", in D. W. Conway and P. S. Groff (ed.) *Nietzsche: Critical Assessments. Vol. 1*, Routledge, London- New York, pp. 124-137

1998c: "Dialogues in Capri", in J. Derrida and G. Vattimo (ed.) *Religion*, Stanford University Press, Stanford, pp. 200-211

1998d: "On the Political Incompetence of Philosophy", in *Diogenes*, 46, pp. 3-11

1999: "Was bleibt? Hans-Georg Gadamer im Gespräch mit Heimo Schwilk und Günter Figal", in *Welt am Sonntag*, 26 December 1999
2000: "Towards a Phenomenology of Ritual and Language", in Schmidt (ed.) 2000, pp. 19-50
2001a: "Weltethos und internationale Gerechtigkeit. Im Gespräch mit Hans-Georg Gadamer", in *Ars Interpretandi*, 6, pp. 9-20
2001b: "'Platone scopritore dell'ermeneutica'. Intervista di Giovanni Reale a Hans-Georg Gadamer", Appendix to Girgenti (ed.) 2001, pp. 117-129
2001c: "'A scuola da Platone'. Un dialogo tra Hans-Georg Gadamer e Giovanni Reale", Appendix to Girgenti (ed.) 2001, pp. 131-141
2001d: "'Es ist mir recht unheimlich geworden'. Mit 101 Jahren sieht der Philosoph Hans-Georg Gadamer den ersten Krieg des 21. Jahrhunderts", in *Die Welt*, 25 September 2001
2002: "Sulla natura e su altre poche cose. Un'intervista a Hans-Georg Gadamer", tr. S. Venuti, in *Paradigmi. Rivista di critica filosofica*, 20/2, n. 59, pp. 217-225
2006: "I tormenti di un maestro. Intervista a Hans-Georg Gadamer", in A. Gnoli and F. Volpi (ed.) *L'ultimo sciamano. Conversazioni su Heidegger*, Bompiani, Milano, pp. 61-93

2. Other Sources

2.1. Collections of Essays on Gadamer's Hermeneutics

AA.VV. 1971. *Hermeneutik und Ideologiekritik*, Suhrkamp, Frankfurt a.M.
AA.VV. 2001. *"Sein, das verstanden werden kann, ist Sprache". Hommage an Hans-Georg Gadamer*, Suhrkamp, Frankfurt a.M.
Cattaneo F., Gentili C. and Marino S. (ed.) 2011. *Domandare con Gadamer. Cinquant'anni di "Verità e metodo"*, Mimesis, Roma
Dostal R. J. (ed.) 2002. *The Cambridge Companion to Gadamer*, Cambridge University Press, Cambridge
Failla M. (ed.) 2008. *Il cammino filosofico di Hans-Georg Gadamer*, in *Paradigmi. Rivista di critica filosofica*, 26/3

Fehér I. M. (ed.) 2003. *Kunst, Hermeneutik, Philosophie. Das Denken Hans-Georg Gadamers im Zusammenhang des 20. Jahrhunderts*, Winter, Heidelberg

Figal G. (ed.) 2000. *Begegnungen mit Hans-Georg Gadamer*, Reclam, Stuttgart

Figal G. (ed.) 2007. *Hans Georg Gadamer: Wahrheit und Methode*, Akademie Verlag, Berlin

Figal G., Grondin J. and Schmidt D. J. (ed.) 2000. *Hermeneutische Wege. Hans-Georg Gadamer zum Hundersten*, Mohr Siebeck, Tübingen

Gardini M. and Matteucci G. (ed.) 2004. *Gadamer: bilanci e prospettive*, Quodlibet, Macerata

Girgenti G. (ed.) 2001. *Platone tra oralità e scrittura. Un dialogo di Hans-Georg Gadamer con la Scuola di Tubinga e Milano e altri studiosi (Tubinga, 3 settembre 1996)*, Bompiani, Milano

Hahn L. E. (ed.) 1997. *The Philosophy of Hans-Georg Gadamer*, Open Court, Chicago-La Salle

Krajewski B. (ed.) 2004. *Gadamer's Repercussions*, University of California Press, Berkeley-Los Angeles-London

Malpas J., Arnswald U. and Kertscher J. (ed.) 2002. *Gadamer's Century. Essays in Honor of Hans-Georg Gadamer*, MIT Press, Cambridge-London

Malpas J. and Zabala S. (ed.) 2010. *Consequences of Hermeneutics: Fifty Years After Gadamer's "Truth and Method"*, Northwestern University Press, Evanston

Orsi G. and Breidbach O. (ed.) 2004. *Ästhetik – Hermeneutik – Neurowissenschaften. Heidelberger Gadamer-Symposium des Istituto Italiano per gli Studi Filosofici*, LIT, Münster

Schmidt L. K. (ed.) 1995. *The Specter of Relativism: Truth, Dialogue, and Phronesis in Philosophical Hermeneutics*, Northwestern University Press, Evanston

Schmidt L. K. (ed.) 2000. *Language and Linguisticality in Gadamer's Hermeneutics*, Lexington Books, Lanham-Oxford

Silverman H. J. (ed.) 1991. *Gadamer and Hermeneutics: Science, Culture, Literature*, Routledge, London-New York

Vattimo G. and Chiurazzi G. (ed.) 2009. *Gadamer: 50 anni di "Verità e metodo"*, in *Trópos. Rivista di ermeneutica e critica filosofica*, 2/2

Wachterhauser B. (ed.) 1994. *Hermeneutics and Truth*, Northwestern University Press, Evanston

Wischke M. and Hofer M. (ed.) 2003. *Gadamer verstehen. Understanding Gadamer*, Wissenschaftliche Buchgesellschaft, Darmstadt

Wright K. (ed.) 1990. *Festival of Interpretations. Essays on Hans-Georg Gadamer's Work*, SUNY Press, Albany

2.2. Books, Articles and Reviews

Adorno Th. W. 1998: *Metaphysik. Begriff und Probleme*, in *Nachgelassene Schriften. Vol. 14* [1965], Suhrkamp, Frankfurt a.M.; tr. E. Jephcott, *Metaphysics: Concept and Problems*, Stanford University Press, Stanford 2001

―――, 2003: *Ästhetische Theorie* [1970], in *Gesammelte Werke. Vol. 7*, Suhrkamp, Frankfurt a.M.; tr. R. Hullot-Kentor, *Aesthetic Theory*, Continuum, London-New York 2004

Aeschylus. 2007: *Agamemnon*, in *The Oresteia*, tr. I. Johnston, Richer Resourcers Publications, Arlington, pp. 7-68

Alexander T. M. 1997: "Eros and Understanding: Gadamer's Aesthetic Ontology of the Community", in Hahn (ed.) 1997, pp. 323-345

Antiseri D. 1997: "Epistemologia ed ermeneutica: il problema del metodo in K. R. Popper e H.-G. Gadamer", in *Hermeneutica*, pp. 255-275

Arendt H. 1959: *The Human Condition* [1958], Doubleday Anchor Books, Garden City

―――, 1992: *Lectures on Kant's Political Philosophy* [1982], ed. R. Beiner, University of Chicago Press, Chicago

Aristotle. *Posterior Analytics* (tr. J. Barnes), *Topics* (tr. W. A. Pickard-Cambridge), *Metaphysics* (tr. W. D. Ross), and *Nicomachean Ethics* (tr. W. D. Ross revised by J. O. Urmson), in *The Complete Works of Aristotle*, ed. J. Barnes, Princeton University Press, Princeton 1991, respectively pp. 114-166, 167-277, 1552-1728 and 1729-1867

Arnswald U. 2002: "On the Certainty of Uncertainty: Language Games and Forms of Life in Gadamer and Wittgenstein", in Malpas, Arnswald and Kertscher (ed.) 2002, pp. 25-44

Ataman K. 2008: *Understanding Other Religions: Al-Biruni and Gadamer's "Fusion of Horizons"*, The Council for Research in Values and Philosophy, Washington

Auerochs B. 1995: "Gadamer über Tradition", in *Zeitschrift für philosophische Forschung*, 49/2, pp. 294-311

Bacon F. 2004: *Instauratio Magna. Pars secunda: Novum Organum* [1620], in *The Oxford Francis Bacon. Vol. 11*, ed. G. Rees and M. Wakely, Clarendon Press, Oxford, pp. 2-446; tr. G. Rees, *Great Instauration. Part II: Novum Organum*, in *The Oxford Francis Bacon. Vol. 11*, pp. 3-447

Barbarić D. 2007: "Die Grenze zum Unsagbaren", in Figal (ed.) 2007, pp. 199-218

Baudrillard J. 2001: "The Spirit of Terrorism", tr. R. Boul. Available at: www.egs.edu/faculty/jean-baudrillard/articles/the-spirit-of-terrorism/

Bauman Z. 1989: *Modernity and the Holocaust*, Polity Press, Cambridge

———, 2000: *Liquid Modernity*, Polity Press, Cambridge

Beck U. 2007: *Weltrisikogesellschaft. Auf der Suche nach der verlorenen Sicherheit*, Suhrkamp, Frankfurt a.M.

Becker O. 1962: "Die Fragwürdigkeit der Transzendierung der ästhetischen Dimension der Kunst", in *Philosophische Rundschau*, 10, pp. 225-238

Beiner R. 1992: "Hannah Arendt on Judging", Appendix to H. Arendt, *Lectures on Kant's Political Philosophy*, University of Chicago Press, Chicago, pp. 89-156

———, 2004: "Gadamer's Philosophy of Dialogue and Its Relation to the Postmodernism of Nietzsche, Heidegger, Derrida, and Strauss", in Krajewski (ed.) 2004, pp. 123-144

Bergson H. 1962: *Le deux sources de la morale et de la religion* [1932], Presses Universitaires de France, Paris; tr. K. A. Pearson and J. Mullarkey, *The Two Sources of Morality and Religion* (excerpts), in *Bergson: Key Writings*, Continuum, London-New York 2002, pp. 295-343

Berman M. 1983: *All That Is Solid Melts Into Air: The Experience Of Modernity*, Verso, London-New York

Bernet R., Kern I. and Marbach E. 1989: *Edmund Husserl. Darstellung seines Denkens*, Meiner, Hamburg; tr. *An Introduction to Husserlian Phenomenology*, Northwestern University Press, Evanston 1999

Bernstein R. J. 1983: *Beyond Objectivism and Relativism: Science, Hermeneutics and Praxis*, University of Pennsylvania Press, Philadelphia

———, 2002: "The Constellation of Hermeneutics, Critical Theory and Deconstruction", in Dostal (ed.) 2002, pp. 267-282

Berti E. 1987: *Le vie della ragione*, Il Mulino, Bologna

———, 1992: *Aristotele nel Novecento*, Laterza, Roma-Bari

———, 2001: "La ricezione delle virtù dianoetiche nell'ermeneutica contemporanea", in *Paradigmi. Rivista di critica filosofica*, 19/3, n. 57, pp. 375-392

Bianco F. 1992: *Pensare l'interpretazione. Temi e figure dell'ermeneutica contemporanea*, Editori Riuniti, Roma

———, 1997: "L'universalità dell'ermeneutica e il problema della sua giustificazione", in *Hermeneutica*, pp. 9-21

———, 2004: *Introduzione a Gadamer*, Laterza, Roma-Bari

Bleicher J. 1980: *Contemporary Hermeneutics: Hermeneutics as Method, Philosophy and Critique*, Routledge and Kegan, London

Blumenberg H. 1966: *Die Legitimität der Neuzeit*, Suhrkamp, Frankfurt a.M.; tr. R. M. Wallace, *The Legitimacy of the Modern Age*, MIT Press, Cambridge-London 1985

Bonanni G. 2004: "Che cos'è un'esperienza ermeneutica?", in Gardini and Matteucci (ed.) 2004, pp. 31-46

Bormann C. von. 1971: "Die Zweideutigkeit der hermeneutischen Erfahrung", in AA.VV. 1971, pp. 83-119

Brandom R. B. 2000: *Articulating Reasons: An Introduction to Inferentialism*, Harvard University Press, Cambridge-London

———, 2002: *Tales of the Mighty Dead. Historical Essays in the Metaphysics of Intentionality*, Harvard University Press, Cambridge-London

Bruneteau B. 2004: *Le siècle des génocides. Violences, massacres et processus génocidaires de l'Arménie au Rwanda*, Colin, Paris

Bruns G. L. 1992: *Hermeneutics Ancient & Modern*, Yale University Press, New Haven-London

———, 2004: "On the Coherence of Hermeneutics and Ethics: An Essay on Gadamer and Levinas", in Krajewski (ed.) 2004, pp. 30-54

Bubner R. 1971: "Philosophie ist ihre Zeit, in Gedanken erfaßt", in AA.VV. 1971, pp. 210-243

Buruma I. and Margalit A. 2004: *Occidentalism: The West in the Eyes of Its Enemies*, Penguin Press, New York

Cambiano G. 1988: *Il classicismo animistico di Gadamer*, in *Il ritorno degli antichi*, Laterza, Roma-Bari, pp. 41-72

Camera F. 1991: "*Erfahrung als Verstehen. Verstehen als Erfahrung* nell'ermeneutica filosofica di Hans-Georg Gadamer", in *Laboratorio di filosofia*, 1, pp. 193-199

Caputo J. D. 1987: *Radical Hermeneutics. Repetition, Deconstruction, and the Hermeneutic Project*, Indiana University Press, Bloomington-Indianapolis

Cassirer E. 1972: *An Essay on Man: An Introduction to a Philosophy of Human Culture* [1944], Yale University Press, New Haven

Cattaneo F. 2011: "Ermeneutica e libertà dell'esperienza. Un percorso tra Gadamer e Heidegger", in Cattaneo, Gentili and Marino (ed.) 2011, pp. 203-228

Chang T. K. 1994: *Geschichte, Verstehen und Praxis. Eine Untersuchung zur philosophischen Hermeneutik Hans-Georg Gadamers unter besonderer Berücksichtigung ihrer Annäherung an die Tradition der praktischen Philosophie*, Tectum, Marburg

Coltman R. 1998: *The Language of Hermeneutics: Gadamer and Heidegger in Dialogue*, SUNY Press, Albany

Cottingham J. 1986: *Descartes*, Blackwell, Oxford-Malden

D'Agostini F. 2002: *Disavventure della verità*, Einaudi, Torino

―――, 2009: *The Last Fumes: Nihilism and the Nature of Philosophical Concepts*, Davies Group Publishers, Aurora

Dahl G. 1999: *Radical Conservatism and the Future of Politics*, Sage Publications, London

Dallmayr F. 2002: *Dialogue Among Civilizations: Some Exemplary Voices*, Palgrave Macmillan, New York

D'Angelo P. 2003: "L'estetica di Gadamer", in *Paradigmi. Rivista di critica filosofica*, 21/2, n. 62, pp. 419-428

Da Re A. 2001: "Figure dell'etica", in C. Vigna (ed.), *Introduzione all'etica*, Vita e Pensiero, Milano, pp. 3-117

Davey N. 2003: "Art's Enigma: Adorno, Gadamer and Iser on Interpretation", in Wischke and Hofer (ed.) 2003, pp. 232-247

―――, 2006: *Unquiet Understanding: Gadamer's Philosophical Hermeneutics*, SUNY Press, Albany

Davidson D. 2001a: *Inquiries Into Truth and Interpretation* [1984], Oxford University Press, Oxford

―――, 2001b: *Subjective, Intersubjective, Objective*, Oxford University Press, Oxford

Deniau G. 2009: "Comprendere e interpretare. Della teoria dell'esperienza ermeneutica", in Vattimo and Chiurazzi (ed.) 2009, pp. 37-54

Derksen L. D. 1983: *On Universal Hermeneutics: A Study in the Philosophy of Hans-Georg Gadamer*, VU Boeckhandel, Amsterdam

Derrida J. 1984: *Bonnes volontés de puissance (Une réponse à Hans-Georg Gadamer)*, in "Revue international de philosophie", 38/4, n. 151, pp. 341-343; tr. D. Michelfelder and R. E. Palmer, *Three Questions to Hans-Georg Gadamer*, in DDGD, pp. 52-54

Descartes R. 1973a: *Discours de la methode* [1637], in *Œuvres de Descartes. Vol. 6*, ed. C. Adam and P. Tannery, Vrin, Paris, pp. 1-78; tr. E. S. Haldane, *Discourse on the Method of Rightly Conducting the Reason*, in *The Philosophical Works of Descartes. Vol. 1*, ed. E. S. Haldane and G. R. T. Ross, Cambridge University Press, Cambridge 1979, pp. 79-130

———, 1973b: *Meditationes de prima philosophia* [1641], in *Œuvres de Descartes. Vol. 7*, Vrin, Paris; tr. E. S. Haldane, *Meditations on First Philosophy*, in *The Philosophical Works of Descartes. Vol. 1*, Cambridge University Press, Cambridge 1979, pp. 131-199

———, 1973c: *Principia philosophiae* [1644], in *Œuvres de Descartes. Vol. 8/1*, Vrin, Paris; tr. E. S. Haldane, *The Principles of Philosophy*, in *The Philosophical Works of Descartes. Vol. 1*, Cambridge University Press, Cambridge 1979, pp. 200-302

———, 1974: *Regulae ad directionem ingenii* [1628-1629 ca.], in *Œuvres de Descartes. Vol. 10*, Vrin, Paris, pp. 359-488; tr. G. R. T. Ross, *Rules for the Direction of the Mind*, in *The Philosophical Works of Descartes. Vol. 1*, Cambridge University Press, Cambridge 1979, pp. 1-77

De Simone A. 1995: *Dalla metafora alla storia: modelli ermeneutici, filosofia e scienze umane. Saggi su Ricoeur, Gadamer e Habermas*, QuattroVenti, Urbino

Detmer D. 1997: "Gadamer's Critique of the Enlightenment", in Hahn (ed.) 1997, pp. 275-286

Dewey J. 1988: *Experience and Nature* [1925], in *The Collected Works of John Dewey. The Later Works, 1925-1953. Vol. 1*, Southern Illinois University Press, Carbondale

———, 1989: *Art as Experience* [1934], in *The Collected Works of John Dewey. The Later Works, 1925-1953. Vol. 10*, Southern Illinois University Press, Carbondale

———, 2008: *Reconstruction in Philosophy* [1920], in *The Collected Works of John Dewey. The Middle Works, 1899-1924. Vol. 12*, Southern Illinois University Press, Carbondale, pp. 77-202

Di Cesare D. 2002: "'Cittadini di due mondi'. L'istanza religiosa nell'ermeneutica filosofica di Gadamer", in *Sophia*, 5, pp. 59-74

———, 2004: *Ermeneutica della finitezza*, Guerini, Milano

———, 2007: *Gadamer*, il Mulino, Bologna; tr. *Gadamer. Ein philosophisches Porträt*, Mohr Siebeck, Tübingen 2009

———, 2008: "Un altro Gadamer. Retrospettive per una futura ermeneutica", in Failla (ed.) 2008, pp. 21-28

———, 2009: "*Verità e metodo* – cinquant'anni dopo. La filosofia contemporanea fra il comprendere e l'altro", in Vattimo and Chiurazzi (ed.) 2009, pp. 55-73

Dilthey W. 1924: *Das Wesen der Philosophie* [1907], in *Gesammelte Schriften. Vol. 5*, Teubner, Leipzig-Berlin, pp. 339-416

Donadio F. 2002: "Dell'ermeneutica, ovvero del problema dell'uno e dei molti", in *Sophia*, 5, pp. 75-80

Dottori R. 1996: "La questione della dialettica in Hegel, Heidegger, Gadamer", Appendix to H.-G. Gadamer, *La dialettica di Hegel*, tr. and ed. R. Dottori, Marietti, Genova, pp. 189-214

———, 2004: "L'eredità di Gadamer. Interpretazione, legittimazione di sé e dialogo interculturale", in Gardini and Matteucci (ed.) 2004, pp. 169-192

———, 2008, "Il concetto di *phronesis* e l'inizio dell'ermeneutica", in Failla (ed.) 2008, pp. 53-66

Drake S. 2001: *Galileo: A Very Short Introduction* [1980], Oxford University Press, Oxford-New York

Dupré J. 2001: *Human Nature and the Limits of Science*, Oxford University Press, Oxford

Eagleton T. 1983: *Literary Theory: An Introduction*, Blackwell, Oxford

Elm R. 2007: "Schenkung, Entzug und die Kunst des schöpferischen Fragens. Zum Phänomen der Geschichtlichkeit des Verstehens in Gadamers 'Analyse des wirkungsgeschichtlichen Bewußtseins'", in Figal (ed.) 2007, pp. 151-176

Failla M. 2008: *Microscopia. Gadamer: la musica nel commento al "Filebo"*, Quodlibet, Macerata; tr. L. Schröder, *Hans-Georg Gadamer als Platon-Interpret. Die Musik*, Peter Lang, Frankfurt a.M. 2009

Fehér I. M. 1996: "Gibt es die Hermeneutik? Zur Selbstreflexion und Aktualität der Hermeneutik Gadamerscher-Prägung", in *Internationale Zeitschrift für Philosophie*, 2, pp. 236-259

———, 1999: "Hermeneutics and the Sciences", in M. Fehér, O. Kiss and L. Ropolyi (ed.), *Hermeneutics and Science. Proceedings of the First Conference of the International Society for Hermeneutics and Science*, Kluwer, Dordrecht-Boston-London, pp. 1-12

———, 2003: "Ästhetik, Hermeneutik, Philosophie. Das Hermeneutisch-Werden der Philosophie im 20. Jahrhundert", in Fehér (ed.) 2003, pp. 15-32

Ferraris M. 1997, *Storia dell'ermeneutica* [1988], Bompiani, Milano; tr. L. Somigli, *History of Hermeneutics*, Humanities Press, Atlantic Highlands

Feyerabend P. K. 1993: *Against Method: Outline of an Anarchist Theory of Knowledge* [1975], Verso, London-New York

Figal G. 1992: "Verstehen als geschichtliche *Phronesis*. Eine Erörterung der philosophischen Hermeneutik", in *Internationale Zeitschrift für Philosophie*, 1, pp. 24-37

———, 1996: *Der Sinn des Verstehens. Beiträge zur hermeneutischen Philosophie*, Reclam, Stuttgart

———, 2000: "Philosophische Hermeneutik – hermeneutische Philosophie. Ein Problemaufriß", in Figal, Grondin and Schmidt (ed.) 2000, pp. 335-344

———, 2001: "Phänomenologie der Kultur. *Wahrheit und Methode* nach vierzig Jahren", in AA.VV. 2001, pp. 100-106

———, 2002a: "Nella tenue luce del passaggio delle stagioni. Hans-Georg Gadamer, maestro di filosofia", in *Sophia*, 5, pp. 81-86

———, 2002b: "The Doing of the Thing Itself: Gadamer's Hermeneutic Ontology of Language", in Dostal (ed.) 2002, pp. 102-125

———, 2003: "Gadamer im Kontext. Zur Gestalt und Perspektiven philosophischer Hermeneutik", in Wischke and Hofer (ed.) 2003, pp. 141-156

———, 2005: "La totalizzazione della filosofia pratica. Riflessioni sul rapporto fra etica ed ermeneutica a partire dal *Natorp-Bericht*", Appendix to M. Heidegger, *Interpretazioni fenomenologiche di Aristotele*, tr. and ed. A. P. Ruoppo, Guida, Napoli, pp. 133-152

———, 2006: *Gegenständlichkeit. Das Hermeneutische und die Philosophie*, Mohr Siebeck, Tübingen; tr. Th. D. George, *Objectivity: The Hermeneutical and Philosophy*, SUNY Press, Albany 2010

———, 2007a: "*Wahrheit und Methode* zur Einführung", in Figal (ed.) 2007, pp. 1-8

———, 2007b: "*Wahrheit und Methode* als ontologischer Entwurf", in Figal (ed.) 2007, pp. 219-235

——, 2007c: "Gadamer als Phänomenologe", in *Phänomenologische Forschungen*, pp. 95-107

——, 2009: "Hermeneutics as Phenomenology", in *The Journal of the British Society for Phenomenology*, 40/3, pp. 255-262

——, 2010: *Erscheinungsdinge. Ästhetik als Phänomenologie*, Mohr Siebeck, Tübingen

——, 2011: "Hermeneutische Wahrheit: Gadamers Frage und ihre phänomenologische Antwort", in *Internationales Jahrbuch für Hermeneutik. Schwerpunkt: 50 Jahre "Wahrheit und Methode"*

Flatscher M. 2003: "Das Spiel der Kunst als die Kunst des Spiels. Bemerkungen zum Spiel bei Gadamer und Wittgenstein", in R. Esterbauer (ed.), *Orte des Schönen. Phänomenologische Annäherungen*, Königshausen & Neumann, Würzburg, pp. 125 ff.

Fleury P. 1993: "Lumière et Tradition. Jürgen Habermas face à Hans-Georg Gadamer", in J. Greisch (ed.) *Comprendre et interpréter. Le paradigme herméneutique de la raison*, Beauchesne, Paris, pp. 343-360

Fornet-Ponse R. 2000: *Wahrheit und ästhetische Wahrheit. Untersuchungen zu Hans-Georg Gadamer und Theodor W. Adorno*, Mainz, Aachen

Forti S. 2006: *Hannah Arendt tra filosofia e politica*, Bruno Mondadori, Milano

Foster M. R. 1991: *Gadamer and Practical Philosophy. The Hermeneutics of Moral Confidence*, Scholars Press, Atlanta

Foucault M. 1966: *Les mots et le choses. Une archéologie des sciences humaines*, Gallimard, Paris; tr. *The Order of Things: An Archaeology of the Human Sciences*, Vintage Books, New York 1994

——, 1984: "What is Enlightenment?", in P. Rabinow (ed.) *The Foucault Reader*, Penguin Books, Harmondsworth, pp. 32-50

Früchtl J. 1996: *Ästhetische Erfahrung und moralisches Urteil. Eine Rehabilitierung*, Suhrkamp, Frankfurt a.M.

Fukuyama F. 1998: *The End of History and the Last Man* [1992], Avon Books, New York

Galilei G. 2005a: *Lettera copernicana. A Cristina di Lorena granduchessa di Toscana* [1615], in *Opere. Vol. 1*, ed. F. Brunetti, UTET, Torino, pp. 551-593; tr. M. A. Finocchiaro, *Letter to the Grand Duchess Christina*, in *The Essential Galileo*, ed. M. A. Finocchiaro, Hackett, Indianapolis 2008, pp. 109-145

―――, 2005b: *Il Saggiatore* [1623], in *Opere. Vol. 1*, UTET, Torino, pp. 605-807; tr. M. A. Finocchiaro, *The Assayer* (excerpts), in *The Essential Galileo*, Hackett, Indianapolis 2008, pp. 179-189

―――, 2005c: *Dialogo sopra i due massimi sistemi del mondo* [1632], in *Opere. Vol. 2*, UTET, Torino, pp. 13-552; tr. S. Drake, *Dialogue Concerning the Two Chief World Systems*, University of California Press, London-Berkeley-Los Angeles 1967

―――, 2005d: *Discorsi intorno a due nuove scienze* [1638], in *Opere. Vol. 2*, UTET, Torino, pp. 561-839; tr. H. Crew and A. De Salvio, *Dialogues Concerning Two New Sciences*, Cosimo Inc., New York 2010

Gamble A. 2000: *Politics and Fate*, Polity Press, Cambridge

Garelli G. 2005: *Il Cosmo dell'ingiustizia. Fine della teleologia e fini della responsabilità*, Il Melangolo, Genova

Geertz C. 2000: *Available Light: Anthropological Reflections on Philosophical Topics*, Princeton University Press, Princeton

Gentili C. 1996: *Ermeneutica e metodica. Studi sulla metodologia del comprendere*, Marietti, Genova

―――, 2006: "Fare i conti con il maestro. Sul ritorno di Gadamer a Heidegger", in *Studi di estetica*, 34/1, n. 33, pp. 75-107

Giddens A. 1991: *The Consequences of Modernity*, Polity Press, Cambridge

Ginev D. J. 1997: *A Passage to the Hermeneutic Philosophy of Science*, Rodopi, Amsterdam

Giurlanda P. 1987: "Habermas' Critique of Gadamer: Does It Stand Up?", in *International Philosophical Quarterly*, 27/1, n. 105, pp. 33-41

Gregorio G. 2008: *Hans-Georg Gadamer e la declinazione ermeneutica della fenomenologia*, Rubbettino, Soveria Mannelli

―――, 2011: "Il concetto di vita in *Verità e metodo*", in Cattaneo, Gentili and Marino (ed.) 2011, pp. 17-38

Greisch J. 2000: "Le phénomène du jeu et les enjeux ontologiques de l'herméneutique", in *Revue Internationale de Philosophie*, 54/3, n. 213, pp. 447-468

Griffero T. 2004: "Dal sentire al (credere di) sapere. Gadamer e i paradossi del senso comune", in Gardini and Matteucci (ed.) 2004, pp. 47-74

Grondin J. 1992-93: "Zur Komposition von *Wahrheit und Methode*", in *Dilthey Jahrbuch*, 6, pp. 57-74; tr. L. K. Schmidt, "On the Composition of *"Truth and Method"*, in Schmidt (ed.) 1995, pp. 23-38

———, 1997: "Gadamer on Humanism", in Hahn (ed.) 1997, pp. 157-170

———, 1999: *Hans-Georg Gadamer. Eine Biographie*, Mohr Siebeck, Tübingen; tr. J. Weinsheimer, *Hans-Georg Gadamer: A Biography*, Yale University Press, New Haven-London 2003

———, 2000a: *Einführung zu Gadamer*, Mohr Siebeck, Tübingen

———, 2000b: "Hans-Georg Gadamer und die französische Welt", in Figal (ed.) 2000, pp. 147-159

———, 2001: *Von Heidegger zu Gadamer. Unterwegs zur Hermeneutik*, Wissenschaftliche Buchgesellschaft, Darmstadt

———, 2002: "Gadamer's Basic Understanding of Understanding", in Dostal (ed.) 2002, pp. 36-51

———, 2003: *The Philosophy of Gadamer*, Acumen, Chesham

———, 2008: "Hans-Georg Gadamer e la metafisica", tr. A. Lossi, in Failla (ed.) 2008, pp. 97-108

———, 2009: "L'incerta eredità di Gadamer", tr. P. Stagi, in Vattimo and Chiurazzi (ed.) 2009, pp. 25-36

———, 2010a: "The Neo-Kantian Heritage in Gadamer", in R. Makreel and S. Luft (ed.) *Neo-Kantianism in Contemporary Philosophy*, Indiana University Press, Bloomington, pp. 92-111

———, 2010b: "Nihilistic or Metaphysical Consequences of Hermeneutics?", in Malpas and Zabala (ed.) 2010, pp. 190-201

Grossner C. 1971: "Die Philosophie des Vorurteils (Hans-Georg Gadamer)", in C. Grossner (ed.) *Verfall der Philosophie. Politik deutscher Philosophen*, Wegner, Reinbeck bei Hamburg, pp. 53-63

Guignon C. B. 1993: "Introduction" to C. B. Guignon (ed.) *The Cambridge Companion to Heidegger*, Cambridge University Press, Cambridge, pp. 1-41

Guyer P. 2006: *Kant*, Routledge, London-New York

Habermas J. 1971: "Der Universalitätsanspruch der Hermeneutik", in AA.VV. 1971, pp. 120-159

———, 1981a: "Die Moderne – ein unvollendetes Projekt", in *Kleine politische Schriften I-IV*, Suhrkamp, Frankfurt a.M., pp. 444-464

———, 1981b: "Urbanisierung der Heideggerschen Provinz", in *Philosophisch-politische Profile*, Suhrkamp, Frankfurt a.M., pp. 392-401

———, 1985: *Der philosophische Diskurs der Moderne. Zwölf Vorlesungen*, Suhrkamp, Frankfurt a.M.; tr. F. Lawrence, *The Philosophical Discourse of Modernity: Twelve Lectures*, Polity Press, Cambridge 1987

———, 1999: *Wahrheit und Rechtfertigung. Philosophische Aufsätze*, Suhrkamp, Frankfurt a.M.; tr. B. Fultner, *Truth and Justification*, MIT Press, Cambridge-London 2003

———, 2000: "Wie ist nach dem Historismus noch Metaphysik möglich?", in AA.VV. 2001, pp. 89-99

———, 2001a: "Der liberale Geist. Eine Reminiszenz an unbeschwerte Heidelberger Anfänge", in Figal (ed.) 2000, pp. 51-54

———, 2001b: *Die Zukunft der menschlichen Natur. Auf dem Weg zu einer liberalen Eugenik?*, Suhrkamp, Frankfurt a.M.; tr. H. Beister, M. Pensky and W. Rehg, *The Future of Human Nature*, Polity Press, Cambridge 2003

———, 2005: *Zwischen Naturalismus und Religion. Philosophische Aufsätze*, Suhrkamp, Frankfurt a.M

Hammermeister K. 1999: *Hans-Georg Gadamer*, Beck, München

Hance A. 1997: "The Hermeneutic Significance of the *Sensus Communis*", in *International Philosophical Quarterly*, 37/2, n. 146, pp. 133-148

Harvey D. 1990: *The Condition of Postmodernity: An Inquiry into The Origins of Cultural Change*, Basil Blackwell, Oxford

Heelan P. A. 2002: "Afterword" to B. Babich (ed.) *Hermeneutic Philosophy of Science, Van Gogh's Eyes, and God: Essays in Honor of Patrick A. Heelan*, Kluwer, Dordrecht, pp. 445-460

Hegel G. W. F. 1970a: *Phänomenologie des Geistes* [1807], in *Werke. Vol. 3*, Suhrkamp, Frankfurt a.M.; tr. A. V. Miller, *Phenomenology of Spirit*, Oxford University Press, Oxford 1977

———, 1970b: *Enzyklopädie der philosophischen Wissenschaften im Grundrisse* [1830], in *Werke. Vol. 10/3*, Suhrkamp, Frankfurt a.M.; tr. W. Wallace and A. V. Miller, *Hegel's Philosophy of mind: Being Part Three of the Encyclopaedia of the Philosophical Sciences*, Clarendon Press, Oxford 1971

———, 1970c: *Vorlesungen über die Philosophie der Geschichte* [1837], in *Werke. Vol. 12*, Suhrkamp, Frankfurt a.M.; tr. *The Philosophy of Right. The Philosophy of History*, Enciclopædia Britannica Inc., Chicago-London-Toronto 1952

——, 1970d: *Vorlesungen über die Ästhetik* [1835-38], in *Werke. Vol. 13/1*, Suhrkamp, Frankfurt a.M.; tr. T. M. Knox, *Aesthetics. Lectures on Fine Art. Vol. 1*, Oxford University Press, Oxford-New York 1998

Heidegger M. 1976: *Wegmarken* [1967], *Gesamtausgabe. Vol. 9*, Klostermann, Frankfurt a.M.; tr. W. McNeill, *Pathmarks*, Cambridge University Press, Cambridge 1998

——, 1977a: *Sein und Zeit* [1927], in *Gesamtausgabe. Vol. 2*, Klostermann, Frankfurt a.M.; tr. J. Stambaugh revised by D. J. Schmidt, *Being and Time*, SUNY Press, Albany 2010

——, 1977b: *Holzwege* [1950], in *Gesamtausgabe. Vol. 5*, Klostermann, Frankfurt a.M.; tr. J. Young and K. Haynes, *Off the Beaten Track*, Cambridge University Press, Cambridge 2002

——, 1982: *Unterwegs zur Sprache* [1959], Neske, Pfullingen; tr. P. D. Hertz, *On the Way to Language*, Harper & Row, San Francisco 1982

——, 1983: *Einführung in die Metaphysik* [1953], in *Gesamtausgabe. Vol. 40*, Klostermann, Frankfurt a.M.; tr. G. Fried and R. Polt, *Introduction to Metaphysics*, Yale University Press, New Haven-London 2000

——, 1988: *Ontologie (Hermeneutik der Faktizität)* [1923], in *Gesamtausgabe. Vol. 63*, Klostermann, Frankfurt a.M.; tr. J. van Buren, *Ontology: The Hermeneutics of Facticity*, Indiana University Press, Bloomington 1999

——, 1990: *Einleitung in die Philosophie. Denken und Dichten* [1944-45], in *Gesamtausgabe. Vol. 50*, Klostermann, Frankfurt a.M.

——, 1991: *Kant und das Problem der Metaphysik* [1929], in *Gesamtausgabe. Vol. 3*, Klostermann, Frankfurt a.M.; tr. R. Taft, *Kant and the Problem of Metaphysics*, Indiana University Press, Bloomington 1997

——, 1997a: *Nietzsche. Zweiter Band* [1961], in *Gesamtausgabe. Vol. 6.2*, Klostermann, Frankfurt a.M.; tr. F. A. Capuzzi, ed. D. Farrell Krell, *Nietzsche. Volume 4: Nihilism*, Harper & Row, San Francisco 1982

——, 1997b: *Der Satz vom Grund* [1957], in *Gesamtausgabe. Vol. 10*, Klostermann, Frankfurt a.M.; tr. R. Lilly, *The Principle of Reason*, Indiana University Press, Bloomington 1996

——, 2000a: *Vorträge und Aufsätze* [1954], in *Gesamtausgabe. Vol. 7*, Klostermann, Frankfurt a.M.; tr. D. Farrell Krell, *Basic Writings* (excerpts), Harper & Row, San Francisco 1993; tr. J. Stambaugh, *The End of Philosophy* (excerpts), University of Chicago Press, Chicago 2003

——, 2000b: "Gelassenheit" [1959], in *Gesamtausgabe. Vol. 16*, Klostermann, Frankfurt a.M., pp. 517-529; tr. J. M. Anderson and E. H. Freund, *Discourse on Thinking*, Harper & Row, New York 1966

——, 2000c: "Empfehlungen für Gadamer, Krüger und Löwith" [1945], in *Gesamtausgabe. Vol. 16*, Klostermann, Frankfurt a.M., pp. 395-397

——, 2005: "Phänomenologische Interpretationen zu Aristoteles (Anzeige der hermeneutischen Situation). Ausarbeitung für die Marburger und die Göttinger Philosophische Fakultät" [1922], in *Gesamtausgabe. Vol. 62*, Klostermann, Frankfurt a.M., pp. 343-419; tr. M. Baur, "Phenomenological Interpretations with Respect to Aristotle: Indication of the Hermeneutical Situation", in *Man and World*, n. 3/4 1992, pp. 355-393

——, 2005-2006: "Ausgewählte Briefe Martin Heideggers an Hans-Georg Gadamer", in *Jahresgabe der Martin-Heidegger Gesellschaft*

Hobsbawm E. J. 1996: *Age of Extremes: The Short Twentieth Century 1914-1991* [1994], Vintage Books, New York

Hollinger R. 1985: "Introduction: Hermeneutics and Pragmatism", in R. Hollinger (ed.) *Hermeneutics and Praxis*, University of Notre Dame Press, Notre Dame, pp. IX-XX

Honneth A. 2000: "Von der zerstörischen Kraft des Dritten. Gadamer und die Intersubjektivitätslehre Heideggers", in Figal, Grondin and Schmidt (ed.) 2000, pp. 307-324

——, 2005: *Verdinglichung. Eine anerkennungstheoretische Studie*, Suhrkamp, Frankfurt a.M.; tr. J. Ganahl, *Reification: A New Look At An Old Idea*, Oxford University Press, Oxford-New York 2008

Horkheimer M. 2004: *Eclipse of Reason* [1947], Continuum, London-New York

Horkheimer M. and Adorno Th. W. 2003: *Dialektik der Aufklärung. Philosophische Fragmente* [1947], in Th. W. Adorno, *Gesammelte Werke. Vol. 3*, Suhrkamp, Frankfurt a.M.; tr. E. Jephcott, *Dialectic of Enlightenment: Philosophical Fragments*, Stanford University Press, Stanford 2002

Horkheimer M., Adorno Th. W., and Gadamer H.-G. 1989: "Über Nietzsche und uns: Zum 50. Todestag des Philosophen" [1950], in M. Horkheimer, *Gesammelte Schriften. Vol. 13*, Fischer, Frankfurt a.M., pp. 111-120

Hösle V. 1991: *Philosophie der ökologischen Krise*, Beck, München

Hoy D. C. 1997: "Post-Cartesian Interpretation: Hans-Georg Gadamer and Donald Davidson", in Hahn (ed.) 1997, pp. 111-128

Huntington S. 1998: *The Clash of Civilizations and the Remaking of World Order* [1996], Simon & Schuster, New York

Husserl E. 1969: *Ideen zu einer reinen Phänomenologie und phänomenologischen Philosophie. Zweites Buch: Phänomenologische Untersuchungen zur Konstitution* [1912-1928 ca.], in *Husserliana. Gesammelte Werke. Vol. 4*, Nijhoff, Den Haag; tr. R. Rojcewicz and A. Schuwer, *Ideas Pertaining to a Pure Phenomenology and to a Phenomenological Philosophy*, Kluwer, Dordrecht 1989

———, 1976: *Die Krisis der europäischen Wissenschaften und die transzendentale Phänomenologie. Eine Einleitung in die phänomenologische Philosophie* [1936], in *Husserliana. Gesammelte Werke. Vol. 6*, Nijhoff, Den Haag; tr. D. Carr, *The Crisis of European Sciences and Transcendental Phenomenology*, Northwestern University Press, Evanston 1970

———, 1987: "Philosophie als strenge Wissenschaft" [1911], in *Husserliana. Gesammelte Werke. Vol. 25*, Kluwer, Dordrecht, pp. 3-62; tr. Q. Lauer, "Philosophy as Rigorous Science", in *Husserl: Shorter Works*, ed. by P. McCormick and F. Elliston, University of Notre Dame Press, Notre Dame 1981, pp. 166-199

Ipperciel D. 2004: "La pensée de Gadamer est-elle conservatrice?", in *Revue Philosophique de Louvain*, 102/4, pp. 610-629. Available at: http://www2.csj.ualberta.ca/Ipperciel/PagePersonnelle/textes/GadamerConservateur.pdf

Janik A. 2002: "Wittgenstein, Hertz, and Hermeneutics", in B. Babich (ed.) *Hermeneutic Philosophy of Science, Van Gogh's Eyes, and God: Essays in Honor of Patrick A. Heelan*, Kluwer, Dordrecht, pp. 79-95

Jonas H. 1984: *Das Prinzip Verantwortung. Versuch einer Ethik für die technologische Zivilisation* [1979], Insel, Frankfurt a.M.; tr. H. Jonas and D. Herr, *The Imperative of Responsibility: In Search of an Ethics for the Technological Age*, University of Chicago Press, Chicago-London 1984

———, 1996: "The Burden and Blessing of Mortality", in *Mortality and Morality: A Search for the Good after Auschwitz*, ed. I. Fogel, Northwestern University Press, Evanston, pp. 87-98

Jung M. 2001: *Hermeneutik zur Einführung*, Junius, Hamburg

Kant I. 1911a: *Kritik der reinen Vernunft. Zweite Auflage* [1787], in *Kant's gesammelte Schriften. Vol. 3*, Reimer, Berlin; tr. M. Weigelt, *Critique of Pure Reason*, Penguin Books, London 2007

——, 1911b: *Grundlegung zur Metaphysik der Sitten* [1785], in *Kant's gesammelte Schriften. Vol. 4*, Reimer, Berlin, pp. 385-463; tr. M. Gregor and J. Timmermann, *Groundwork of the Metaphysics of Morals*, Cambridge University Press, Cambridge 2011

——, 1913a: *Kritik der praktischen Vernunft* [1788], in *Kant's gesammelte Schriften. Vol. 5*, Reimer, Berlin, pp. 1-163; tr. M. J. Gregor, *Critique of Practical Philosophy*, in *Practical Philosophy*, Cambridge, Cambridge University Press 1999, pp. 133-271

——, 1913b: *Kritik der Urtheilskraft* [1790], in *Kant's gesammelte Schriften. Vol. 5*, Reimer, Berlin, pp. 165-485; tr. P. Guyer, *Critique of the Power of Judgement*, Cambridge University Press, Cambridge 2000

——, 1923: "Beantwortung der Frage: Was ist Aufklärung?" [1784], in *Kant's gesammelte Schriften. Vol. 8*, De Gruyter, Berlin, pp. 33-42; tr. H. S. Reiss, "An Answer to the Question: 'What is Enlightenment?'", in *Kant. Political Writings*, ed. H. S. Reiss and H. B. Nisbet, Cambridge University Press, Cambridge 1991, pp. 54-60

Kelly M. 1995: "Gadamer, Foucault and Habermas on Ethical Critique", in Schmidt (ed.) 1995, pp. 224-235

——, 2004: "A Critique of Gadamer's Aesthetics", in Krajewski (ed.) 2004, pp. 103-120

Keuth H. 1998: "Zur Kritik am Anspruch einer universellen Hermeneutik", in B. Kanitscheider e F. J. Wetz (ed.), *Hermeneutik und Naturalismus*, Mohr Siebeck, Tübingen, pp. 63-82

Kumar K. 1995: *From Post-Industrial to Post-Modern Society: New Theories of The Contemporary World*, Blackwell, Oxford

Kusch M. 1989: *Language as Calculus VS. Language as Universal Medium: A Study in Husserl, Heidegger and Gadamer*, Kluwert, Dordrecht-Boston-London

Lang P. C. 1981: *Hermeneutik Ideologiekritik Ästhetik. Über Gadamer und Adorno sowie Fragen einer aktuellen Ästhetik*, Forum Academicum, Königstein

Lawn C. 2004: *Wittgenstein and Gadamer: Towards a Post-Analytic Philosophy of Language*, Continuum, London-New York

——, 2006: *Gadamer: A Guide for the Perplexed*, Continuum, London-New York

Lee H. Y. 2004: *Geschichtlichkeit und Sprachlichkeit des Verstehens. Eine Untersuchung zur Wesensstruktur und Grundlage der hermeneutischen Erfahrung bei H.-G. Gadamer*, Peter Lang, Frankfurt a.M.-Berlin-Bern-Bruxelles-New York-Oxford-Wien

Lembeck K.-H. 2008: "Gadamer e il neokantismo", tr. A. Lossi, in Failla (ed.) 2008, pp. 29-42

Liessmann K. P. 2003: "Die Sollbruchstelle. Die Destruktion des ästhetischen Bewußtseins und die Stellung der Kunst in Hans-Georg Gadamers *Wahrheit und Methode*", in Wischke and Hofer (ed.) 2003, pp. 211-232

Löwith K. 1983: "Der europäische Nihilismus. Betrachtungen zur geistigen Vorgeschichte des europäischen Krieges" [1940], in *Sämtliche Schriften. Vol. 2*, Metzler, Stuttgart, pp. 473-540; tr. G. Steiner, "European Nihilism: Reflections on the Spiritual and Historical Background of the European War", in *Martin Heidegger and European Nihilism*, ed. R. Wolin, Columbia University Press, New York 1995

Lukács G. 1968: *Geschichte und Klassenbewusstsein* [1923], in *Werke. Vol. 2*, Luchterhand, Darmstadt-Neuwied, pp. 161-517; tr. R. Livingstone, *History and Class Consciousness: Studies in Marxist Dialectics*, Merlin Press, London 1971

Lyotard J.-F. 1979: *La condition postmoderne*, Éditions de Minuit, Paris; tr. G. Bennington and B. Massumi, *The Postmodern Condition*, University of Minnesota Press, Minneapolis 1999

MacIntyre A. 1985: *After Virtue: A Study in Moral Theory* [1981], Duckworth, London

——, 1988: *Whose Justice? Which Rationality?*, University of Notre Dame Press, Notre Dame

——, 1994: "Nietzsche or Aristotle?", in G. Borradori (ed.) *The American Philosopher*, University of Chicago Press, Chicago-London, pp. 137-152

——, 2002: "On Not Having the Last Word: Thoughts on our Debts to Gadamer", in Malpas, Arnswald and Kertscher J. (ed.) 2002, pp. 157-172

Madison G. B. 1995: "Is Hermeneutics Necessarily Conservative?", in *Bulletin de la Societé canadienne d'herméneutique*, 10. Available at: http://www.ualberta.ca/~di/csh/csh10/csh10.html

——, 1997: "Hermeneutics' Claim to Universality", in Hahn (ed.) 1997, pp. 349-365

Makkreel R. A. 1990: *Imagination and Interpretation in Kant: The Hermeneutical Import of the "Critique of Judgment"*, University of Chicago Press, Chicago-London

Malpas J. 2002: "Gadamer, Davidson, and the Ground of Understanding", in Malpas, Arnswald and Kertscher J. (ed.) 2002, pp. 195-216

———, 2009: "Ethics and the Commitment to Truth", in *Trópos. Rivista di ermeneutica e critica filosofica*, 2/1, pp. 19-32

Malpas J. and Zabala S. 2010: "Introduction: Consequences of Hermeneutics", in Malpas and Zabala (ed.) 2010, pp. XI-XVIII

Mantzavinos C. 2006: *Naturalistische Hermeneutik*, Mohr Siebeck, Tübingen; tr. D. Arnold, *Naturalistic Hermeneutics*, Cambridge University Press, Cambridge 2005

Marcuse H. 1991: *One-Dimensional Man: Studies in the Ideology of Advanced Industrial Society* [1964], Beacon Press, Boston

Marino S. 2008: "Il paradigma del gioco in Gadamer: tra estetica e filosofia del linguaggio", in *Estetica*, 2, pp. 5-20

———, 2009a: "La moralità del bello: etica ed estetica in Hans-Georg Gadamer", in S. Bertolini and R. Formisano (ed.) *Filosofia, estetica ed etica: otto percorsi di ricerca*, Aracne, Roma, pp. 13-29

———, 2009b: "La saggezza che canta di Zarathustra e l'irredimibile finitezza dell'uomo: Hans-Georg Gadamer interprete di Nietzsche", in F. Cattaneo and S. Marino (ed.) *I sentieri di Zarathustra*, Pendragon, Bologna, pp. 205-221

———, 2010a: "Gadamer on Heidegger: Is the History of Being 'just' Another Philosophy of History?", in *The Journal of the British Society for Phenomenology*, 41/3, pp. 287-303

———, 2010b: *Un intreccio dialettico: teoresi, estetica, etica e metafisica in Theodor W. Adorno*, Aracne, Roma

———, 2011a: "Philosophy *and* Poetry – Philosophy *as* a Kind of Writing: Some Remarks on Richard Rorty's Heidegger Interpretation", in D. Espinet (ed.) *Schreiben Dichten Denken. Zu Heideggers Sprachdenken*, Klostermann, Frankfurt a.M., pp. 56-68

———, 2011b: "Seconda natura e linguaggio: Gadamer, McDowell e l'antropologia filosofica", in Cattaneo, Gentili and Marino (ed.) 2011, pp. 39-57

―――, 2011c: "Seconda natura, libertà e corporeità: alcune considerazioni su Gadamer e McDowell", in *Philosophical Readings. Philosophical Online Journal*, 3/1. Available at: http://philosophicalreadings.wordpress.com

Marquard O. 1981: *Abschied vom Prinzipiellen. Philosophische Studien*, Reclam, Stuttgart; tr. R. M. Wallace, S. Bernstein and J. I. Porter, *Farewell to Matters of Principle: Philosophical Studies*, Oxford University Press, Oxford 1989

Matteucci G. 2004: "Processi formativi e ontologia dell'arte", in Gardini and Matteucci (ed.) 2004, pp. 133-156

―――, 2010: *Il sapere estetico come prassi antropologica. Cassirer, Gehlen e la configurazione del sensibile*, ETS, Pisa

―――, 2011: "Gadamer e la questione dell'immagine", in Cattaneo, Gentili and Marino (ed.) 2011, pp. 73-91

McDowell J. 1996: *Mind and World* [1994], Harvard University Press, Cambridge-London

―――, 2002: "Gadamer and Davidson on Understanding and Relativism", in Malpas, Arnswald and Kertscher J. (ed.) 2002, pp. 173-193

Menegoni F. 2008 : *La "Critica del Giudizio" di Kant. Introduzione alla lettura*, Carocci, Roma

Merleau-Ponty M. 1964, *Le visible et l'invisible*, Gallimard, Paris; tr. A. Lingis, *The Visible and the Invisible*, Northwestern University Press, Evanston 1968

Michon P. 2000 : *Poétique d'une anti-anthropologie. L'herméneutique de Gadamer*, Vrin, Paris

Misgeld D. 1990: "Poetry, Dialogue, and Negotiation: Liberal Culture and Conservative Politics in Hans-Georg Gadamer's Thought", in Wright (ed.) 1990, pp. 161-181

―――, 1991: "Modernity and Hermeneutics: A Critical-Theoretical Rejoinder", in Silverman (ed.) 1991, pp. 163-177

Mittelstrass J. 1970: *Neuzeit und Aufklärung. Studien zur Entstehung der neuzeitlichen Wissenschaft und Philosophie*, De Gruyter, Berlin-New York

Moda A. 2000, *Lettura di "Verità e metodo" di Gadamer*, Utet, Torino

Morin E. and Kern A. B. 1993. *Terre Patrie*, Seuil, Paris

Mura G. 1997: *Ermeneutica e verità. Storia e problemi della filosofia dell'interpretazione*, Città Nuova, Roma

Nacci M. 2000: *Pensare la tecnica. Un secolo di incomprensioni*, Laterza, Roma-Bari

Nagl-Docekal H. 1997: "Towards a New Theory of the Historical Sciences: The Relevance of *Truth and Method*", in Hahn (ed.) 1997, pp. 193-204

Natali C. 2007: "Etica", in E. Berti (ed.) *Aristotele*, Laterza, Roma-Bari pp. 241-282

Neuser W. 2004: "Natur und Hermeneutik", in Orsi and Breidbach (ed.) 2004, pp. 31-50

Nicholson G. 1991: "Answers to Critical Theory", in Silverman (ed.) 1991, pp. 151-162

Oldroyd D. 1986: *The Arch of Knowledge: An Introductory Study of the History of the Philosophy and Methodology of Science*, Methuen, New York-London

Orozco T. 1995: *Platonische Gewalt: Gadamers politische Hermeneutik der NS-Zeit*, Argument, Hamburg

———, 2004: "The Art of Allusion: Hans-Georg Gadamer's Philosophical Interventions Under National Socialism", in Krajewski (ed.) 2004, pp. 212-228

Palmer R. E. 2003: "Moving Beyond Modernity: The Contribution of Gadamer's Philosophical Hermeneutics", in Fehér (ed.) 2003, pp. 159-174

———, 2010: "Two Contrasting Heideggerian Elements in Gadamer's Philosophical Hermeneutics", in Malpas and Zabala (ed.) 2010, pp. 121-131

Pannenberg W. 1963: "Hermeneutik und Universalgeschichte", in *Zeitschrift für Theologie und Kirche*, 60, pp. 90-121

Philipse H. 1995: "Transcendental Idealism", in B. Smith and D. W. Smith (ed.) *The Cambridge Companion to Husserl*, Cambridge University Press, Cambridge, pp. 239-322

Picardi E. 2004: "La verità nell'interpretazione. Alcune osservazioni su Gadamer e Davidson", in Gardini and Matteucci (ed.) 2004, pp. 275-286

Piccini D. 2003: "Hans-Georg Gadamer verso un'ermeneutica filosofica", in *Paradigmi. Rivista di critica filosofica*, 21/3, n. 63, pp. 691-719

Pippin R. 2002: "Gadamer's Hegel", in Dostal (ed.) 2002, pp. 225-246

Plato. *Phaedo* (tr. G. M. A. Grube), *Statesman* (tr. C. J. Rowe), *Philebus* (tr. D. Frede), *Symposium* (tr. A. Nehamas and P. Woodruff), *Phaedrus* (tr. A. Nehamas and P. Woodruff), and *Meno* (tr. G. M. A. Grube), in *Plato. Complete Works*, ed. J. M. Cooper, Hackett Publishing Company, Indianapolis-Cambridge 1997, respectively pp. 49-100, 294-358, 398-456, 457-505, 506-556, and 870-897

Pöggeler O. 1983: *Heidegger und die hermeneutische Philosophie*, Alber, Freiburg-München

Popper K. R. 1971: "Philosophische Selbstinterpretation und Polemik gegen die Dialektiker. Brief an Klaus Grossner", in C. Grossner (ed.) *Verfall der Philosophie. Politik deutscher Philosophen*, Wegner, Reinbeck bei Hamburg, pp. 278-289

———, 1994: *The Myth of the Framework: In Defence of Science and Rationality*, Routledge, London-New York

———, 2002: *The Poverty of Historicism* [1957], Routledge, London-New York

Putnam H. 1981: *Reason, Truth, and History*, Cambridge University Press, Cambridge

———, 1992: *Renewing Philosophy*, Harvard University Press, Cambridge-London

———, 1995: *Pragmatism: An Open Question*, Blackwell, Oxford

———, 2005: *Ethics Without Ontology*, Harvard University Press, Cambridge

Qualizza G. 1992: "Il gioco in Gadamer tra rischio e simmetria", in *Fenomenologia e società*, 15/1, pp. 149-166

Rese F. 2007: "*Phronesis* als Modell der Hermeneutik. Die hermeneutische Aktualität Aristoteles", in Figal (ed.) 2007, pp. 127-150

Ricoeur P. 1986: *Du texte à l'action. Essais d'herméneutique II*, Seuil, Paris; tr. K. Blamey and J. B. Thompson, *From Text to Action: Essays in Hermeneutics II*, Northwestern University Press, Evanston 1991

Ripanti G. 1999: *Gadamer*, Milella, Lecce

Risser J. 2000: "Philosophical Hermeneutics and the Question of the Community", in C. E. Scott and J. Sallis (ed.) *Interrogating the Tradition. Hermeneutics and the History of Philosophy*, SUNY Press, Albany, pp. 19-35

———, 2010: "Gadamer's Hidden Doctrine: The Simplicity and Humility of Philosophy", in Malpas and Zabala (ed.) 2010, pp. 5-24

Rodi F. 2004: "Problemi della comprensione interculturale. Alcune domande critiche alla filosofia ermeneutica", in Gardini and Matteucci (ed.) 2004, pp. 15-30

Rorty R. 1982: *Consequences of Pragmatism: Essays 1972-1980*, University of Minnesota Press, Minneapolis

———, 1989: *Contingency, Irony, and Solidarity*, Cambridge University Press, Cambridge

———, 1990: *Pragmatism as Anti-Representationalism: Introduction* to J. P. Murphy, *Pragmatism: From Peirce to Davidson*, Westview Press, Boulder 1990, pp. 1-19

———, 1991a: *Objectivity, Relativism, and Truth: Philosophical Papers 1*, Cambridge University Press, Cambridge

———, 1991b: *Essays on Heidegger and Others: Philosophical Papers 2*, Cambridge University Press, Cambridge

———, 2004: "Being That Can Be Understood Is Language", in Krajewski (ed.) 2004, pp. 21-29

———, 2005: "What is Religion's Future After Metaphysics?" (Dialogue with G. Vattimo and S. Zabala), in R. Rorty and G. Vattimo, *The Future of Religion*, Columbia University Press, New York, pp. 55-82

———, 2006: *Take Care of Freedom and Freedom Will Take Care of Itself*, ed. E. Mendieta, Stanford University Press, Stanford

———, 2007: "Main Statement", in P. Engel and R. Rorty, *What's the Use of Truth?*, Columbia University Press, New York

———, 2009: *Philosophy and the Mirror of Nature. Thirtieth-Anniversary Edition* [1979], Princeton University Press, Princeton

Said E. 1994: *Orientalism: 25th Anniversary Edition* [1978], Vintage Books, New York

Sallis J. 2007: "The Hermeneutics of the Artwork", in Figal (ed.) 2007, pp. 45-57

Scheibler I. 2000: *Gadamer: Between Heidegger and Habermas*, Rowman & Littlefield, Lanham-Oxford

Schiller J. C. F. 1962: *Über die ästhetische Erziehung des Menschen in einer Reihe von Briefen* [1795], in *Schiller's Werke. Nationalausgabe. Vol. 20*, Böhlau, Weimar, pp. 309-412; tr. E. M. Wilkinson and L. A. Willoughby, *On the Aesthetic Education of Man In a Series of Letters*, Oxford University Press, Oxford-New York 1983

Schmidt L. K. 2010: "Critique: The Heart of Philosophical Hermeneutics", in Malpas and Zabala (ed.) 2010, pp. 202-217

Schönherr-Mann H.-M. 2004: "Hermeneutik als Antwort auf die Krise der Ethik", and "Ethik des Verstehens. Perspektiven der Interpretation", in H.-M. Schönherr-Mann (ed.) *Hermeneutik als Ethik*, Fink, München, pp. 9-29 and 181-205

Schulz W. 1970: "Anmerkungen zur Hermeneutik Gadamers", in R. Bubner, K. Cramer and R. Wiehl (ed.) *Hermeneutik und Dialektik. Hans-Georg Gadamer zum 70. Geburtstag. Vol. 1*, Mohr Siebeck, Tübingen, pp. 305-316

Sen A. 2006: *Identity and Violence: The Illusion of Destiny*, Norton & Company, New York-London

Shusterman R. 2000: *Pragmatist Aesthetics: Living Beauty, Rethinking Art* [1992], Rowman & Littlefield, Lanham

Singer P. 1995: *Rethinking Life and Death: The Collapse of Our Traditional Ethics* [1994], St. Martin's Press, New York

———, 2000: *Moral Experts* [1972], in *Writings on an Ethical Life*, HarperCollins, New York, pp. 3-6

———, 2002: *One World: The Ethics of Globalization*, Yale University Press, New Haven-London

Smith P. C. 1991: *Hermeneutics and Human Finitude: Toward a Theory of Ethical Understanding*, Fordham University Press, New York

———, 2003: "*Phronesis*, the Individual, and the Community: Divergent Appropriations of Aristotle's Ethical Discernment in Heidegger's and Gadamer's Hermeneutics", in Wischke and Hofer (ed.) 2003, pp. 169-185

Sokolowski R. 1997: "Gadamer's Theory of Hermeneutics", in Hahn (ed.) 1997, pp. 223-234

Sonderegger R. 2000: *Für eine Ästhetik des Spiels. Hermeneutik, Dekonstruktion und der Eigensinn der Kunst*, Suhrkamp, Frankfurt a.M.

———, 2003: "Gadamers Wahrheitsbegriffe", in Wischke and Hofer (ed.) 2003, pp. 248-267

Stolzenberg J. 2005: "Hermeneutik der praktischen Vernunft. Hans-Georg Gadamer interpretiert Martin Heideggers Aristoteles-Interpretation", in G. Figal and H.-H. Gander (ed.), *"Dimensionen des Hermeneutischen". Heidegger und Gadamer*, Klostermann, Frankfurt a.M., pp. 133-152

Stueber K. R. 1994: "Understanding Truth and Objectivity: A Dialogue between Donald Davidson and Hans-Georg Gadamer", in Wachterhauser (ed.) 1994, pp. 172-189

Sullivan R. R. 1989: *Political Hermeneutics: The Early Thinking of Hans-Georg Gadamer*, Pennsylvania State University Press, University Park

———, 1997: "Gadamer's Early and Distinctively Political Hermeneutics", in Hahn (ed.) 1997, pp. 237-255

Taylor C. 1979: *Hegel and Modern Society*, Cambridge University Press, Cambridge

———, 1992: *The Malaise of Modernity: The Ethics of Authenticity* [1991], Harvard University Press, Cambridge-London

———, 1994: "The Politics of Recognition", in A. Gutmann (ed.) *Multiculturalism: Examining the Politics of Recognition*, Princeton University Press, Princeton, pp. 25-74

Teichert D. 1991: *Erfahrung, Erinnerung, Erkenntnis: Untersuchungen zum Wahrheitsbegriff der Hermeneutik Hans-Georg Gadamers*, Metzler, Stuttgart

Theunissen M. 2001: "Philosophische Hermeneutik als Phänomenologie der Traditionsaneignung", in AA.VV. 2001, pp. 61-88

Tietz U. 1999: *Hans-Georg Gadamer zur Einführung*, Junius, Hamburg

Toulmin S. 2002: "The Hermeneutics of the Natural Sciences", in B. Babich (ed.) *Hermeneutic Philosophy of Science, Van Gogh's Eyes, and God: Essays in Honor of Patrick A. Heelan*, Kluwer, Dordrecht, pp. 25-31

Touraine A. 1992: *Critique de la modernité*, Librairie Fayard, Paris

Tugendhat E. 1984: *Probleme der Ethik*, Reclam, Stuttgart

Vasilache A. 2003: *Interkulturelles Verstehen nach Gadamer und Foucault*, Campus, Frankfurt a.M.-New York

Vattimo G. 1967: *Poesia e ontologia*, Mursia, Milano; tr. L. D'Isanto, ed. S. Zabala, *Art's Claim to Truth*, Columbia University Press, New York 2010

———, 1998: *La fine della modernità* [1985], Garzanti, Milano; tr. J. R. Snyder, *The End of Modernity: Nihilism and Hermeneutics in Postmodern Culture*, Johns Hopkins University Press, Baltimore 1991

———, 2002: *Oltre l'interpretazione. Il significato dell'ermeneutica per la filosofia* [1994], Laterza, Roma-Bari; tr. D. Webb, *Beyond Interpretation: The Meaning of Hermeneutics for Philosophy*, Stanford University Press, Stanford 1997

———, 2008: *Non essere Dio. Un'autobiografia a quattro mani* (con P. Paterlini), Aliberti, Reggio Emilia; tr. W. McCuaig, *Not Being God: A Collaborative Autobiography* (with P. Paterlini), Columbia University Press, New York

———, 2009a: *Addio alla verità*, Meltemi, Roma; tr. W. McCuaig, *A Farewell to Truth*, Columbia University Press, New York 2011

———, 2009b: "Dal dialogo al conflitto", in *Trópos. Rivista di ermeneutica e critica filosofica*, 2/1, pp. 9-17

———, 2010: "The Political Outcome of Hermeneutics: To Politics Through Art and Religion", in Malpas and Zabala (ed.) 2010, pp. 281-287

Volpi F. 1992: "Praktische Klugheit im Nihilismus der Technik: Hermeneutik, praktische Philosophie, Neoaristotelismus", in *Internationale Zeitschrift für Philosophie*, 1, pp. 5-23

———, 2000: "Warum praktische Philosophie? Zum Problem einer Sinnorientierung im Zeitalter der Technik", in Figal, Grondin and Schmidt (ed.) 2000, pp. 325-333

———, 2005, *Il nichilismo*, Laterza, Roma-Bari

Wachterhauser B. R. 1999: *Beyond Being. Gadamer's Post-Platonic Hermeneutical Ontology*, Northwestern University Press, Evanston

Waite G. 2004: "Radio Nietzsche, or How to Fall Short of Philosophy", in Krajewski B. (ed.) 2004, pp. 169-211

Waldenfels B. 1999: *Vielstimmigkeit der Rede. Studien zur Phänomenologie des Fremden 4*, Suhrkamp, Frankfurt a.M.

Warnke G. 1987: *Gadamer: Hermeneutics, Tradition and Reason*, Polity Press, Oxford

———, 1990: "Walzer, Rawls, and Gadamer: Hermeneutics and Political Theory", in Wright (ed.) 1990, pp. 136-160

———, 2002: "Hermeneutics, Ethics, and Politics", in Dostal (ed.) 2002, pp. 79-101

Weber M. 1972: *Wirtschaft und Gesellschaft: Grundriss der verstehenden Soziologie* [1922], Mohr Siebeck, Tübingen; tr. T. Parsons et al., ed. G. Roth and C. Wittich, *Economy and Society: An Outline of Interpretive Sociology. Vol. 1*, University of California Press, Berkeley-Los Angeles-London 1978

———, 1978: *Die protestantische Ethik und der Geist des Kapitalismus* [1905], in *Gesammelte Aufsätze zur Religionssoziologie*, Mohr Siebeck, Tübingen, pp. 17-206; tr. P. Baehr and G. C. Wells, *The Protestant Ethic and the "Spirit" of Capitalism and Other Writings*, Penguin Books, London 2002

Weberman D. 2003: "Is Hermeneutics Really Universal despite the Heterogeneity of its Objects?", in Wischke and Hofer (ed.) 2003, pp. 35-56

Weinsheimer J. 2000: "Charity Militant: Gadamer, Davidson, and Post-critical Hermeneutics", in *Revue Internationale de Philosophie*, 54/3, n. 213, pp. 405-422

Wiehl R. 2006: "Ästhetische Theorie oder Hermeneutische Ästhetik. Zu einer nicht stattgefundenen Diskussion zwischen Adorno und Gadamer", in *Philosophical Problems Today*, 2, 163-179

———, 2009: "Metodo e dialogo: verità nel discorso, verità del discorso", tr. P. Stagi, in Vattimo and Chiurazzi (ed.) 2009, pp. 11-24

Wiggershaus R. 1986: *Die Frankfurt Schule: Geschichte. Theoretische Entwicklung. Politische Bedeutung*, Hanser, München-Wien; tr. M. Robertson, *The Frankfurt*

School: Its History, Theories, and Political Significance, MIT Press, Cambridge-London 1995

Wilson E. 2003: *Adorned in Dreams: Fashion and Modernity* [1985], Tauris & Co., London-New York

Wittgenstein L. 1989: *Philosophische Untersuchungen* [1953], in *Werkausgabe. Vol. 1*, Suhrkamp, Frankfurt a.M., pp. 225-618; tr. G. E. M. Anscombe, *Philosophical Investigations. 50th Anniversary Commemorative Edition*, Blackwell, Oxford 2003

Wolin R. 2004: *The Seduction of Unreason: The Intellectual Romance with Fascism from Nietzsche to Postmodernism*, Princeton University Press, Princeton-Oxford

Zaccaria G. 2008: "Pluralismo, ermeneutica, multiculturalismo: una triade concettuale", in *Ragion pratica*, 2, n. 31, pp. 559-584

Zuckert C. H. 1996: *Postmodern Platos: Nietzsche, Heidegger, Gadamer, Strauss, Derrida*, University of Chicago Press, Chicago-London

Index

Adorno, T. W. – 56 and note, 57 and note, 107 and note, 108 note, 111 note, 140, 141 note, 154 and note, 172 note
Aeschylus – 191, 192 and note
Alexander, T. M. – 235 note
Anders, G. – 12, 76
Antiseri, D. – 48 note
Aquinas, T. – 130
Arendt, H. – 12, 55 and note, 97 note, 201 note
Aristotle – 17, 24, 25 note, 38, 39, 92 and note, 93 and note, 94, 126, 127 note, 149, 153, 155, 168, 191 and note, 192 and note, 200 and note, 201 note, 202 and note, 203 and note, 204 and note, 214, 217 and note, 218 and note, 220, 222, 223, 225, 226 and note, 227 and note, 228, 229 and note, 230 and note, 234
Arnswald, U. – 181 note
Ataman, K. – 72 note
Auerochs, B. – 163 note
Augustine – 130
Bach, J. S. – 111 note
Bacon, F. – 37 note, 39 note, 40 note, 182, 185, 191 note
Barbarić, D. – 181 and note
Baudrillard, J. – 238 and note

Bauman, Z. – 125 note, 142 and note
Beaufret, J. – 220
Beck, U. – 75 and note, 76 note
Becker, O. – 103, 104 note
Beiner, R. – 72 note, 97 note
Benjamin, W. – 107, 108, 109 and note
Bentham, J. – 222
Bergson, H. – 54 and note, 55 note
Berman, M. – 11 note
Bernet, R. – 211 note, 212 note
Bernstein, R. J. – 32 note, 115 note, 165, 166 and note, 218 and note
Berti, E. – 159 and note, 230 and note, 231 note
Betti, E. – 197 note, 198 note
Bianco, F. – 117 note, 147 note, 181 and note
Bleicher, J. – 150 and note
Blumenberg, H. – 24 note
Bonanni, G. – 194 note
Bormann, C. von – 162 note
Bourdieu, P. – 121
Brandom, R. B. – 242 note
Brumlik, M. – 236 note
Bruneteau, B. – 141 and note
Bruns, G. – 13 note, 205 note
Bubner, R. – 179 note
Bultmann, R. – 130, 133, 149 note
Buruma, I. – 70 note
Butterfield, J. – 26

289

Cambiano, G. – 32 note, 143 note
Camera, F. – 177 note
Caputo, J. D. – 155 note
Cassirer, E. – 207 and note
Cattaneo, F. – 182 note
Celan, P. – 98 note, 119 note, 181 note
Chang, T. K. – 202 note, 208 note, 211 note
Colli, G. – 17 note
Coltman, R. – 203 note
Copernicus, N. – 38 note, 39 and note, 169
Cottingham, J. – 29 note
Cristina (Grand Duchess of Tuscany) – 34
Crombie, A. C. – 26
Dahl, G. – 62 note
Dallmayr, F. – 68 note
D'Agostini, F. – 116 note, 119 note
D'Angelo, P. – 111 note
Danto, A. C. – 103 note
Da Re, A. – 241 note
Davey, N. – 108 note, 125 note
Davidson, D. – 119 and note, 120 and note
Deniau, G. – 178 note
Derksen, L. D. – 88 note
Derrida, J. – 146 note, 160 and note, 161 and note, 181 note
Descartes, R. (Cartesius) – 24 note, 28 and note, 29 and note, 30 and note, 31 and note, 34 and note, 39 note, 41, 42, 43, 44 note, 99, 191 note
De Simone, A. – 177 note
Detmer, D. – 165 note, 173

Dewey, J. – 101 and note, 102 and note, 170 note, 183, 184 and note, 185 and note, 235 note
Di Cesare, D. – 16 note, 86 note, 116 and note, 117 note, 129 note, 130 note, 189 note, 203 note, 239, 240 note
Dilthey, W. – 28 note, 118 and note, 190 note, 195, 199, 200 note, 244
Donadio, F. – 155 note
Dottori, R. – 68, 73, 121 note, 128, 133, 195, 196 note, 201 note, 225
Drake, S. – 37 note
Droysen, J. G. – 244
Duhem, P. – 26
Dupré, J. – 149 note
Dutt, C. – 62, 167
Eagleton, T. – 162, 163 and note
Elm, R. – 193 note
Ernst, P. – 21
Epicurus – 123
Failla, M. – 131 note
Fehér, I. M. – 103 note, 153 note, 234, 235 note
Ferraris, M. – 161 note
Feuerbach, L. – 123
Feyerabend, P. K. – 146, 148 and note
Figal, G. – 15 note, 16 note, 104, 105 note, 108 note, 120 note, 134 note, 136 note, 173 note, 198, 199 note, 201 note, 203 and note, 204 note, 206 and note, 207 note, 208 note, 209 note
Flatscher, M. – 181 note
Fleury, P. – 166 note

Fornet-Ponse, R. – 108 note
Forti, S. – 97 note
Foster, M. R. – 88 note
Foucault, M. – 12, 72 note, 172 note, 238 and note
Freud, S. – 12, 123, 159
Freyer, H. – 62
Früchtl, J. – 183 note
Fukuyama, F. – 12, 248 and note, 249 and note, 250 note
Galilei, G. – 25 note, 29, 34 and note, 35 note, 37 and note, 38 note, 39 note, 43, 44 and note, 45 note, 157, 168, 185, 191 note
Gamble, A. – 248 and note, 250 note, 251 note
Garelli, G. – 72 note
Geertz, C. – 77 and note, 78 note
Gehlen, A. – 12, 62, 107, 108 and note, 109 note, 134 note, 152 note
Gentili, C. – 149 note, 155 note
Giddens, A. – 12 note
Ginev, D. J. – 24 note
Giurlanda, P. – 147 and note
Goethe, J. W. – 149 note
Gorgias – 169
Graeser, A. – 236 note
Gregorio, G. – 43 note, 189 note
Greisch, J. – 180 note
Griffero, T. – 39 note
Grondin, J. – 13 note, 14 note, 15 note, 17 note, 19 and note, 20 note, 29, 30 and note, 44 note, 57 note, 65 and note, 78 note, 79 note, 98 note, 99 note, 100 note, 102 note, 120 note, 129 note, 130 and note, 131 and note, 133 and note, 134 note, 147, 148 and note, 149 note, 177 and note, 195 note, 198 and note, 200 note, 202 note, 233 note, 238 note, 239 and note, 241 note
Grossner, C. – 47, 62 note, 103 and note, 231 note
Guignon, C. B. – 143 note
Guyer, P. – 113 note
Habermas, J. – 86 and note, 87 note, 119 note, 120 note, 127, 147 and note, 161 note, 162 and note, 164 and note, 166 and note, 172 note, 220 note, 233 and note, 234, 251 note
Hammermeister, K. – 99 note
Hance, A. – 99 note
Hartmann, N. – 92, 103
Harvey, D. – 12 note
Hausmann, F.-R. – 236 note
Heelan, P. – 47 note
Hegel, G.W.F. – 57, 92, 94, 114 note, 140 note, 191 and note, 192 and note, 209 note, 223, 224 and note, 225, 229 note, 242, 243 and note, 244, 245 and note, 246, 247 and note, 248, 249, 250, 251, 252, 253
Heidegger, M. – 12, 16 note, 17 note, 40, 41 and note, 42 and note, 48 note, 56 note, 57 and note, 65, 80, 96, 103 and note, 105 note, 109 note, 115 note, 116, 121, 127 note, 129 and note, 131 and note, 132 and note, 133 and note, 134 note, 143 and note, 144 note, 146 note, 154 and

note, 155 and note, 156 and note, 164 note, 191 note, 195 and note, 196 and note, 197 note, 200 note, 201 and note, 202 and note, 203 and note, 204 and note, 209 and note, 210 and note, 213, 220 and note, 237 and note, 238 and note, 240 and note, 247 note
Herder, J. G. – 66 note, 237 and note, 240 note
Hippocrates – 84
Hitler, A. – 20 note, 78, 121, 240, 250
Hobbes, T. – 43
Hobsbawm, E. J. – 18 note, 77 note
Hölderlin, J. C. F. – 133
Hollinger, R. – 184 note
Honneth, A. – 55 and note, 56 and note, 178 note, 183 and note, 184, 193 note
Horkheimer, M. – 12, 56 and note, 57 note, 154 and note, 155 and note, 172 note
Hösle, V. – 79 note
Hoy, D. C. – 119 note
Huizinga, J. – 12
Humboldt, W. von – 235
Hume, D. – 28
Huntington, S. P. – 67 and note, 68 note
Husserl, E. – 12, 42 and note, 43 and note, 44 and note, 121 note, 143, 207, 211 and note, 213 and note
Immermann, K. L. – 106
Ipperciel, D. – 164 note
Iser, W. – 108 note
James, W. – 172 note

Janik, A. – 47 note
Jaspers, K. – 76, 124
Jonas, H. – 80 and note, 81 and note, 82 and note, 86 note,
Jung, M. – 190 and note
Jünger, E. – 240
Kant, I. – 15 note, 44, 45, 81, 82 and note, 91, 92 and note, 95 and note, 96, 97 and note, 98 and note, 113 and note, 146 note, 165, 172 note, 173 and note, 174, 179 note, 186 and note, 187 and note, 207 note, 223, 224, 227 note, 242, 243, 252
Kelly, M. – 100 note, 104 note, 172 note, 173 note
Kern, A. B. – 75 note, 158 note
Kern, I. – 211 note, 212 note
Keuth, H. – 165 note
Kojève, A. – 12, 248
Kuhn, T. – 26, 48 and note, 49
Kumar, K. – 13 note
Kusch M. – 155 note
Lang, P. C. – 108 note
Lawn, C. – 181 note, 240 note
Lee H. Y. – 194 note
Leibniz, G. W. – 43, 121
Lembeck, K.-H. – 15 note, 44 note
Lessing, T. – 21
Liessmann, K. P. – 102 note
Locke, J. – 235
Lorenz, K. – 12
Löwith, K. – 12, 19 and note, 240, 245
Luhmann, N. – 12
Lukács, G. – 55, 154 and note
Lyotard, J.-F. – 12, 247 note

MacIntyre, A. – 12, 125, 126 and note, 127 note
Madison, G. B. – 46 note, 233 note
Makkreel, R. – 98 note
Malpas, J. – 119 and note, 120 note
Mann, T. – 21
Mantzavinos, C. – 190 note, 191 note
Marbach, E. – 211 note, 212 note
Marcuse, H. – 56 and note, 57 note, 154 note
Margalit, A. – 70 note
Marino, S. – 103 note, 113 note, 115 note, 146 note, 152 note, 153 note, 154 note, 180 note
Marquard, O. – 197 note
Marx, K. – 53, 55, 56 note, 69, 123, 159
Matteucci, G. – 104 and note, 109 note, 194 note
McDowell, J. – 119 note, 151 and note, 152 note, 153 and note, 187 and note
Menegoni, F. – 97 note
Merleau-Ponty, M. – 193 note
Michon, P. – 164 and note
Mill, J. S. – 28, 46 note, 235
Misgeld, D. – 234 note, 251 note
Mittelstrass, J. – 168 and note
Moda, A. – 147 note
Montinari, M. – 17 note
Morin, E. – 75 note, 158 and note
Most, G. – 93 note
Motzkin, G. – 236 note
Mura, G. – 188 note
Nacci, M. – 144 note
Nagl-Docekal, H. – 46 note

Natali, C. – 229 note
Natorp, P. – 44, 45, 131, 202, 203
Neuser, W. – 46 note
Newton, I. – 44, 185
Nicholson, G. – 162 note
Nicolas of Cusa – 130
Nietzsche, F.W. – 12 and note, 17 note, 56 and note, 57 note, 115 and note, 116, 118, 121 and note, 122, 126, 132, 159 and note, 160, 236, 237, 248
Oldroyd, D. – 26 note
Orozco, T. – 236 and note, 237 note, 239
Qualizza, G. – 180 note
Palmer, R. E. – 13 and note, 18 note, 45 note, 195 and note
Pannenberg, W. – 163 note
Parmenides – 146 note
Philipse, H. – 44 note
Picardi, E. – 119 note
Piccini, D. – 118 note
Pippin, R. – 246 note
Plato – 17, 24, 25 note, 36 and note, 37 note, 44, 92, 93 and note, 94, 113 note, 133, 136, 137 note, 151, 168, 170 note, 187, 188 and note, 203 note, 222, 226 note, 229, 236, 240 note
Plessner, H. – 134 note, 190 note
Pöggeler, O. 195 note, 210 note
Polanyi, M. – 48 and note
Pol Pot (Saloth Sar) – 250
Popper, K. – 46 note, 47, 48 note, 235, 246 and note
Protagoras – 169

293

Putnam, H. − 151 and note, 170 note, 251 and note
Pythagoras − 169
Ranke, L. von − 244, 252 note
Rawls, J. − 235
Reale, G. − 130 note, 133
Rese, F. − 201 note
Ricoeur, P. − 147 and note, 159 note
Ripanti, G. − 222 note
Risser, J. − 178, 179 note, 203 note
Rodi, F. − 72 note
Rorty, R. − 71 note, 116 note, 119 and note, 120, 146 and note, 148 note, 151 note, 183, 238 note
Rovatti, P. A. − 116 note
Russell, B. − 158
Said, E. W. − 69 note
Sallis, J. − 103 note
Scheibler, I. − 166 note
Scheler, M. − 92, 134 note, 152 note
Schelling, F. W. J. − 209 note, 210
Schelsky, H. − 62
Schiller, J. C. F. − 52 and note, 53 note, 105 note, 111
Schmidt, L. K. − 147 and note
Schmitt, C. − 109
Schönherr-Mann, H.-M. − 72 note
Schulz, W. − 163 note
Schwilk, H. − 136
Sen, A. − 68 note, 70 note
Shusterman, R. − 101 note
Singer, P. − 79 note, 84 note, 141 and note, 142 note, 221, 222 and note
Smith, P. C. − 127 note, 203 note
Snow, C. P. − 186 and note

Socrates − 36 note, 93, 130, 170 note, 188 note, 203 note
Sokolowski, R. − 125 note, 205 note
Sonderegger, R. − 120 note, 180 note
Spengler, O. − 11, 21, 238, 246
Spinoza, B. − 43
Stadelmann, R. − 196 note
Stolzenberg, J. − 203 note
Strauss, L. − 196 note
Stueber, K.-H. − 119 note, 120 note
Sullivan, R. R. − 17 note, 235 and note, 236 note
Taylor, C. − 11 note, 72 and note, 243 and note
Teichert, D. − 177 note
Thales − 168
Theunissen, M. − 167 note
Tietz, U. − 241 note
Toulmin, S. − 47 note, 48 and note
Touraine, A. − 144, 145 note
Tugendhat, E. − 92 note
Üxkull, J. J. − 152 note
Valèry, P. − 12
Vasilache, A. − 72 note
Vattimo, G. − 12, 100 note, 101 note, 111 note, 116 and note, 117 note, 119 and note, 120,
Vietta, S. − 59 note, 87, 108 note, 195 note
Volpi, F. − 91 note, 201 note
Wachterhauser, B. R. − 120 note, 164, 165 note
Waite, G. − 57 note
Waldenfels, B. − 163 note

Warnke, G. – 18 note, 62 note, 236 note, 242 note
Weber, M. – 59 note, 154 and note, 162, 228
Weberman, D. – 179 note
Weinsheimer, J. – 119 note
Wiehl, R. – 15 note, 57, 108 note
Wiggershaus, R. – 56 note, 154 note
Wilson, E. – 59 note, 60 note

Wittgenstein, L. – 180 and note, 181 note
Wolin, R. – 233 note, 236 and note, 237 and note, 238 and note, 239
Zabala, S. – 119 note
Zaccaria, G. – 72 note
Zuckert, C. H. – 233 note

Berner Reihe philosophischer Studien

Band 1: Gerhard Heinzmann
Schematisierte Strukturen. Eine Untersuchung über den Idoneismus Ferdinand Gonseths auf dem Hintergrund eines konstruktivistischen Ansatzes. 185 S., 1982.

Band 2: Vincent F. Brunner
Probleme der Kausalerklärung menschlichen Handelns. 112 S., 1983.

Band 3: Jean-Claude Wolf
Sprachanalyse und Ethik. Eine Kritik der Methode und einiger Folgeprobleme sowie der Anwendung des universalen Präskriptivismus von Richard Mervyn Hare. 142 S., 1983.

Band 4: Duen Jau Marti-Huang
Die Gegenstandstheorie von Alexius Meinong als Ansatz zu einer ontologisch neutralen Logik. 136 S., 1984.

Band 5: Claudia Risch
Die Identität des Kunstwerks. VIII, 189 S., 1986.

Band 6: Andreas Graeser (ed.)
Mathematics and Metaphysics in Aristotle/Mathematik und Metaphysik bei Aristoteles. 333 S., 1987.

Band 7: Stephan Hottinger
Nelson Goodmans Nominalismus und Methodologie. 94 S., 1988.

Band 8: Michael Schrijvers
Spinozas Affektenlehre. 233 S., 1989.

Band 9: Andreas Gunkel
Spontaneität und moralische Autonomie. Kants Philosophie der Freiheit. IX, 238 S., 1989.

Band 10: Andreas Bächli
Untersuchungen zur pyrrhonischen Skepsis. XI, 90 S., 1990.

Band 11: Hansueli Flückiger
Sextus Empiricus. Grundriss der pyrrhonischen Skepsis. Buch I – Selektiver Kommentar. 126 S., 1990.

Band 12: Gérard Bornet
Naive Semantik und Realismus. Sprachphilosophische Untersuchung der Frühphilosophie von Bertrand Russell (1903–04). 315 S., 1991.

Band 13: Herbert Schweizer
Bedeutung. Grundzüge einer internalistischen Semantik. 201 S., 1991.

Band 14: Jürg Freudiger
Kants Begründung der praktischen Philosophie: systematische Stellung, Methode und Argumentationsstruktur der „Grundlegung zur Metaphysik der Sitten". 123 S., 1993.

Band 15: Erwin Sonderegger
Aristoteles, Metaphysik Z 1-12: philosophische und philologische Erwägungen zum Text. VIII, 369 S., 1993

Band 16: Lutz Danneberg / Andreas Graeser / Klaus Petrus (Hg.)
Metapher und Innovation: die Rolle der Metapher im Wandel von Sprache und Wissenschaft. 324 S., 1995.

Band 17: Gérard Bornet
Die Bedeutung von „Sinn" und der Sinn von „Bedeutung": auf dem Weg zu einem gemeinsprachlichen Wörterbuch für formale Philosophie.
XVI, 246 S., 1996.

Band 18: Cinzia Ferrini
Guida al „De orbitis planetarum" di Hegel ed alle sue edizioni e traduzioni. 259 S., 1995

Band 19: Urs Bruderer
Verstehen ohne Sprache. Zu Donald Davidsons Szenario der radikalen Interpretation. 80 S., 1997.

Band 20: Peter Zimmermann
Soziologie als Erkenntniskritik. Die Wissenssoziologie Karl Mannheims.
64 S., 1998.

Band 21: Thomas Gfeller
Was ist wichtig: Beschreibung, Wertung und ethische Theorie. 112 S., 1998.

Band 22: Gerald Bechtle
The Anonymous Commentary on Plato's „Parmenides". 285 S., 1999.

Band 23: Ursula Thomet
Kunstwerk, Kunstwelt, Weltsicht. Arthur C. Dantos Philosophie der Kunst und Kunstgeschichte. 112 S., 1999.

Band 24: Pierfrancesco Basile
Experience and Relations. An Examination of F.H. Bradley's Conception of Reality. 197 S., 1999.

Band 25: Andreas Graeser
Prolegomena zu einer Interpretation des zweiten Teils des Platonischen Parmenides. 60 S., 1999

Band 26: Martin Flügel / Thomas Gfeller / Charlotte Walser
Werte und Fakten. Eine Dichotomie im Spiegel philosophischer Kontroversen.
268 S., 1999.

Band 27: Rebecca Iseli
Kants Philosophie der Mathematik. Rekonstruktion – Kritik – Verteidigung.
110 S., 2001.

Band 28: Helen Plüss
Bedeutungstheorie und philosophische Psychologie bei Paul Grice.
76 S., 2001.

Band 29: Alain Metry
Speusippos. Zahl – Erkenntnis – Sein. 198 S., 2002.

Band 30: Heiko Holweg
Methodologie der qualitativen Sozialforschung. Eine Kritik. 176 S., 2005.

Band 31: Thomas Ruprecht
Die Unbestimmtheit der Verursachung. Ein philosophischer Essay über Kausalität. 138 S., 2003.

Band 32: Evangelos Zoidis
Notes on a Metaphysics of Presence. 113 S., 2003.

Band 33: Philipp Keller
Ein Dritter Blick auf Descartes' Erste Philosophie. Eine analytische Interpretation der cartesianischen Metaphysik.
In Vorbereitung.

Band 34: Marcel van Ackeren
Heraklit. Vielfalt und Einheit seiner Philosophie. 167 S., 2006.
ISBN 978-3-03910-815-2.

Band 35: Mika Ojakangas
A Philosophy of Concrete Life. Carl Schmitt and the Political Thought of Late Modernity. 2nd revised edition, 225 S., 2006.
ISBN 978-3-03910-963-0 / US-ISBN 978-0-8204-8362-7.

Band 36: Erwin Sonderegger
Aristoteles' Metaphysik Λ: Ein spekulativer Entwurf. Einführung, Übersetzung, Kommentar. XXXII, 514 S., 2008. ISBN 978-3-03911-477-1.

Band 37: Thomas Schindler-Wunderlich
Kritik der neuzeitlichen Wunderkritik. Eine religionsphilosophische Studie.
217 S., 2008. ISBN 978-3-03911-510-5.

Band 38: Gianluigi Segalerba: Semantik und Ontologie. Drei Studien zu Aristoteles.
In Vorbereitung.
Band 39: François Grandjean: Aristoteles' Theorie der praktischen Rationalität.
346 S., 2009. ISBN 978-3-03911-674-4
Band 40: Charlotte Walser: Personen – Inwiefern wir sind, wofür wir uns halten.
235 S., 2009. ISBN 978-3-0343-0080-3
Band 41: Paul Taborsky: The Logic of Cultures. Three Structures of Philosophical Thought.
266 S., 2010. ISBN 978-3-0343-0378-1
Band 42: Alba Papa-Grimaldi: Orphans of the One or the Deception of the Immanence.
Essays on the Roots of Secularization. 239 S., 2010. ISBN 978-3-0343-0410-8
Band 43: Stefano Marino: Gadamer and the Limits of the Modern Techno-Scientific Civilization.
295 S., 2011. ISBN 978-3-0343-0663-8

Bände 1–32 erschienen im Paul Haupt Verlag, Bern